VICTORIAN MODERNISM
Pragmatism and the Varieties of Aesthetic Experience

In *Victorian Modernism: Pragmatism and the Varieties of Aesthetic Experience* Jessica Feldman sheds a pragmatist light on the relation between the Victorian age and Modernism by dislodging truistic notions of Modernism as an art of crisis, rupture, elitism, and loss. She examines aesthetic sites of Victorian Modernism – including workrooms, parlours, friendships, and family relations as well as printed texts and paintings – as they develop through interminglings and continuities as well as gaps and breaks. Examining the works of John Ruskin (art critic and social thinker), Dante Gabriel Rossetti (poet and painter), Augusta Evans (best-selling domestic novelist), and William James (philosopher and psychologist), Feldman relates them to selected twentieth-century creations. She reveals these sentimental, domestic, and sublime works to be pragmatist explorations of aesthetic realms. This study, which leads Modernism back into the Victorian age, will be of interest to scholars of literature, art history, and philosophy.

JESSICA FELDMAN is Associate Professor of English at the University of Virginia. She is the author of *Gender on the Divide: the Dandy in Modernist Literature* (1993).

VICTORIAN MODERNISM

Pragmatism and the Varieties of Aesthetic Experience

JESSICA R. FELDMAN

CAMBRIDGE
UNIVERSITY PRESS

PUBLISHED BY THE PRESS SYNDICATE OF THE UNIVERSITY OF CAMBRIDGE
The Pitt Building, Trumpington Street, Cambridge, United Kingdom

CAMBRIDGE UNIVERSITY PRESS
The Edinburgh Building, Cambridge CB2 2RU, UK
40 West 20th Street, New York, NY 10011-4211, USA
477 Williamstown Road, Port Melbourne, VIC 3207, Australia
Ruiz de Alarcón 13, 28014 Madrid, Spain
Dock House, The Waterfront, Cape Town 8001, South Africa

http://www.cambridge.org

First published 2002

Printed in the United Kingdom at the University Press, Cambridge

Typeface Baskerville Monotype 11 / 12.5 pt   *System* LATEX 2ε   [TB]

A catalogue record for this book is available from the British Library

ISBN 0 521 81581 9 hardback

To the memory of
Milly Feldman, Jonathan Feldman, Joseph Simko

"*And shall my sense pierce love, – the last relay*
And ultimate outpost of eternity?"
Dante Gabriel Rossetti

Contents

List of illustrations   *page* ix
Acknowledgments   x
List of abbreviations   xii

1 Introduction   1

2 A sweet continuance: John Ruskin's Victorian Modernism   17

   Meditation: aestheticism and pragmatism   56

3 Arrangements: Dante Gabriel Rossetti's Victorian
   Modernism   66

   Meditation: domesticity   112

4 Recondite analogies: The Victorian Modernism of Augusta
   Evans   123

   Meditation: sentimentality   164

5 Positions of repose: The Victorian Modernism of
   William James   172

   Meditation: sublimity   213

6 Afterword   223

Notes   229
Index   258

vii

Illustrations

1   "Santa Zita and the Angel," Francesca Alexander,   *page* 53
    Plate VI, vol. 32, *The Complete Works of John Ruskin*,
    Edited by E. T. Cook and Alexander Wedderburn
    (London: George Allen, 1907).

2   *Monna Rosa*, Dante Gabriel Rossetti. Reproduced by
    permission of Sotheby's.   70

3   *Marigolds*, Dante Gabriel Rossetti. Reproduced by
    permission of Nottingham City Museum and Galleries;
    The Castle Museum and Art Gallery.   80

4   *The Day Dream*, Dante Gabriel Rossetti. Reproduced by
    permission of the Victoria and Albert Museum, London.   104

5   *Olana: Court Hall View*. Reproduced by permission of
    the Olana Partnership. Photo credit: Kurt Dolnier.   142

Acknowledgments

Marigolds, Dante Gabriel Rossetti, with the permission of Nottingham City Museum and Galleries; the Castle Museum and Art Gallery.
Monna Rosa, Dante Gabriel Rossetti, with the permission of Sotheby's.
"Olana, Court Hall View," with the permission of the Olana Partnership. Photo credit: Kurt Dolnier.
Part Seen, Part Imagined, Charles Rennie Mackintosh, with the permission of the Glasgow Museums.
"Santa Zita and the Angel," Francesca Alexander, Plate VI, vol. 32, *The Complete Works of John Ruskin*, eds. E. T. Cook and Alexander Wedderburn (London, George Allen: 1907), with the permission of the Ruskin Foundation.
The Day Dream, Dante Gabriel Rossetti, with the permission of the Victoria and Albert Museum.

Letters of Augusta Evans quoted with the permission of W. Stanley Hoole Special Collections Library, University of Alabama.

Portions of Chapters 1 and 3 three appeared in *Modernism/Modernity* 8, no. 3 (September 2001), pp. 453–470. Reprinted by permission of the Johns Hopkins University Press.
Portions of Chapter 5 appeared in Ruth Anna Putnam, ed., *The Cambridge Companion to William James* (Cambridge University Press, 1997), pp. 300–321.

* * *

For bearing the lamps in whose light I wrote this book, I thank Reid Adams, Stephen Arata, Karen and Michael Chase-Levenson, Roger Cohen, Margaret Croskery, Virginia Germino, Cecil Lang, Melvyn Leffler, Gena McKinley, Karen Marshall, Joan Simko, Patricia Meyer Spacks, Mabel Timberlake, Herbert Tucker, and Melissa White. I am grateful to Paul Barolsky for his unwavering illumination and generosity, to Susannah Rutherglen for careful editing and shimmering conversation, and to Michael Rutherglen for his grace in guiding me toward easy street, even though I usually got lost on the way. Above all, I thank George Rutherglen, who is present in every arrangement I make.

Abbreviations

Dante Gabriel Rossetti

Contents	*16, Cheyne Walk, Chelsea. The Valuable Contents of the Residence of Dante G. Rossetti*
CW	*The Collected Works of Dante Gabriel Rossetti*
LDGR	*Letters of Dante Gabriel Rossetti*
Surtees	*The Paintings and Drawings of Dante Gabriel Rossetti 1828–1882: a Catalogue Raisonné*

Augusta Evans

Hoole	*Letters to Rachel Heustis*, Hoole Special Collections Library, University of Alabama
Curry	*Letters to the Honorable J. L. M. Curry*, Curry Collection, Library of Congress

William James

CWJ	*The Correspondence of William James, vols. 1–4*
ECR	*Essays, Comments, and Reviews*
ERE	*Essays in Radical Empiricism and A Pluralistic Universe*
ERM	*Essays in Religion and Morality*
Houghton	*Correspondence.* James Family Collection. Houghton Library
MEN	*Manuscript Essays and Notes*
P	*Pragmatism: A New Name for Some Old Ways of Thinking*
PP	*The Principles of Psychology*
TT	*Talks to Teachers on Psychology and to Students on Some of Life's Ideals*

VRE *The Varieties of Religious Experience: A Study in Human Nature*
WB *The Will to Believe and Other Essays in Popular Philosophy*

Wallace Stevens

CP *Collected Poems*

CHAPTER I

Introduction

She is completely genial. She will entertain any hypothesis, she will consider any evidence.

William James, Pragmatism[1]

The more that is gathered together in a confused representation, the more extensive clarity the representation has.

Alexander Baumgarten, Reflections on Poetry[2]

Marcel Proust, exemplary high Modernist, saw himself as more than an admirer of the Victorian sage John Ruskin, explaining in the "Preface" to his translation and creative annotation of Ruskin's *The Bible of Amiens* that he mingled his being with that of Ruskin in an actual, if aesthetic, lovemaking. Proust teaches, in a tangle of pronouns and antecedents, that Ruskin's thought has "[M]ade the universe more beautiful for us, or at least certain individual parts of the universe, because it touched upon them, and because it introduce[d] us to them by obliging us, if we want to understand it, to love them."[3] Love, understanding, beauty; a universe in parts; touching and obligation: Proust speaks of a world of intense and complicated interrelations.

Proust never met Ruskin face to face, but his "Preface" describes an intimate relationship. To know Ruskin, Proust tells us, we must love what he has loved. Ruskin, by visiting places and works of art and by sketching them and writing about them, inhabits them: "It was the soul of Ruskin I went to seek there, which he imparted to the stones of Amiens as deeply as their sculptors had imparted theirs, for the words of genius can give, as well as does the chisel, an immortal form to things."[4] For Proust, the experience of art is a pilgrimage in which we touch the holy relics – stones and words.

When we feel beauty as Ruskin discovered and made it, when we touch him as we visit and touch objects he loved, Proust continues, we share in Ruskin's aesthetic sensibility which is his very being. He becomes part of

I

us as we weave ourselves into a chain bound, embarrassingly enough to our professional sensibilities, by love. Reading Proust reading Ruskin as Ruskin himself reads statues and buildings, we enter a chain of embodied beauty that invites our creations, including our works of literary commentary, as the next link. Intimacy, reverence, and creativity, Proust tells us, will forge the links. Proust's "Preface," in its open references to love as the engine and reward of art, might easily have become cloying. What mitigates the sweetness is his fascination with the substance of the chain itself, with the works of art created when artists and aesthetes know one another – even mystically inhabit one another – across continents, centuries, and artistic media.

Art which is complex, always under construction yet providing dwelling places, satisfying in its very lack of simplicity and closure: Proust and Ruskin found these ideas *useful*. Together they have suggested to me the hypotheses I have set out to explore, these acts of exploration themselves grouping, for the moment, under the term "Victorian Modernism." It is meant to signal an exploration of mid-nineteenth- to mid-twentieth-century literature, with an emphasis on the earlier century, in which both the artists studied and the critics doing the studying are pragmatists. The upper-case Pragmatism of such classic American philosophers as Charles Sanders Peirce, William James, and John Dewey is a category that may itself expand, as I shall explain, to include lower-case pragmatists writing in other times and places.[5] It is easier to say what pragmatist truth-seeking is not, than to say what it is. Pragmatism tends to be anti-dogmatic, anti-metaphysical, anti-foundational, anti-positivist, anti-systematic. Suspicious of traditional dualisms (subject–object, mind–world, theory–practice), it eschews monisms; tends toward meliorism (the idea that human effort may improve the world) rather than optimism or pessimism; and involves an evolutionary view of truth that examines how truth is made and remade over time – and always in the "light of human needs and interests."[6]

Rather than assuming the successful work of art to be the product of a unifying imagination, a seminal and quasi-mystical power superior to mere emotion and mere fancy, Victorian Modernists fuel their pragmatist search for linked and contingent truths with the energies of fancy and tender feeling: superfluous, sentimental, over- or under-wrought as that feeling might appear when held to the standard of modernist purification. The pragmatist hypotheses of Victorian Modernism, the network of paths down which I have chosen to set foot, are as follows. Whether they are true in a pragmatist sense – that is, whether they add to existing bodies of critical truth in ways that speak effectively to our "human needs and interests" – it will be the work of this study to discover, and for readers themselves to judge.

First path: the Victorian period and the Modern period, each so complex as to resist intellectual containment almost successfully, may be studied fruitfully as one continuous period, Victorian Modernism. Such a study will lean more heavily on intricate, intermingling patterns – on nuance, detail, and plenitude – than it will on sturdier critical constructions such as "The Victorian Novel" or "The Crisis of Modernity." Nor are the boundaries of this "period" themselves firm; the method of finding relations between Victorian and Modern will naturally lead outside the artificial limits I have set (and exceeded): 1837 to 1945. Implicit in this study is a questioning of the periodization of literary study – a questioning, not a conclusion.

Second, Victorian Modernist criticism will find multiple links and overlappings of hitherto separate critical discourses such as those of sentiment, sublimity, domesticity, and aestheticism. When we are able to see that a sublime sentimentality intermingles with a domestic aestheticism in a given work, we will find ourselves experiencing multiple centers, at home in the pragmatist realm of Victorian Modernism where sharp breaks between categories and concepts are usually softened. Similarly, chronologically separate categories such as aestheticism and decadence or Pre-Raphaelitism and Abstractionism will lose their hard edges. National divisions will not disappear, but will be less useful sorting devices, as Victorian Modernism not only links the art of England, America, and France, but also follows each country's linkages with multiple and always contingent centers in many countries. Phrases such as "Victorian America" will feel more comfortable to our ears. Victorian Modernism will also turn some disciplinary tables. To the list of philosophers who made the aestheticist turn,[7] we will add such artists as John Ruskin and Oscar Wilde, who made the philosophical turn. "Theory" will be as much an exercise of artists and artistic creations as it is an exercise of critical schools of thought.

Third, in Victorian Modernist works, frames of art and frames of reality overlap. Artists' everyday lives at home are not lived in contradistinction to their works; the artistic and the ordinary mingle. To the extent that the quotidian (often seen as trivial) in the nineteenth and twentieth centuries has been traditionally gendered feminine and imagined in domestic terms, its importance in the patterns of Victorian Modernism returns a measure of female experience to our critical narratives. Because public (masculine) and private (feminine) spheres have never actually been separate in "Victorian" or "Modern" culture, critics of Victorian Modernism simply remember to look harder for the aspects of every-day life within works of art, and of art within everyday life, aspects that have been occulted by many critical narratives. Furthermore, Victorian Modernist critics will work to bring their daily lives and their profes-sional worlds into convergence by writing what helps them (and if they are talented and lucky, may help others) to discover, in Wallace Stevens's words, "how to live" and "what to do."[8]

Fourth, neither simply mimetic of everyday life nor sleekly au-tonomous and therefore apart from everyday life, literary works of Victorian Modernism seek what will work by exploring and expressing a filigree of four major, and many minor, strands: the artist herself, the "actual" worlds in which that artist participates (including but not limited to the most mundane), the work of art, and the audience.[9] By examining any one of these strands in isolation, we as critics fail to address the plen-itude of relations of Victorian Modernism. Victorian Modernism will reveal artists' ability to dwell in complexity and even seeming paradox: incoherent coherence, controlled disorganization, concatenated union, patchworks, and filigrees. It will involve literary scholars in a related mak-ing of patterns-in-progress that are playful but also serious, sentimental but also restrained.

But, it will be asked, is there not already a rich critical literature reading Modernism across the nineteenth and twentieth centuries? The answer, of course, is yes. I use the term "Victorian Modernism," however, to signal my intention of *adding to* the body of dominant beliefs, methods, and conclusions of those who have already made such connections, by whatever tag we may choose to know them: Critical, Queer, and Post-Colonial Theorists; New Historicists and Literary Historians; Feminist, Psychoanalytic, and Cultural Studies critics, and so on. I began to write this book because some words seemed to me to be missing from the contemporary critical scene, at least in their positive connotations. Dare I say them? Tenderness, pleasure, beauty, playfulness, fascination.[10]

In bringing the Victorian period into relation with twentieth-century modernity and post-modernity, we have created critical narratives that have for the most part featured strife, loss, rupture, and a perpetual disorientation caused by often over-powering forces. Furthermore, a preeminent critical stance of the past thirty years – whatever one's methodology and subject matter – has been adversarial. Modernism has often been about resistances, and who would deny the significance of such work? Even when resistance is joined by submission or active acceptance, critical narratives have tended to the strenuous. What has not clashed in the night? I do not wish to eliminate the energy that comes from living and writing *à rebours*; as a feminist I continue to try to think against the grain of accepted truths and customs. In fact, I too, have written a work of resistance: to argue is to resist. Yet I have felt another need – the desire not just to react *against*, but also to react *with*, that is, to appreciate. Pragmatist receptivity requires geniality and inclusiveness. Personifying Pragmatism as a woman, William James assures us that "she will entertain any hypothesis, she will consider any evidence." Aestheticist impulses, for all we have been taught of their ideological work and their market value (and I will be discussing both) need not always be dramatized as economic, social, and psychological agon and alienation. We also need to explore in a variety of ways the pleasurable swoons and feelings of reverence that sometimes occur as we experience art.

Victorian Modernist appreciation does not mean turning away from or correcting the critical explorations conducted since the New Criticism began to feel inadequate to our needs. Rather, I take my cues from William James's Pragmatist philosophy which, read across his writings, advocates not so much a method of finding the truth as an openness to various methods, a reactive tendency, a pluralist and changing set of positions. Appreciation as criticism takes place in the time signatures of finding, making, testing, and dwelling; in textures of finely grained and evolving relations interrupted by both dwellings in plenitude and sharp breaks; in colors both shimmering and opaque. It is escapist and utopian when it needs to be; it is angry, socially aware, rebellious, and recuperative when it needs to be, and sometimes it is playful, hedonistic, irresponsible, or passive.

Victorian Modernism is, then, a provisional set of leadings that may prove useful to scholars and critics. It signals, as well, a set of intermingling pathways and resting places explored by the artists I have chosen to study. So I emphasize for the moment, and at length in my chapters about authors, not what the critic does, but what the artists studied have done, although the two are never fully separable. Works of modern art have been richly interpreted as phenomena that express strife, rupture, loss, and gap – but they have been insufficiently appreciated as figurings forth of peaceful dwelling, plenitude, and continuities that reach across gaps.[11] The very Victorian qualities that Modernists purportedly had to overcome – conventionality of form, sentimentality and coziness, discursiveness, didacticism – have, like Poe's purloined letter, been hidden for

all to see on the very surfaces of Modernist works.[12] Faulkner abstractly
spreads the conventional nineteenth-century melodrama of beset womanhood across *Light in August* as he teaches us about the poisonous notion
of the color line. Willa Cather's sentimental and domestic fiction so deliberately wrings the heart that it took critics a long while to recognize
its Modernist sophistications.

But of which Modernism do I speak? The answer, of course, depends
on one's own Modernism, since there is so little agreement about modern
literature's formal qualities, its years of origin (1490s? 1880s?), its longevity
(has it ended?), and its groupings of artists and texts, whether generic, national, philosophical, or historical.[13] Every argument about modernism
can thus be seen as a straw-man argument since its assumptions are
eminently open to challenge. I have had to choose. The understanding
of modernism to which I wish to add often goes by the name "high
Modernism," and its dates are roughly 1880–1945. It features a literary
work that, having been conceived in a time of spiritual crisis, communicates an exile from the homeland of certainty as it sits high on the shelf of
autonomous art. An object to be admired (or in some cases excoriated)
for its self-sufficiency and self-involvement, the Modern work has often
been imagined, by artists and critics alike, as purely sculpted, paradoxically spiritual or cerebral for all its hardness, and preferably not for sale.
Its internal incoherencies are bounded by its autonomy, made whole
by its separation, at times its rupture, from the familiar. It takes the long
and impersonal view, turning away from the ordinary and the fleshly, the
vulgarly emotional and the preachy. This autonomy may also be viewed
as false in the sense that the work expresses important, if often denied or
unconscious, relations to capitalist society or the dehumanizing aspects
of technological or profane culture. One must work hard to understand
and appreciate such a Modernist work of art, and most people will fail
to do so.

This portrait is as false as any other composite, but as a way to begin
examining Victorian Modernism it is one that I choose to take down
and handle – not because I wish to reject it but because I wish to work
with it, to place it in relation to some other ideas. I shall wish to explore
what John Ruskin described as an "art of the wayside," a space and an
energy within Modernism that differs from both the maelstrom and the
serene island of the autonomous.

In addition to hypothesizing the importance of tender relation to
nineteenth- and twentieth-century literature, I have also attempted to
add to the body of understandings of "the aesthetic" by asking whether

it would be useful to regard it as something in addition to a (philosophical, political, historical, or social) problem to be solved. Problem became a verb, problematize, through the needs of a varied and instructive theoretical literature that does just that – "takes" things as problems, and often as evidence of social injustice. Some of this professional literature embodies what George Levine has called the "appropriation of the aesthetic by politics," a practice which he sees as ignoring questions of literary value and of literature's distinctiveness.[14] His goal in collecting the essays of *Aesthetics & Ideology*, he tells us, has been to reconsider the "category of the aesthetic" (p. 13) and to urge us to ask a set of questions that moves beyond noting the "politico-historical purposes" of literature (p. 13) in favor of questions about how we place value on what we read.

Instead of reconsidering, as Levine urges, what the "category of the aesthetic" refers to, I have begun by hypothesizing that I could do without the category, without "*the* aesthetic" itself. I have tried to understand what happens when we replace aesthetics as an object of study with aestheticism: the beliefs, customs, experiments, and actual creations in words and paint of nineteenth-century artists such as Ruskin and Rossetti. For attempts to understand an abstract aesthetic, I have substituted a pragmatist approach, asking how particular artists made their art in relation to their own specific human needs and interests – and their own notions, always embodied in works of art, of what art is and does, what artists do and are. The question, "What is the aesthetic?" metamorphoses to "How have artists lived, what have they made?".[15]

This pragmatist receptivity to the complex ways in which aestheticism answers in imagery or tone or rhythm our questions about the artistic enterprise also rescues us from a dualism that haunts talk about art. "The aesthetic" in nineteenth- and twentieth-century thought has been understood in two opposing ways: as a self-contained realm entirely apart from everyday concerns or reality, and as the whole of reality, the "tendency to see 'art' or 'language' or 'discourse' or 'text' as constituting the primary realm of human experience."[16] Thus on the one hand, the relation of "reality" to "the aesthetic" has been seen as absent, attenuated or threatening, e.g., "Rossetti knows the nearness of human life in the concrete world only as that which besieges the house of aesthetic life and threatens it with death and disruption."[17] On the other hand, the relation of reality to the aesthetic is one of identity: reality just *is* the aesthetic. In this view, we live, inescapably, inside and through texts and performances. To regard the figures of my study as four artists whose delights and terrors, intellectual explorations and physical habits at home bring into complex relation the lives they led and the works of art they made is to study aestheticism rather than aesthetics, to engage in tentative and varied strolls, flights, and dwellings in the neighborhood of art. It is to avoid the all-or-nothing views of aesthetics.

Nabokov's butterflies famously display the finely patterned wing of art-and-science, beauty-and-morality, arabesque-and-grid; indeed, they bring into intricate proximities, not synthesis, any of a number of erstwhile dichotomies. Such a butterfly has, in my fond imaginings, occasionally fluttered through the work that follows. Mine is a work of pattern, and it does not shy away from complication or even entanglement. In the spirit of Alexander Baumgarten ("The more that is gathered together in a confused representation, the more extensive clarity the representation has.") it looks for and embraces clarity which is not necessarily simplicity. This study itself has been conceived as a large pattern. Meditations on four artistic phenomena – sentimentality, domesticity, sublimity, aestheticism – appear between chapters addressing the study's principal writers: Ruskin, Dante Gabriel Rossetti, Augusta Evans, and William James. Because this is a work of *arrangement* rather than an organic or fused whole, it is open to rearrangement and repetition with a difference. Any of its elements may, for a time, figure as center. *Beyond this introduction, meditations and chapters may be read in any order.* This is a work that tends to begin again and again, although it provides opportunities for dwelling. It is meant not to define Victorian Modernism, but to suggest its own revision.

But why primarily nineteenth-century writers in a study that also addresses the issues of twentieth-century modernisms? I have in passing sketched relations to twentieth-century writers such as Proust, James Joyce, Wallace Stevens, Gertrude Stein, and Elizabeth Bishop. A fuller treatment of that century would have required a second volume. But more important than the issue of length is the issue of critical mode. Much of what I have seen in nineteenth-century texts I have seen because I looked at them through a twentieth-century lens. The latter century is in this way everywhere implied, but not always stated. Further, each of the chapters and each of the meditations may be treated as, to borrow a phrase from William James, "little hangings-together" within the larger hanging-together of the book. The partial stories of the world "mutually interlace and interfere at points" (*P*, p. 71) – and if others find it useful to link their stories of twentieth-century literature to this study, it will have fulfilled a pragmatist goal by at least presenting Victorian Modernism as what William James would call a "live option."

There is another reason, though, why I have chosen these four writers in particular. They present a pleasing historical pattern as they group about one American publication of their day, *The Crayon*, forming less than a cohesive coterie, more than a random set. Art critic William Michael Rossetti (Dante Gabriel Rossetti's brother, an original member of the Pre-Raphaelite brotherhood, and its self-appointed publicist) appeared in its pages, as did Henry James, Sr., whose religious philosophy and personality influenced his son William. *The Crayon* also presented to the American public much of Ruskin's work, sometimes before it appeared in book form in the United States.[18] And Evans clearly chose him as a teacher; he provides the epigraph to *St. Elmo*.

Ruskin we might liken to a moving spider in the web of arguments that stretches across this study, perhaps because as both a critic and an artist he so frequently presents and explores hypotheses about what art and artists are and do. Of the four writers I discuss, he is the only one read by all the others. His relationship with Dante Gabriel Rossetti and Elizabeth Siddal has been well documented, and he also provides a strong link between the two principal literatures of this work, English and American.[19] He was exceedingly well known throughout America during the Victorian period – we know that not only Evans and James, but also most educated readers of the day, would have read at least some of his work.[20]

Augusta Evans took Ruskin's words to heart before Proust did. Characters in one of her novels model a "school of design" where people may see "specimens of the best decorative art of the world" on the school which Rossetti, William Morris, and Ruskin created in Red Lion Square.[21] The heroine of Evans's *St. Elmo* borrows Ruskin's passion for world mythology, specifically imitating his fascination with the mythologies of William Tell and the Egyptian goddess Neith.[22] In such admiration for Ruskin, Evans, as a domestic novelist, was not alone. Harriet Beecher Stowe, for example, was proud to announce that she had visited Ruskin in England. While the Bible was the most important book to nineteenth-century American women who wrote domestic and sentimental novels, they schooled themselves fervently in the works of John Bunyan, Charlotte Brontë, Lord Byron, and John Ruskin. Why Ruskin? They saw in him a good Christian man who loved the Bible and preached the virtues. Further, he taught Americans, and American women in particular, that a man could discuss the affections of the human heart, and, what is more, could mention such affections in the varied contexts of judging high art, explaining the natural world, and writing history. What he did it was safe for them to do.

Whatever his subject, and however pious he may have been, Ruskin preached an experiential approach to the world, not a dogmatic one, counseling his readers, as Dante Rossetti had earlier, to look accurately, but to think of accuracy as a matter of actual, tender experience. Ruskin reassured women when he made such pronouncements as "It is not feeling, nor fancy, nor imagination . . . that I have put before science, but watchfulness, experience, affection, and trust in nature".[23] In these terms, women writers who lacked systematic education or doubted their right or ability to engage in describing the world could find confidence in their own human goodness. Taking a degree mattered less than taking care, sincerity mattered more than science. Furthermore, Ruskin demonstrated that a good Christian could take a fervent interest in art, that beauty and morality were entwined. To women writers who feared novel reading and writing, Ruskin's message came as good news.

William James, too, read and admired Ruskin. Even without claiming Ruskin as a source, we may see ample similarities between their ideas. Both wondered about the nature of faith and looked for answers not in Church doctrine but in the actual experiences of people, in what, for example, James called the "buildings out" of faith and Ruskin called the Gothic impulse in architecture. James's essay "The Will to Believe" describes the way in which a decision to believe can bring the repose of faith; Ruskin describes a similar insight in an 1852 letter to his father. "I resolved," Ruskin writes, "that at any rate I would act as if the Bible *were* true; that if it were not, at all events I should be no worse off than I was before; that I would believe in Christ, and take Him for my Master in whatever I did . . . When I rose in the morning the cold and cough were gone; and – I felt a peace and spirit in me I had never known before" (10.xxxix). James explained "The Sentiment of Rationality"; Ruskin spent a lifetime telling his audience that their sentiments mattered, that they must express their feelings through their thought and work.

Ruskin, however, provides only one of several centers for my investigations. Studying Victorian Modernism, I believe, we will learn to ponder works of art as webs of relations and ideas with multiple centers and gaps, a filigree-in-progress. Or, in weightier terms, we will learn to pay attention to collections of things, arranged but subject to rearrangement. In parallel, our critical goal will be to chart coherences that begin and end with critical scintillations, not solid blocks. Like the structural designs of buildings that Ruskin often found less interesting than their surface ornamentations, the solidities of this study exist for the patterns they make possible, not the patterns for the solid blocks.

One important pragmatist pattern has been provided by James when he asks us to consider

the world ... as a collection, some parts of which are conjunctively and others disjunctively related. Two parts, themselves disjoined, may nevertheless hang together by intermediaries with which they are severally connected, and the whole world eventually may hang together similarly, inasmuch as *some* path of conjunctive transition by which to pass from one of its parts to another may always be discernible. Such determinately various hanging-together may be called *concatenated* union, to distinguish it from the 'through-and-through' type of union, 'each in all and all in each' ... which monistic systems hold to obtain when things are taken in their absolute reality.[24]

Such a union, James's notion of Pragmatist and Radical Empiricist unity, describes both a central practice of Victorian Modernist writers and a central practice of this study as well. It is a process of recentralization, rearrangement, and tactile meaning, and one might imagine it as lace-making or interior decoration.[25]

Concatenated union is more closely related to Romantic notions of Fancy than to Imagination. The Victorian Modernists' Romantic fore-bear, Coleridge, describes the supreme, God-the-Father-like powers of the Secondary Imagination. He even coins a term, "esemplastic" – "to shape into one," – both to describe such imagination and to enact it as he collapses two Greek words into one Angloid word. The Secondary Imagination "dissolves, diffuses, dissipates, in order to re-create ... struggles to idealize and to unify. It is essentially *vital*, even as all objects (*as* objects) are essentially dead and fixed." In contrast to Imagination, Fancy is of the kingdom of death, for it "has no other counters to play with, but fixities and definites ... [like ordinary memory] the Fancy must receive all its materials ready made from the law of association."[26] Fancy is, as it were, the interior decorator of the art world – it never creates from unformed matter paintings or poems of the first order, but merely rearranges existing artistic furniture. Surely moving received, dead objects about is, in comparison to the vast seminal power of the unifying and idealizing Imagination, woman's work.[27]

Indeed, the very notion of decorative art, ornamentation and detail work – as opposed to one central infusion of breath that, like God creating the world, makes a work whole – has a gendered history.[28] To the extent that detailed ornamentation can obscure the central subject, or even take on an important life of its own, to decorate or ornament is intrinsically to challenge the notion of unified, mastering form.

"Hanging together" implies less than total union. James uses it to describe the very process of consciousness, suggesting that we are all artists in our sensory lives: "Out of what is in itself an undistinguishable, swarming *continuum* devoid of distinction or emphasis, our senses make for us by attending to this motion, and ignoring that, a world full of contrasts, of sharp accents, of abrupt changes, of picturesque light and shade (*PP*, I:284). For James, philosophy is what we all do in making sense of the world, and it is a process linked to the making of art: we explore and test possibilities, we try to maintain the "richest intimacy" with the world, we trace the practical consequences of a notion and judge it by our impressions and feelings as we dwell in them. We taste experience, judge the flavor, and move according to another part of our experience, "linking things satisfactorily" (*P*, p. 34) into the creation of our world. In this way we all compose patterns; and these patterns we relate to the (already mentioned) "innumerable little hangings-together of the world's parts within the larger hangings-together, little worlds, not only of discourse but of operation, within the wider universe." (*P*, p. 67).

These hangings-together James takes aesthetically, as well: "Things tell a story. Their parts hang together so as to work out a climax. They play into each other's hands expressively. . . . The world is full of partial stories that run parallel to one another, beginning and ending at odd times. . . . we cannot unify them completely in our minds" (*P*, p. 71).

John Shade, poet laureate of the country of lost souls and partial stories in Nabokov's *Pale Fire*, chooses pattern upon pattern:

> My picture book was at an early age
> The painted parchment papering our cage:
> Mauve rings around the moon; blood-orange sun;
> Twinned Iris; and that rare phenomenon
> The iridule—when, beautiful and strange,
> In a bright sky above a mountain range
> One opal cloudlet in an oval form
> Reflects the rainbow of a thunderstorm
> Which in a distant valley has been staged –
> For we are most artistically caged.[29]

John Shade is at this moment both poet and art critic. His "iridule," made of water, light, printed word and imagination, is also a version of the rainbow, nature's own work of art, translated by a young aesthete's yearning to oval, opal form. His cage is also his space of freedom and his home; and he imagines it as abundantly filled, like a Victorian parlour, with as many shapes and patterns as he needs.

Dante Rossetti similarly writes and paints the story of "[t]enderness, the constant unison of wonder and familiarity so mysteriously allied in nature, the sense of fullness and abundance such as we feel in a field, not because we pry into it at all, but because it is all there. . . . " Tenderness is "the inestimable prize to be secured".[30] Ruskin, too, describes his experience of tender pattern in the landscape of northern climes when he sees: "Not the diffused perpetual presence of the burden of mist, but the going and returning of intermittent cloud. All turns upon that intermittence. Soft moss on stone and rock; – cave fern of tangled glen; – wayside well – perennial, patient, silent, clear;" (7.178).

Proust not only touches Ruskin when he reads his work with love and visits the places Ruskin has touched, but he also creates, with Ruskin's intermittent help, *A la Recherche du Temps Perdu.* The paralyzed narcissist and aesthete Charles Swann is, like Ruskin himself, a wealthy man, an art critic, and an unlucky lover. Swann has realized that (though not why) his love affair with Odette has failed. Fitfully asleep in his own life, he is about to be awakened by Beauty incarnate in the musical art of the composer Vinteuil, himself victimized by love. Tenderness between suffering men through the medium of art is about to replace in Swann's imagination and heart – at this moment indistinguishable from each other – regret for his lost love. Alone at a party, Swann hears once again "the little phrase," anthem of his and Odette's *amour.* The poignant sound awakens him:

And Swann's thoughts were borne for the first time on a wave of pity and tenderness towards Vinteuil, towards that unknown, exalted brother who must also have suffered so greatly. What could his life have been? From the depths of what well of sorrow could he have drawn that god-like strength, that unlimited power of creation?[31]

Proust rewrites in high-Modernist fashion a literary form from the past: the sentimental tableau. Its elements include a suffering victim and a sensitive spectator who can read the victim's body in order to know, even empathically inhabit, that person's mind, spirit, and heart. Action halts for a time, and the author, narrator, and reader (if all goes well) are overcome, almost beyond the ability of language to communicate. In this expanding moment only feelings matter.[32]

For eighteenth-century readers, a sentimental scene such as Proust's would have required the actual presence of the suffering Vinteuil, with the pitying, empathizing gaze of Swann focused directly upon him. By the mid-nineteenth century, writers create more abstract sentimental tableaux. Here, for example, Vinteuil's work of art stands in for him, expressing, even embodying, his innermost self. A little thing that is a great thing happens: in hearing these notes, the souls of Swann and Vinteuil meet in an expanding moment created by Swann's sympathetic curiosity, a pooling of time in which music and sympathy together free him from the prison of his own dormant imagination.

Implicit in Proust's tableau, and finally inseparable from one another, are four complex notions which we may, for a moment, artificially separate: sentiment, as we have already seen, along with aestheticism, domesticity, and sublimity. Together they comprise much of the wisdom Proust culled from his Victorian teacher, and they will help to structure my study as well. *Sentiment*: Swann feels acutely the sorrows of Vinteuil, the local Combray music master whose lesbian daughter makes him the subject of malicious gossip. *Aestheticism*: Swann is potentially capable of deep and generous feeling because he is a sensitive gentleman of consummate good taste and artistic judgment who can fully savor a phrase of beautiful music. His love of art, hallowed by Vinteuil's musical presence, allows him to grow morally, to pose at this moment a question about the humanity of another, and by so asking, to begin to save himself. *Sublimity*: "that god-like strength, that unlimited power of expression" that Swann believes Vinteuil to possess removes him from the company of mere mortals and places him in an elevated realm apart – but not completely. Vinteuil's sublimity is extensive. It reaches through space and time, not above or beyond them, as Swann feels a deep and specifically human tie to him: "that unknown, that exalted brother who must have suffered so greatly." *Domesticity*: Vinteuil's art issues from the richness of daily life in Combray. The home truths of Vinteuil's musical existence – his careful cottage existence with Mlle. Vinteuil, his direct connection to "Swann's Way," (the landscape of an almost lost Eden of familial tenderness that presents a well-prepared lunch as a work of art), the hiddenness of his public success – have infused Vinteuil's ethereal art as Proust imagines it. Vinteuil makes his art at the wayside in Combray and not in the nineteenth-century capital of culture, Paris.

Proust links notions of sentiment, aestheticism, sublimity, and domesticity not just in this tableau, but throughout the diffuse and interlocking tableaux of his complex, multi-centered novel. By early in the twentieth century, these elements may mingle as equals: the weave is so tight and the pattern so fine that the reader barely stops to examine its parti-colored texture. A major inspiration for such an undertaking has been another vast, nearly static set of tableaux mingling the same elements: the *oeuvre* of John Ruskin.

Contemplate, for example, Ruskin's memory of the Col de la Faucille, which rises like a sublime peak among the many reminiscences of *Praeterita*:

the Col de la Faucille, on that day of 1835, opened to me in distinct vision the Holy Land of my future work and true home in this world. My eyes had been opened, and my heart with them, to see and to possess royally such a kingdom! Far as the eye could reach – that land and its moving or pausing waters; Arve, and his gates of Cluse, and his glacier fountains; Rhone, and the infinitude of his sapphire lake, – his peace beneath the narcissus meads of Vevay – his cruelty beneath the promontories of Sierre. And all that rose against and melted into the sky, of mountain and mountain snow; and all that living plain, burning with human gladness – studded with white homes, – a milky way of star-dwellings cast across its sunlit blue. (35.167–168)

Ruskin recounts an experience of montane sublimity whose conventions he would expect his audience to recognize and share. From this pass in the Jura mountains, he can see "the chain of the Alps along a hundred miles of horizon" (35.167). The passage delivers the diction and imagery of sublimity: nobility, cruelty, vastness, extremes of temperature. Not limited to verticality (what Longinus called *hypsos*, the elevated), this sublime also leads the eye outward to a vast plain (what I shall call *platos*, the extended).

Ruskin, however, intertwines with these conventions another set: those of sentimentality. His heart has been opened, it beats with the shapes of what he sees, and what he sees is infused with "human gladness" as well as a more sublime awe. Hearts burn, personified rivers take their rest, and the viewer has lovingly connected with joy, rather than fainted from grandeur. Given the insistently domestic focus of all of *Praeterita*, and especially of the passages immediately preceding this moment of vision, it comes as no surprise that we are asked to understand such sublimity and sentimentality within the context of domesticity. The passage begins with "my true home in the world," gestures toward the shared home of the "Holy Land," and extends to an image of homes as stars. These three intertwinings of immanence (the familiarity of home) and transcendence (the visionary quality of home) echo the larger pattern of intertwining sentiment and sublimity. Finally aestheticism infuses the whole without effacing its separate, but linked, discourses. The boy's work, his home, is to be the home of art, the cultivation of good taste, pleasure, and morality in his own life and in that of his readers. What matters is the making and loving of art, and Ruskin sees nature twice, once as wild, and again as artificial: rivers are gems and mythical beings, glaciers are fountains, mountains are a kingdom.

The Victorian Modern finds a voice. Both Proust and Ruskin create what George Eliot independently described in 1868 as a particular kind of unity:

And as knowledge continues to grow by its alternating processes of distinction and combination, seeing smaller and smaller likenesses and grouping or associating these under a common likeness, it arrives at the conception of wholes composed of parts more and more multiplied and highly differenced, yet more and more absolutely bound together by various conditions of common likeness or mutual dependence. *And the fullest example of such a whole is the highest example of Form: in other words, the relation of multiplex interdependent parts to a whole which is itself in the most varied and therefore the fullest relation to other wholes.* . . . . The highest Form, then, is the highest organism, that is to say, the most varied group of relations bound together in a wholeness which again has the most varied relations with all other phenomena.[33]

When Eliot describes complex wholes that are themselves formed in relation to other complex wholes, she offers us a useful way in which to think about the relation of Proust's and Ruskin's already internally complex works to each other.

Eliot's description offers us as well a way of thinking about the four authors who provide interlinking centers for my own study of "multiplex interdependent parts": Ruskin, Rossetti, Evans, and James. I have chosen these figures for their differences as well as their similarities. Two are American, two are British. Evans is a popular, domestic novelist, Ruskin an art critic, Rossetti a poet and painter, James a scientist and philosopher. Three carry out their work within the confines of the nineteenth century; James publishes through 1910 and has been much more closely associated with Modernism than the others. Of their similarities and historical connections, more later.

For Victorian Modernists, the process of art is something like the process of life. Yeats's old man does say, "Consume my heart away," but the artist who forges the aesthetic object, the wonderous bric-à-brac of the Byzantine bird, continues to burn the hotter for that wish. Let us turn to sharp accents and clouds, intermittences, entanglements, and partial stories – the wayside worlds of Victorian Modernism.

CHAPTER 2

A sweet continuance: John Ruskin's Victorian Modernism

In order to teach men how to be satisfied, it is necessary fully to understand the art and joy of humble life, – this, at present, of all arts or sciences being the one most needing study. Humble life, – that is to say, proposing to itself no future exaltation, but only a sweet continuance ... the life of domestic affection and domestic peace, full of sensitiveness to all elements of costless and kind pleasure.

John Ruskin, *Modern Painters*, v[1]

To read Ruskin is to enter a world of fluid commixtures in which we can observe Victorian Modernism in the making. As he considers the arrangements of nature, art, and society, Ruskin links them to the making of delicate, labyrinthine, sometimes even entangled patterns. Whether Ruskin looks at a Gothic workman's sculpture or the book of nature, he feels

love of all sorts of filigree and embroidery, from hoarfrost to the high clouds. The intricacies of virgin silver, of arborescent gold, the weaving of birds'-nests, the netting of lace, the basket capitals of Byzantium, and most of all the taberna-cle work of the French flamboyant school, possessed from the first, and possess still, a charm for me. (35.157n3)

One might add to his list of filigreed work his own prose. He describes himself as a girl working a sampler, "quietly and methodically as a piece of tapestry," placing the words "firmly in their places like so many stitches, hemm[ing] the edges of chapter round" (35.367–368).[2]

For all Ruskin's lists, numbered categories, definitions, and anatomies, he is not a systematic writer. It has been a tradition among Ruskin scholars to attempt to pin down the excesses and digressions of his expository prose long enough to extract his ideas on given subjects.[3] This study does not jettison that effort, but adds to it by attempting to study the fluid connections among Ruskin's discrete ideas as seriously as those ideas themselves. Differentiating and rationalizing will give way to a host of less tidy activities: mixing, analogizing, linking, wandering, and pausing at the waysides. Ruskin as an artist and critic can teach us his own method, that of exploration rather than system, of intricate and spreading mazes rather than hierarchical orderings, of continual burgeoning into states of repose rather than achieved organic unity. Once we look seriously at relations, at Ruskin's prepositional rather than propositional life, once we acknowledge Ruskin's confusions as his insights, we will recognize him for the aesthetic pragmatist and Victorian Modernist that he was.

To establish Ruskin as a pragmatist, we will follow the multiple and intersecting paths he explored as he sought always contingent truths about beauty, right action, and human identity. He shows his pragmatist credentials when he writes, "an affected Thinker, who supposes his thinking of any other importance than as it tends to work, is about the vainest kind of person that can be found in the occupied classes. Nay, I believe that metaphysicians and philosophers are, on the whole, the greatest troubles the world has got to deal with" (5.333).

The pattern of this chapter presents three interconnected centers. First, Ruskin's interweaving of the conventional rhetorics of domesticity and sentiment. Then, beginning again with a biographical perusal of Ruskin's poignant difficulties in human relations (his needs for personal solitude and a stony integrity conflicting with his needs for community and tender relations), we shall proceed to ask why and how he developed a Victorian Modernist notion of artistic impersonality that was, through Pater, the French Symbolists, and the Parnassians, to mingle in the imaginations of William Butler Yeats, James Joyce, and others. The lapis Chinamen's stony gaiety, the gray isolation in which each Dubliner fantasizes – these are patterned in relation to Ruskin's experiments in feeling. We shall come to understand impersonality as sublime sentimentality, Ruskin's feelings for people extended to vast and important webs of relation spun across his lifetime's work as an aesthetic thinker at, and about, home. To close, we shall dwell in one of Ruskin's late texts, *Roadside Songs of Tuscany* (1884–1885), in which he exemplifies the making of intimate, pragmatic truth over his lifetime. Viewing Ruskin as a pragmatist will lead us to see that, rather than slipping into ineffectual raving as the lights of sanity dimmed, he explored until he could write no more.

For all his fascination with architectural structure, Ruskin loves watery mixtures of things more than solid constructions. He prefers the fluid flutings of capitals to the right angles formed by sturdy walls. Considering San Marco in Venice as perhaps the greatest example of the domestic transformed into "lovely order," he imagines its stone as water: "the crests of the arches break into a marble foam, and toss themselves far into the blue sky in flashes and wreaths of sculptured spray" (10.83). San Marco is, he tells us, "a confusion of delight" (10.83).

Ruskin creates minglings whose separate elements are neither wholly distinct nor wholly merged: water and stone. He prefers unstable mixtures to stable solutions. In this way Ruskin the writer follows his own advice to painters, that those who would capture the truth must understand that nature "is never distinct and never vacant, she is always mysterious, but always abundant; you always see something, but you never see all" (3.329). By analogy, artists and critics – Ruskin was both – must find a way that, whatever the polarities involved, leads them toward neither an ordered and complete synthesis nor an unchecked chaos.

As a pragmatist, Ruskin questions monistic unities and master plans, even though he believes in God.[4] From early on, he praises God as the author and sustainer of all creation yet continuously (and even contradictorily) works his way toward an understanding of creation as a set of fascinating contingencies. Ruskin's monist or essentialist thinking is tempered by pluralist and empiricist leanings; in James's terms, Ruskin is both "tender minded" (going by principles, religious) and "tough-minded" (going by facts, materialist) (*P*, p. 13). He imagines artistic creation itself as a matter of contingent arrangements: "A poet, or creator, is . . . a person who puts things together" (7.215). The artist is one who collects in the storehouse of his memory all the images he has ever seen, and then relaxes into reverie as "over all this unindexed and immeasurable mass of treasure, the imagination [moves,] brooding and wandering, but dream-gifted, so as to summon at any moment exactly such groups of ideas as shall justly fit each other" (6.42). Dreamily, fancifully, precisely and carefully – so the artist places and replaces found images and idea. If those adverbs seem inconsistent, Ruskin minds less than we do. Echoing the Coleridgean notion of Fancy as subordinate to Imagination, he nevertheless presents a notion of creativity as arrangement, not godlike creation *ex nihilo*. This notion is a feminizing one, and we may think of it as interior decoration rather than seminal construction, as housekeeping rather than house-building and as inextricable from his understanding of domesticity's nurturing and sentimental powers.

Arrangement for Ruskin often has a specifically moral quality; "The Law of Help" decrees that "composition may be best defined as the help of everything in the picture by everything else" (7.205).[5] To paint well is to bring into nurturing relation. He frequently views the external walls of domestic buildings as part of a landscape, remaining true to the title of his early work *The Poetry of Architecture*, subtitled *The Architecture of the Nations of Europe Considered in Its Association with Natural Scenery and National Character* (1.1). Throughout Ruskin's oeuvre, Nature presents itself to the careful and loving artist–naturalist in the arrangements and patterns of domestic tenderness: "Every leaf has assuredly an infant bud to take care of, laid tenderly, as in a cradle, just where the leaf-stalk forms a safe niche between it and the main stem" (7.25). Having learned a "'sentimental' love of nature" from Rousseau (35.115), Ruskin often describes nature itself as sentimental tableau:

passing to the edge of a sheet [of unsullied snow] upon the lower Alps, early in May . . . we . . . find two or three little round openings pierced in it, and through these emergent, a slender, pensive, fragile flower, whose small, dark purple, fringed bell hangs down and shudders over the icy cleft that it has cloven, as if . . . partly dying of very fatigue. (4.146)

The viewer's delicate sympathies flow out to flowers as surely as they will on later occasions to dying women, impoverished men, and undernourished children.[6]

Beyond their moral import, arrangements for Ruskin often speak of matters domestic. While he considers domesticity as the ordering and sustaining activities of home life and as the site of the individual's first society, he also sees it as free and abstracted interminglings – filigrees, embroideries, carvings, lacework. These patterns in turn attenuate further, moving toward a place in which discrete human identity in particular disappears toward a limit of self-effacing intimacy. Approaching that limit, Ruskin feels that he has come home. It is this spatial rather than chronological progression – domestic sites (houses, nests) to domestic patterns (lacework, stone-carving) to domestic states (closeness, intimacy that are paradoxically abstract) – and its attendant confusions, that this study will trace.

As he investigates the domestic, Ruskin confronts what was for him an overwhelming personal dilemma, itself an entanglement of questions about identity, intimacy, and personality. What Ruskin cannot achieve in life, finding his being in another person, he achieves in art. Of water Ruskin writes, "how shall we follow its eternal changefulness of feeling? It is like trying to paint a soul" (3.494). We shall observe Ruskin as he creates his own watery confusion, attempting a self-portrayal that delivers him to the mysteries of psychological surface and depth that would soon be explored by Freud. His Tory propensities did not render him from the first

an aesthetic reactionary, the Whistler affair notwithstanding. Like many
early twentieth-century artists, he superimposed reaction and rebellion,
tradition and experimentation. And to the extent that he engaged in a
lifelong meditation on domesticity, he is also part of the feminization of
Modernism which we have yet to understand fully.

To trace the importance of domesticity to Ruskin's self-discovery and
to his participation in Victorian Modernism, we must ask: what did
the domestic allow Ruskin to attempt and even achieve, what was it
good for? In Ruskin's case, as we shall see, domesticity prompted him to
mingle the elements of two powerful literary modes, each with a long
history: sentiment and sublimity. It was for him a force in almost every
tale he told, and its presence, whether literal or metaphorical, veiled
or direct, shifting or solid, suggests it as an important watery medium
for his thought. Neither foundational nor teleological, the scenes and
experiences of domesticity provide pragmatist testing grounds for truths
that are never systematic, wholly rational, or complete.

Ruskin is capable of describing a good painter as one who can by the
power of imagination draw one thread from the "entangled" mass of
a discordant natural scene, "spin it stouter," and then weave it into his
painted scene "so that all its work looks as pure and true as nature itself"
(4.246). Touching the tapestry of his prose, we may choose to tug on the
thread of domesticity. Doing so, we notice its enlacement with a central
question of his day and of his own scene of writing: how do my heartfelt
feelings of sympathy for others (sentimentality) enter into relation with
a universe of larger forces (sublimity), whether those forces be seen as
human or inhuman?[7] That the answer would for Ruskin always involve
studying and making art implies the aesthetic. Sentiment and sublimity
for him meet in the domestic – a sufficient intricacy. Domestic sentiment
and domestic sublimity will each have their moments in this study, but
it is important to realize that, absent clear distinctions between them,
we may yet trace the fluid patterns these notions create, forming and
reforming Ruskin's aesthetic experience.

From juvenilia through *Praeterita* (1885), domesticity appears on the
face of Ruskin's works. It is from the beginning critical to his aesthetic
understanding of architecture. *The Poetry of Architecture* (1837–1838) describes cottages and villas, and although he announces sequels to discuss
"fortress and palace," (1.30) and "Homes of the Mighty" (1.78n1), these
he never writes.

At the height of his middle period, Ruskin describes the surviving pre-
Renaissance architecture of Venice, San Marco included, as domestic

in origin. He argues that sacred Gothic architecture is "not, in the total spirit of it, more devotional than humane"; that "all the beautiful forms of it will condescend to the simplest domestic comfort" (33.245); and that "no style of noble architecture *can* be exclusively ecclesiastical. It must be practised in the dwelling before it be perfected in the church" (10.123). Lest there be any doubt as to the importance of domestic expression, Ruskin states,

once for all, I would desire here clearly and forcibly to assert, that wherever Christian church architecture has been good and lovely, it has been merely the perfect development of the common dwelling-house architecture of the period; that when the pointed arch was used in the street, it was used in the church ... [churches] were never built in any separate, mystical, and religious style; they were built in the manner that was common and familiar to everybody at the same time. (10.120)

Thus San Marco "when it was built ... rose in the midst of other work fanciful and beautiful as itself ... every dwelling-house in the middle ages was rich with the same ornaments and quaint with the same grotesques" (10.118).[8] While Ruskin argues that the most exalted Gothic architecture is the *perfection* of domestic architecture, he simultaneously instructs us in the fundamental quality of the domestic; the Gothic cathedral is the "continuation ... of a style ... familiar to every eye throughout all [Venice's] lanes and streets." (10.118–119). Ruskin maintains this position as late as 1864, when, in "Traffic," he lectures the burghers of Bradford on the need to build all their buildings in the spirit of the sacred: not the clergy's idea of the sacred, but the laborer's and warrior king's understanding of it as continuous with domestic cottage and castle (18.444).

As Ruskin attempts to bring closure to his five-volume study, *Modern Painters*, he depicts a hopeless figure – part J. M. W. Turner, part Ruskin – who, having battled the military, pseudo-religious, and monetary "dragons" of modern society, teaches us the value of "sweet continuance," of "the life of domestic affection and domestic peace" (7.427). Long before *Praeterita*'s encomia to life at home, Ruskin writes that great artists such as Veronese, "delight ... in slight, sweet, every-day incident, but hide ... deep meaning underneath it" (7.295). Even when Ruskin imagines repairing the modern city, he continues to think in cottage-sized plans: to organize a squad of broom men, to keep a little bit of London as "perfectly clean" as Utopia (28.xvi–xviii).

Yet domesticity in Ruskin's writings has a peculiar quality: it is almost always described abstractly, or from a distance. Facades of cottages, nests of birds, or concepts such as industrious repose, affection, and humility replace the physical objects and human dramas of hearth-side domestic arrangements. Unlike Dante Gabriel Rossetti, who transforms the intimacies of domestic activities, relations, and things into poetry and painting as he brings nature itself half-indoors in his paintings, Ruskin describes primarily the *exteriors* of humble people's homes. Late in life, writing of the thatched cottages of the Dole, he comments on his characteristic aloofness toward people's home-lives: "Strange, that I never inquired into the special reason of that form, nor looked into a single cottage to see the mode of its inhabitation!" (35.159).

Like Rossetti, who insists that feeling is the mark of true poetry ("All poetry, that is really poetry, affects me deeply and often to tears") and who loves details, ornamentation, and arrangements, Ruskin, too, searches for feeling in small things and patterns.[9] Looking for the ornamental and the arranged in an unexpected dimension of domesticity – on the surfaces of those external walls – he often examines them inch by inch.[10] The contrast of Ruskin's love of detail, presented at close range and described in the language of traditionally feminine relation or intimacy, to the rarity in his writing of descriptions of interior, domestic details, seems at first simply contradictory. *Praeterita* represents a great (and significantly late) exception to Ruskin's more common exterior perspective. It will be part of our task to understand that such a turn required a lifetime of pragmatist exploration, specifically on the subject of the rewards and dangers of intimacy. Ruskin often contradicts himself in print, but, as we shall see, this particular contradiction – between love of domestic detail and unwillingness to depict life at the hearthside in any but the most general terms – occurs so frequently as to become an important pattern as his works unfold.

It is as if Ruskin lived emotionally in an English landscape painting with a cottage or church in the near distance. He seems incapable, however, of finding his way into a Dutch painting of luminous interiors, and he even scorns such painting as he begins his career as an art critic (3.90). Abstract terms veil the particularities of private life: work, affection, steadfastness, order, kindness, community, care, family, sympathy. Although Ruskin chooses distance, he worries about where to stand. To solve the problems of point of view and perspective, major preoccupations of Victorian Modernism, Ruskin develops two artistic modes: sentiment and sublimity. Through them, Ruskin will create a self in relation both to other individuals and to communities that are simultaneously social and aesthetic.

THE WAYS OF SENTIMENT

Throughout his work Ruskin meditates on the possibility of a force, an artful energy, that would aid him in reading the exteriors of buildings, and, analogically, the exteriors of people, as evidence of their interiors. This force is sentiment, a strong presence whenever Ruskin refers to the domestic, and finally inseparable from it and from his pragmatist method of filigreed connection. Ruskin repeatedly teaches his readers that sentiment is a necessary quality of true art. Composition and arrangement carried out without emotion are mere "watchmaking" (7.215), while a great composition always has a "leading emotional purpose" (7.217). Artists who matter possess imagination that is "based upon, and appeals to, a deep heart feeling" (4.298). Like other nineteenth-century writers who commingle the already complex literary phenomena of sensibility and sentiment, Ruskin is capable of contempt for their qualities, especially in popular literature.[11] Yet once Ruskin learns to widen and deepen its venue, sentiment becomes a pervasive presence in his works. It enables him to approach difficult problems by insisting on the power of tenderness, receptivity, and relation: the feminized efficacy of heart's knowledge. Richly developing a sentimental tendency toward the reflexive – a feeling portrayal of those who feel – Ruskin seeks answers to related questions about human intimacy, human identity, and human artistic creation.

Ruskin's sentimental talk grows out of domestic concerns, and, circularly, domesticity matters because it is infused with sentiment. We can use the terms "domestic sentimentality" and "sentimental domesticity" interchangeably to describe an energy pulsing, now delicately, now passionately, throughout Ruskin's oeuvre. The diction and cadences of sentiment and domesticity often merge as Ruskin makes aesthetic judgments. For example, Ruskin describes Samuel Prout as "trained among the rough rocks and simple cottages of Cornwall. . . . [He was] gifted with infinite readiness in composition, but also with infinite affection for the kind of subjects he had to portray" (12.362). As Ruskin tells his aesthetic rosary – artist, drawings, rough rocks, simple cottages, infinite affection – his affection for his own subject, Prout, draws together art, nature, and domestic dwelling into his own composition.[12]

To demonstrate that Ruskin writes in a sentimental tradition is to present one context for his pragmatist efforts. He imagines sentimental relation as a flux in which traditional hierarchies of being partially dissolve along with the traditional unitary subject, man made in the image of God. Simply by insisting repeatedly and passionately that, whatever the subject at hand, feeling matters, Ruskin establishes sentiment as an engine that drives the pragmatist truth-making process. So, too, to choose a twentieth-century example, does Flannery O'Connor. Hazel Motes of *Wise Blood*, propelled by a bodily wisdom that runs counter to his principled atheism, travels picaresque routes until he finds his way to the only home that matters, with Christ. O'Connor imagines a grotesque sentimentality – obscene relations between people, victims tortured by their observers – in order to figure forth Motes's homecoming, what James would call in *The Varieties of Religious Experience* a sense of repose in the faith-state.

The traditions of sentiment and sensibility – between which Ruskin does not always make a clear distinction – provide a significant literary element of his "scene of writing," the microculture within which he formulated his ideas of what it means to be a writer.[13] He went to school in Samuel Richardson, Henry Fielding, and Laurence Sterne, even noting in his diary that *Sir Charles Grandison* has had "a greater practical effect on me for good than anything I ever read in my life."[14] In 1836 he works out his allegiance to sentiment and sensibility in "Essay on Literature." A forceful apology for sentimental writing in Bulwer, Scott, and Byron, "Essay on Literature" defends sentiment in sentimental terms. The seventeen-year-old Ruskin instructs us, for example, that Bulwer "revels in the deep waters of the human heart, where all is seen misty and dim, but most beautiful, by the pale motion of the half lost light of the outward sun through the softly sobbing waves of our thoughts" (1.371). Yeats in his early years could have written this passage. Simply stated, the more sentiment, the more beauty: "The more we can feel, the more beauty we shall perceive in this universal frame" (1.371).

By 1853, Ruskin has refined but not substantially altered his juvenile notion of sentiment:

The whole function of the artist in the world is to be a seeing and feeling creature, to be an instrument of such tenderness and sensitiveness, that . . . no instantaneous and evanescent expression of the visible things around him, nor any of the emotions which they are capable of conveying to the spirit which has been given him, shall either be left unrecorded, or fade from the book of record . . . The work of his life is to be two-fold only; to see, to feel. (11.49)

He might have added, "to read," for both Ruskin's sentimental writing and his discussions of sentiment depends on other writers. All books of record are for Ruskin but commentary on *the* book of record: we know that the most influential book in his life was the Bible. Any intense expression of sentiment (love, fear, delight, or anger) is also for Ruskin an upswelling of religious feeling, and often accompanied by Biblical quotation or allusion. He also read Sir Walter Scott and William Wordsworth with fervor; Byron, he tells us, "felt the facts" (35.150).[15]

Beyond them, he knew the popular literature of sentiment. A far from exhaustive list would begin with gift books such as *Friendship's Offering*, to which he himself contributed.[16] Ruskin dares to refer his readers to *Aunt Judy's Magazine*, and mentions approvingly such sentimental and popular writers as J. H. B. de Saint Pierre, Eugene Sue, Ouida (Louise De La Ramée) and Flora (Lady Lugard) Shaw.

We must pause here to consider how to identify in Ruskin's art sentimental expression that is protean and pervasive. His sentimental writing changes form in order to accomplish the particular task at hand, whether it be to explain the natural history of a mountain or to recount for us an 1867 *Daily Telegraph* story of a starving father and son (18.90–92). We can, however, identify a range of sentimental rhetoric, one which proceeds in parallel with the increasing abstraction of domesticity as Ruskin sees it in things, then textures, then abstractions. His sentimental writing begins with the literal and figural, extends through degrees of indirection and abstraction, and trails into space with the invisible or inaudible.

To begin, the literal or figural. As Ruskin describes Sir Edwin Landseer's "Old Shepherd's Chief-mourner" (3.88–89), the rhetoric of sentiment flows from the legible, "realistic" subject of the painting, a dog weeping at the coffin side of his master:

the close pressure of the dog's breast against the wood, the convulsive clinging of the paws, which has dragged the blanket off the trestle, the total powerlessness of the head laid, close and motionless, upon its folds, the fixed and tearful fall of the eye in its utter hopelessness . . . these are all thoughts . . . by which the picture is separated at once from hundreds of equal merit. . . . (3.89)

Part of Ruskin's campaign to convince his English readers that painting matters because it contains ideas important to their own lives, this passage appears in a section of *Modern Painters* 1 entitled "Definition of Greatness in Art." It teaches that painterly thought involves embodied feeling: the weight and tears of the innocent victim, the dog. Ruskin invites his audience to substitute, for the so-called greatness of neo-classical painting of the Italianate school, a portrait of an anthropomorphic dog. And in this *mise-en-abîme* of sentimental looking by the reader, Ruskin, Landseer, and the dog, relation grows. Through such layered sentimentality, Ruskin the art critic can attempt to translate an actual painting into the world of shared and pulsating life which we all, presumably, know.[17]

Ruskin's rewriting of Landseer's tableau makes it easy to recognize the sentimental – it is a sentimental reading of an already clichéd sentimental subject, the Victorian Fidoesque. The heartfelt can, however, enter both works of art and Ruskin's evocations of them in an almost coded form, by the briefest of allusions. Since Ruskin practices a sentimental aesthetics, often distinguishing good art from mediocre or bad art by the immediacy of feeling it communicates, good paintings need not include figures of dogs or children, grieving mothers or adoring fathers. They can evoke sentiment more abstractly. A bit of throbbing color can do so, or a confusion of clouds, or the grain of wood. In Ruskin's own verbal equivalent of such painted feeling, only a synecdochal word or two is required to place us in the landscape of sentiment, especially because he often moralizes as he describe, e.g., "No air is sweet that is silent; it is only sweet when full of low currents of under sound – triplets of birds, and murmur and chirp of insects, and deep-toned words of men" (17.11). Ruskin's propensity for sentimental diction – noble, tender, sweet, good, kind, bright, heart, humble, true – reminds us that we are never far from a sentimental tableau.

But beyond Ruskin's sentimental susurrus, there is a further degree of abstraction: speaking silence, an insistence on sentiment so pervasive that it need not be specified. To "hear" this silent sentiment in Ruskin's prose, let us consider a characteristic passage, necessarily quoted at length:

Turner was the only painter who had ever represented the surface of calm or the *force* of agitated water. He obtains this expression of force in falling or running water by fearless and full rendering of its forms. He never loses himself and his subject in the splash of the fall, his presence of mind never fails as he goes down; he does not blind us with the spray, or veil the countenance of his fall with its own drapery . . . [In] the Upper Fall of the Tees, though the whole basin of the fall is blue and dim with the rising vapour, yet the attention of the spectator is chiefly directed to the concentric zones and delicate curves of the falling water itself; and it is impossible to express with what exquisite accuracy these are given . . . Now water will leap a little way, it will leap down a weir or over a stone, but it *tumbles* over a high fall like this; and it is when we have lost the parabolic line, and arrived at the catenary, when we have lost . . . the *spring* of the fall, and arrived at the *plunge* of it, that we begin really to feel its weight and wildness. Where water takes its first leap from the top, it is cool, and collected, and uninteresting, and mathematical; but it is when it finds that it has got into a scrape, and has farther to go than it thought, that its character comes out: it is then that it begins to writhe, and twist, and sweep out, zone after zone, in wilder stretching as it falls; and to send down the rocket-like, lance-pointed, whizzing shafts at its sides . . . And it is this prostration, this hopeless abandonment of its ponderous power to the air, which is always peculiarly expressed by Turner. (3.552–554)

To say that a passage is silently sentimental is perhaps to open any passage in Ruskin to such a judgment, to claim that we can "hear" the sentimental wherever we should like. We need not find such a broad claim disturbing, however, because Ruskin himself writes, "In these books of mine, their distinctive character, as essays on art, is their bringing everything to a root in human passion or human hope" (7.257). Human passion and hope are nothing if not sentiments. But how, beyond its structure of spectatorship, does this passage reflect and transform the topoi of literary sentiment? And why should we consider the watery energy of the passage to be specifically the energy of sentiment?

We might begin with the passage's immediate context: the lengthy chapter "Of Water, as Painted by Turner." Like a traditional man of sensibility who has been called upon to give of himself in order to establish and reestablish a world of civic responsibility and moral rectitude,[18] Ruskin is as much concerned with virtue as he is with water. Seeing accurately is a moral act, and Turner is a moral man: "Turner had a heart as intensely kind, and as nobly true, as ever God gave one of his creatures" (7.448). Part of Ruskin's celebration of the painter he has set out to defend, the description requires the reader, like Ruskin himself, to look long at this painting (in our mind's eye, or with an engraving of it nearby), and to sympathize with Turner by touching upon his work, catenary by catenary. So near to the Fall(s), virtue requires labor. As we form this relation to Turner and to Ruskin, we become better people – or so Ruskin would wish.

Affiliation with, rather than power over, matters here, as it frequently does in eighteenth-century sentimental tableaux.[19] Such appreciation can, however, easily give way, as we shall see in the case of *Roadside Songs of Tuscany*, to identification or appropriation. Turner's artistic powers imperceptibly become the powers of the water he views, as sentimental observer and the observed engage in a deep reflexivity. In turn, Ruskin himself melts into the scene he observes: Turner's watery ways and water's Turneresque qualities expand to a triad including Ruskin. The passage anatomizes a power that must be relinquished in order to be won, an activity that becomes passivity. The force of the Falls doesn't conquer, it "is expressed." We don't see water hitting anything; even when it sends down "lance-pointed, whizzing shafts," they are mysteriously transformed into the water's "prostration," "hopeless abandonment." All falls, losing physical power but gaining moral power on the way. Whatever destructive power the "powerful stream" possesses has been tamed by "delicate curves" and "exquisite fidelity." Passivity extends beyond the triad of water, Turner, and Ruskin to include ourselves: our beholding of all this is of course an engaged passivity, too. Nor does Ruskin gives us a sense of Turner's actively painting the scene. To behold nature sympathetically, because accurately, is all that he need do.

Further, the water itself presents a sentimental or sensible instance of victimization, in that it is utterly "self-absorbed" in its experience. Its struggle is a moral struggle, and its success lies in its internalized defeat, presented (not without moral ambiguity) for our delectation. If, as Adam Smith tells us in *Theory of Moral Sentiments*, sympathy involves an "observing subject having experienced that which the sufferer is experiencing,"[20] Ruskin feels the water's pain and triumph, and wishes us to, as well.

Beyond these sentimental implications, Ruskin suggests one more, of startling import: everything in this scene has entered into feeling relation to such an extent that metamorphosis occurs. Every spectator of this scene is also its creator and even one of its subjects: God ("actual" nature), Turner (painted nature), Ruskin (words on the page), and the reader (asked to imagine it all). Like Nabokov's "iridule," this is a scene created by more than one artificer.[21] Actual water and painted water flow together, as do God's love for mankind and Ruskin's love for Turner. Patterns upon patterns: dispassionate study becomes passionate embrace, and Ruskin has begun, in his own novel way, to lessen the distance between himself and others.

Ruskin begins *Modern Painters*, 1, of which the passage quoted above is part, as a work of sentimentality: observing the victimized Turner, Ruskin will display to us, his readers, the appropriate receptive stance for experiencing Turner's art, and through it, his heart. Tutoring us in aesthetic issues and improving our characters constitute a single activity. But a few chapters into the process Ruskin's chapter headings and subheadings, such as "Of the relative importance of truths" or "All truths valuable as they are characteristic" (3.59), prove incapable of containing the teeming ideas, observations, and pronouncements that follow. Ever the meliorist and sentimental moralist, Ruskin first beholds a tableau, painted or otherwise, then attempts to discourse on the virtues. His message of sentimental salvation begins in the literal, moves through the metaphorical, and diffuses into abstraction. Like the brush strokes in Turner's painting, his lessons are "confused, odd, incomprehensible; having neither beginning nor end, – melting into each other, or straggling over each other, or going wrong and coming right again, or fading away altogether" (6.83).

A full appreciation of Ruskin's sentimentality, however, requires more than taxonomies of sentimental sources and techniques; we must ask what difference sentiment made to his thinking as he pragmatically sought and made the truths of human identity. Such an inquiry will lead us to tug, once again, on the strand of domesticity in his works.

DOMESTIC SENTIMENT AND PRAGMATISM

Because Ruskin's "scene of writing," is always, simply, home – *wherever* he felt or created intensely he labeled as "home" – and because he associates home with love, domestic sentiment is as necessary an idea for him as is God. As Ruskin matures, his Protestant and evangelical love of God broadens and diversifies, initially spurred by his heartfelt admiration for the monuments of Roman Catholicism, and encouraged through the years by his mythography. He never loses his interest in the type or the essence, but he does dwell with increasing confidence in particulars which are not wholly subsumed by God's plan. Contingency joins with Creation. He repeatedly chooses – over fixities and certainties – the ability to move in eccentric ways among varieties of places, concepts, artists, and things. However appealing it may be to locate his "unconversion" in 1858, however true it may be that he adopted evangelical rhetoric in his writing, it is *also* true that Ruskin the believer mingled with Ruskin the apostate throughout his life. The "unconversion" was not the well-defined experience of a day, as he would have us believe; it had slowly evolved. Furthermore, Ruskin never lost his faith: the prefix "un" captures only part of the truth. The two Ruskins, Protestant and post-Protestant, child at home and man without his own home, struggle throughout his life, and his writings themselves present the best evidence of this fertile confusion.

Loving concern is for Ruskin first among the sentiments, a nineteenth-century form of benevolence. Love is for him the presence of creative energy which is both sacred and secular, a feeling of intensity that, like the flux he so often invokes, rearranges things, metamorphically dissolves things, one into another, or makes connections between them. As we have seen, this sentiment often takes domestic forms, for from the first, Ruskin associates it with home and family. Ruskin and a host of nineteenth-century novelists, including the American "domestic" novelists who read him fervently, figure sentiment as much through coziness as sorrow. Ruskin includes his share of dark tableaux of suffering – we think, for example, of his description of a Highland scene that at first appears beautiful, but then reveals an undernourished child, the father who lost his wife in childbirth, and their hovel (7.268–271). Yet the amelioration of such tragedy is everywhere to be found, in humble domesticity, whether it be actual or only nostalgically recalled. Even when Gothic purity lies ravaged by Renaissance brutality, Ruskin teaches that domesticity can effect, cottage by cottage, a sweet continuance.

Like sentiment, which can expand or shrink to fill available space, domesticity is for Ruskin a flexible notion. Domesticity expands into the sophistications of Chartres Cathedral or the economy of the good state, yet shrinks to the comforting idea that in the ordinary and the local our salvation lies. It expands to describe nations and shrinks to describe a tiny bit of sculpture on a cathedral. "Heart-sight deep as eyesight" (7.377) we learn at home; but such heart-sight gives us leave to recognize much of what we look feelingly upon – wherever it may be – *as* home. "Repose," feeling peacefully in place, at home, is a favorite word of Ruskin's. It is the domestic grail of sentiment.

Ruskin *used* domestic sentiment, however conservative a formula it may appear, to think beyond available cultural truths. Sentiment, although we expect it to be tiresomely formulaic or self-indulgent, hides at its heart difficult questions and brave experiments, not just easy answers and self-indulgent emotion.[22] Conventional forms, he demonstrates, may actually free us to imagine a world beyond the given.

Through domestic sentiment Ruskin tests familiar forms of thought, especially those involving dichotomies, and develops both the ways in which he thinks and also the range of subjects he can consider. Having inherited a world of such stark polarities as Herne Hill and world, good and evil, orthodoxy and blasphemy, and public and private, Ruskin seeks a middle way—not through synthesis, but through the creation of a manifold of relations. He finds it in the entwinement of aestheticism and domesticity, an available form for thinking of a place or situation neither wholly private nor fully public; neither entirely sacred yet not profane, neither altogether open to the elements nor altogether free from them; neither given to us nor made by us, and so on.

When Ruskin follows aesthetic paths between extremes, houses tend to appear. Let us return for a moment to a passage previously examined, in which Ruskin counsels that painters must paint what they see and love, and explains that nature "is never distinct and never vacant . . . you always see something, but you never see all" (3.329). The illustration he happens to present is, tellingly, that of a house in a Poussin landscape. Ruskin finds it improperly painted because the artist has painted "dead square masses," vacancies, instead of the abundance nature would have given us:

> She would have let us see the Indian corn hanging on the walls, and the image of the Virgin at the angles, and the sharp, broken, broad shadows of the tiled eaves . . . and the white and blue stripes of the mattresses stuffed out of the windows, and the flapping corners of the mat blinds. All would have been there . . . not to be comprehended or understood, but a confusion of yellow and black spots and strokes, carried far too fine for the eye to follow, microscopic in its minuteness, . . . out of which would have arranged itself the general impression of truth and life. (3.330–331)

This middle way, a proto-impressionist mingling, is a requirement for painters. But we notice that the passage includes a specifically domestic confusion of inside and outside: mattresses hanging out of the windows, mat blinds flapping. This mixture of inner household furnishings and outer architectural surfaces functions as a material emblem for the collapsed oppositions in the passage – distinct and muddled, something and nothing, large and minute – insisting, as does the import of the whole description, that absolute polarities are not the vehicle of "truth and life."

After Ruskin has relaxed polarities through what William James might consider a struggle with "the serpent of rationalism" (*P*, p. 16), a new way of thinking, an analogical method that takes him far beyond the Biblical exegetical tradition, can develop. Domestic sentiment makes possible the freedoms of this new method. The very melting quality of heart's feeling expressed through the topoi and textures of sentiment encourages Ruskin to range pragmatically among categories and orders of things, creating a disorder that brings him ever closer to the multitudinous "world of concrete personal experiences" (*P*, p. 17).

Because, for example, a cathedral and a mountain elicit similar emotions in him (one the house of the Lord, the other formed and unformed by nature's housekeeping), he may begin to blur the categories of man made and divinely made.[23] Ruskin pragmatically makes and tests truth by viewing things sympathetically and analogically, from the structure of a fragile plant, to Turner's misunderstood paintings, to a pastoral and spiritual England oppressed by the evil forces of laissez-faire capitalism.[24]

He elides differences of scale and kind by an implied sentimental axiom: whatever is, is capable of being sympathetically, sentimentally, passionately, imaginatively (and these shade, imperceptibly, one into the other) inhabited by what he calls heart-sight. And the tenderness of heart-sight gathers disparate things to its throbbing breast, forming them into more than a random collection, less than a final order: an arrangement. Every time Ruskin leaps from one order of things to another – for example, from birds in nature to birds in myth, or from families in cottages to the family of the English nation – such metamorphic style "argues" for the availability of connection, of a common ground which promisingly shifts at our feet.

In this way domestic sentiment enables a Victorian Modernist, pragmatist receptivity. Paying attention to the arabesques of sentimental domesticity, Ruskin explores and tests unions as they form and reform within the currents of experience. He considers the subject of unity in several ways, moving metamorphically among metaphysics (the unity of what is), aesthetics (the unity of works of art), ethics (what gives a person moral integrity), and history (the larger story of which his moment is but a part). His philosophy inheres in the very filigree of the domestic ornamentation he first lovingly sees and then describes in his own embroidered prose. The unities he presents are periodic, discontinuous, incomplete, in process – *and* experienced as dwellings in truth. As William James imagines a wholeness made by "things partly joined and partly disjoined," he, too, positions himself within the domestic.[25]

Ruskin counsels in *The Poetry of Architecture* that a house "must NOT be a noun substantive" [Ruskin's emphasis]; indeed, it "must not even be seen all at once; and he who sees one end should feel that, from the given data, he can arrive at no conclusion respecting the other, yet be impressed with a feeling of a universal energy" (1.187).[26] Such immarginate unity is that of process and connection, always "hanging together," as James would say, for a while, then suggesting its own reformation. It seems to describe, as we shall see, Rossetti's *The House of Life* as well as the interior decoration of his own house at 16 Cheyne Walk. Never seeing all at once is one of Ruskin's favorite ideas – it is implicit in his digressions, his unstable categorizations, and the huge volume of criticism he produced. It is an idea later favored by, for example, Joseph Conrad, whose *Lord Jim* offers layers of narrators spinning story within story, all of which gradually converge on the exquisite torture of Jim's rediscoveries of himself – that is, on a Ruskinian absence of conclusion. Through the intertwining conventions of sentiment and domestic life, Ruskin embraces, gathers, imagines many things into poolings of energy, familial arrangements that last for a while. That his own family life was in some ways freeing, in others imprisoning, only adds to the intensity and pathos of his artistic imaginings.

Together the topoi of sentiment and the intricacies of domestic surfaces lead Ruskin to undermine his own yearning for an absolute and fully divulged order and to become the pragmatist that he now appears to be. He admires Byzantine architecture, whose spaces were carved through "an art of weaving," into "the semblance of interwoven fillets." (10.163). And such an architecture is in no wise superior to that of birds' nests: both allow "inhabitation" of the world. Such an architecture speaks to our "innate love of mystery and unity; in the joy that the human mind has in contemplating any kind of maze or entanglement, so long as it can discern, through its confusion, any guiding clue or connecting plan" (10.163). This is the clarity, for example, of Elizabeth Bishop's "At the Fishhouses": "the silver of the benches, / the lobster pots, and masts, scattered / among the wild jagged rocks, / is of an apparent translucence / like the small old buildings with an emerald moss / growing on their shoreward walls." Such silver patterning includes the sea, which is "like what we imagine knowledge to be . . . "[27] A revision, even a revocation, of clear law and certain knowledge through substitution, qualification, or even contradiction will always occur, if feeling dictates. Feeling almost always does.

SUBLIME IMPERSONALITY

For all his talk of sentiment, for all his love (however troubled) of family and friends, Ruskin apparently also wished to shun Romantic, transcendental egotism with its baring of souls. Eager to say what he feels, he does so by a particular kind of indirection: the intimacy of distance, or what, after Gustave Flaubert, T. S. Eliot, and Joyce, we have called impersonality. Ruskin often expresses such impersonality not only in domestic images (homes passionately examined, yet seldom fully entered), but also in the sentimental language we have already noted. The clichés and conventions of sentimentality – eyes brimming with tears and all the rest – need not be regarded as simply debasement of the language. They may also be a testing ground for the expression of personal feeling in abstract terms: their very off-the-rack quality may invite readers to infuse these containers with their own emotional histories.[28]

Although Ruskin writes repeatedly and enthusiastically of heartfelt connection, when he attempts such connection himself, he is notoriously troubled by what William James describes as "the world of concrete personal experiences to which the street belongs," because this world is "multitudinous beyond imagination, tangled, muddy, painful, and per-plexed" (*P*, pp. 17–18). Ruskin shuttles between approaching others and withdrawing from actual contact, and many passages of domestic de-scription speak in strangely generalized and arid terms of his emotional involvement, e.g., "My delight in these cottages, and in the sense of hu-man industry and enjoyment through the whole scene, was at the root of all pleasure in its beauty" (35.165). Introducing what will become a lifelong undertaking, he warns, "[We] shall be more interested in build-ings raised by feeling, than in those corrected by rule" (1.9). The passive "raised by feeling" reveals a lack: those who presumably do the feeling, the Swiss or English cottager, the Italian villa owner, remain in Ruskin's exposition cardboard figures. He simply cannot touch them. At the same time, it is clear that Ruskin wants to connect houses to their inhabitants' innermost feelings, or Gothic churches with the feelings of their original workmen – "was the carver happy while he was about it?" he character-istically asks (8.218).

Insisting that it is his way "to admire through sympathy" Ruskin be-moans those who "wherever they find themselves, think only 'of their position'" (36.165). Yet he does continually think of position; it is the awareness of his own aesthetic position that accompanies him on his travels. As a critic, should he make closer contact? If so, how can he get inside buildings and close to people, yet take their measure without physical or emotional contact? In *Praeterita* he reminisces,

My entire delight was in observing without being myself noticed, – if I could have been invisible, all the better. I was absolutely interested in men and their ways, as I was interested in marmots and chamois, in tomtits and trout. If only they would stay still and let me look at them, and not get into their holes and up their heights! (35.166)

Hesitation at following men into their private abodes develops into the decision to avoid intimacy with them, to remain invisible and "abso-lutely interested" rather than actually involved, whatever the cost in lost opportunities: "if only." Aesthetic distance and emotional distance are one.

Ruskin perseveres, however, in attempting to make human contact from a distance, combining several methods or strategies over a lifetime of writing. One of these, which we may call the geometrical, he reaches by a strange logic. If, for whatever emotional reasons, Ruskin is unable to enter actually or imaginatively through the portals of other people's houses, or, by analogy, through the doorways to their private selves, he will achieve intimacy by transforming inner and outer into one complicated surface. Experimenting with a largely flattened view of the world (for him, happily similar to Gothic as opposed to Renaissance perspective), he discovers that the dimension of depth may be reconceived, however paradoxically, as deep superficiality. Intimacy will be his once the people he observes cannot "get into their holes and up their heights."

Ruskin also invents a deliberate aloofness which he represents as stony objectivity. Making use of this tactile method, he can talk about himself and other people by talking about mountains and cathedrals instead. The artist must become stony, lest he become one of those who analyze and describe their emotions at length in "the mass of sentimental literature." Here is a way to make feeling safe for high culture: the true artist or "seer," "feels as intensely as any one [sic] else; but he does not much describe his feelings" (5.334). In fact, Turner as Ruskin's representative artist experiences "the greatest of all feelings – an utter forgetfulness of self" (12.370).

People and buildings begin to share qualities. Silence is, after all, a commonplace of sentiment or sensibility: when feelings are too strong for words, victims and observers alike "speak" in elisions, interruptions, even in the total speechlessness and immobility of swoons and unconsciousness.[29] The analogy runs in two directions; from his earliest architectural criticism, Ruskin likens the external surfaces of buildings to human faces, "I do with a building as I do with a man, watch the eye and the lips" (12.89). Personification of architectural elements abound; "The poor round arch is still kept to do all the hard work" he writes of a Venetian window, "and the fantastic ogee takes its pleasure above in the form of a moulding merely" (10.294). Architectural ornamentation, Ruskin teaches, is a book to be read, telling the story of the workmen who labored there as well as Bible stories. Ruskin's own story is similarly evident in the vast edifice of his works.

Not only does he silently watch buildings to see their human stories, but those buildings can turn the tables, watching him as they silently speak. Ruskin imagines a reflexivity of observer and observed in which it is hard to say who is the personifier, who the personified:

"For, indeed, the greatest glory of a building is not in its stones, nor in its gold." Its glory is in its Age, and in that deep sense of voicefulness, of stern watching, of mysterious sympathy, nay, even of approval or condemnation, which we feel in walls that have long been washed by the passing waves of humanity. It is . . . in the strength which . . . maintains its sculptured shapeliness for a time insuperable, connects forgotten and following ages with each other, and half constitutes the identity, as it concentrates the sympathy, of nations. (8.233–234)

The sublimity of Ruskinian impersonality becomes evident. The diction of sublimity – greatest glory, stern, mysterious, time insuperable – joins the diction of sentimentality: passing humanity, shapeliness, connection, sympathy. Spirits in stones are a religious archetype, but when Ruskin personifies buildings, he also makes a claim about human emotion: stony, aloof people may nonetheless be infused with human stories and soulful feelings. The quiet, because non-effusive surfaces of good painting or writing also express emotion. One need not express introspection by a Romantic rhetoric of personal feeling, nor make use of the egotistical sublime to link personal depth to transcendent height. Of this sublimity, more later.

Throughout his oeuvre, Ruskin combines the two strategies of searching for human relations in deepened surfaces and experiencing them as cool, hard, or distanced. In *The Seven Lamps of Architecture*, for example, he writes:

All our interest in the carved work, our sense of its richness . . . results from our consciousness of its being the work of poor, clumsy, toilsome man. Its true delightfulness depends on our discovering in it the record of thoughts, and intents, and trials, and heart-breakings – all this *can* be traced by a practised eye; but granting it even obscure, it is presumed or understood. (8.82)

Here Ruskin moves from a generalized man to a list of thoughts, feelings, and situations that can be experienced only by actual people. Yet as he invites "a practised eye" to "presume" or "understand," the actual person disappears into the passive voice. The "record" of others' feelings may well remain obscure, but at least Ruskin himself will never be lost therein.

Ruskin's third strategy for seeking human contact, after the geometrical and the tactile, is, unsurprisingly, the sentimental. Aware of his own "incapacity" (33.274) in matters of personal expression, Ruskin's sentimental language is all the more poignant. The "tomtits and trout" passage about invisibility (quoted above) ends in this way:

The living inhabitation of the world – the grazing and nesting in it, – the spiritual power of the air, the rocks, the waters, to be in the midst of it, and rejoice and wonder at it, and help it if I could, – happier if it needed no help of mine, – this was the essential love *of Nature* in me, this the root of all that I have usefully become, and the light of all that I have rightly learned. (35.166)

As incapable of following people into their homes as he is marmots into their holes, Ruskin takes the domestic grazing and nesting, the "inhabitation of the world," as his subject. In his art the good parent and family man he could not be in life, Ruskin stands by, but at a freeing distance.

This ideally invisible, hovering Ruskin imagines seeing as a form of generosity, a quasi-universal and creative bestowal of love: "every healthy state of nations and of individual minds consists in the unselfish presence of the human spirit everywhere, energizing over all things; speaking and living through all things" (7.264). Not God's spirit alone, but man's also. The notion of the autonomous work of art, with the artist as a god-like figure, makes an early appearance in Ruskin's attraction to the oddly impersonal form of love known as sentiment and in his lifelong, yearning admiration for "inhabitation," domesticity achieved. "*My* times of happiness," he writes, "had always been when *nobody* was thinking of me" (35.165). And, we might add, when he was "*nobody*," thinking in a god-like – yet tender, feminized, contingent – way of the world.

Now, in the blessedly abstract form of energy rather than individual ego, the artist gathers into his embrace things and people alike. Turner's greatness, he tells us in his essay on Pre-Raphaelitism,

depends on his taking possession of everything that he sees, – on his grasping all . . . – on his forgetting himself, and forgetting nothing else. I wish it to be understood how every great man paints what he sees or did see, his greatness being indeed little else than his intense sense of fact. And thus Pre-Raphaelitism and Raphaelitism, and Turnerism, are all one and the same. (12.385)

And Ruskinism, one might add. In forgetting himself he may be spared the agonies of artistic narcissism and self-consciousness, the fear of solipsism, that haunted Rossetti and Pater, for example. The true artist views his own work with loving, yet impersonal intensity, divided within himself into sentimental observed and observer. He recognizes in his work "its precise value, or no value, from that outer standpoint" (22.144).

Not only will the impersonal artist gain control of himself, but he will also exercise power over other people. For as well as enabling Ruskin to imagine distanced intimacy, impersonality also invites him to claim a gentle sympathy for the world. He becomes a beneficent *Weltonkel* marveling at the world's inhabitation at the same time as he claims a nearly cosmic superiority. Never need he stoop to enter the humble doorway of a cottage. Never speaking the native tongue, he effectively silences the world for himself. Relation to doubles back as passive power over; sympathy offers the gift of autonomy. Ruskin has found an aesthetic *via media* between independence and relation, between knowing and being known. A good pragmatist in the Jamesian sense, he inhabits connections with as much fervor as he seeks destinations.

Thus Ruskin interweaves the traditions of sentiment and sublimity as he invents, out of emotional and aesthetic needs, the strategies of superficial intimacy and passionate impersonality, first tested by him on the exteriors of personified houses. His is a sublimity of the ordinary, of household objects and truths, including those intricacies of filigree, carving, and embroidery with which we began. He reimagines the traditional and terrible sublime, with its "isolated, stationary observer" overcome by "a single view of overwhelming power."[30] Despite Ruskin's depiction of peaks and valleys, he often presents a levelling exploration of the world's surface. Mountains crumble gradually into the sea; with his first view of the Alps as he remembers it in *Praeterita*, the mountains melt into a "living plain . . . studded with white homes" (35.167–168). We might subtitle many of his works *Peri Platous*, "On the Extended."

Given Ruskin's obsessions, his perspectives often involve views of domestic dwellings in the near distance, as they expand within sentimental tableaux. One of his great themes is the need to make familiar, to learn how to be at home on the Continent, in the country, the local landscape, the town, the church, or even in the bit of sculpture on the church facade. Carefully examining the minutiae of domestic exteriors, including those of churches, rather than sublimely ravished by their size, he finds himself transfixed but not conquered by suffering and love. He is no longer estranged from humanity. At the same time, the utter intensity of his response removes these moments from the old category of the picturesque, traditionally considered inferior in power to the sublime.

While Ruskin creates multiple terms for this new notion of the sublime, his message is simple: if "sublime" means ravishing in spiritually and aesthetically important ways, it may now apply not just to, say, Turner's paintings of storms at sea, but also to Turner's scenes of pastoral life. It may apply to hills, not just mountains, to cottages, not just cathedrals. Clear distinctions among sublimity, beauty, and picturesqueness no longer work very well in considering the creation and appreciation of art. Like Rossetti, who combines in his sonnet sequences *Five English Poets*

and *The House of Life* traditional images of sublime awe such as storms
at sea with sentimental topoi of loved ones at home, Ruskin insists upon
the mingling of awe and fellow feeling. Victorian Modernist sentimental sublimity is now firmly in place: the vastness and mystery of what is
closest to us, the confused lives of joy, boredom, wrath, and sorrow that
we actually live, inside the rooms of our houses.[31] Across the Atlantic,
domestic novelists such as Augusta Evans and Harriet Beecher Stowe are
taking careful note. Iris Murdoch will continue the tradition in novels
that are overfilled with intricate mazes of emotion.

Although he retains some allegiance to neo-classical ideas of beauty,
Ruskin's attacks on Sir Joshua Reynolds's neo-classical dicta, especially
Reynolds's hierarchical ideas of high and low art, prove crucial to Ruskin's
developing aesthetic. It is not true, Ruskin argues, that lowly, small
details don't matter, or that high art seeks only the invariable in elevated
subjects, or that an accurate picture of reality is most easily painted
by dullards (5.42). As Longinian *hypsos* (elevation) metamorphoses into
Ruskinian *platos* (extension or breadth), vertical relations simply matter
less. There are no high and low subjects, only degrees of sentimental
intensity in the artist himself: "It does not matter whether he paint the
petal of a rose, or the chasms of a precipice, so that Love and Admiration attend him as he labours" (5.42). Great art may depict "peasants or
nobles" (5.42). All the world – God's creation, artists' creations, Ruskin's
interpretations of both – can be wrought and rewrought as a series of
linked surfaces. Thus can an aloof Ruskin touch all the world.

The more he discovers that the lowly and textured may be aesthetically
praiseworthy, and the more his writing touches the world's surfaces in
performances of intimacy which he largely describes in domestic terms,
the more he tends to blur the category of the sublime with those of the
grotesque, the noble picturesque, or the parasitic sublime.[32] Elizabeth
Helsinger shows us that Ruskin reconceives the overwhelming Burkean
sublime as an "excursive sublime" of multiple viewpoints and partial
opportunities: "First grotesque and then picturesque art became a co-
operative effort between artist and spectator to comprehend greatness
and enlarge sympathies."[33] Ruskin invites us to consider such art, in
its comprehension of greatness, as sublime. And in its enlargement of
sympathies, we may see it as part of Ruskin's sentimental and domestic
explorations.

But what did such a revision of the sublime accomplish? It allowed
Ruskin to locate the realm of ultimate value in the spaces and practices of
ordinary life. Although Ruskin states a hierarchical relation between two

types of sublimity he labels – "There is a Divine beauty, and a terribleness of sublimity coequal with it in rank . . . and there is an inferior or ornamental beauty [the grotesque], and an inferior terribleness coequal with it in rank" (11.165–166) – reader beware. Once again, Ruskin classifies things, only to have "the squamous facts exceed the squirming mind."[34] If rank in Ruskin be measured by admiring attention paid, by fullness or intensity of treatment, "merely" ornamental or grotesque beauty is easily superior to the traditional sublime.

At the same time, sentimental sublimity allows Ruskin to move easily, horizontally, as it were, between aesthetic and social concerns, stimulating him to sympathize with the marginal or dispossessed. Flowers, he typically tells us, are precious to nuns, cottagers, children, and disorderly people – all those of humble stature – but they are seldom precious to "the men of supreme power and thoughtfulness" and even then "rarely for [the flowers'] own sake" (7.119–120). Admirers of flowers live at the wayside of power – along with weeds, mosses, watchers of clouds, and folk artists.[35]

FRANCESCA'S CABINET

If Victorian Modernism is to earn its pragmatist keep, it must reveal to us useful and previously unnoticed aspects of writers and their works. Let us close this chapter by dwelling in one work – *Roadside Songs of Tuscany* (1884–1885) – which has been largely invisible to twentieth-century critics of Ruskin. Read in the light of Victorian Modernism, however, it reveals methods and ideas that we can no longer afford to ignore as we write the history of such notions as pragmatism, the feminized origins of Modernism, the questioning of the unitary nature of the self, and the inseparability of so-called "low" and "high" art. To be able to see these aspects in the "minor" work of a Victorian writer, we must amend previous accounts of Ruskin's life itself in order to detect that he is in motion, following pragmatist paths of inquiry, during the period commonly considered his decline.

The most widely accepted view of Ruskin's trajectory requires of the reader a saddened, downward glance at his final years. This perspective has the advantage of placing the writer himself within the sentimental tableau of suffering that characterizes his work. Although critics have been loath to admire sentiment in the work, they have been eager to see it in the life. Even before mental illness wholly robs Ruskin of his faculties, so the story often goes, he is out of touch with his audience in

Fors Clavigera, pessimistic about the future of England, sunk even more deeply in the doubt he communicated in the closing volumes of *Modern Painters* where "the face of God seems to withdraw from nature and in His stead emerges a 'multitudinous, marred humanity'" (7.384). "One feels the whole hinge of sensibility turn from lyric exultation to tragic despair" as we trace Ruskin's "growth from a youthful, ecstatic, evangelical, ego-oriented worshipper of nature to a brooding, guilt-burdened observer of the brutality of man."[36] Eventually, Ruskin's brooding shades into the mental illness that brings all to a close.

Such a trajectory implies a set of expectations about the Victorian sage and the shape of his career: that he is heroically masculine, energetic, and individualistic, and that the reduction of his power over time is a phenomenon that he and we necessarily greet with sadness. Yet it is important to examine our own received assumptions, to realize that "when Victorian nonfiction prose enters the academic canon, it comes clothed in a garb of heroic masculinity akin to Carlyle's."[37] The notion of the Victorian sage as a strong and great spiritual leader defending human dignity reflects the 1930s and 40s climate in American and British letters – the period when the figure enters the critical literature – as much as it does any quality intrinsic to the prose.

My purpose is not simply to replace the masculine, heroic sage with a feminized Ruskin, but rather to *add* important elements – call them senti-mentality, domesticity, passivity – to an overly masculinized portrait. We have seen Ruskin throughout his career challenge notions of transcen-dently heroic power by making claims for the tender and the modest. As a sage he asks us to value sympathetic being more than rational in-strumentality, myth more than technology, and fragile ornamentation as well as structural soundness. Preach and prophesy he does, but the very excesses, digressions, and circularities of his prose require that we choose our own way.

That way, he suggests by the tableaux through which he instructs us, often involves dwelling rather than going. Indeed, midway through his career, he praises what he calls the "art of the wayside" (11.157). Such art is grotesque, one of the sibling terms for sublimity in Ruskin's word family, and must be judged

according to the tone of the minds which have produced it, and in proportion to their knowledge, wit, love of truth, and kindness; secondly, according to the degree of strength they have been able to give forth; but yet, however much we may find in it needing to be forgiven, always delightful so long as it is the work of good and ordinarily intelligent men. (11.158)

This always imperfect art, "done in times of rest" rather than created by heroic measures, is to be judged "not [by] its own merit so much as [by] the enjoyment of him who produced it" (11.158). A work of wayside art appeals, in a traditionally sentimental mode, to our sympathetic reading of the inner man.

In four works of his closing years, the lectures at Oxford collected as *The Art of England, Fors Clavigera, Studies of Peasant Life* (including *Roadside Songs of Tuscany*), and *Praeterita*, Ruskin settles himself at the wayside, yet his interest in that position develops through the practices of a lifetime. In a self-consciously sentimental mode, he continues his needlework. One figure appears in all four of these works: Francesca Alexander. It is in her stories, which *become by repeated acts of aesthetic will Ruskin's story*, that Ruskin wishes finally to dwell. This is a story of sweet continuance, linked works of art, and wreathed identities.

We may read the tale clearly in *Roadside Songs of Tuscany* (32.41–252), "Translated and Illustrated by Francesca Alexander, and Edited by John Ruskin" (32.ix), although to attempt to describe it critically is to be caught in the static intricacies of its wayside world.[38] *Roadside Songs of Tuscany* has an involved history, multiple in its origins, confusing in its development, and crucial to a reconsideration of the trajectory of Ruskin's career. To trace *Roadside Songs*' publication history is perhaps the most fruitful way to understand it.

Francesca Alexander (1837–1917) was the daughter of Francis Alexander, a painter who emigrated from Boston to Italy.[39] Francesca lived in Florence, with lengthy stays in other regions of Italy, all her life. Part artist, part amateur ethnographer, and altogether a good Christian lady, Francesca befriended the peasants of Tuscany and the Veneto. From her childhood on, she drew their portraits, fondled their babies, listened to their stories and told them hers, translated their traditional ballads and songs into English, and channeled to them the philanthropic gifts that she received primarily from American visitors to Florence.

In gratitude for such gifts, Francesca, while still a girl, created for an American benefactress a handmade book telling the personal histories of the poor people who had received the aid, along with an illustration of each. This was a juvenile version of Francesca's principal work, *Tuscan Songs*, renamed *Roadside Songs of Tuscany* by its editor, John Ruskin, after he appropriated and changed it. *Roadside Songs* includes several elements, and is something of a hodge-podge. Italian ballads and songs (with facing English translations) transcribed by Francesca, are accompanied by her illustrations of scenes from them. She also wrote short biographies of the

Italian peasants whom she used as models for her illustrations, and these appear, along with various brief essays and introductions written, as will become clear, by both Francesca and Ruskin.

Ruskin met Francesca Alexander and her mother in Florence in October 1882, and, impressed by *Tuscan Songs*, purchased it for £600. Delighted by both his purchase and his friendship with Francesca and her mother (he called them, during a correspondence conducted fervently on both sides, "Sorella" and "Mammina"), Ruskin proceeded to make Francesca's creations in part his own. He lectured about Francesca and her work – both artistic and charitable – when he resumed the Slade Professorship at Oxford. She appears repeatedly in *The Art of England* (March 1883) and *Fors Clavigera*, and also in at least one of Ruskin's private lectures to distinguished audiences.[40] Throughout, he depicts her as an ideal of gentle womanhood: "a girl of quite peculiar gift, whose life has hitherto been spent in quiet and unassuming devotion to her art, and to its subjects . . . she is an American!" (33.282). Francesca is in Ruskin's telling the very type of the sentimental woman artist, one whose artistic creations are but the overflow of her primary activities of Christian devotion.

After purchasing *Tuscan Songs*, Francesca's original manuscript book of 109 illustrated leaves, Ruskin edited it with a heavy hand – even brutally, to feminist eyes over a century later. He dispersed her illustrations to various destinations, chose twenty of them for photographic reproduction as *Roadside Songs of Tuscany*, and as he himself writes in his "Editor's Preface" decided "to print, together with them, so much of the text as immediately relates to their subjects, *adding any further elucidation of them which may be in my own power*" (32.51, emphasis added). This work he released in ten parts, from April 1884 through August 1885, and it is these that Cook and Wedderburn have collected as *Roadside Songs of Tuscany*.

That the resulting text as we know it in the *Library Edition*, whether collaboration or butchery, contains the work of both Francesca and Ruskin is beyond dispute. Yet it is also the work of the folk artists who passed on the old songs ("rispetti") and ballads that Francesca translated. The apparently simple, chronological flow of creation and presentation – hypothetical "Ur artist" to folk tradition to Francesca and on through Ruskin and Cook and Wedderburn to the reader – widens to a more static estuary of complex notions about artistic identity and creation.[41] In that process, discrete human identity begins to waver and disappear. When Virginia Woolf grants some characters in *Mrs. Dalloway* the ability to know directly the thoughts of other characters, when Samuel Beckett and Gertrude Stein create characters as patterns of words on paper, we may link their efforts to those of Ruskin.

Describing and explaining such notions, we will find ourselves tracing familiar complexities: the intertwinings of sentiment, aestheticism, sublimity, and domesticity mingling with those of identity, intimacy, and artistic creation to form Ruskin's Victorian Modernist filigree. We will move from domestic things through these patterns to states of intimacy so thorough-going that Ruskin might be said to merge his very self happily into the (sentimentally domestic) works of another, Francesca Alexander, who has herself recorded the lives and artistic works of others. Far from the despairing gasp of a defeated man, *Roadside Songs*, like the Italian peasants it sentimentally portrays, acknowledges the victory of simply continuing.

It is the tradition of sentiment that permits Ruskin in *Roadside Songs* to approach more closely than ever before an opening of the unitary self to multiple identifications and intimate appropriations, especially the appropriation of a woman's consciousness. Since the final volume of *Modern Painters*, Ruskin had been insisting that Turner's art was valuable for its feminine qualities, noting that "his exquisite tenderness in sight and touch are ... exponents of his kindness of heart" (7.443n). Now he turns to a woman artist whose tenderness in life is inseparable from her tenderness in art. Francesca actually embodies the analogy of beauty and moral goodness that Ruskin has been at pains to establish throughout his many volumes. And, even better, she may be imaginatively inhabited by Ruskin because, as we shall see, she welcomes him, invites him into both her art and her home. He may in good faith choose to enter, because his writing has all along been made of the same sentimental stuff as hers. "All my writing is only the effort to distinguish what is constantly, and to all men, lovable, and if they will look, lovely" (33.273) he writes, the same year as he edits Francesca's work.

What, exactly, do we have before us in this congeries of drawing and photograph, calligraphy and typeface, English and Italian dialects, prose and poetry, artists and editors, people and personae, history and myth? An aesthetic confusion ("The more that is gathered together in a confused representation, the more extensive clarity the representation has"), to be sure.[42] Two introductory essays greet us: first, Ruskin's "Editor's Preface," and then Francesca's "Preface" to the original *Tuscan Songs*, the latter appearing here in print rather than in her original calligraphy and labeled by Ruskin "The Author's Preface." Ruskin's essay, written from his home, Brantwood, on New Year's Day 1884, in effect

claims a new beginning for the work that follows. He appropriates
Francesca's text by explaining how he came to possess the manuscript
and how he manipulated its pages, sending some away and photograph-
ing others.

He also explains that part of what follows exists only because he requested it. He has solicited from Francesca additions of a particular sort:

> I asked her to furnish me, for what use I might be able to make of them, with
> such particulars as she knew, or might with little pains remember, of the real lives
> and characters of the peasants whom she had taken for her principal models.
> (32.54–55)

Francesca complies by writing *another work*, sending him a little
manuscript book of biographical stories about the peasants who are the
life models for her illustrations of the religious ballads she has transcribed.
If she is the creator of this work, so is he; their lives have mingled in this off-
spring. Furthermore, this humble work cannot be cleanly distinguished
from high art; at least since the writing of *Modern Painters* III, Ruskin has
noticed that the most beautiful paintings used local models, pointing out,
for example, that in Tintoretto's *Adoration of the Magi*, " . . . the Madonna is
an unaltered portrait of a Venetian girl, the Magi are unaltered Venetian
senators, and the figure with the basket, an unaltered market-woman of
Mestre" (5.112). Francesca's book of similarly "unaltered" figures Ruskin
then cuts up and distributes among his already chosen pieces of her
Tuscan Songs, reassembling the truncated whole as *Roadside Songs*.

In addition to an account of the work's genesis, Ruskin's introduction
also contains brief critical passages that place Francesca's drawings in the
context of Pre-Raphaelism [sic] and defend their artistic faults. As art of
the wayside (here, "roadside"), Francesca's art must be justified by the
very goodness of its creator, not by its formal qualities. Ruskin's praise
of Francesca's character blends syntactically into a personification of the
work itself: "Miss Alexander's work is . . . industrious, with an energy as
steady as that by which a plant grows in spring; modest and unselfish, as
ever was good servant's work for a beloved Master" (32.53). Very much
the manly Victorian sage in this preface, Ruskin has wielded scissors,
printing press, camera, and judgment in a spirit of unselfconscious entitlement. Yet he has also done so, as we shall see, in the tradition of the
feminized man of feeling.[43]

Francesca's own "Preface" to her original *Tuscan Songs* follows. In contrast to Ruskin's introduction, it reveals Francesca's awareness of the
appropriative nature of her creation. She makes explicit the lovingly

subordinate relation of herself to the people and texts she presents – the very relation that Ruskin himself wishes to practice on Francesca's behalf, even as he forthrightly buys, cuts, pastes, and renames. Appropriating Francesca's words, he can have it both ways. Francesca speaks for Ruskin, as it were, and she says that in art, gentle intimacy is all:

These songs and hymns of the poor people have been collected, little by little, in the course of a great many years which I have passed in constant intercourse with the Tuscan contadini. They are but the *siftings*, so to say, of hundreds and hundreds which I have heard and learnt, most from old people: many of them have never, so far as I know, been written down before, and others it would be impossible now to find. (32.57)

Francesca's art is a domestic operation (the sifting of wheat from chaff) inextricable from the tender methods by which she has harvested songs: listening to, touching, speaking with, sometimes aiding, and above all, loving, the old and the poor. *They* provide the bounty; she is but winnower and scribe.

 Taking Ruskin's and Francesca's prefaces together, then, *Roadside Songs of Tuscany* announces itself as a field of linked agreements and contradictions, created through Ruskin's own love of "filigree . . . embroidery . . . intricacies of virgin silver . . . the netting of lace" (35.157n3). It is not only a work about the domestic lives of peasants, but also a rendering of domesticity as texture, texture as domesticity. It is a heartfelt, direct presentation of simple songs by two loving collectors, Ruskin and Francesca, yet it is also a painstaking arrangement of elements that have been inspired, self-consciously created, retrieved, copied, translated, altered, and juxtaposed. Originally composed as a private gift, it is a collection of works of art to be bought and sold. To name its author is to enter a Jamesian flux of renaming.

 The two introductions made, Ruskin's next task is to present Francesca's transcription of the "Ballad of Santa Zita." A series of digressions appears instead: another introduction, then Ruskin's meditation on the meaning of sainthood, followed by a passage from Francesca's story about Lucia Santi (the peasant woman who models for her illustration of Santa Zita), and Ruskin's preface to the ballad, this preface itself opening out to a series of allusions to other books. As surely as Ruskin earlier mingled God, waterfall, Turner, himself, and reader (3.552–554), he here mixes multiple creators and creations. Wandering through an ever-burgeoning field of artists, works of art, and audiences, we arrive at the ballad itself, only to find it a palimpsest. From Bible story or saint's life to

sung ballad to seventeenth-century transcription by one Guaspari de
Bartolomeo Casenti to Francesca's facing Italian and English tran-
scriptions to Ruskin's edited version: this is the house of art that
Ruskin believes love has built. Francesca/Casenti joins Lucia/Zita and
Ruskin/Francesca in the by now kaleidoscopic focus of Ruskin's edited
work.

A verse tale of the life of a poor servant, the miracles in which she
participates and her eventual burial as a beloved folk-saint and protectress
of the town of Lucca, the "Ballad of Santa Zita" in both languages
occupies a total of seventeen pages (including Francesca's illustrations).
Its language is simple and pious; here is a characteristic verse, in which
she offers her borrowed cloak to a begger:

> She looked awhile, her heart with pity led,
> Then called him, saying: "Brother, come to me;
> Come, take this cloak, and wear it in my stead:
> It is not mine, or I would give it thee.
> Then kneel beside me till the prayers be said;
> Pray with me, and God's love shall with us be.
> Then matins over, I would much desire
> To lead thee home and warm thee by our fire.
>
> (32.89)

Ruskin's made and borrowed material, including his "Postscript," occupies twenty-three pages. In striking contrast to the Ruskinian machinery,
the ballad moves quickly, rhythmically, and seamlessly from beginning
to end. It seems anticlimactic, over almost before it begins. With the
next ballad cluster, the process of arranging diverse materials begins
again.

Tempted as we might be upon first leafing through *Roadside Songs*
to assess it as the condescendingly imagined, hastily assembled, and
rambling work of a man no longer in control of his faculties, such a
judgment would be a mistake. If we approach the work instead with
the hypothesis that in it Ruskin makes a series of artistic choices that
are the fruition, not the decay, of his lifelong imaginative adventures in
aestheticism, we will find ourselves richly rewarded.

With intensity, purpose, and even a poignant bravery, Ruskin in *Roadside Songs* explores the most radical implications of his earlier critical
positions, practices and fantasies. Consider his actual scene of writing in
these closing years. While he had all along imagined a feminized, because
tender, stance for the artist (Turner reaches his zenith, Ruskin tells us,
when he paints the creation in "the tenderest, kindest, most feminine of
its aspects" [7.410]), in his last years he entered a female world itself. In his

own home at last, Ruskin at Brantwood surrounded himself with female friends, family members, and correspondents: Kate Greenaway, Susan Beever, Mrs. Arthur Severn (Joanie), Amy Yule, Francesca Alexander and Mrs. Alexander, Julia Firth, Katie MacDonald, and Mary Russell Mitford. While a lecture such as "The Mystery of Life and its Arts" (18.145–187) is a cry of despair at his failure to change the hearts and minds of English people, he records in *Fors* a different story:

I thought myself speaking to a crowd which could only be influenced by visible utility; nor was I the least aware how many entirely good and holy persons were living in the faith and love of God as vividly and practically now as ever in the early enthusiasm of Christendom, until, chiefly in consequence of the great illnesses which... forbade my accustomed literary labor, I was brought into closer personal relations with the friends in America, Scotland, Ireland, and Italy, to whom... I owe the best hopes and highest thoughts.... (29.527–528)

If we pay attention to this kind of language without denying the bitter ravings of *Fors*, we can see that *Roadside Songs* is Ruskin's effort to *make true* the "Spirit of Mercy and Truth" (28.102). It is a lived experience of what Ruskin's admirer William James would call "The Will to Believe."

In the acts of owning, presenting, and writing about the lives of victimized but gentle, loving, and humbly triumphant peasants whose culture he believes to be beautifully medieval in quality, Ruskin inserts himself (however harshly, to our eyes) into their world. It is a world of relationship that, precisely in its confusion of artifice and reality, original and derivative, Francesca and himself, fantasy and fact, high and low, makes him feel welcome, able at last to experience intimacy.[44] Ruskin writes to Francesca, "I have opened your book today in my old nursery, where I found it – waiting for me."[45] Books and rooms now welcome him equally; friends become loving mothers. Even the dismemberment of Francesca's book is in Ruskin's mind an act of loving domesticity: he assures her that he will "instantly order frames for the main drawings and cabinets for the whole, out of which separate pages may be shown on different days" (p. 28).

What in part makes the experiment of *Roadside Songs of Tuscany* possible is Francesca's willingness to include him in *her* drama of human relations. She writes in 1882 to a friend:

But what surprised me most of all was that he [Ruskin] talked to me in the most familiar and even confidential manner.... and seemed even to find a certain comfort in doing so, just exactly as the poor women who came in from the country to bring me a bunch of flowers and have an hour's gossip talk to me of their own troubles and cares and pleasures. (p. 376)

As Ruskin writes *Roadside Songs*, then, he inhabits *mundus muliebris*, a world of women, that makes actual domestic sentiment artistically available to him. He writes primarily of women; men appear as background characters in this work – as good or bad husbands, healthy or dying sons and fiancés. The one ballad in the collection that contains no female figures, "St. Christopher," Ruskin asks Francesca not to transcribe, but to tell as a story in her own words, as if literally to transform it into a woman's story. We may read *Roadside Songs* together with "Of Queens' Gardens" in order to enrich our notion of Ruskin's woman-centered art and to correct critical views of him as a thorough misogynist. At times, and in certain writings, he was misogynist by early twenty-first-century standards. He was also, at times, and over the course of nearly everything he wrote, profoundly sympathetic to what was (and still largely is) considered to be a feminized view of the world: domestic, sentimental, relational.[46] Into this female world Ruskin introduces the one male who troubles him most: himself.

Roadside Songs is a work of pragmatist and fanciful arrangement rather than seminal wholeness. When Ruskin writes in *Modern Painters V*, as we have seen above, that the creator is "a person who puts things together," one whose work of "gathering and arranging of material" has "in it at last the harmony or helpfulness of life, and the passion or emotion of life," (7.215), the "at last" here applies to Ruskin's own artistic development. At last, and in a work that is itself highly discontinuous and enticingly confusing, Ruskin has created an arrangement that is, in his view, tender in every aspect. This arrangement's origins (his feelings for Francesca, hers for the peasants) are admiration, love, and charity. Its subject matter is humble virtue and the ordinary made holy. This arrangement's audiences are multiple, and they overlap with its creators: peasants, Francesca, Ruskin, and ourselves. Looking and listening, these people gather in an accord of aesthetic pleasure through time and space, becoming a harmonious human arrangement. Before we leap to the judgment that this is a story about the exercise of hegemonic power (male over female, British upper class over Italian lower class, written over oral) we ought to linger long enough to experience it as a work impelled by conflicting motivations.

Roadside Songs is a culmination of Ruskin's metamorphic mode of analysis, his yearning for one being or thing to melt into another rather than to belong to a strictly patrolled category. Melting is what characterizes this work at many levels: one author melts into another, Francesca and Ruskin as spectators of suffering and saintly love feel their own hearts melt with charity, figures in ballads soften their hearts with the love of Christ, lovers in "Rispetti" melt for each another. Ruskin's story is not simply *about* the peasants or Francesca, it is in its convoluted structure and rhetoric *of* them, as, for example, the Ovidian laurel tree is not a representation of Daphne, but Daphne "herself."

But perhaps the most important form of metamorphosis for Ruskin is that between the real and the imaginary. Just as ballads, myths, and symbols occur at the intersection of something real and something ideal or imaginary, so all of *Roadside Songs* – a work about saints and martyrs – becomes itself a myth, a fiction that is truth. For Ruskin in this work, telling a story and living a story merge. Victorian Modernist myth-making is well underway.[47]

By thus confusing the frames of art and life, Ruskin's stories make it possible for him to experience more fully than ever before the intimacy that he has sought, through the very impersonality he has so painstakingly developed over time. Touching another bodily and touching the artistic creation of another are not so very different – as they weren't for Proust, who professed to learning this lesson in Ruskin. Texts of tenderness blend into, touch upon, the experience of actual, embodied intimacy. The verbal and visual art object has dissipated to become both the externalization of one's own emotions and a place where others' emotions may be vividly felt. Where Eliot would achieve through poetry a departure from emotion and personality, Ruskin imagines an escape into emotion, into personality – that of another who cannot be fully distinguished from himself. Ruskin discovers in his own way Rimbaud's "I is someone else" and he implies what Baudelaire dreams aloud in his journal: "Of the vaporization and centralization of the Self. That is everything."[48] Let there be no mistake: as surely as Baudelaire's dandy loses himself in the Parisian crowd in order to find himself as an artist, Ruskin the Victorian Modernist loses himself among the ladies of the Lake District and among the contadini of Francesca's Italy in order to find himself within art. With the making of *Roadside Songs*, the tableau of sentimental art – always still and pulsating, artificially posed and painfully, pleasurably real – actually melts into emotional, iconic life for Ruskin.

While this is a project of immense sentimental pathos and narcissism, it is also a project of fortitude. Ruskin remains true to his earlier teaching that the virtue of a work of art depends on the artist's "being able to quit his own personality, and enter successively into the hearts and thoughts of each person, and in all this he is still passive" (5.124–125). The mere "editor" of *Roadside Songs*, Ruskin – despite his intrusive editing – can

believe that he witnesses, mirrors or passes on, rather than actively creating in his own image, what he presents. This work expresses what he
feels once he understands his identity as a pleasurable entanglement in
his relations to others. The *Roadside* saints teach that one must lose oneself
not only to find God, but also to find other people.

Now, as earlier, Ruskin seeks the repose of domesticity. Francesca's
art of domestic storytelling begins with her drawings. Ruskin as art critic
(and draughtsman) has over the course of a lifetime considered primarily
landscape and architecture, but Francesca is a portraitist. As Ruskin
incorporates Francesca's work into his own, he replaces buildings and
landscapes with people. Yet part of Ruskin's attraction to her art must
have been her own interest in domestic and architectural settings for the
people she draws. With the exception of generalized backdrops of fields,
nature has been flattened and reduced to flowers twining artificially
as decorations or stylized plants ornamenting the exteriors of buildings.
Surface carries its own kind of depth. Like Ruskin, Francesca often draws
the exteriors of cottages and churches – but she sees them as settings for
her people.

In fact, domesticity in *Roadside Songs* becomes the proving ground for
an impassioned impersonality, always Ruskin's paradoxical goal. Inhabitants of Francesca's houses may stand in doorways, but they are touching
people who stand outside, placing specific domestic objects such as food
or articles of clothing, directly into their hands. Women holding pots of
herbs lean from windows, replacing the statues of Ruskin's architectural
facades. Francesca's courtyards, crowded squares, town wells, and streets
outnumber her scenes of bedrooms and sitting rooms, but they become
so many stage settings, like Henry James's Venice of *The Aspern Papers*,
for layered domestic dramas. Courtship, marriage, children, work, and
death: Francesca knows and tells, through the curious impersonality of
the sentimental tableau, the "inside" story. Ruskin is there with her.

Roadside Songs is also domestic in its larger conception. As a cultural
history of the "hill-people" of Tuscany and the Veneto that shows the
interrelations of their religious beliefs, artistic creations, and agricultural
practices, the work fulfills Ruskin's yearning for a new kind of history.
Beyond the "apparent... the only recognized world history" of wars,
leaders, institutions, Ruskin finds "the real history [that] is underneath
all this," in the " low-nestling, speechless, harmless, infinitely submissive,
infinitely serviceable order of being," of which "no Historian ever takes
the smallest notice" (33.59–60). *This* historian does. Because Ruskin
frames a contemporaneous document, *Praeterita*, with the statement that

Figure 1   "Santa Zita and the Angel," Francesca Alexander (*The Complete Works of John Ruskin*, plate vi, vol. 32)

"the personal feeling and native instinct of me had been fastened, irrevo-
cably, long before, to things modest, humble, and pure in peace," (35.33)
we may understand the need of these humble folk for love as Ruskin's
need, too. Such love infuses artistic practice and human interaction alike;
the two are wholly entwined in Ruskin's sentimental aestheticism.

Ruskin learns to imagine himself *through* and *as* Francesca, as he has
previously done with Turner and again with Sir Walter Scott.[49] As early
as *Modern Painters* I Ruskin has insisted that "Love" is the *sine qua non* of the
true artist (3.169). Now the love of the artist for his subject has ripened
into a love between people that dissolves the spaces between their beings,
a love which is itself a form of art. The venerable balladic "I," voice of
the individual who, through art, gives voice to the community, has been
reclaimed by Ruskin, among others, for the modern artist. This is not to
argue that Ruskin's voice disappears from *Roadside Songs*. It is rather to
pay attention to the beliefs and yearnings informing Ruskin's decision
to arrange his own words among the words, images, musical notes of
others. For it is finally in the pattern of the expanding whole that Ruskin
loses himself in order to find himself.

Ruskin has taken pains to mingle his life with Francesca's in several
ways: by the exchange of letters with her, by sending her a picture of
Rose La Touche which she hangs in her room, and by the act of craft-
ing *Roadside Songs*. "The little supplementary bits enable me to fit it all
together into what will be the loveliest thing ever seen, and do more good
than the Fioretti de San Francisco," he tells her.[50] Ruskin's mosaic work
doubles at a humble remove that of the Byzantine builders of San Marco
just as Francesca's work doubles that of St. Francis.

The setting of stones, the drawing out of filaments – these skills, translated into verbal art, Ruskin has developed over his lifetime. His oeuvre
exemplifies the primacy of ornamentation and the centrality of works
of art that grow out of, reflect, create, and embody "purity of heart and
sentiment" (27.631). Both his filigreed textual arrangements and his daily
work of art criticism depend on the paradox of deep surfaces, of stability
without foundation.

Finally, we must ask to what extent *Roadside Songs* represents a culmination of desire articulated rather than of desire fulfilled. Certainly
we would not wish to argue that Ruskin solved the puzzles of a lifetime
during his closing years. Yet the very recapitulation of so many of his
heartfelt needs in frame after frame of this edition constitutes a kind
of victory. His appropriation is also his appreciation, that aestheticist
donnée. For Ruskin, appreciation is a love best expressed through the

richest confusion between the poverty of loneliness and the wealth of full possession. In literary terms, appreciation marks the wavering ways among the arts of self-expression, mimesis, and autonomy. Above all, Ruskin shows us in *Roadside Songs* that sentimentality, "feeling in excess of the facts," does not mark the failure of art. Our feelings, he teaches, are always in excess of the facts; that is what makes them feelings. Thus the patterns of Victorian Modernism grow.

Meditation: aestheticism and pragmatism

Aestheticism, like Modernism, suffers from chronological disarray: some critics consider it a turn-of-the-century movement, others trace it back as far as the Pre-Raphaelites, John Ruskin, Théophile Gautier, and even John Keats. It has been difficult to distinguish aestheticism from Aestheticism: which artists carved a movement from a set of more general artistic concerns, and what were their particular beliefs and representative works of art? Rather than viewing aestheticism as a set (or multiple sets) of authors, texts, and positions, this study begins with the hypothesis that aestheticism is the pragmatist exploration, within works of art themselves, of what art might be and do. In other words, aestheticism is aesthetics pursued by pragmatist means. As Victorian Modernist writers and artists explore the meanings of beauty, taste, imagination and artistic truth, each one creates a pragmatist aestheticism in relation to his or her particular purposes, questions, or needs.[1]

In addition, pragmatism allows those of us who study art (including literature) to engage in shaping a useful critical eclecticism. Pragmatist receptivity enables us to entertain a variety of critical schools and methods. William James explains, borrowing an image from the Italian pragmatist Giovanni Papini, "[Pragmatism] lies in the midst of our theories, like a corridor in a hotel. Innumerable chambers open out of it." Many different philosophical schools and theories "own the corridor, and all must pass through it if they want a practicable way of getting into or out of their respective rooms."[2]

If we imagine that corridor, for a moment, as connecting the many rooms of critical approaches to aestheticism, a preliminary passage through it will reveal some stark choices. Three large antechambers – each deliberately painted here in only the broadest of strokes, and each in turn potentially leading to many smaller rooms – seem worth a visit. They are the antechambers of *l'art pour l'art*, Marxism, and Poststructuralism.[3]

Aestheticism's commentators have often understood it to be a creation centering about the notion of *l'art pour l'art* and predicated, after Kant, on disinterestedness or purposiveness without purpose rather than on verisimilitude, usefulness, or ethical soundness. Questions of the nature of aesthetic judgment metamorphose into statements about works of art, artists, and audiences, most of which presuppose that art defines something called an "aesthetic realm" and must be judged accordingly. Pragmatists might choose to explore the usefulness to artists and critics of the concepts of the purity, uselessness, and autonomy of art. Those seeking a religion in or of art, as well as those drawn to the mysterious qualities of beauty that distinguish it from the workaday world, find notions of art for its own sake rewarding. Others have been drawn to it precisely because they wish to show how, in one way or another, those who professed a belief in the purity of beauty or the exaltation of refined taste did so in ways that brought such aesthetic separatism squarely into the impure marketplace.[4]

Within the Marxist antechamber, such refutation of *l'art pour l'art* proceeds with vigor, and "pure" beauty is often its target – although it is never totally vanquished. Here we must understand aestheticism within its historical, social, and cultural setting. Only when we hypothesize that the (supposedly) pure and autonomous realm of beauty is in fact dependent on or constitutive of dominant ideologies, those ideologies themselves supportive of the flawed material arrangements of a society, will we come to understand aestheticism adequately. Some Marxist studies of aestheticism actually begin by tracking the autonomist view of our first antechamber. The aestheticist work of art turns inward, away from the materialist conditions of life: "Aestheticism had made the distance from the praxis of life the content of [its] works. The praxis of life to which Aestheticism refers and which it negates is the means–ends rationality [of bourgeois life]."[5] In this interpretation, beauty encourages us to avoid or deny the problems of capitalism rather than to face up to them. Far from offering a haven, beauty is a symptom of the disease of aestheticism, and revolutionary consciousness is the best medicine. Aestheticism is debased and suspect, a form (like sentimentality) of false emotion, nothing but evidence that capitalism has been internalized and the artistic impulse co-opted: "The ultimate binding forces of the bourgeois social order, in contrast to the coercive apparatus of absolutism, will be habits, pieties, sentiments, and affections. And this is equivalent to saying that power in such an order has become aestheticized."[6] Aestheticism in this view is complicit with – even constitutive of – capitalist hegemony.

If critics (often themselves artists) who believe in *l'art pour l'art* seek pure Beauty and an aesthetic realm apart, and if critics who believe in Marxism want to unmask beauty as part of the apparatus of capitalism, critics of the Poststructuralist/post-modernist schools want to explain the aesthetic as, in one way or another, nothing but reality. Rather than referring to separation and enclosure, aestheticism in this mode points to the tendency of philosopher-artists to claim that all of reality is aesthetic, that there is no escaping an artfully made world. Wallace Stevens suggests "it is a world of words to the end of it" (*CP*, p. 345). Textual worlds, including but certainly not limited to literary texts, make and unmake themselves. "Reality" is but an artifact of our interpretation and creation; we live in a "free-floating aesthetic universe."[7]

Each of these views tends toward exclusivity. The aesthetic exists in a world apart from everyday life; or, the aesthetic seduces us all unwittingly into the debasements of bourgeois reality; or the aesthetic has always already overtaken reality, because it is the condition of our knowing it. Pragmatist aestheticism, however, enables us to make choices of, not between, these and other theoretical groupings, depending on what it is we wish to accomplish. We may work *as* aesthetic purists/formalists, Marxists, deconstructionists, and other critical types too numerous to catalogue, and that can mean borrowing hypotheses from or even joining forces with those who dwell in certainties different from our own.

This is certainly not the first study to seek connections among various methods or schools; to the extent that others have done so, they have adopted a pragmatist receptivity. Much of this work has, however, been conducted under the aegis of literary theory, which in the past few decades has often meant using literary texts as handmaidens, speaking through us when we need them to make a conceptual point, otherwise silent. This study, too, makes use of texts as illustrations, but it also allows the texts a power capable of ventriloquizing us, their would-be interlocutors. Sonnets, paintings, even interior decorations may be works of critical statement. Art may mingle on an equal footing with theories about art – and either one may serve the other. That one person may be simultaneously artist and critic is a lesson that Oscar Wilde attempted to teach; a pragmatist refresher course will perhaps encourage us to regard our own critical work as art, and to be mindful that its form is part of its meaning – as well as its political positioning or philosophical import.

Learning to be pragmatists, we will find that certain sturdy critical commonplaces begin to require revision by nuance. For example, late nineteenth-century aestheticism has been considered a masculine movement of high culture in which women were reduced to caricature or used by male aesthetic artists as models. And when women were presumptuous enough to make art themselves, men forced them to the sidelines. Women were in fact victimized by male aesthetes, but that is only part of the story; some male aesthetes chose to feminize themselves; some women artists held sway.[8] Another established and useful critical narrative has it that aestheticist artists wished to place their works of art (often including themselves in that category) apart from the marketplace and above the works of lesser artists who pandered to the masses. They failed in this undertaking; or, through commercial failure, succeeded; or actually wanted to sell well in mass markets.[9] But the evidence, as we shall see, also indicates that not all of them posed the question of aestheticist superiority in just these ways: some measured it by the quality of their friendships, or by the number of souls or buildings they saved, or by regional loyalty. Other story-lines emerge.

We shall also, perhaps, decide to reconsider the limiting reading of aestheticism that posits self-referential purity as its *sine qua non*, whether to champion it or to attack it. Instead we might question the very idea of such a sign and to ask whether aesthetes themselves not only demanded autonomy of the work of art or witnessed for pure Beauty, but also explored artistic didacticisms. Aesthetics in the British tradition has historically mixed what we would now call aesthetics, ethics, psychology, and sociology, and traces of this intermingling appear in Victorian Modernist texts.[10] While the movements of literary aestheticism have frequently been viewed as creations of "high" culture, the aesthetic in its wider meaning has often concerned itself with the possibilities of a "low" – because sensuous, ordinary, or material – critique of rationality.[11] Aestheticist writers in practice followed suit in this suspicion of cerebralism and abstraction: when Baudelaire, Poe, or Swinburne desired to "efface" moralism from literature, it was the abstract law of bourgeois culture they sought to counterbalance with improving moral "arguments" made of the sensuous elements of sound, rhythm, and imagery.

Furthermore, to say that a writer is aestheticist will involve a close look at what that term means across time and text. Ruskin, for example, both attacks and embraces aestheticist conventions of *l'art pour l'art*, defining and redefining aestheticism as he goes. At times he describes beauty as distinct from usefulness, insisting, for example, that "I had got at the principle ... that the seeds and fruits of them were for the sake of the flowers, not the flowers for the fruit"[12]; or, "Remember that the most beautiful things in the world are the most useless; peacocks and lilies for instance" (9.72). Yet he mingles such statements with a moralizing insistence that beauty can be grasped only within a framework of right belief and Christian action: "The Christian Theoria seeks not... what the Epicurean sought; but finds it food and the objects of its love everywhere... even in all that seems coarse and commonplace" (4.50). In the realm of Theoria, the flower exists for the seeds and fruits. One may "consider the lilies" but not stroll about with them in hand. Ruskin's statements of Evangelical moralism often appear to silence his trills of *l'art pour l'art*; yet those trills not only periodically revive, but they do so in relation to moralizing pronouncements, thus forming a moral aestheticism.[13] The principal writers studied here celebrate beauty; but they also ask how beauty means in relation to any of a number of issues such as regional identity, gender arrangements, professionalism, religious belief, friendship, and financial security.

In order to understand how nineteenth-century aestheticisms developed in two rhetorics – one of abstract autonomy, the other of embodied relatedness – we may look to the traditions of sublimity and sentimentality, as well as to German aesthetics of the same period. Since a full study of the latter tradition's importance to Victorian Modernism lies beyond the scope of this discussion, we'll proceed here by examining Friedrich Schiller's *Letters on the Aesthetic Education of Man* (1965) not as the exemplary text, but as a promising starting place.[14]

Throughout Schiller's work of anthropological aesthetics, he describes man as a set of polarities. In one mode, man hews to reason, form, being, objectivity, and ideality, and in another mode he involves himself with feeling, energy, animal desire, subjectivity, and brute existence. In sets of shifting terms and subtle rhetorical moves within and between these modes, Schiller gradually develops, both logically and poetically, the notion of Beauty as the realm where these two aspects of humanity can mingle, thus freeing each man and the concept of man from two slaveries: that of reason and that of nature.[15] This realm of beauty or semblance Schiller labels as the aesthetic, taking care to establish that it is not a place of final synthesis or compromise, but rather a mode of experience that is both conjunctive and disjunctive.

In an enthrallingly metamorphic display of metaphor composed in the cadences of logical analysis, Schiller sounds the (to him, magic and mysterious) chord of beauty as a space or a process that enables human beings to live productively by entertaining the possibilities of both reason and nature. From the first, this realm of freedom is meant to address what Schiller saw as the fiasco of the French Revolution, in which he had initially placed great hope. In the end, his *Letters* address the "realm of aesthetic semblance" as a utopian political idea. "The aesthetic state," true to its own aesthetic semblance and sense of play, is mysteriously less than a reality but more than a possibility (p. 178).

We shall refer to this Schillerian aesthetic realm as a "third way" that richly confuses polarities through the impulse of play, analogous in some ways to Wallace Stevens's search for a supreme fiction in the dance of imagination and world; and analogous in other ways to William James's desire to find a rationalistic philosophy that is "in touch with concrete facts and joys and sorrows" and an empiricist philosophy which is also humanistic and religious (*P*, p. 17).

For all the writers of this study, aestheticisms develop within the *domus*, the physical structure of home and the related people who live there, perhaps because it enables them to imagine an aestheticism of possibility rather than aesthetic orthodoxy of one school or another. As Stevens writes, "Within the actual, the warm, the near, / So great a unity, that it is bliss, / Ties us to those we love."[16] Home becomes the place in which the "phrases compounded of dear relation" speak into intermingled existence beauty, knowledge, and love. Home is sometimes the poem itself where readers may dwell: "The house was quiet and the world was calm. / The reader became the book; and summer night / Was like the conscious being of the book" (*CP*, p. 358).

Schiller's association of the aesthetic mode with home figures forth such a patterning. His "Twenty-Sixth Letter," dramatizes anthropological development as a movement (ostensibly across vast sweeps of time) into the time and space of the aesthetic mode. Man begins in a savage, physical stage and moves toward beauty, and he does so at home, in a domestic realm that is neither savage nor civilized, but a location where such polarities may potentially converge. In Schiller's view, the domestic mediates in the way that the aesthetic itself mediates, and the list of polarities that both deliberately confuse is long. Aesthetic man comes into being as one who, by living in the *domus* of a hut, avoids the extremes of utter individuality (hiding in a cave) and utter loss of individuality (roaming the world as part of a nomadic horde). Schiller explains that the germ of beauty develops:

Not where man hides himself, a *troglodyte*, in caves, eternally an isolated unit, never finding humanity outside *himself*; nor yet there where, a nomad, he roams in vast hordes over the face of the earth, eternally but one of a number, never finding humanity *within himself* – but only there, where, in his own hut, he discourses silently with himself and, from the moment he steps out of it, with all the rest of his kind, only there will the tender blossom of beauty unfold. There, where a limpid atmosphere opens his senses to every delicate contact, and an energizing warmth animates the exuberance of matter . . . there . . . where out of life itself the sanctity of order springs, and out of the law of order nothing but life can develop.[17]

"There," in the domestic "Là-bas" of aestheticism, beauty is a matter of "dear relation" between contraries.

As domesticity entwines with the celebration of beauty to create the domestic aestheticism of Victorian Modernism, the Schillerian aesthetic tradition is taken up and revivified. We think of Ruskin's claims that domestic architecture gives rise to the great Gothic cathedrals; of Wilde's advice to the Americans, "At least let the pitcher that stands by the well be beautiful";[18] of William James's search for a renewal of his failing energies by an exploration of intense, aesthetic experience within the home; and of the invention of their own forms of literary aestheticism by American domestic novelists.[19] Considering the twentieth century, we think, too, of Gertrude Stein's "Objects" of *Tender Buttons*: "A substance in a cushion," "Mildred's umbrella," "A new cup and saucer," "A seltzer bottle." Or, "Anything that is decent, anything that is present, a calm and a cook and more singularly still a shelter, all these show the need of clamor. What is the custom, the custom is in the center."[20] "An energizing warmth animates the exuberance of matter": Schiller dreams Stein.

The realm of beauty that both respects and defies dichotomies is eccentrically central to Victorian Modernism. Born of oxymoron, contradiction, irony, and even paradox, Victorian Modernist aestheticism dramatizes emotional ambivalence. Like Ruskin, who intertwines the beauty of Christian morality with that of epicurean delight, other Victorian Modernists often think and create as aesthetes who value beauty in contrary ways. They range, as does Schiller's "man," between form and feeling, law and desire. Art may be for itself, but it is also for others. It is patterns of interrelation, including conflict, that matter, not the sorting into one category called the beautiful, another called the good. Augusta Evans's pure, Christian heroine Edna Earl conducts research into world mythologies that is not wholly unlike her reprobate St. Elmo's worldwide dabblings in evil. Both are fascinated aesthetes who make their sentimental home together at novel's end. Rossetti's poetry mingles personifications of intense feeling with personifications of moral abstractions until he is sure that they cannot ever be pulled apart.

How far, then, does aestheticism extend? In a broad sense, aestheticism exists wherever people both make and think about art: aesthetes are the clan of the art society that makes claims about the importance of beauty. They may be artists whose style tends to announce itself as such, those who like to explore through their works of art the idea that art is never a transparent rendering of the world. Hellenistic sculptors, Mannerist painters such as Bronzino and Parmigianino, writers of Euphuistic prose or the English Metaphysical poets, Shakespeare as he creates the romances – all like to think about an art that announces the importance of art. All might be said to practice aestheticism. Beyond this extremely broad and therefore unwieldy notion of aestheticism across the centuries, we are left with collections of local aestheticisms – in this case, the aestheticisms of Victorian Modernists.

One final note. To the extent that aestheticism has attracted varied and conflicting descriptions, definitions, and judgments, so, too, has decadence. It has often been seen as a subcategory of aestheticism itself – the love of beauty and the cult of art in the "late" period of movements or centuries. Decadence in this reading is aestheticism that has evidently dabbled in the lurid or the strange as it has become more intensely itself, and it is usually considered (in English literature) as a phenomenon of the 'nineties, the bridge from Victorianism to high Modernism. Given Victorian Modernism's reluctance to privilege the turn of the century as the scene of Modernism's awakening, decadence begins to look somewhat different. We might consider it usefully not as a later, over-developed or even hysterical stage of aestheticism, but rather as aestheticism's darker side, present, as Mario Praz has taught us, since the Romantic era and traceable back to the Gothic and the Grotesque in earlier centuries.[21] Rossetti, then, would be both aestheticist and decadent, depending on what we were looking for in his paintings, poems, and life. Surely his mysterious women can be as unsettling as anything dreamt by arch-decadents such as Beardsley or Huysmans.

However we try to describe decadence, a return to the scene of writing in which it appears will enrich our understanding of it. Formalist criteria and conventional practices of decadence – sultry atmospherics, self-reflexive narratives, paradox, grotesqueries, and sensationalisms, continuously refined registers of feeling, and the dwelling on form at the expense of subject – can, after all, be found in one another's company elsewhere in literature.[22]

For Victorian Modernists, particularly those who were women, decadence was often aestheticism yearned for. It represents a difficulty and intensity in their efforts to make art and to claim the title of artist, and it returns us to the plot of Modernism's agon in a new form, and well before the fin-de-siècle. We may add some sweetness and light to our critical picture of Modernism instead of regarding it as primarily a phenomenon of rupture or conflict, because male Victorian Modernists wove what we would still consider "feminized" strands of feeling into their multiplex creations. Now, in considering female Victorian Modernists we will at times need to reverse the process: beginning with the sweetness, conventionality, and connectedness (to audience, to "everyday life") of their writing, we will also need to understand its processes of darkness, rupture, and experimentation. Domestic novelists such as Augusta Evans, for example, created decadent works in order to relate the conventions of domesticity in their own lives to something that felt like an artistic leap to freedom.

As male Victorian Modernists embraced and made use of the feminine, sometimes to exploit it and thereby diminish themselves, sometimes to enrich it and themselves, female Victorian Modernists made connections that moved in another direction. They imagined the move from a strongly didactic literary culture to one that was also expressive and autonomous, and they imagined this move both within and apart from conventional forms of domesticity. The making of art felt dangerous and sometimes delicious, its cultural paths unmarked, and so they imagined it as a process of darkness and intensity. Just as we have to examine our critical tendency to view Ruskin as a patriarchal Sage whose "masculine" powers failed him toward the end, so we should also examine our critical tendency to see domestic novelists as doing something primarily "feminine" in nature. Now that they have been taken up as a serious subject for critical exploration, we should remove them from the critical ghetto that made such a move possible in the first place. Victorian Modernism reveals male writers who preached the virtues of the heart, vastly expanding sentimentality into a sublime of its own. Victorian Modernism reveals female writers who deliberately "fell" from sincerity "into" the abstract surfaces of various practices, including a deliberate trifling with their audiences, the self-conscious frame-breaking that allows characters to speak as if they have grasped their own fictionality, and irony twisted and intensified to paradox. In short, Victorian Modernists practiced in mid-century what literary critics would later label turn-of-the-century "decadence."[23]

Once decadence is understood as arising from multiple sources and situations, our understandings of it must be adjusted to accommodate its complexities. Although decadent artists present images of Circe, Leda, "knowledgeable" female children, and vampirish women, although they plumb domesticity to its darkest depths, many of their techniques, themes, and images retain the presence of morality, didacticism, tenderness, and sentiment.[24] This can happen at the level of plot: in Bram Stoker's vampire-haunted world, the corruptible Lucy is destroyed, while Mina, the exemplary Christian woman, lives on. That neither character is without moral ambiguity only increases the intermingling of wholesomeness and depravity.

The very ambiguity and paradox of decadent literature enable a tender, relational sublimity. One of the personae of Wilde's *De Profundis* desires a loving, empathetic and tender relationship. "He" cannot be fully distinguished from the other voices of that work – or from the entanglement of voices across Wilde's oeuvre. As we now well recognize, Wilde's denial of morality is in part an insistence on an even finer and stronger morality – he does want to improve us. His satire implies, if it does not describe, a kinder world, where people combine artistic taste with genuine, not hypocritical, caring for others. Just as Wilde kept an eye to the marketplace, he also kept an eye to the Bible and to Greek tragedy. The strange flower of decadent moralism is moralism none the less, and it is so because of and not just despite its fascination with the bizarre or the nihilistic.

Victorian Modernist aestheticism: pragmatist explorations conducted by artists as they make art. The process often involves creating works that enable artist and audience to know by feeling. Victorian Modernists' aestheticism frequently figures forth the vague, the melting, or the fluid: wavering movement, metamorphosis, reverie. It also presents the detailed, particular, and highly patterned: ornamentation, pattern, linkage, concatenation. Whatever the practices, the effects are to allow whatever seem the most satisfying matings to hang together, for a while, in a discontinuous unity. Aestheticism may perhaps be storied more successfully than it has been categorized; and it is a few of these developing narratives, across multiple centuries, countries, and artists, that this study traces.

CHAPTER 3

Arrangements: Dante Gabriel Rossetti's Victorian Modernism

> For Rossetti, then, the great affections of persons to each other, swayed and determined, in the case of his highly pictorial genius, mainly by that so-called material loveliness, formed the great undeniable reality in things, the solid resisting substance, in a world where all beside might be but shadow.
>
> Walter Pater, "Dante Gabriel Rossetti"[1]

Walter Pater's Rossetti bears only a slight resemblance to our own turn-of-the-century figure. His Rossetti locates solid reality in the "affections of persons to each other," while ours struggles with tales of erotic love and death, fatal women narcissistically claimed, fragmentation of identity challenging the very notion of "person," and treasons of friendship and of time. While Pater speaks of Rossetti's belief in "the great undeniable reality in things," we know better: Rossetti's crippling subjectivism led him to doubt the existence of a world outside his mind. Rossetti may have possessed "pictorial genius," but didn't that gift wane as he prostituted it in the marketplace?

However off-key Pater's description of reciprocated affections, material loveliness, and an undeniable reality may at first sound, eventually its reverberations ring true to the careful listener – without silencing the conclusions of more recent criticism. It is possible to describe a Rossetti conjunct with both nineteenth- and late twentieth-century understandings, that is, a Victorian Modernist Rossetti; and it can be demonstrated that a complex process of sentimental domesticity involving several overlapping activities was central to Rossetti's aestheticism. First, he decorated the interiors of his homes, most notably that of 16 Cheyne Walk, Chelsea. Second, Rossetti depicted, intensely and repeatedly, domestic spaces and objects in both his poetry and his painting. Bedrooms, halls, sitting rooms; nests, bowers, cages; windows, doors, thresholds; cups, washbasins, chairs, cabinets, screens, mirrors: his "fine art" on its face represents a choice of spaces and things resolutely quotidian in nature, if frequently exoticized. Third, and in a sense encompassing these two domestic exercises, Rossetti passionately made "arrangements." I choose the word precisely because of its flexibility of meaning, its ability to capture the activities of "applied" art (interior decoration, crafts), "high" art (painting, poetry) and "household" art (practical affairs of home, hospitality). These three arenas of aesthetic arrangements intermingled in Rossetti's creative life, and as they did so, fueled specifically by tender sentiments, they enabled him to create a domestic sublimity that periodically redeemed for him a life of pain and terror. To save himself, Rossetti sought truth through the making of Victorian Modernist art.

Rossetti, like Ruskin, believed that "arrangements" could establish one's credentials as a major painter. Writing in May 1855 to his friend William Allingham, Rossetti describes the painting *Cimabue's Madonna Carried in Procession through the Streets of Florence* by Frederick Leighton which he has just seen at the Royal Academy:

It was *very* uninteresting to me at first sight; but on looking more at it, I think there is great richness of arrangement – a quality which, when *really* existing, as it does in the best old Masters, and perhaps hitherto in no living man . . . ranks among the great qualities.[2]

"Richness of arrangement" is a phrase like "truth to nature" which can only point toward an ineffable quality of goodness in painting. Yet it appears to be related in Rossetti's mind to composition or structure as opposed to content. Fourteen years later he will write, this time of poetry, "The quality of complex structure in art is more touching and pathetic to me always than even the emotional appeal of the subject matter" (*LDGR*, 750).

Arrangement and complex structure succeed in Rossetti's view only if they emotionally engage the audience, and Rossetti clearly relates arrangement to feeling rather than thought as he judges *Cimabue*: "As for purely intellectual qualities, expression, intention, etc., there is little as yet of them," he writes (*LDGR*, 252). Richness of arrangement elicits sentiment, just as the quality of complex structure in poetry matters because it is "touching and pathetic to me." Arrangement has to do with the private world of sentiment and thus indicates a feminization of the nineteenth-century artist which is actually a return to the eighteenth-century roots of sensibility in which sympathetic feeling was a part of every gentleman's civic repertoire. Deviating from the Victorian type of the stalwart man of affairs, the artist in Rossetti's view must enable his melting emotions to infuse his work so that his audience may feel them too, perhaps even learn the language of the heart.[3]

In fact, as this study will reveal, Rossetti's sentiment-laden arrangements in art, the choices he makes about how to fill a canvas or the sonnet form, are inseparable from the actual arrangements – choices of interior decoration and servants, renovations and invitations – he makes at 16 Cheyne Walk. Further, Rossetti values, and even practices so far as he is able, the once Christian, lately femininized, virtues of charity, duty, and selflessness. This is not to deny his nervous breakdowns and suicide attempt, chloral addiction, anguished relationships with women, or selfish use of his brother William and his friends – all the self-destructive qualities that tended to damage others in his sphere. Yet we may illuminate with Paterian notions of loveliness and affection, and with Victorian notions of duty and rectitude sincerely practiced, a picture that has become too *noir*, to choose a favorite term of our own century's turn.

To approach the question of domestic arrangements widely construed is certainly to tread on time-honored values of masculinity in art. As we have seen, Coleridge implies that Fancy, gendered feminine, is the inferior of masculine Imagination, with its through-and-through, unifying, and mastering form. Rossettian arrangement is the work of Fancy. The notion of arrangement itself involves the often hierarchy-challenging placement of entities in complex relation, whether they be, as in Rossetti's case, feathers, foliage, and bodies in a painting; friends and family members in the guest rooms of 16 Cheyne Walk; lyric "songs" within ballads; or paintings in highly wrought frames on specific walls in the rooms of his patrons' grand houses.

A common criticism of Rossetti's poetry and painting has been its tendency to lapse into "mere" or "unnecessary" ornamentation, a complaint implying that there is an important meaning (central, unified, living) that is obscured by tacked on, deadening details. This study refutes such a position, setting out the reasons for valuing ornamentation and decoration as an intrinsic part of aesthetic arrangement in Rossetti's practice of several, interlinking arts. For Rossetti, objects are not, as Coleridge programmatically states, dead. Rossetti understands the "vital" as a free-floating energy that can infuse (and ebb from) people, objects, rooms, paintings, and poems alike, as he arranges them in complex patterns.

While there is an impressive literature on the relation of Rossetti's poetry and painting, such recognition of artistic complexity must, if we are to understand Rossetti more fully and accurately, expand even farther. His eclecticism within a given work of art has been appreciated and puzzled over ever since Ruskin first wrote of the Pre-Raphaelite tendency to combine different orders of reality, perception, and artistic style within a single work.[4] Certainly we register a functional complexity in both Rossetti's painting and poetry: for example, a scene may have both a rolling narrative quality and near-static symbolist reverberation. Any given detail may gain, lose, and regain (a new) significance as we view it in different contexts. It is precisely Rossetti's eclecticisms of mode, technique, and detail that require us to consider his "arrangements" freely, crossing not only formalist lines within a given work of art, but also moving back and forth from arrangements within a painting or poem to those surrounding it in "real" life. Conducting a search for what would suffice, Rossetti mingles the frames of art and life.

One brief example: the hawthorn pot in *Monna Rosa* (Fig. 2), a bit of the "blue and white" china that has become the emblem of aestheticism itself.[5] Our understanding of the painting might begin with a formalist appreciation of the pot's decorative texture in relation to figures on the woman's robe and the background of peacock feathers and roses. We might then proceed to an appreciation of the pot as an incipiently Symbolist image of imagination and artisanry, and from there to a meditation on the woman herself as a beautiful, "vital object" and so on. But we should also attend to the aesthetic arrangements Rossetti made beyond the painting's frame, at the center of which the pot still beautifully rests. Rossetti's carefully cultivated and deeply affectionate relationship with the arts dealer and collector Murray Marks, one of his principal suppliers of Oriental ware; his own collector's obsession that led him to entertain other collectors to dinner and thus people his solitude meaningfully; his feeling that an earlier and better culture of beauty and virtue inhabits the hawthorn pot, and that such significant beauty can be placed both in his home and on his canvases (themselves to be placed in homes, not public galleries): all these and other arrangements must inform our appreciation of *Monna Rosa* precisely because Rossetti painted and lived them simultaneously, interchangeably.

Above all, the hawthorn pot reminds us that translation is one of Rossetti's defining practices. The "bringing home" or domesticating of foreign speech is central to his intense practice of domestic aestheticism. He translated not only Italian poetry into English poetry, but also real Chinese pots (already translated from the Chinese when Rossetti named them "hawthorn") into items of English domesticity – part of the ensemble of his sitting room – and then into painted pots, themselves carefully placed in painted bowers and rooms. While many high Modernists

Figure 2　*Monna Rosa*, Dante Gabriel Rossetti

tended in theory, following Kant, to assume that the successful work of art is "a fairly small perceptual object" beautiful because of its distance from everyday life, in practice they often wrote of ordinary things.[6] Marcel Proust, Henry James, Virginia Woolf, William Butler Yeats, and James

Joyce translated humble objects into writing: railroad timetables, cracked teacups, heather-mixture stockings, Connemara cloth, vaseline, and orangeflowers. And they moved these fixities about as objects requiring us to rethink the nature of artistic unity as we come to grasp the avant-garde notion of discontinuous continuity. Gertrude Stein's patterns of words on a page *as objects* on a page continue this tradition: "What does literature do and how does it do it. And what does English literature do and how does it do it. And what ways does it use to do what it does do."[7] Despite our own critical narratives of these artists' search for pure and autonomous art, they used real things, and often to teach (moral) lessons about how to live.

But why trace these metamorphoses? Are not the paintings and poems subtle enough to fascinate us without adding domestic mythology and practice to all the others Rossetti explored – Classical, Gothic, Arthurian, Assyrian, etc.? I believe that what might at first appear merely a complication of an already difficult oeuvre will eventually reveal an important "reading" of Rossetti's creations. We have tended to unduly extreme interpretations, most of which, as I have mentioned, insist upon Rossetti's despair, periodic madness, and wandering about in precisely that world of shadows that Pater believes he kept at bay. Our tales of Rossetti have chronicled his loss of religious faith, his entry into a world of endlessly replicating signs and his agony upon realizing that "pure" art cannot be created in the fallen world of commerce.[8] This critical focus on bleakness has often been accompanied by polarizing conceptions: Rossetti chooses wrongly between selling out (pot-boiling) and artistic integrity; during a given creative period he creates either Christian typological or secular "psychological" works; *Lilith* represents the feminine principle of evil in the world and *Sibylla Palmifera* the feminine purity of soul, etc.

Often the critical narratives of bleakness and polarization go hand in hand:

His poetry is torn by his conflicting desires to be self-expressive yet to remain within the "standing-point" of Victorian values, to be avant-garde and yet not too much at odds with his age, to be transcendently "aesthetic" and yet not too far from the "passion-woven complexities" of actual experience.[9]

Why "torn"? Here Riede assumes that self-expression would necessarily be at odds with Victorian values, and he implies that the aesthetic must exist in opposition to actual experience. However, domesticity, construed as a process of making arrangements, provides Rossetti with a middle way between avant-garde rebellion and stifling Victorian propriety, the aesthetic and the ordinary – thus relaxing, if not collapsing, such polarities. Once we begin to trace the forms and energies of his domestic aestheticism a more complex, but ultimately a more balanced, picture of Rossetti emerges.[10]

In order to pursue such an extended exploration, we must begin by questioning some of our critical assumptions. The first is that the Victorian middle-class home is only a place of Philistine prejudices begging for revision by iconoclasts and that Victorian domesticity must mean claustrophobic enclosure – or at the least anxiety or ennui – in overstuffed rooms.[11] That the room within the "typical" middle-class home might be a testing ground for modern culture, that it might provide both the space of reaction and the space of rebellion, is a possibility we would do well to keep in mind as we explore Rossetti's arrangements. Watercolors of interiors at 16 Cheyne Walk, verbal descriptions in friends' memoirs, and the auction catalogue of his belongings all suggest both rooms filled to bursting with furniture and bric-à-brac *and* rooms carefully arranged, tasteful, and interesting in the very oddity or special beauty of articles displayed there. Rossetti's letters, his brother's diaries, and memoirs of friends depict a prickly Victorian *pater familias* without a family, a manipulator, a brother and son arrogantly claiming respect, attention, and funds for his projects. At the same time we may read there, as we shall see, of a man who demanded real, rather than hypocritical, Christian charity of himself. Furthermore, Rossetti arranged with great care a workroom within each of his homes. There he envisioned the very aesthetic values that would, transformed by both decadent artists in England and the creators of *art nouveau* in France, enter the mainstream of Modernism.[12] Rossetti stayed at home, worked at home, and created a home as he imagined the shapes and patterns of mid-century Victorian Modernism. Between accounts of Rossetti that assume on one hand Victorian claustrophobia and stultification, and on the other hand a perilous aestheticist challenge, fall the shadows of the critics; we must take care to examine both positions critically.

A second and related assumption has to do with aestheticism as a movement of *l'art pour l'art*, a coterie practice separating itself from the largely Philistine religious and moral thought of the day. Once again, the critical tendency has been to organize a complex reality into overly simplified polarities. Art is assumed either to worship and instruct or to exist only for the sake of its own beauty.[13] Here the evidence overwhelmingly supports Rossetti's difficult negotiation of both elitist separatism and popular participation. As we shall see, he continually gathers sentimental mass culture into the ever slackening arms, the deliberately failing embrace, of elitist high culture.

A third assumption: that Rossetti's Victorian tendency to idolize, fear, and (attempt to) control "woman" captures the most important aspect of his sexual politics. Certainly Rossetti repeatedly rehearsed the deadliest of Victorian sexual schematics: the heads of his women are as likely to spawn Medusa-like strangling hair as they are to radiate angelic auras from velvety, boneless faces. Yet his own feminization – his deliberate choice of female roles and values – suggests a more complicated story. Objectify women he did, but given his rich and strange notions of what objects could be, this is not a simple issue to judge. The several aspects of his freely chosen self-feminization, which I will lay out in the course of this chapter, indicate that Rossetti not only lost himself in narcissistic mirror worlds of feminine beauty (he indisputably did), but also found himself in daily acts and beliefs that celebrated Victorian notions of female virtue.[14]

Domesticity, it must be said, is a good thing, for Rossetti and for the development of his aestheticism. Although domesticity promises little, although it neither arches over nor undergirds Rossetti's life and art but rather fuels a process without an outcome, it does supply a healing energy, the agonies of Rossetti's life at home notwithstanding. To contemplate sympathetically Rossetti's domestic arrangements is not to sentimentalize an already mawkish Victorian culture. It is to discern a salutary energy of domestic arrangement that might account for Rossetti's productivity (however tainted), his friendship and social intimacy (however flawed and ultimately decaying), and his capacity to love (however frustrated).

This description will involve readings of life and works that cannot be completely distinguished from each other. But then aestheticism is "about" just this creation of self, surroundings, and work of art as a continuum, all joining in the task of renewing the world. Such a process is deliberately scaled down from the great imaginative projects of early Romanticism. Rossetti's arrangements replace transcendent Beauty with a notion of good taste, thus enabling him to skip Romantic grandiosities for a more modest task: the making of a pleasing and protecting nest or bower as preparation for a leap not to the transcendent, but to an anti-transcendent domestic sublime.

THE DOUBLE ROOM OF THE DOMESTIC SUBLIME

Rossetti's revisionary art turned to the private, interiorized and feminine as a way of countering the pressures of modernization. His fascination with objects is especially revelatory of his strategies for dealing with the "master plots" of religion, science, and empire. When John Ruskin writes after Rossetti's death that he "wilfully perverted and lacerated his powers of conception with Chinese puzzles and Japanese monsters, until his foliage looked fit for nothing but a firescreen" (33.271), he quite misses the point. Rossetti loved and admired an attractive firescreen. Similarly, when Ruskin attempts to educate a generation of art consumers by cautioning them that "real love of the picture" is not "the same sort of fancy which we would take to a pretty arm-chair or a newly-shaped decanter" (16.187), Rossetti's need to break with Ruskin becomes more comprehensible than ever. While Ruskin sought domesticity in the exterior surfaces of houses, Rossetti wrote and painted from an indoor perspective, even when his subject was nature.

Rossetti never accepted, much less assumed, the distinction between applied and fine art. As he replaces idealist imagination with pluralist taste, as he replaces the notion of fixed composition with a medley of interesting objects in a room – some coming, some going, all subject to rearrangement – Ruskin's suspicion of interior decoration simply makes little sense to him. Consider, for example, Rossetti's "Introductory Sonnet" to *The House of Life*:

> *A Sonnet is a moment's monument,–*
> *Memorial from the Soul's eternity*
> *To one dead deathless hour. Look that it be,*
> *Whether for lustral rite or dire portent,*
> *Of its own arduous fulness reverent:*
> *Carve it in ivory or in ebony,*
> *As Day or Night may rule; and let Time see*
> *Its flowering crest impearled and orient.*
>
> *A Sonnet is a coin: its face reveals*
> *The soul,–its converse, to what Power 'tis due:–*
> *Whether for tribute to the august appeals*
> *Of Life, or dower in Love's high retinue,*
> *It serve; or, 'mid the dark wharf's cavernous breath,*
> *In Charon's palm it pay the toll to Death.*[15]

Rossetti includes among the aims of poetry the creation of an autonomous object "of its own arduous fulness reverent" *and the care of art's readers or viewers* "for lustral rite or dire portent" – and all this by placing them in the presence of special, even magical objects. The view of art as "lustral rite" bespeaks a cyclical process (the lustrum was originally conducted every five years by the censors at Rome), meant to purify a people, a piece of land, or even the community's home, the city. A ritual cleansing, it conducts us to the realm of the spiritulized domestic.[16] Sonnets themselves become the objects used in lustral rites or as dire portents, warning readers of the need to amend the present; and they must be carved, decorated, full. Yet the sonnet as object implies other, even conflicting, notions of art: beyond its autonomous and didactic qualities, its face reveals "the soul" as deeply as any Romantic poet could wish.

In the end, the sonnet as Rossetti conceives it is both a medley of critical ideas and a "medley of bric-à-brac" like that of the paintings.[17] "The Sonnet" is, to summarize, arduously full, carved in ivory or ebony with a flowered and impearled crest, and also rounded, flattish, and engraved differently on each side. Such a medley, an instance of what William James would later call "things partly joined and partly disjoined" (*P*, p. 79), might then be recognized for what it is: the jumble of life sanctified, arranged by the artist–priest–householder into an intimacy of related but contingent aspects rather than an organically conceived unity. Details and ornaments cannot be clearly distinguished from the things themselves (who can tell the engraving from the coin?), and we feel ourselves moving toward an abstraction of texture that signals the advent of the modern. As Riede acutely notes, "the paradox is that [Rossetti] consistently saw surfaces as the most profound symbols of emotional and psychological depths."[18]

A prose poem of the same period, Baudelaire's "The Double Room," eloquently reveals just the trap Rossetti has, with his bric-à-brac, avoided. Baudelaire's speaker imagines "a room that is like a dream, a truly *spiritual* room" where even the furniture dreams. Here he experiences an eternity of sensual bliss, until a knock on the door awakens him to a "filthy hole, this abode of eternal boredom."[19] Rossetti's rooms refuse such harsh contrasts. The double room of art and life is for him an artful disunity in which overwrought ornamentation and changing arrangements deny both blissful "spiritual" dream and punishing wakefulness. It is also the double room of pleasure and education: Rossetti means to teach his audiences of the life-giving qualities of art and beauty. Certainly he turns away from stern Christian moralizing, but he turns toward intense aestheticist "preaching" through color, pattern, composition, and rhythm. Rossetti infuses his art with notions of familial duty and domestic charity – sentiments meant to be accessible and improving. Pater once again gets it right when he remarks on Rossetti's "sincerity" and "transparency in language."[20] Rossetti could say what he felt, and he meant what he said. His art does not represent a turning away from moral issues, but rather a sentimental relocation of the moral impulse from orthodoxies of the head to feelings of the heart.

Rossetti's double room shelters and impels reverie, for him the preferred mode of experiencing a domestic site as more than real, less than fully transcendent: Rossetti's version of the domestic sublime. Domesticity is in his mind often connected to the pleasures of reverie, of strolling about London looking in shops, of imagining the proper setting for a curious object. He writes to his friend Miss Losh of her lover William Bell Scott:

Of course the luxury of planning and working out arrangements in Bellevue House is still far from over for its inmates, and yet Scotus exists all day long in that Paradise of pottering which as you know is so sweet to him. (*LDGR*, p. 926)

To arrange is a luxury and to potter in the midst of arrangements is for some a version of Paradise – a dream-like process as slow, unmethodical, and inefficient as the relaxations of a perpetual summer's afternoon.

The nature of Rossetti's reverie-induced domestic sublime may best be conveyed by example rather than definition. Late in life Rossetti wrote a series of sonnets entitled *Five English Poets* (*CW*, pp. 337–339). They read as a gloss on one of Rossetti's earliest pronouncements, from "Heart and Soul": "in all that thou doest, work from thine own heart, simply" (*CW*, p. 394). How does one know the imperatives of the heart? All five poems suggest that greatness in writers demands the sentimental notion of home as a place of tenderness, nurture, and heart-won inspiration. Rossetti writes of "Thy nested home-loves, noble Chatterton" (*CW*, p. 337). Coleridge's soul fares like a father bird "as from the deep home-grove," who feeds his soul-brood while Coleridge's "warm heart, the mother-bird" hovers protectingly above (*CW*, p. 338). The very structure of the sonnet on Keats depends on a list of his various homes, both actual and imaginary. The sonnet for Shelley is written as an inscription for his couch, his last earthly support.

Together the sonnets testify to the sacred power of artists' domestic experience. The poems share an incessant movement from the humble, sheltered and familiar to the vast and mysterious, and back again. Sweet, radiant, loving, dreaming, blest, kindling, fostering, true: here is the sentimental language of home. Wild, noble, dauntless, pain, eclipse, flood, dread, deathly, Truth: here is the language of leave-taking to something sublimely large, frightening, and profound. In the *relations* between these sets of words, embedded as so many markers of feeling rather than expository terms, inheres the domestic sublime.

The sonnet on Blake presents such mixed sublimity:

William Blake

(To Fredrick Shields, on his sketch of Blake's work-room and death-room, 3 Fountain Court, Strand)

> This is the place. Even here the dauntless soul,
>   The unflinching hand, wrought on; till in that nook,
>   As on that very bed, his life partook
> New birth, and passed. Yon river's dusky shoal,
> Whereto the close-built coiling lanes unroll,
>   Faced his work-window, whence his eyes would stare,
>   Thought-wandering, unto nought that met them there,
> But to the unfettered irreversible goal.
>
> This cupboard, Holy of Holies, held the cloud
>   Of his soul writ and limned; this other one,
> His true wife's charge, full oft to their abode
>   Yielded for daily bread the martyr's stone,
>   Ere yet their food might be that Bread alone,
> The words now home-speech of the mouth of God.

(CW, p. 338)

"This is the place": Rossetti allows himself to dream a bit in response to a sketch by his friend. To be at home, in an actual room with cupboards, a table, a familiar view from the "work-window" is, for the true artist, to take flight into a sacramental and aesthetic sphere in which the cupboard holding the writing becomes the "Holy of Holies." While "thought-wandering" leads to "the unfettered irreversible goal," the turn of the sonnet reverses and confuses that goal by relating it to Blake's cupboard of writings, and further connects that cupboard to an empty larder. In a similar pattern of linked oppositions, Blake dies in the sonnet's first quatrain, but lives again, on earth, in the second. The contents of both cupboards, one holding scanty food, the other art, ensure that the Blakes (like two baby birds) will be nourished by the "home-speech of the mouth of God." Sentimentalized and domestic, this Heaven awaits the great writer whose "thought wandering" will always lead him home. Elevation and breadth, heavenly mystery and earthly poverty, mingle. Rossetti would have us experience the "Nothing that is not there and the nothing that is."[21]

Furthermore, the sonnet itself, beginning with its dedication to Frederick Shields, traces a filigreed pattern that includes, in an implied *mise-en-abîme*, the art of both Rossetti and his friends. As one artist writing about another, Rossetti does not address Blake's poetry or pictures directly, nor does he himself visit 3 Fountain Court. Instead he turns to a "picture by another artist of a room once inhabited by Blake."[22] Such a choice indicates Rossetti's love of arrangements as part of his fascination with domestic scenes. That Frederick Shields probably made the sketch after Rossetti suggested he do so; that Shields sent him the sketch and the floorplan of the rooms; that Rossetti could then reciprocate with the gift of a sonnet based on Shields's gift; that both Shields and Rossetti, along with his brother William Michael Rossetti, helped the widowed Mrs. Alexander Gilchrist complete her husband's *Life of William Blake*: all of these circumstances speak of Rossetti's continual efforts to create bonds of mutual affection through art that would, in their own way, create a sense of family. The activities of Mrs. Blake, supporting and encouraging as the "true wife," interested Rossetti greatly. An "equivocal being" in his own household at 16 Cheyne Walk, he played the parts of both husband and wife.[23]

The domestic may be understood as a site of narcissism, commodity culture, and gender politics – a space as sequestered as the mind turned in upon itself, reflective of buying and selling in capitalist culture, denominated "woman's realm" for better and for worse.[24] Whatever our interpretive approach, the domestic is a process of mediation between the individual and the world, and certainly for Rossetti, as for Ruskin, it is the important site of beauty. Rossetti's aestheticist tableaux of reverie – their spaces, events, faces, ornaments – place the individual in a logic-defying daydream, a world that confuses private and public, elitist and popular, conscious and unconscious. Indeed, the dreamy connections between these concepts matter more to the pragmatist Rossetti than do the waking distinctions that others make.

To understand more fully the waking dream of the double room, it is necessary to study Rossetti's willing participation in sentimental and feminized aspects of Victorian culture, including his intense and puzzling admiration for an artist much his inferior, Charles J. Wells; the actual domestic and decorative arrangements Rossetti makes at 16 Cheyne Walk; and the arrangements he makes with other people that enable him to paint and write. After sketching these domestic scenes of creation, we shall find their characteristic reflections and refractions within Rossetti's painting (*The Day Dream*) and poetry (*The House of Life*).

SENTIMENTAL ARTIFICE

Rossetti paints in *Marigolds* (Surtees, II:335), a subject domestic on its face (Fig. 3). In it a young serving girl clothed in a rustic gown places a jar of marsh marigolds on a shelf. Her simplicity contrasts with the lushness of carvings and tapestries that surround her, but echoes affectively a form in the lower right-hand corner, a cat playing with a ball of worsted. The figure jars our sensibilities, for here is the *Ur*-cat of generations of cheaply printed calendars, greetings cards, and advertisements. Perceiving the kitten as sentimental, we remember a host of related moments in our experiences of Rossetti's paintings. For all their complex fascinations, the subject of many of Rossetti's paintings might be aptly described as "hearts and flowers." Ponder the sweetness of all those roses, honeysuckles, lilies, camellias, etc., suggesting the Victorian language of flowers.[25] Notice heart-shaped lockets and bracelets, appearing in *Joli Coeur, Vision of Fiammetta, Aurea Catena* (Surtees, II:286, 366, 297) – and the philodendron of *The Loving Cup* (II:291), "heart" and "flower" combined. Doves and children, too, can give us pause – especially in a story painting such as *The Gate of Memory* (II: 136) in which a fallen woman watches innocent little girls play as she clutches a shawl into a heart shape over her very heart. And so on.

These popular iconic renderings of the tender emotions can be off-putting. Sentimentality throbs faintly throughout Rossetti's oeuvre. The term "sentimental," however, often functions not as a formalist assessment, but rather as a marker for emotional discomfort in the viewer. It can be a term of aesthetic scapegoating – art that displays kittens and balls of yarn or hearts and flowers, and therefore calls directly and naively on our "feminine" emotions, is inferior art, "sentimental" art. And like woman herself, it elicits embarrassing feeling in excess of the facts.

Yet Rossetti tells us in letters, reviews, and poetry such as the sonnet on William Blake that he believes sentiment to be a crucial ingredient in artistic genius. Indeed, the Pre-Raphaelite criticism of British painting of the day might be boiled down to its failure to communicate real feeling. That Rossetti's sentiment sometimes registers with us as (low) "sentimentality" is the very issue that requires us to consider his painting in its cultural context as both popular and elitist, domestic and sublime, rebellious and reactionary.

Rossetti admired the sentimental. He applauded his friend Dr. Thomas Gordon Hake's *Madeline and Other Poems* for their "tender

Figure 3   *Marigolds*, Dante Gabriel Rossetti

thought for human suffering" (*CW*, p. 493), and even quotes a choice passage from Hakes's "The Cripple": "As a wrecked vessel on the sand / The cripple to his mother clung. / Close to the tub he took his stand / While she the linen washed and wrung." (*CW*, p. 503). Hake has, Rossetti defensively assures us, a "manly human heart."

This review moves beyond friendly puffery. Rossetti formulates as a general quality of good art a desire he has always had: to take care of his audience by connecting with them, establishing a rapport that will ensure their ability to receive what he has created. They must understand his work, in the sense of *kennen* or *connaître*. Perhaps his most eloquent expression of this desire appears in a letter to Jane Morris: "Do not say that poetry is far from you. It should be nearest to us when we need it most."[26]

In his review of Hake's poetry, Rossetti insists upon the artist's sympathy with his reader: "Above all ideal personalities with which the poet must learn to identify himself, there is one supremely real which is the most imperative of all; namely, that of his reader" (*CW*, p. 489). For such "assimilation" with his reader, the writer must exercise "practical watchfulness." "Spiritual contact" must be "part of the very act of production" (*CW*, p. 489). Assimilation of artist to audience involves sentimental heart-to-heart intercourse with what Rossetti calls "the general reader" (*CW*, p. 489) – and thus he speaks his willingness to court audiences in familiar, even clichéd, images. Like the hearts, flowers, children and kittens of his paintings, the swoons, tears, sighs, and souls of his poems are meant as familiar vessels into which readers may pour their own emotions, and thus be assimilated to the writer.[27]

Such an ideal is clearly anti-subjectivist. Rossetti may have chronicled a descent into the maelstrom of narcissism in his poetry, but he also believed the very act of writing that poetry to be an antidote to narcissism. Rossetti wanted to write to and for others, not just echoing notes to himself. Sentimentality is for him the very program of emotional health and artistic success.

Rossetti has, however, his sentimental limits. He criticizes Dr. Hake for his "most extraordinarily conventional (or once conventional) use of Della-Cruscan [turn-of-the-eighteenth-century sentimental] phrases" (*LDGR*, p. 936) and believes some of Allingham's verse to be "a trifle *too* homely, a little in the broadsheet-song style" (*LDGR*, p. 212). Mere mass appeal could never be sufficient to the assimilative goal – Tennyson, he writes, can get away with a "rude aiming at the . . . popular view" but "it's not my vocation" (*LDGR*, p. 958). Rossetti's translation of Italian poets, his epistolary conversations with Jane Morris, and ultimately the sale catalogue for his library all reveal a man far removed from the popular or easily assimilable. He clearly inhabited intellectual and aesthetic heights in his own appreciation of art. Yet it is important to note that, like other Victorian Modernists, he also read widely in popular fiction. He mentions admiringly, for example, Mary Elizabeth Braddon's *Vixen*, *Aurora Floyd*, and *Charlotte's Inheritance*; Paul de Kock's *Ce Monsieur*, Samuel Warren's *Ten Thousand a Year*, and "Beasley's" *Violet or the Danseuse*. Still, Rossetti consciously employs sentiment as a strategy for selling books, asking his editor Frederick Startridge Ellis to place "The Blessed Damozel," "Troy Town," and "The Burden of Nineveh" at the beginning of *Poems and Ballads* (1870), "and so secure three sentimental or moral things at the outset" (*LDGR*, p. 821).

But the work that most inspired Rossetti's sentimentalism never sold well to a mass audience: Charles J. Wells's verse drama, *Joseph and His Brethren* (1824). Wells's earlier work, *Stories After Nature* (1822), appeared in the "list of Immortals" that Rossetti prepared for the Brotherhood, "to be pasted up in our study for the affixing of all decent fellows' signatures."[28] (Theodore Watts avowed that "No young poet at one time dare show his face at 16 Cheyne Walk... who could not utter the Shibboleth" of Wells's name."[29])

It seems that Rossetti could not praise Wells highly enough; he was, quite simply, "the greatest English poet since Shakespeare" (*LDGR*, p. 1626). "In what may be called the Anglo-hebraic order of aphoristic truth," Rossetti writes, "Shakespeare, Blake, and Wells are nearly akin" (*CW*, p. 455). To read Wells's verse drama *Joseph and His Brethren* and to learn of his life is akin to perusing a sourcebook of Rossettian materials.

Why Wells? An element of narcissism must have been involved; late in life, Rossetti, who had buried his manuscript poetry with his wife, remarks that Wells "burnt at his wife's death eight or ten MS. volumes of poetry" (*LDGR*, p. 1627). But the shock of recognition for Rossetti upon first reading Wells was evidently great enough to fuel on its own a life-long hyperbolic appreciation. Wells's characters stride about the Biblical lands in appropriate costume, spouting Elizabethanesque English which imitates endlessly the gorgeous surface of some of Shakespeare's language, minus all its other qualities, including acuity and profundity. In rhetorical voice *faux* Elizabethan-Biblical, Joseph, Jacob, Potiphar and the rest express nineteenth-century British sentiments. Wells takes liberties with the past in order to convey a modern scene; his drama's very motive power is anachronism.

Every costumed figure in Rossetti's paintings, every medievalesque figure within the traditionally flattened form of his ballads, owes a debt to Wells. Certainly Potiphar's lewd wife Phraxanor, with her silk of gossamer like tawny gold, precious jewels, beflowered hair, and fragrant oils is, along with Tennyson's women, the big sister of Rossetti's fatal women. Rachel seems the very type of the Pre-Raphaelite beauty: "her full dark eye ... / Her slanting head curv'd like the maiden moon /And hung with hair luxuriant as a vine / and blacker than a storm."[30] Gorgeousness for its own sake, the deep purple of much of the poem's figurative language, suggests that the poet might as well enjoy too much of a good thing. A perverse amplitude, figured as "eastern" and borrowed from Shakespeare's *Cleopatra*, reigns. Rossetti over-fills his canvases as Wells packs his pages.

But the key to Rossetti's fascination has to do with Wells's license in celebrating linguistic lushness both for its own sake and for its links to a sentimentally moralizing set of characters and incidents. Wells, Rossetti maintains, "had a firmer hold on the human heart and a more piercing gaze into the springs of human action than belonged to any predecessor" (*LDGR*, p. 1727). It is the disparity between the message of simple virtues and the complex, derivative style that rapidly and permanently charmed Rossetti.

For example, when Phraxanor all but rapes Joseph, he responds with the brief cries of a heroine of melodrama who has been tied to the railroad tracks, but he also responds at length by moralizing. Joseph cannot give in to Phraxanor's lewd advances because her husband, Potiphar, has treated him tenderly when he first arrived in Egypt: "through my sufferings he read my heart / And all his features melted at the sight.... / ... / He took me to his house, put me in trust / [and changed] A broken heart to love and tenderness."[31] Joseph (the effeminate male) and Potiphar have melted into each other's hearts as tenderly as two innocent girls; mere lustful embrace with the masculine woman, Phraxanor, cannot begin to compare. The entire scene is repetitious to the point of stasis, a free-for-all of shifting gender roles and luxuriantly sexual in its diction. It is also a scene whose outcome we know from the first, an occasion for speeches on the nature of duty and responsibility, and a call for the viewer to feel sentimental pity for the endangered Joseph.

Joseph, throughout all his tests, triumphs by the application of a few simple ideas: to obey God, tell the truth, love his family, and forbear, utterly forbear. By working responsibly for his master and by rejecting the advances of Phraxanor, Joseph's rewards are both domestic and aesthetic in nature. He can pardon the family that sold him into bondage as well as feed that family in its famished state: "Therefore grieve not, nor fret upon your act / For I declare 'twas God who sent me forth."[32] Rossetti admires Wells for the complexities of the cross-currents he creates.

Wells also arranges for his hero a more public award. The grateful Pharaoh whose dream Joseph has aptly interpreted stages in his honor a decadently magnificent festival in which the pharaoh's "crimson robe, / Deep edg'd with silver, and with golden thread, / Upon a bear-skin kirtle deeply blush'd, / Whose broad resplendent braid and shield-like clasps / Were boss'd with diamonds large, by rubies fir'd" contrasts with Joseph's robes, "simple, but . . . full of grace" (p. 174). Standing as a moral exemplar in a silver car pulled by eight white horses (a suitably understated gorgeousness for the man of moral principle), Joseph observes, among many other splendors, a "vast platform" on a thousand springs and a thousand wheels,

> Drawn by some hundred trainèd elephants
> All hous'd in velvet and in cloth of gold,
> And on it was bestow'd with wondrous art
> Forest and rocky fastness, wood and glen,
> Peopled with all that nature could bestow
> Of savage beauty, beast or bird or fish.
> Behold a mimic Nile appear'd to flow
> From end to end. . . . [33]

Wells thus situates the temperate and dutiful son at the center of a vastly excessive theater of praise, that pageant where all of nature has been killed into art. Far from causing Joseph to excoriate such worldly display, Wells insists that Joseph belongs both in this elaborate foreign scene and in the tent where he quietly pardons his brothers and is reunited with his father. Wells's moral universe (in *Stories After Nature*, too) is as simple, accessible, and sentimental as his poetic vehicle is encrusted with splendors. Overwrought artifice itself, Wells demonstrates, can bear the human messages of duty, tenderness, and fortitude.

Taking Wells's work into account, we begin to see a different Rossetti. Not only his images of simple tenderness, but also his complex, artificial, deathly images, might convey a tale of duty and fortitude. Like Wells's Phraxanor, Rossetti's band of fatal women might be placed in the service of heart-felt messages of virtuous redemption. Jewels and gold, fabrics, exotic animals, royalty: by the magic of artful arrangement these can be translated into the ornamental furnishings of 16 Cheyne Walk, including its doomed menagerie of imported animals. Wells's images appear again in the painted images of *The Beloved* (jewels, virgins in three styles – Jewish, English, Gypsy – black child, gold vase, gold and scarlet aigrettes of Peruvian featherwork). Wells's language and morals together provide one of many sources of inspiration for *The House of Life*. Compare, for example, "The Soul's Sphere": "Lo! the soul's sphere of infinite images!/ What sense shall count them? /.... / Visions of golden futures: or that last/Wild pageant of the accumulated past...." (*CW*, p. 208).

Rossetti, like Wells before him (and, as we shall see, like Augusta Evans across the Atlantic), blends sentiment, sincerity and artful pose. Just as the absent Rachel figures largely in Wells's drama, two Victorian women are the wellsprings of Rossetti's moral earnestness: Rossetti's internalized "True Woman" and Mrs. Gabriele Rossetti, his mother. The first woman inspires Rossetti's chosen feminization, the second elicits an answering manliness, but both enable him to learn the domestic virtues he will so lavishly preach to the general audience whose hearts he wishes to touch.

CHOOSING THE FEMININE

Modernism's putative rupture from the Victorian has been in part a divorce of masculine from feminine, with the masculine triumphant. Rejecting the fussy, overstuffed, and moralizing Victorian feminine, Modernism, so the critical stories imply, is man's creation: the building of new structures with clean lines and hard surfaces. Mere housekeeping cannot compete. In tracing the more complex tale of Victorian Modernism, another plot-line may be added to this tale: the deliberate feminization of artist and work of art, parsed clearly in their relation to audience. The truths of Victorian Modernism are often tested and made in *mundus muliebris*, the world of women.

In keeping with his emphasis on the artist's need to speak directly from the heart to a general audience, Rossetti also believed that the quality of tenderness best described nature's own gift to the suitably receptive artist: "Tenderness, the constant unison of wonder and familiarity so mysteriously allied in nature, the sense of fulness and abundance such as we feel in a field, not because we pry into it at all but because it is all there: these are the inestimable prizes to be secured" (*CW*, p. 444). Artist, audience, and world form a love triangle. But what of his own eye and heart – was he capable of securing the prize?

To questions of Rossetti's character and personality we may find as many answers as he had acquaintances. Theodore Watts-Dunton testifies to Rossetti's sweetness: "so irresistible was he, so winsome, and so affectionate, so open of heart (save when in the grip of the terrible and unmanning drug ...), so generous, so free from all rivalries and jealousies. ... " [34] William describes him as the "genial despot" capable of many generosities once his superiority was established.[35] Hall Caine testifies to his repeated acts of altruism. Yet others describe him as manipulative, tortured, selfish, or infantile.[36] Even if it were possible, we should not wish to reach a final judgment of Rossetti's character based on these conflicting reports. We would perhaps do better to explore the ways in which Rossetti displayed feminine attitudes and carried out charitable and tender acts, whatever his very real and frequent lapses from sympathy and generosity might have been. A biographical cameo will help to explain the man who created a sentimentalized art, rather than merely putting a shine on tarnished personal credentials.

Accounts of Rossetti's feminization have been largely negative, and premised upon the subordinate position of women in Victorian culture – i.e., what man in his right mind would *choose* to identify himself with women? Some see him as an hysteric, a man who struggled against his feminized role as an artist dependent, like women, on masculine capital.[37] Others regard his seemingly intimate relation to the women in his portraits as narcissistic, but the term is usually applied as normative shorthand for "disturbed," without ever asking whether needs and goals beyond neurotic shadow-chasing might inspire such an identification.

Far from railing against the feminine positions he sometimes inhabited, Rossetti defended them. Even factoring out his jealousy toward William Morris, the following passage from a letter to Jane still suggests that Rossetti practiced a feminized, private, person-to-person charity that he himself viewed as a contrast to action of the public sort:

I know it is vain to try and interest you in such a subject as the sale of Smetham's pictures, or anything one is able to do for any poor unit like oneself and not for wholesale mankind. I suppose Topsy [Morris] never gave one farthing to Keats's sister, but then he writes long epistles on every public event.[38]

The record of Rossetti's activity on behalf of James Smetham, a painter who suffered a nervous collapse from which he never recovered, reads today as a tale of doing good in the private, Christian/feminine sphere of Victorian society. Rossetti carefully selected books to send to the hospitalized Smetham and asked William to do the same. He arranged for sales of Smetham's paintings, and even before they sold considered "making some advance and reckoning on sales" in the event that Mrs. Smetham needed immediate funds (*LDGR*, p. 1553). He approached friends for funds. In 1878 he agreed to show the *Proserpine* at Manchester, violating his deep need to keep his paintings private, because Turner urged him to do so, and Turner had worked on Smetham's behalf.[39] We have records of similar, if less lavish, good works on behalf of the families of James Hannay and Walter H. Deverell.

Although we can document Rossetti's abusive behavior, his letters provide a complementary record of a man who inquired carefully after the health of his friends, sent them prescriptions and medicines, puffed their writing, and forwarded to them the favorable reviews of their work that he came across. He commented on their sonnets and paintings carefully, which is to say often negatively, but never without some encouraging words. He hung their pictures on his studio walls and spent evenings by the fire trading sonnets. He solicited from them advice on his own writing, and sometimes followed it.

Certainly Rossetti enjoyed the feeling of reproducing the legendary fellowship of the Italian poets he translated. But he also practiced his art in such contexts of intimacy because he needed to feel connected to others, to take care and to be attended to. Implicitly acknowledging his feminized role, he even explains in a letter to Caine that "I do not attain to the more active and practical of the mental functions of manhood" – such an assessment explaining his "sloth" in producing few works of art as well as his choice of the private over the public, political realm. He likens himself to a Michelangelo, who did participate in the fortification of Florence, but who eventually turned his back on public life when he "retired to a certain trackless and forgotten tower, and there stayed in some sort of peace."[40] Rossetti's tower, ultimately a hermitage, was for many years also a place of welcome to friends and fellow artists. His comparison of himself to Michelangelo – a premier nineteenth-century mythic figure of the artist – suggests that Rossetti wished to explain his (tender, passive, or impractically time-consuming) choices in the best of all possible lights.

Perhaps his most feminine quality is the privacy he claimed for his paintings. Feminine, because culturally appropriate for women, who were denied a public voice or stage, and encouraged to cultivate a horror of exposure.[41] Feminine, too, because Rossetti saw solitude as the space of gestation in which the artistic vision may be nurtured rather than sent prematurely into the world where others may kidnap – i.e., plagiarize – it.

(*CW*, p. 467; *LDGR*, p. 1825). Although Rossetti believed that writers, including himself, should connect directly with wide audiences, he took a far more protective view of his painting.

Rossetti chose feminization, too, in his daily life. That Rossetti, like the "general reader," the male of his day, feared, idolized, loved, and despised women is undoubtedly true. That he was involved with them narcissistically in a dance of love and death is apparent on the very face of *The House of Life* as well as in his relationship with Elizabeth Siddal. But women were more to him than erotic beings: he empathized with their position because he did their work. Even when Lizzie was alive, and later with Fanny Cornforth and Treffry Dunn on the scene, Rossetti still managed servants, watched (however sporadically) the budget, ordered meals, furnished rooms, invited guests, and, as we have seen, "visited" the poor and the sick. He was, in an uncharacteristically intense version for a man of his day, "in the house," and something of an angel besides.

In tracing Rossetti's assimilation of the feminine, we will find it useful to examine, too, the presence in Rossetti's life of the "warm Heart, the mother-bird" (*CW*, p. 338), actually embodied in Mrs. Gabriele Rossetti. Although an expansive account of the complex relations among the Rossetti family members lies beyond the compass of this study, we cannot ignore the relation his mother bore to Rossetti's own nesting instincts. To read as an isolated group the letters Rossetti wrote to his mother is to experience an oddly pleasurable sense of distance. The often formal expressions of respect, the stilted avowals of gratitude and concern, coming from a man who frequently wrote relaxed, even slangy, letters to others, tend to surprise us. They seem to waft from some ideal Victorian family scene that never was: "it was sweet indeed to me to receive this day, and written in so fine a hand, the reassurance of what was the first thing I learned to know in this world – my Mother's love," Rossetti writes soon after his mother's eightieth birthday (*LDGR*, p. 1760). Such a rhetoric of respect and affection, moving judiciously and serenely toward its sentimental climax in "my Mother's love" captures the substance of a relationship that Rossetti appears to cultivate as emotional and moral ballast.

Worried about the slothfulness and unmanly impracticality of his ways, Rossetti assuages his anxiety by writing regularly to his mother of money matters, often confiding his fears but just as frequently reporting triumphant sales of pictures or discoursing on his prospects. He even poses as a man interested in heady issues of finance: "I hear there is a decided improvement in trade. Even cotton at Manchester is looking up. Iron, copper, and coal mines on the mend. . . . I view it as vitally wound up with the picture-market" (*LDGR*, p. 1688). To be at peace with himself, Rossetti must establish "masculine" credentials of fiscal responsibility with the woman who is his moral lodestar ("I assure you that your first inculcations on many points are still the standard of criticism with me" [*LDGR*, p. 1402]).

While Rossetti for long periods of time involves William in the concerns, however trivial, of his daily life, he tends to reserve letters to his mother for specific occasions. Formal thank-you notes – "you brought me as much consolatory tending during a time of sickness as at any period of my earlier life" (*LDGR*, p. 1566) – mingle with invitations for Christmas festivities extended or accepted and courtly observations on her birthdays. But these carefully timed and worded letters tend to open doorways into more intimate encounters, arrangements for one thing or another – to draw her portrait, to have an object delivered, to see her, to request a favor.

Whatever the occasion, the inner repose she embodies provides a sanctuary for her son and a sacrament that he half receives and half creates, much as Wordsworth in the presence of that larger Mother, nature. But where Wordsworth must efface his Mother so that he might become Creator, Rossetti himself practices motherly prerogatives.[42] He notes, characteristically, that the "pleasant peaceful hours" he has recently spent with his mother are "the first happy ones I have passed for months" (*LDGR*, p. 1074). What sounds like a gift is, however, frequently in part of his own creating:

I have often and often thought of you since we last met, – always whenever my path in the garden lies by the window of that summer-room at which I used to see your dear beautiful old face last summer, reading or enjoying the garden prospect. (*LDGR*, p. 1263)

A guest in his home by his invitation, his mother has been placed, framed there by his arrangements, then recaptured as the beloved object of his framing memory. Object and creation, she is also cherished audience and judge of his idyllic domestic life at Kelmscott. Muse and moral exemplar, she is the origin of his artistic method of tenderness and assimilation. He speaks in his study of Blake of "rapport," and certainly the original rapport of mother and son is here reimagined as the locus of art.

Rossetti can assimilate his mother's ways to his own through what is at first a natural flow of objects such as spare beds from the parental house to the newlyweds' house, but that immanation slowly develops into Rossetti's reciprocal furnishing of his mother's house. He can show his gratitude and provide for his ongoing presence within her warm, steadying light by sending objects of his choosing, design, and construction to reside where he cannot himself be, with her. Curtains, chairs, cabinets, carts, centerpieces, and work-boxes will enable her to recollect her devoted son as one who paints, draws, writes, and in the widest sense, designs, for an appreciative private audience. Rossetti's gifts of fine art flow homeward with gifts of decoration and furnishings as he feathers the maternal nest. To make family contact is to decorate, to create the summer scene of his mother's repose at the garden window year round, in London as well as at Kelmscott. He tells her where to place objects, how to have them improved – "I send you the other things. Stennet had better make covers for the settees similar to those he is putting on the chair cushions" (*LDGR*, p. 601) – and to what uses they might be put: "The little square spaces would do for a series of family *cartes de visite*" (*LDGR*, p. 574).

Such painstaking attention, respect, and loving connection form the pattern within which Rossetti will conduct his artistic life. With a notion of a mother held at arm's length precisely so that he might both worship her and rehearse aesthetic acts of reverent connection, Rossetti is able to furnish worlds upon worlds.

Beyond practicing the tender virtues and placing himself in moral, emotional, and artistic relation to his mother, Rossetti explored the art of homemaking. He conducted daily household affairs because he had to, and since he worked at home, his domestic concerns and his artistic practice blended. Like many a middle-class Victorian woman, Rossetti felt harassed by the "servant problem." But for him the issue had a twist: he continually felt the lack of models, and sought them either on the street (the "stunners" were both sexual and artistic prey) or among the serving class. "What I really want," he writes to Mrs. Alexander Gilchrist, who has been advising him on the servant issue, "is a very handy man or youth, capable of turning his hand to odd jobs of carpentry, etc. . . . another desirable quality would be that he should be fit for a model" (*LDGR*, p. 483). Just as such a handyman must be fit to enter the studio, so the women hired as models must be fit for the workroom; he requests, for example, that Alexa Wilding mend the fabric and then remake the dress to be worn as she sits to him. Fanny Cornforth acts not only as model, but also as housekeeper, for several years. At Kelmscott Manor a local serving girl becomes the model for *Marigolds*.

A curious circularity of domestic and artistic activity develops. As completed paintings are sold and money flows in, it must be disbursed to cover household and studio expenses; such expenses make it possible for the next painting to be completed but also bring on the next round of bills for canvas, paint, artists' dinners, and models'/servants' wages.

Over the course of the years, Rossetti engaged three men to ease his dual domestic and aesthetic burdens: W. J. Knewstub, Treffry Dunn, and toward the end, T. Hall Caine. Rossetti required Dunn, in particular, to find his way among the complexities of a household that was part nest, part artistic factory (with Rossetti himself the principal piece-worker) and part artistic *salon*. Dunn's memoirs indicate his initial enthusiasm for the job of artistic factotum, because he feels at last that he is entering the world of London art. He reminisces about a particularly vivid scene of domestic sublimity that takes place in Rossetti's studio as a thunderstorm crescendos, and with it, Swinburne's verse declamation:

Faint electric sparks played round the wavy masses of his luxuriant hair. . . . I lay in the sofa in a corner of the studio and listened in wonder . . . for it appeared to me as though the very figures in the pictures that were on the easels standing about the room were conscious of and sympathised with the poet. . . . The "Proserpine" gazed out more mournfully than I had been wont to see her gaze.[43]

Dunn understands that the sympathetic vibrations of weather, fellowship (Rossetti returns soon after and he and Swinburne sit up until dawn together), and works of art are not to be distinguished at 16 Cheyne Walk.

Dunn not only fabricates frames, scale models, and drawings to Rossetti's specifications, but also shops for artistic props, advises Rossetti on appropriate household budgets, and searches the house for misplaced items during his employer's absences. He absorbs visits from angry merchants, kills rats, mails information, books, and furniture, and even goes househunting for Rossetti, making sketches of promising properties. But all of his activities require of him artistic talent, aesthetic judgment, or at the very least sympathy with his artist-employer's special needs. Spaces must be filled with appropriate light, objects must be located or bid upon, projects must be finished so that "tin" for Dunn's own, at best intermittent, salary might be forthcoming.

Although the term exploitation comes to mind, it is important to remember that Rossetti himself never drew a sharp line between work on paintings and domestic concerns. William finds in his brother's writing-book the following contiguous scraps:

5. From John Marshall. Eat meat, poultry, game, fish, oysters, kidneys, green vegetables, stewed fruit, ripe fruit. . . . Avoid or reduce much bread, potatoes, sugar, beer, spirits, cocoa, chocolate, olive oil, eggs, bacon.
6. For plain scarlet: try laying ground with venetian or Indian red, and white, to the full depth of tone, and glazing with orange-vermilion.[44]

The slimming man and the accomplished artist are one. Domestic upsets easily became artistic incidents – such as Fanny's breakage (or hiding) of a blue-and-white jar he needs for a painting. A misplaced medieval costume means a slowdown in work.

But household matters may also have unexpected value for artistic work. When he receives a sofa ordered through Howell, he discovers it "covered with the most lovely chintz of a Japanese pattern admirably designed and coloured like greyish blue china" (*LDGR*, p. 1205). To pay for actual blue-and-white china – cherished as decoration for both paintings and living quarters – he paints a picture, and makes it worth £200 "to cover a previous account."[45] It is perhaps only part of the story to say that Rossetti knew at heart that he had "sold out" as an artist by engaging in the impure world of the marketplace. If he sold out, he also, as homemaker, bought in. Pots, paintings, sofas, pounds sterling, models, dresses, achieve an aesthetic fungibility based in the domestic. To keep house, however frantically, is to manage affairs in the name of beauty. And to paint and write poetry is to make aesthetic arrangements that include, as part of their very composition, personal and domestic arrangements.

Two major modes of such aesthetic and domestic composition emerge, and they must inform any biographical discussion of the poems and pictures themselves. The first mode involves the complex and artful arrangements Rossetti makes with people outside his home – these living tableaux often composed of acts of generosity performed or received that make it possible to paint or write. Simply stated, for Rossetti the personal favor becomes an element of creation that works in tandem with inspiration – his insistence on "fundamental brainwork" – and execution. The second mode consists of the making of artful arrangements at 16 Cheyne Walk, the creating, collecting, and displaying of objects that bear witness to his urge to create a visible order whose artifice tells the story of its own construction, element by beautiful element. It would be inaccurate to think of the first as an issue of "people" and the second as an issue of "things." The two are mirror images of each other. His dealings with people can be viewed as so many scripted dramas, first acted, then captured forever in beautiful *objects*: poems and paintings which themselves insist on their source in a personal, contingent, and often sentimental milieu. Correspondingly, we can think of the rooms and decorations of Rossetti's home as the *process* by which he infuses things with feelings, making them sentimental intensifications of experience itself. Such a metamorphic tendency between things and beings characterizes the space of the domestic sublime.

The first mode, the aesthetic composition of human relations, is the important beginning of such a line of analysis. Every artist paints in some relation to other people – but understanding Rossetti's social "compositions" leads to a significant reinterpretation of his works, especially those of the later portraits of women which are often discussed as problematical. Rossetti, in his move from quasi-historical, mythological, or sacred paintings to the post-1858 depictions of women, takes a dangerous step down the hierarchy of painting, from respectable history painting of a sort to mere genre painting. The discomfort has been expressed in a number of ways: these later paintings are judged repetitive, called potboilers (even by Rossetti himself), or deciphered as images of his own despair – crowded, even claustrophobic canvases. While a few of them are considered great, many are seen as evidence of artistic slackening.

Indeed, after 1858 his pictures of women often lack a compelling narrative framework, and the quality of their emotion seems odd rather than inspiring or moving. Rossetti seems to withhold emotion, denying it to the viewer by sheer lushness (*Monna Vanna*), a sense of repression (*Bower Meadow*), attenuation into a self-involved melancholy (*La Donna della Fiamma*), or some combination of the three (Surtees, II:281, 330, 308).

Given their strange emotional excess and reticence (the pictures seem to say too little and too much), our tendency has been to read into these paintings what Rossetti might call "an arduous fulness": that is, a sense of dangerous fascination with the fatal woman and her sister of the mirror world, the angelic woman. In a largely overlooked parallel plot, that of arrangement, in which Rossetti conveys another kind of intensity, one discovers a quieter passion arising cumulatively from small acts that enable him to travel freely among the realms of poetry and painting, friendship, domestic activity, and business as he creates his own pragmatist filigree. In other words, the highly wrought canvas with figures and textures filling the space is not necessarily threatening or claustrophobic. It might be simply full of many things, all of them connected by feeling. Rossetti's arrangements deliberately juxtapose in close quarters the traces of several worlds, until the kinds and even orders of experience they represent begin to blend, even as they continue to insist on their differences. This is the opposite of transcendental vision rendered visible; it is instead the ordinary seen as in a daydream, the gates of ivory and the gates of horn interlinked.

Personal arrangements that together inform Rossetti's pictures and poems include, for example, business relations. Although Rossetti refers contemptuously and despairingly to merchants and patrons, he cultivates two of them, Murray Marks and Frederick Leyland. Whether it be truth or legend that Rossetti "knew in a moment when he saw Marks that he was of an artistic temperament and a man of fine taste, because of the extreme beauty of his hands,"[46] we do know that Rossetti valued him as friend, business associate, and artistic collaborator. He introduced some important clients to Marks, and asked him for the loan of objects for his pictures, practical advice, monetary loans, and personal visits. Marks for his part admired Rossetti's work ("the *Venus Verticordia* arrested my attention and almost took my breath away" [52]), enjoyed an *entrée* into the artistic community, and even expanded the range of his professional services at Rossetti's suggestion. Thus between the two men a friendship, business association, and mutual aesthetic mentorship developed. This rich relationship centered about the beautiful object – hawthorn pot or exquisite tapestry – destined alike for Rossetti's rooms and paintings. And these decorated spaces in turn expressed the intense inspection of things and people in complex intimacy which inspired them.

Similarly, that Frederick Leyland was primarily a buyer of Rossetti's work does not diminish the quality of their friendship, their many visits, the portraits of Leyland in chalk that Rossetti executes, or Rossetti's intimate advice about where and why Leyland should hang paintings. When they are made in the practice of the sentimental art of friendship, "pot boilers" and replicas are not so artistically debased a form as they otherwise might be. And by many accounts, friendship was an art that Rossetti cared deeply to perfect, though the results were sometimes disappointing.

Perhaps Rossetti could sustain friendships with business associates because he could make business agreements with friends. Here a lengthy record of favors asked, to be paid presumably in the coin of friendship and favors returned, indicates Rossetti's desire to make his canvases and poems group productions. He frequently sends friends and family members in search of props: fresh flowers, dress fabrics, draperies, embroidery frames and picture frames, pots, jewelry, chandeliers. For his writing he requests books, help with historical research, and even images for poems. To Miss Alice Boyd he writes:

could [you] bring to mind any feature or incident particularly characteristic of the Penkill glen at nightfall. In my poem ["Stream's Secret"] I have made the speaker towards the close suddenly perceive that the night is coming on, and have had to give a descriptive touch or two. (*LDGR*, p. 818)

He asks for images as he asks for objects: here, in the experience of creation, lies an important relation between his painting and his poetry. Favors flow outward as well; Rossetti enjoyed lending and giving objects and aid to others. Such generosity replicates his relationship with his mother: pieces of tapestry and blue pots go to Alice Boyd at Penkill Castle; pictures to Fanny Cornforth (in lieu of salary) and to Jane (in lieu of his own presence); a frame or a book to William; and a chair, an African carved stool, and two African robes to Ford Madox Brown.

Perhaps best of all is the favor of a visit from Maria Spartali, a beautiful woman, herself a painter, whom he wishes to paint. She visits Rossetti (in his slang) "to see the crib and appurtenances" (*LDGR*, p. 502); her appreciation of his surroundings will encourage her participation in his art. When she sits, she will figure in an especially rich "arrangement": as viewer or audience, as artist, as beautiful object within his painting, as beautiful woman seated among the paintings and other exquisite objects of his studio. It is no wonder that Rossetti's portraits of women mystify; such complexity, in which frames of art and frames of reality merge, cannot be easily restated. And so it is, not just with Maria Spartali's visit, but with every small favor asked and granted.

Thus is Rossetti's creation of an intimate and fluid composition brought to life in the space between his daily life and the formal techniques of writing and painting. To complete the picture of arrangements made with people, it is helpful to examine a second, related sketch of things: Rossetti's arranging of his home at 16 Cheyne Walk, where he lived from 1862 until his death in 1882. To understand Rossetti's house, by many accounts strangely or fascinatingly decorated, and to appreciate its relation to his aestheticism, we should begin with a few facts, listen to the opinions of Rossetti's friends, and then examine some of the best evidence we have as to its appearance: the catalogue of the contents of 16 Cheyne Walk that was produced for the auction held shortly after Rossetti's death.

The London City Council tells us that the house, Georgian in style, was built in 1717, that it was called Queen's House because of its association with the flight of Queen Catherine Parr on the death of Henry VIII, and that it has especially well-preserved and beautiful wrought ironwork.[47]

Rossetti's studio evidently occupied the dining room on the ground floor; a vast drawing room on the first floor runs along the entire front of the house, and the second floor is primarily given over to bedrooms. Judging by exterior and interior photographs taken by the Council, the house is large and elegant, a gentleman's residence. In addition to these photographs, we have paintings by Dunn of the studio, dining room, drawing room, and (reflected by one of Rossetti's many convex mirrors), part of his bedroom.[48] In addition we have several written accounts of the house.

Descriptions of 16 Cheyne Walk have tended to focus on the mysterious quality of its bedrooms, probably because for observers of the house's strange hodgepodge of furnishings, the concept of the Gothic was most available as a descriptive device. Hall Caine described it as a fairytale castle: "the brickwork seemed to be falling into decay; . . . the windows to be dull with the accumulation of the dust of years; the sills to bear the suspicion of cob web . . . and round the walls and up the reveals of doors and windows were creeping the tangled branches of the wildest ivy that ever grew untouched by shears."[49]

George Meredith preferred to think of its luxury: "a strange, quaint, grand old place, with an immense garden, magnificent pannelled staircases and rooms, – a palace" (*LDGR*, p. 464).

Dunn bewails the unhealthy darkness, airlessness, and gruesome picture of the bedrooms. But the rest of the house strikes him as above all filled with interesting and beautiful objects, which he breathlessly catalogues:

The mantelpiece was a most original compound of Chinese black-laquered [sic] panels, bearing designs of birds, animals, flowers and fruit in gold relief, which had a very good effect, and on either side of the grate a series of old blue Dutch tiles, mostly displaying Biblical subjects treated in the serio-comic fashion that existed at the period, were inlaid. The fire-grate itself was a beautifully-wrought example of eighteenth century design and workmanship in brass . . . in one corner of the room stood an old English china cupboard, inside of which was displayed a quantity of Spode ware. I sat down on a cosy little sofa. . . . [50]

Like Dunn as he awaits his first glimpse of the great man, others describe coziness rather than gothic horror; William perhaps sums up this position when he passes judgment on the house: "old-fashioned, many-roomed, homelike, and comfortable."[51] A comparatively recent critic, Mario Praz (himself a house-obsessed man), looks at Dunn's paintings and complains of the eclecticism of the house: "in the end there was no style at all. Non-style was created from an excess of styles."[52]

The common thread among these varying assessments is the striking number and variety of decorative things in Rossetti's house. These he collected (in excursions ranging from the elegance of Marks's premises to the junk shops of the East End), received as gifts, ordered to specification, and sometimes made himself. To trace this thread, we can reflect on the auction catalogue, with a bit of contextual help from Dunn's paintings.[53] An impressionistic perspective is helpful here, not only because discussion of the material history of Rossetti's belongings is beyond the scope of this study, but also because there is no evidence to suggest that Rossetti regarded himself as an expert in anything but blue-and-white china. He bought what he liked, and the evidence suggests a happily roving rather than a professionally focused taste.

Even allowing for the randomness of anyone's household belongings, the list of Rossetti's household effects indicates an aesthetic of incoherence, repetition, and complication. Almost everything in the house is out of context, collected from other places, times, and cultures. One particularly intriguing page of the catalogue lists Indian, Japanese, Albanian, Venetian, Chinese, and Irish objects. Perhaps the candidate for the most stunning example of the unassimilated "other" would be a foreign object that also announces itself as freakish: "A curiously carved mahogany frame chair with cane seat, formerly belonging to the Chinese Giant 'Chang'" (*Contents*, item 104). We hear the babble of *Finnegans Wake*.

At the same time, Dunn's paintings portray a mood of serenity and sumptuous ease. How to reconcile these two accounts? These objects' unequivocal presence together throws the sentimental context of "home" into high relief. Rossetti liked, even adored, these things – his feelings about them provide the only aesthetic principle informing his acts of acquisition and arrangement. Many parts are here gathered, however loosely, into a whole. Certainly that is one tide of energy within 16 Cheyne Walk. But complication within individual objects can create confusing cross-currents. The Elgin Marbles these are not. Consider "Pair of Chinese antique girandoles [the very descriptive terminology appears to fail], fitted with 4 shelves each, elaborately carved and heavily gilt" (*Contents*, item 257). Or "A very handsome plated centre stand, inlaid with reflected glass, fitted at the ends with 3-light candelabra with serpentine arms, the centre supporting a cut glass flower dish" (*Contents*, item 400). Rossetti liked this kind of complexity: such an item sits quietly, bursting with multiple shapes and reflections. And he liked repetition as well. Although classification can be a problem, a conservative count of items in the catalogue reveals twenty-five cabinets, chests, and cupboards, and thirty-one glasses and mirrors. Such repetition has, like incoherence within a house, two contesting qualities: mirrors everywhere indicate either a comforting similarity or an unnerving replication both of the mirrors themselves and the scenes they endlessly reflect. They can make us feel at home, eerily unhoused, or even entrapped. As for the cabinets, the issue is not just numbers – after all, this era antedates the built-in closet. Most of these cabinets, however, have interior shelves and drawers enclosed by highly decorated folding doors in various arrangements: within cabinets are smaller enclosures, themselves holding discrete items, repetition within repetition.

This spreading, multiplex pattern, repeating what is never precisely the same, makes of Rossetti's house a patchwork of borrowings that announce both their common ground (they rest with a sigh in the sentimental space of home) and their ineluctable strangeness. Furthermore, his house is in flux as items come and go, or are moved about. Even the status of items within the house can never be clear. How heavily carved or exquisitely veneered must a chest be before it metamorphoses from storage bin to *objet*? Or perhaps at the very limits of artful impracticality the ordinary suddenly reappears: "A curious cabinet of Burmese glass workmanship, having grotesque figures, with stand for same (suitable for a hall as a receptacle for carriage rugs)" (*Contents*, item 217).

The complicated arrangement of Rossetti's house represents an artistic experiment. It announces itself as a language of objects in a syntax we can learn only by taking context seriously: Rossetti's relations to other people; his love of Arthurian, Asian, and Gothic mythologies and motifs; his use of his house as studio, art dealer's shop, literary salon, family gathering place, stage set, and shelter from nature, the indoors to which he flees from Nature's no longer transcendent messages.

Here is the site of the domestic sublime: threatening in its foreign-ness and grotesque replication, yet comforting in its presentness. Not huge or powerful, as traditional forms of the sublime, but complex in-stead, an analogue of Ruskin's horizontally spreading sublime. Not a lonely, incommunicable experience, but "curious," as the catalogue so often says, something to show off and chat about with friends. This sublime beckons and resists, like the look in the eyes of Rossetti's por-traits of women. These are the textures of the Victorian Modernist parlor and together they exemplify Rossetti's "*Peri Platous*," "On the Extended."

THE DAY DREAM OF ART

The aestheticist intertwining of life and art prevents a neat transition from biographical to textual analysis: the turn to two representative works of art by Rossetti, the painting, *The Day Dream*, and the sonnet sequence, *The House of Life*, is not a step out of life and into art. We have dwelt on the aesthetic quality of Rossetti's quotidian life, and now we must acknowledge and celebrate the ordinary quality of his artistic oeuvre, its tendency actually to entwine with the world it also represents. The satisfyingly pure identity expressed by the phrase *l'art pour l'art* must come under scrutiny; and, in keeping with our understanding of the embodied and sensational rather than the abstractly transcendental nature of aestheticist beauty, we should seek a sentimentally nuanced *l'art pour l'autre* that takes into account the needs of its audience. It is time to explain how Rossetti's texts and canvases themselves argue for the importance of day-to-day domestic life, how they place a high value on sentimental tenderness, and how they represent an anti-transcendent sublimity experienced at home, through reverie, as the very process of making arrangements.

The women of Rossetti's painted portraits are nothing if not complex. Rossetti places them in rooms often lacking walls and ceilings, and he surrounds them by things that appear to be both pretty and sinister at the same time. These women seem at home in their often mysterious settings, but also as coolly abstract and inhuman as the very decorated surfaces in which they find their only existence.

From the first Rossetti drew and painted domestic scenes in which the viewer is asked to catalog a variety of objects for their religious symbolism (*Ecce Ancilla Domini!*); for their specifically typological significance (*Passover in the Holy Family*); or most often simply in an attempt to bring order into an overstocked space (*"Hist!", Said Kate the Queen*) (Surtees, II:29, 84, 38). Rossetti tended to furnish these paintings as he did 16 Cheyne Walk – with an eclecticism meant to convey both a break-up of cohesion and a new kind of arrangement emphasizing the intriguing qualities of fragmentation, repetition, and juxtaposition. In fact, he did furnish these paintings with domestic objects. *Ecce Ancilla Domini!*, for example, featured "a curious lamp [Ford Madox] Brown has got" and "a gilt saucer behind [the angel's] head, which crowns the *China*-ese character of the picture" (*LDGR*, p. 126).

From early on, Rossetti expressed his interest in domestic spaces in part by painting them in ambiguous relation to the "outer" or public world: the pleasure tent, the balcony, the open door giving onto a sunlit outdoor scene. Greenery grows into a room to provide part of ceiling or wall, or spirits drift through walls not quite there. And what at first appear to be simply the interior spaces of palace halls and chambers become themselves the outer shells of numerous smaller spaces within: cupboards and chests, curtained alcoves, bookcases, deep chairs, and shadowy corners.

Indeed, space and its uses have been central to the major line of interpretation of Rossetti's post-1858 pictures of women. These paintings of alluring but self-absorbed women have been understandably interpreted as painted parables of sexual seduction and rejection, or of body and soul. Since Rossetti often indicates by title mythological and literary personae for these women – Venus, Lilith, La Pia de'Tolomei, Penelope, Mariana – our interest in them as seductive, wronged, dangerous, or pure women, but always women with a sexual story to tell, has been justified.

William Michael Rossetti reached a conclusion about these paintings that has not been substantially altered from his day to ours:

Their titles casually allude to characters from literature, legend, and, infrequently, myth, but the actual object seems to be the search for some primal goddess. Her presence dominates the pictorial space. Usually we see only the torso, sometimes only the face. . . . Surrounding the women are emblematic details. Sometimes they have a narrative function, filling in elements of the woman's story; sometimes they symbolically suggest aspects of her character.[54]

We should observe, however, that as time went by Rossetti increasingly resented having to name or identify these women and did so primarily to please potential patrons. What he wished to express often had little to do with the ostensible mythological or literary subject of each painting, and thus our tendency to join William in reading details only for their narrowly emblematic function should give us pause. We would be mistaken, too, in regarding Rossetti's decorative details and objects as so much irritating bric-à-brac that tends to detract from the paintings' depictions of mysterious and powerful women.[55] What to do with these things that do not fit neatly into the "plots" of the "primal goddess"? Only in a wider account of the paintings' meanings can such details reveal the importance they possessed for Rossetti, who painted them painstakingly and repeatedly throughout his oeuvre. The arabesques of greenery, the burnished objects and decorative backgrounds are not mere explanatory decoration or, worse, a kind of detritus, but rather expressions of Rossetti's deeply felt understandings of time, work, home, and human connection. Through them Rossetti creates paintings as arrangements that express the (feminized) sentiments of everyday life as well as the primal plots of the goddess-woman's other-worldly powers.

Let us observe for a moment the details surrounding these women of the later paintings: flowers and leaves, jewelry, furnishings (especially mirrors, carvings, hangings, chairs, cabinets), and, mostly at the behest of Frederick Leyland, musical instruments. Some, such as Proserpine's pomegranate, are clearly painted for the emblematic value that William discusses. But objects tend to proliferate far beyond such explanatory value.

Rossetti, it seems, had another idea of what he meant to accomplish. He wanted to "raise" his work. He writes to Ford Madox Brown in 1874:

> [Henri] Regnault has some admirable remarks, in one of his admirable letters, on the invaluable importance of beautiful objects to paint from, and how the surface and colour of such things will often at once raise one's work to a tone which it would not otherwise attain but does not then recede from. That book of Regnault's [*Correspondance*, 1872] I have read with the deepest interest. (*LDGR*, p. 1278)

Seeking a higher "tone," Ruskin believes that the surface and color of beautiful objects would improve his painting, and so powerful is this faith that he makes of each painting *itself* a beautiful object of surface and color – albeit one that must exist in relation to its surroundings.

Indeed, when the founders of *Art Nouveau* in France borrowed an eighteenth-century aristocratic ideal of art as "technical wizardry for fashioning surfaces" including those of walls, picture frames, and furniture; and when they followed an eighteenth-century lead in seeing the coifed, costumed, bejeweled woman as an *objet d'art* to be coordinated with interior decoration, they discovered that Rossetti had already provided a contemporary version of this aesthetic.[56] His paintings, filled with beautiful decorative objects and designs, draw no clear distinction between beautiful women and their surroundings. Baudelaire writes in the same period, "All the things that adorn woman, all the things that go to enhance her beauty, are part of herself; and the artists who have made a special study of this enigmatic being are just as enchanted by the whole *mundus muliebris* as by woman herself."[57] While Baudelaire argues for the union of woman and her apparel, Rossetti, as we shall see, paints his own vision of *mundus muliebris*, "the world of women" – woman, her apparel, her fans, mirrors, and chairs, and her floating "background" of flowers – in a dreamy identity he calls reverie.

The self-absorption we detect in Rossetti's paintings is not, then, merely his identification with women, but also his love of the beautiful surroundings and things in which their feelings might be known. His painted women are distant not just because they are self-absorbed, but also because they are, in a sense, beautiful objects. It is crucial at this point to appreciate the complex nature of objects in Rossetti's imagination. For a man who, as we have seen, viewed people and things in fluid, even fungible relation, for a man who spoke to others through the exchange of things and placed those things in his paintings only after they had absorbed the attention, friendship, and even love of other people, objectification joins hands with humanization. This is not to deny the dangerous aspects of confusing people (usually, as it turns out, women) and things, but we must complicate, refine, and in a sense detoxify our understanding of Rossetti's relation to the material world. It was, for him, infused with sentiment, with meaning and value that arose directly from his domestic impulses. Perhaps the spaces of Rossetti's paintings feel "suffocating" or "claustrophobic," but we should also allow ourselves to register their intimate, sheltering qualities.

The gap between the rooms of 16 Cheyne Walk and the gloriously filled spaces of Rossetti's paintings, often bearing little immediate resemblance to domestic rooms, must be crossed, if we are to appreciate the domestic quality of these paintings. In some of the paintings, most notably *The Loving Cup* (Surtees, II, plate 201) and *Marigolds*, Rossetti himself closes the gap, portraying domestic scenes as rich and inviting as those of Memling and Van Eyck, whom he so admired.[58] *La Bella Mano* (Surtees, II, plate 341) appears to depict Rossetti's own bedroom at 16 Cheyne Walk reflected in a mirror.[59]

But when Rossetti is not depicting clearly identifiable domestic milieux, he often presents ambiguously domestic spaces in which it is impossible to decide what is inside and what is "outside" architectural structures. *The Wedding of St. George and the Princess Sabra* (Surtees, II, plate 132) is, for example, a visual riddle of interiority. *Lady Lilith* (Surtees, II, plate 293) conducts her toilette in a chamber that has been invaded, as it were, by a rose plant – a chamber whose mirror reflects not, as we would expect, the room's interior, but a forest glade. The figures of *Rosa Triplex* (Surtees, II, plate 348) appear to lean on a window sill, but the inner space they inhabit is filled with "real" rose plants that also suggest rose-patterned wall paper. Like Francesca Alexander, so admired by Ruskin, Rossetti presents figures in spatially ambiguous settings such as balconies and courtyards, closely connected to houses but not inside them.

A further degree of abstraction of the domestic reveals itself in scenes in which there are no direct representation of rooms and their contents. Pandora and Venus Astarte, for example, appear to float in a dark ether. But it is in *The Day Dream* (Surtees, II, plate 388), his last serious painting, that Rossetti seems to place his figure in a wholly natural setting, perched in a tree. With the exception of a book lying open in her lap, this woman displays no trappings of the boudoir or the drawing room. She wears no jewelry, holds no mirror, seems to brook no decorative touch. Even *Astarte Syriaca* (Surtees, II, plate 371) is more openly a depiction of interior spaces: her attending angels carry decorated torches, and they also form a decorative enclosed space, a frame-within-a-frame, for the figure of Astarte.

The figure of *The Day Dream*, painted after Jane Morris, sits in the fork of a sycamore tree, staring into the near distance with a pensive and sad look. The portrait, uncharacteristically for this late period, is full length, and as if to call attention to the fact, Rossetti has painted her feet shod in leather shoes, not delicate slippers. This woman touches the ground, yet that ground also seems to merge with her dress and the tree's trunk. Her voluminous leaf-green dress hides her seat, and the whole figure appears, if not to float, at least to blend into its surroundings, the dark hair at the crown of her head shading – never completely – into the foliage. Reminiscent of Daphne, this dreamer is also the dark sister of the fatal blond woman of "The Orchard Pit," who stands "In the largest tree, within the fork whence the limbs divide" (*CW*, p. 427). She also suggests Dante's "Lady of Pity" of the *Vita Nuova*, who Rossetti liked to think might have been Gemina Donati, Dante's future wife.[60] We should not forget that Rossetti placed a framed study of *The Day Dream* over his mantelpiece; it is about his love for Jane in ways which letters and talks could never be.

Here in *The Day Dream* is the domestic scene painted, not as itself, but as the effect which it produces. A kind of shadow room attends the painting; the woman has settled into the tree as if it were a chair. The sycamore leaves behind her appear as flattened "wallpaper," in contrast to the living branches in front. This move from the comparative realism of the leaves in the foreground to the abstracted design in the background is also a move toward the domestic quality of wall covering. The woman holds a branch as if it were one of Rossetti's signature stringed instruments played in an exquisite Mallarméan silence. Living leaves contrast with the spray of honeysuckle in her hands, which has become, in its plucked state, a lovely but dead object, the shadow version of a fan or hair brush.

Figure 4   *The Day Dream*, Dante Gabriel Rossetti

This is the domestic interior itself transformed into a shady, waking dream of that Rossettian paradox, artificial nature. Rossetti disliked painting outdoors; early on he requests of his mother "the looking-glass over the drawing-room mantelpiece" because "without this, I should be obliged either to buy or hire one, as a large scrivanier looking-glass is indispensable to me in my present pictures, being the only means of casting reflexion on objects to imitate an out-of-door effect" (*LDGR*, p. 113). Not only would such a mirror help him paint the outdoors while indoors, it would itself appear in paintings, reflections upon reflections. Mirrors are not only symbols and symbol-making devices, they are also domestic objects *par excellence*. Further, Rossetti looked to photographs of Jane, posed by himself, for inspiration. In these photographs, Jane sits on parlor furniture placed outdoors; he might also have looked to Julia Margaret Cameron's photograph "The Day Dream" (1869) for inspiration.[61] Rather than waiting to travel to Kelmscott again in order to paint Jane in a natural tree, he asks Dunn to "set up a tree or something as substitute" in the studio, because "only your genius is equal to this kind of stage-machinery" (*LDGR*, p. 1712). From the first, the portrait is tied to his love for Jane; to his dependence on Dunn for expertise in bringing the outdoors inside, and for willingness to attend to his needs; to his fascination with photography and the mutually inspiring relations with the photographer Julia Margaret Cameron; and to his plans to paint the outdoors from safely within his own studio at 16 Cheyne Walk. The painting is a domestic arrangement in planning, execution, and (abstract) representation.

Although *The Day Dream* presents a woman as enticing as a summer's afternoon but as forbidding as "woman" in the garden, it is also about summer – that is the seasons, time – itself. Rossetti, in one of his few extended critical meditations, the essay on Blake, links the very notion of pattern and highly wrought surfaces with an escape from time. Looking at colored plates by Blake in the British Museum, the viewer:

will be joyful more and more the longer he looks, and will gain back in that time some things as he first knew them, not encumbered behind the days of his life; things too delicate for memory or years since forgotten; the momentary sense of spring in winter-sunshine, the long sunsets long ago, and falling fires on many distant hills." (*CW*, p. 448)

Here is Proust's *mémoire involuntaire* (itself the product of the intense domestic experience of the narrator) *avant la lettre*. The viewer will be especially entranced, as is Rossetti, by Blake's *Newton*, which "consists in a great part of rock covered with fossil substance . . . the treatment of which is as endlessly varied and intricate as a photograph from a piece of seaweed would be" (pp. 448–449). Patterns that relax rational control open the door to involuntary memory. As our eyes explore the tracery of the sycamore leaves and the folds of the leaf-green dress, Rossetti would wish us to enter a reverie of time redeemed, our own daydream echoing that of his painted subject.

During the creation of the painting and its accompanying poem he actually worries a great deal about the orderly progression of the seasons. He at first calls the painting *Vanna Primavera*, a reference to the *Vita Nuova*, "where Guido Cavalcanti's love named Primavera goes before Beatrice as spring before summer," and he plans to paint a spring sycamore.[62] We can follow an extended review of flowers and leaves through his correspondence: snowdrop, snowdrop and primrose together, convolvulus, honeysuckle, wood anemone – Rossetti considers them all before finally choosing the honeysuckle. The discussion seems to turn on two issues: arranging a variety of leaves and flowers that would all appear at the same season, spring-to-summer, "Not that correctness of literal kind is imperative on this point," and repeatedly soliciting both advice and plant specimens from friends. With Jane, such exchanges are not really about flowers, but about love:

As to the flowers, I feel deeply how good it is of you to interest yourself about them, and the thought is very dear to me, for I am desolate enough, as you know, indeed, without my work, should be lost altogether.[63]

Rossetti weaves the weft of love and work against a warp of time and its seasons to produce a tapestry that joins life and work seamlessly.

The Day Dream is thus a meditation on love and death, but not just an erotically charged death dispensed by a fatal woman. Nor does it represent, by its very genre, Rossetti's own gradual death by capitalism, the need to turn out yet another potboiler to pay the bills. It is also a meditation on how a life has been spent, an important subject of Part II of *The House of Life*, and it occurs day by day as the seasons change, in a late spring that almost unnaturally proffers new birth in summer:

> The thronged boughs of the shadowy sycamore
> Still bear young leaflets half the summer through. . . .
> Still the leaves come new;
> Yet never rosy-sheathed as those which drew
> Their spiral tongues from spring-buds heretofore.
>
> (*CW*, p. 364).

Rossetti removes snowdrops from the painting but has not replaced them, telling Jane: "I may have to put off the flowers to the early part of next year – i.e. if I live."[64] The sycamore leaves, living and killed into highly wrought artifice, unfurling and reaching maturity at once; the drooping honeysuckle chosen because "[i]t seems to be longer in all the year round than anything else" (p. 154); the woman gazing with something that might be pity though her name, Primavera, implies hope and new birth: these comprise Rossetti's visual "Immortality Ode" that must find its inspiration more in a post-Romantic, domestic Byzantium – tree become chair – rather than in the Romantic sway of fountains, meadows, hills and groves.

Rossetti expresses domestic sublimity, the power to move sentimentally through the complexities of home and to experience there the overwhelming mysteries, through the portrait of a woman's reverie. In this sublime practice, one *can* come back and tell; audiences must be reached. The tale is of the hard-won prize, the repose that is rooted in the quotidian, if only we can arrange things properly.

THE HOUSE OF ART

Pater's disciple and Rossetti's friend Swinburne presents in his rapturous study of Rossetti's *The House of Life* a split in critical assessment that has been reproduced in the criticism ever since. On the one hand, the sonnet sequence is a tightly woven fabric – "the woof of each poem is perfect," a ground from which the flowers, "rich surprises of casual ornament and intermittent embroidery," spring. But its warp is "of the sun's spinning, a web not of woven darkness but of molten light." The poem, then, is solid and grounded, but also evanescent, flickering, and fluid. Swinburne repeats the sense of contraries in a second conceit; this house of life is built according to a "solid and harmonious" scheme in which "there is no waste," but it is also a grandly excessive and confusing construction with "so many mansions, so many halls of state and bowers of music, chapels for worship and chambers for festival, that no guest can declare on a first entrance the secret of its scheme."[65] These two conceits of doubleness, sonnet sequence as building (harmonious, random) and sonnet sequence as woven fabric (solid, ephemeral), together form a like opposition: is the sequence the solid shelter of art, Blake's cupboard, the Holy of Holies that is both cabinet and doorway to Heaven, or is the sequence a shimmering fabric of words behind which the self crumbles, a veil over the abyss?

At first the choices seem clear. A tale of loss seeking impossible consolation, tortured, anything but sure, *The House of Life* is the very chronicle of the inaccessible ground, the ever-receding transcendent. Yet why choose? – Swinburne certainly didn't. In his contradictory metaphors, Swinburne searches for a way to express his understanding that the sequence cannot be adequately captured by making a choice between such dichotomies – in a sense, he poetically "argues" that the only adequate critical response to the sequence must entertain the irrationalities and ambiguities of art itself.[66] In sympathetic response both to Swinburne and to the distinguished critics who have read the sequence as either elegy or as account of growing despair, let us develop a useful critical posture for approaching *The House of Life*.

Any adequate response must first face the fact that the sequence of 102 poems begins in hope and love achieved, and despite moments of "regenerate rapture," moves inexorably to the "coverts of dismay." But such a fact does not tally with a full experience of the sequence, in which those earlier raptures seem never to be lost. *The House of Life* is as heartfelt and secure in its raptures as it is burgeoning in fear and pain. To borrow the words of Rossetti's disciple Gerard Manley Hopkins, the world's beauty in *The House of Life* is pregnant "with swift, slow, sweet, sour; adazzle, dim." Like the speaker of "The Monochord," one asks of the poem itself, "Oh! what is this that knows the road I came, / The flame turned cloud, the cloud returned to flame." Rapture and dismay, hope and despair, seem forms of one response – intense feeling, "sentiment" itself – that denies chronological development and binds the sequence into: a sphere of feeling? A constellation of glimmering gems? A garden of monuments? A quincunx of literary modes? Rossetti wrote these poems from the heart ("I hardly ever do produce a sonnet except on some basis of special momentary emotion" [*LDGR*, p. 985]) but often revised them with the same perspicacity he brought to bear on his friends' works.

The sequence affords us frequent glimpses of these elements and, taken together, they require a spatial appreciation of the series in which youth and age, rapture and decay are not consecutive stages, but, like the leaves of the sycamore tree, simultaneous. It is crucial to note that we must not read the sequence as an example of organic form, but instead as an arrangement or collection of things. Just as Rossetti makes of his sycamore tree flattened "wallpaper," a pattern in which to lose our bearings rather than a form expressing nature's unified logic, so the individual sonnets, even phrases within them, can be understood out of context, out of chronology, out of any order but that of the heart's whims and desires.

And, like the patterns of that foliage, in which Rossetti would have us defy time by relaxing the rational mind so that involuntary memory may bind together past and present, the dazzling patterns of language within and across sonnets are meant to make us feel the truth of experience, to know it intimately in a way that puts to rest our yearning for final answers. *The House of Life*, for all its emphasis on change, is also meant to be a place of repose. The questions of existence, the pain of selfhood, are not answered by anything but the pulse of beauty on our senses as it allows us to remember, rather than learn, what we know intimately and feelingly. Consider, for example, a phrase, "The tender glamour of day." Taken as a tiny piece of verbal beauty, a sentimental occasion rather than a description of nature, it invites us to read our own passing experiences of earthly redemption into its words and music. Understood as a phrase in a series of sonnets about sunlight swelling into sunset and dying into night, including "Mid Rapture," "Heart's Compass," "Soul-light," "The Moon Star," and "Last Fire," it conveys not just the one phase of daylight, but the entire cycle of the growth, death, and renewal of light. Such a cycle allows both regret and desire, "wan soul" and "one hope" (*CW*, p. 227) both to enchant us with feeling: the tender, confused glamour of all our days.

If we approach a particular sonnet with sentimental expectations, it will reward us by offering the kind of human connection Rossetti culti- vated throughout his life. Many of the poems are about dead children, loving parents, premature bereavement: the stuff of Victorian parlor sen- timentality. Woman and man in "Stillborn Love" (*CW*, p. 294) mate to produce the dead child "love" which waits for them in heaven; wedded souls now, they "Together tread at last the immortal strand / With eyes where burning memory lights love home" and "the little outcast hour" of their lost love "leaped to them and in their faces yearned: – / 'I am your child: O parents, ye have come.'" Like the patterning Rossetti so admired in Blake, the sonnet's "choral consonancy" – "somewhere sighs and serves . . . together tread . . . hours elect . . . lights love," – effects the very loosening of rational control that will make the message of the son- net, "we'll be reunited in heaven," acceptable not as religious dogma but as sentimental truth. We know it because we have heard and felt it, earlier in the sequence and now. "Burning memory" is the lovers', but it is ours as well, as Rossetti invites us to read a personal message into his sonnet and thus creates the rapport with us that is always his goal. If this is narcissism, it is narcissism transcended – in the visceral world of tears and sighs we all share.

The domestic sublime in *The House of Life* makes explicit this kind of sentimental homecoming. The metaphysical questions of "The Dark Glass," for example, are answered by images of love's small, deep, and sheltering truth:

> Not I myself know all my love for thee:
> How should I reach so far, who cannot weigh
> To-morrow's dower by gage of yesterday?
> Shall birth and death, and all dark names that be
> As doors and windows bared to some loud sea,
> Lash deaf mine ears and blind my face with spray;
> And shall my sense pierce love, – the last relay
> And ultimate outpost of eternity?
>   Lo! what am I to Love, the lord of all?
> One murmuring shell he gathers from the sand,–
> One little heart-flame sheltered in his hand.
> Yet through thine eyes he grants me clearest call
> And veriest touch of powers primordial
> That any hour-girt life may understand.
>
>   (*CW*, p. 193)

The sublime storm at sea here is meant to answer the mystery of love, itself a sentimentalization of the sublime's ineffable Truth. Even more significantly, the speaker, in a somewhat contorted conceit, imagines life as a house, with birth and death as doors and windows onto sublimity. Love in these terms is the "last relay and ultimate outpost of eternity." The most intimate connection between people is also the most distant contact they may have with the metaphysical; but significantly it is the intimate side of the equation that is still the mystery: "not I myself know all my love for thee." The sestet answers the octet's question, "and shall my sense pierce love?", with domestic images. The speaker may not pierce love, but love may minister, attend to, him. Love, the lord of all, gathers a shell, home to both a particular being and the murmuring voice of the sea, and shelters "one little heart-flame" in his hand. Love also vouchsafes him knowledge as synaesthetic union – through the combined senses of sight, sound, and touch he may "understand." Without losing its mystery, the wildest storm of wisdom contracts to a sheltered "hour-girt" life and the known-because-felt truth of love.

Given these poetic tales of sentiment and domestic sublimity, we want to know, in the discursive sense, more. To what do all these heartfelt states tend? Gaining some distance by extricating ourselves from felt truths, Rossetti's and our own, we ask questions about larger design: how do the sonnets fit together, and which questions do they as a group seem to pose?

Our evidence must include the poems as they were written, revised, and published. But we must look as well at Rossetti's scene of writing, the conditions in which he actually came to writing, especially because Rossetti made no clear distinction between life arrangements and artistic arrangements. Certain forays into the formal complexities of the sequence seem daunting in the very richness of discovery. We may trace the changes Rossetti rings in the sonnet form across the sequence. We may trace "unifying" motifs of many sorts: those tied to a specific type of sensory experience; to thematic developments of work, love, will, loneliness; or to rewritings of Italian sonneteers or Poe – to name only a few. We may muse upon the sequence's generic suggestivenesss: epic? elegy? allegory? Or we may begin with a specific problem Rossetti faced in his daily life, e.g., the need to earn a living by his art or his love for another man's wife, and ask how Rossetti plays it out in the sequence's formal effects.

To such explorations of form and meaning *The House of Life* will yield appropriate answers, neither fixed and final nor wholly unmoored. Rossetti's sonnet sequence presents neither a master plot nor a field of randomly shifting signs, and the critical tales we tell pale in contrast to the sheer feeling of relation-in-disparity that his verse offers. This feeling, of intimate relation, is the truth of arrangement: here, today, at home, together. It is as well the feeling of a Poundian contingency: what is arranged may be rearranged. Rossetti tells us in the first, but hardly primary or originary sonnet, "Love Enthroned," that he "marked" "all kindred Powers." "Kindred": related, close, feeling, all the powers worship at "Love's throne," conceived throughout Rossetti's painting and poetry, now as a medievalized royal seat, now as a curiosity in his bedroom, now as the couch James Smetham gave him, now as the trunk of a fallen tree set by Dunn in his studio that he might paint his reveries of love and fear. "The great undeniable reality in things" invoked by Pater is the momentary repose afforded by lovely objects, people, words, and paint after they have been arranged, such repose and loveliness grasped only in the heart's knowledge of sublimity made familiar, of aestheticism – link by link – domesticated.

Meditation: domesticity

Victorian Modernist notions of form converge with those of family, as artists seek to associate "by various conditions of common likeness or mutual dependence" parts with a whole.[1] The domestic scene is for them more than setting; it is also an intertwining of the activities, physical objects, and emotions of the people who live in relation to a house. The medieval notion of the *domus* as the actual house of stone or wood that is "one and the same thing" as its "flesh and blood" inhabitants provides an important layer of the palimpsest that is domesticity in the nineteenth and twentieth centuries.[2] Although domesticity is a process, it is also a collection of things. It enables artists, including writers, to create patterns that intricately connect, and thereby relax, the polarities that haunt modern life and thought: animate/inanimate, inside/outside, and concrete/abstract, among others.

Interiors of selves and interiors of familiar structures seem to have been linked from the first. In painting, detailed interior scenes began to appear frequently only in the sixteenth century. Words having to do with the innerness of self, such as self-love, privacy, disposition, ego, apathy, sentimental, made their appearance in the seventeenth and eighteenth centuries: "The interior furniture of houses appeared together with the interior furniture of minds."[3] Since Victorian Modernism has a pragmatist bent, we might contemplate the aesthetic quality of consciousness itself as home-making, the building out, from the unstructured flux, of a world in which one can satisfactorily dwell. For all its restless seeking and forward-looking qualities, pragmatism also allows for repose. We do not remake our world each day. Furthermore, home is often the actual site in which people begin self-consciously to arrange the flux of experience through the exercise of imagination – the place in which they come to view themselves as artists.

We may, however, well ask whether we are saying anything useful to aesthetic understanding when we note that the domestic scene is both created by and enabling of an inherently artistic exercise of consciousness. Certainly students of philosophical aesthetics don't think so when they split off the realm of art from the world of domestic or everyday affairs. Arthur Danto, for example, demonstrates this move of rupture: mere things elicit a response from us that is different from our response to works of art. Further, when we confuse a mere thing with a work of art, sometimes "an act of disinterpretation may be required."[4] Should we mistake a sugar bowl for a thing of beauty, or, more intriguingly, should we mistake a regular urinal for Duchamp's "Fountain," we need to back up, deny the former's status as aesthetic object. The category of the artwork must be distinct from the category of things that are not art, the latter labeled by Danto as "mere real thing[s]" (p. 94).

It is just such a distinction between what can and cannot be classified as art that John Ruskin and other Victorian Modernists challenge:

A picture is to have harmony of relation among its parts? Yes; and so is a speech well uttered, and an action well ordered, and a company well chosen, and a ragout well mixed. Composition! As if a man were not composing every moment of his life, well or ill, and would not do it instinctively in his picture as well as elsewhere, if he could.[5]

Dante Gabriel Rossetti's domesticity similarly reveals permeable borders between works of art and Danto's world of "mere things." We simply cannot distinguish clearly between the hawthorn vase in Rossetti's paintings and the hawthorn vase that he buys from his friend Murray Marks. They overlap in Rossetti's experience, and not just because the hawthorn vase is itself a work of art. It is a treasured domestic object in Rossetti's experience, not wholly unlike his furniture or the wallpaper he designed for his first home with Elizabeth Siddal. As a vase, it has a function – yet it is neither wholly "pure" art nor wholly practical "thing." Rossetti transforms it into a painted vase, buys and sells it in the marketplace, uses it to develop relations with other people, treasures it for its living qualities, and places it, beautifully, on a real shelf in a real house as part of his ongoing domestic arrangements.

Rather than dividing art and life into two categories, Victorian Modernists experiment with bringing them into intimate relation through the activities of domesticity. For example, Henry James opens *The Portrait of a Lady* with a tea ceremony:

The implements of the little feast had been disposed upon the lawn of an old English country-house, in what I should call the perfect middle of a splendid summer afternoon. . . . The old man had his cup in his hand; it was an unusually

large cup, of a different pattern from the rest of the set and painted in brilliant
colours . . . unconscious of observation [he] rested his eyes upon the rich red
front of his dwelling. The house that rose beyond the lawn was a structure to
repay such consideration and was the most characteristic object in the peculiarly
English picture I have attempted to sketch.[6]

The many minglings and softenings of the scene – light/shadow, time/-
eternity, male/female, outdoors/indoors, British/American – all radiate from a domestic act, the communal taking of tea. James's narrator
presents the activity as neither mere animal nourishment nor as a religious ritual or staged drama, but rather as the act of desiring, and thereby
making, connection among these three possibilities. The cup's function
as a container for liquid makes it a "mere thing," but the context of domesticity in which it appears makes it a work of art. James's scene traces
the third way of a Schillerian aestheticism (mentioned in "Meditation:
aestheticism"), for all its half-hidden anxieties and threats. Its domestic
intercourse, "the ceremony known as afternoon tea" presents its own
most powerful, because lived, claim to artfulness as it brings into complex form kinds and orders of relation. Patterns on tea cups and patterns
in prose mingle in the "perfect middle" of a summer's afternoon.

Several decades earlier, Rossetti fashioned an experimental, Victorian
Modernist aesthetic by interlocking arrangements involving the bric-à-
brac of his parlour, forms in his paintings, images in his poetry, and
friends and family. Ruskin, seeking his own "third way," explained the art
of painting to his largely middle-class readers in England and America.
Nature, he asserts, is "never distinct and never vacant, she is always
mysterious, but always abundant; you always see something, but you
never see all" (3.329). He then illustrates this dictum by choosing to
describe (not by chance, as we shall learn), a house as nature would have
us see it:

She would have let us see the Indian corn hanging on the walls, and the image
of the Virgin at the angles, and the sharp, broken, broad shadows of the tiled
eaves . . . and the white and blue stripes of the mattresses stuffed out of the
windows, and the flapping corners of the mat blinds. (3.330)

Domesticity here relates a realist "truth to nature" to an idealist Catholicism, joining as well the world of art making to the world of everyday
experience, inner to outer. The breeze that flaps the blinds mingles spiritual weather and mundane weather.

"Our God is a household God, as well as a heavenly one; He has an
altar in every man's dwelling," Ruskin preaches (8.227). Although such

a domestication of divinity reveals Ruskin's early training in Evangelical Protestantism, he has more revolutionary ideas in mind. Even the cathedrals of Roman Catholicism are worthy of Protestant admiration, precisely because they are domestic at heart. Ruskin repeatedly insists that Gothic cathedrals are modeled on humble houses. Even St. Mark's in Venice is grandly and humbly domestic in inspiration. Coming upon this cathedral from a narrow side street, Ruskin tells us that it gathers up and transforms, without denying, ordinary human life, "as if the rugged and irregular houses that pressed together above us in the dark alley had been struck back into sudden obedience and lovely order, and all their rude casements and broken walls had been transformed into arches charged with goodly sculpture, and fluted shafts of delicate stone" (10.82).

Domesticity evokes complex responses in many of us, and this is no less true for Ruskin, Rossetti, Augusta Evans, and William James. This study's biographical accounts reveal that they find the *domus* to be a site of ennui, servitude, and fear, yet they also luxuriate in its securities and receive its inspirations. More importantly, however, their aesthetic views and their day-to-day experiences at home are mutually dependent.

Regarding domesticity as an important artistic accomplishment of Victorian Modernism, we would do well to address two critiques of it: feminist and Marxist.[7] Although there is no such thing as "the" feminist position on domesticity, we can address a few of the more common feminist reservations about celebrating life at home. If the dwelling place of humanity is language, then, so one feminist argument goes, men own the dwelling house, name its objects, and dictate its workings. In this way they entrench their power at the expense of women's freedom. Or, other arguments contend, the comforts and securities of home, especially its psychological securities for men, are paid for with women's freedom. Men's active role requires women's nurturance, men's wish to return to a home (womb, childhood, native land) which they can never reach results in their wish to keep women at home, to "preserve" symbolically what they believe they have lost. To these accounts of oppression, we might respond pragmatically: certainly these narratives are useful, but there is more truth to be pursued. We need to entertain the possibility that home has *also* been the site of freedom for men and women alike.

We could begin to muse on such freedom by moving beyond the distinction formulated early on by Simone de Beauvoir, that of men's (active) transcendence and women's (passive) immanence. In this view, men build the houses that entrap women. But perhaps it is true, too, that building (active, creative) and preservation (also active, creative),

involve both men and women. We might also reevaluate the gifts of less
active modes – reverie, memory, meditation, repose, fancy – that men
and women alike have sought out of a need to realize their existence in
story and ritual.[8] As we do so, shifting and complex gender patterns take
shape. Male artists such as Rossetti and Ruskin engage in preservation –
a form of house-keeping, and therefore traditionally considered feminine
in nature. Ruskin proposes the preservation, not the reconstruction, of
old buildings. Rossetti's rearrangements – of mythic figures, antique-store
bargains, or the poems of Dante and his circle – themselves preserve
what others have made. Furthermore, preservation and construction
themselves combine in ornamentation. Of this, more below.

Once we hypothesize that power relations between the sexes take a
more complex form than the struggle of male versus female (with the
male usually victorious), we can begin to view home as a site where
repose, antagonism, exploration, and boredom interact. Further, we can
begin to regard the *domus* as the site of experimentation within the local
and the concrete, not just the enclosure of political and aesthetic reaction.
As feminists, we might call attention to the positive values of home, such as
"safety," "individuation," "privacy," and "preservation."[9] To explore the
positive nature of domesticity for men and women alike is not to engage
in another misogynist fantasy of the glory of housework, but instead to
reexamine a picture that has been too simply charted in conflict. The
artist's workplace within the home – library, study, studio – joins other
modernist *topoi* – urban labyrinth, dreamscape, shores of exile – as places
in which creativity may flourish and pragmatist paths may ramify.

Along with feminist judgments of domesticity as largely a trap for
women, Marxist critiques of bourgeois domesticity have also prolifer-
ated. Critics on the Left look with deep suspicion upon the bric-à-brac of
Victorian parlors, the heavy thingness of material culture that embodies
the imperial, masculine, capitalist practices of nineteenth-century industrial and colonial culture. Marxist narratives often present aestheticism
as primarily or even necessarily involving the contradictions between the
work of art as a commodity and its claim to exist apart from the marketplace. Implicated in this contradiction, domestic aestheticism would
seem to offer a double dose of false consciousness.[10] Because, in this view,
domesticity falsely promises that one can escape the scene of alienated
labor, Marxist critics tend to point to it as a poisonous creation of capitalist ideology.[11] Certainly such a critique of bourgeois materialism will
be part of any picture of Victorian Modernism. Ruskin, for example,
famously railed against the "illth" (17.89), rather than celebrating the

wealth, of the modern industrial state. He particularly disliked machine-made domestic items.

We will, however, wish to pause long enough to ponder other tales of material life beyond those that assert the necessary alienation effected by capitalist ideology. A fuller, if less tidy, picture would include the Victorian parlor as a locus of aesthetic, social, and moral experimentation. Ruskin wrote of the "Storm Cloud" of industrial England, but he also celebrated the loveliness of the British Isles of his day. He attacked and praised English painters. Alienation and "illth" were only part of his story; he also wrote of the social well-being that the tender-hearted could help to create. Rossetti directed his loving energies toward both living beings and the objects he especially cared for, and we would do well to study his deliberate confusing of the two. Evans, in imagining decadent *objets d'art*, the "world-scrapings" of a masculine rake, simultaneously asked why it was that women didn't journey outside the home more frequently themselves – and promptly sent her heroine to New York City.[12] That she closed her novel with a resounding vote for the repressive status quo (Edna marries and gives up writing) only throws into domestic chiaroscuro the dangerous questions she first asked, then stifled.

If Marxist concepts of commodity culture, then, enable us to grasp only a partial truth, what should we add to the search?[13] Perhaps an appreciation of bourgeois beauty itself. We often think of Victorian rooms as ornamented with fringes, heavy fabrics, figured wallpapers and china patterns; and also as cheaply constructed, airless, and thrown into harsh relief by gas lighting. Just as the modifier "mere" often qualifies the words "sentimentality" and "domesticity," so "excessive" dogs the word "ornamentation." Yet such patterns became for the artists who worked among them the first templates for the multiplex wholes or concatenated unions of the sort that George Eliot and William James meditated upon, a source for aesthetic practices that also gave rise to changes in epistemological, metaphysical, and moral understandings. When Poe, for example, criticizes American interior decoration in "The Philosophy of Furniture," he speaks of an aesthetic failure that is also a moral failure. Often linked to sentimentality, Victorian Modernist domesticity mingles an excess of ornament with strong, didactic messages.

The eclectic interior decoration of bourgeois England and America at mid-nineteenth century was largely a product of the imaginations of Christian women. Like the typological sermons they might have heard on Sundays, their lushly decorated rooms both memorialized and prefigured other places and times, other mythologies.[14] Their willingness to explore juxtapositions, details, and palimpsests within one room and from one room to the next in a single house indicated an ability to admire discontinuous continuities or totalities-in-progress. Although the 1880s in America saw a flourishing of "Aesthetic" decoration, we should note that such decorative practices were not new.[15] First, many of the American domestic novelists of the 1850s and '60s had already furnished their novels with such rooms. Second, and more importantly, rather than representing a rupture with Victorian middle-class and upper-class interior decoration, the turn-of-the-century styles that went by the name "Aesthetic" intensified what were already self-consciously artful living spaces of earlier decades. The appropriation in England of (women's) decorative domestic arts by (men's) "connoisseurship" later in the century is a fascinating tale of gender politics.[16]

The ornamentation of rooms mattered to mid-century aestheticism because it provided a vehicle for the celebration of artificiality in general and with "useless" or non-functional artificiality in particular. To oversimplify for a moment, we can observe the Romantic fascination with nature-spirit gradually giving way to the Victorian Modernist fascination with artifice. There is, of course, no sharp distinction between Romantic and Victorian; Wordsworth, for example, describes a glen as a room in "Nutting." By mid-century, however, artifice often trumps "nature." Rossetti either recreates natural settings inside his studio, asking his assistant to bring logs and plants into the studio, or moves furniture out onto the lawn as settings for his paintings or the photographs from which he painted. His paintings themselves regularly confuse indoors and outdoors. Ruskin describes natural phenomena, but often metaphorically, as processes of building and furnishing the world. To a monistic nature he prefers a highly wrought, pluralist concatenation of designers: God, nature, artist, and critic.

As the first decade of the twentieth century ended, it became a Modernist article of faith that the ornamentation of houses and their furnishings revealed a vulgarity and complacency best left behind, along with materialist fussiness in prose and poetry.[17] The notion that serious artists rejected detail and ornamentation in favor of pure, significant, or ephemeral form lives on in many accounts of Modernism. The desired abstraction or impressionism consisted of a clearing away of clunky realist detail, a rejection of what Virginia Woolf famously diagnosed as, "[the spending of] immense skill and immense industry making the trivial and the transitory appear the true and the enduring."[18] The materialist, mere "thingness" of buttons and gig lamps lit must go.

Yet it is worth asking whether such plodding detail work was, in fact, rejected by Modernists. Decoration and ornamentation often form pluralist unities – a useful oxymoron for a discussion of Victorian Modernism. This study reveals that the entanglements of daily lives at home and literary works often involve domestic items that are themselves already complicated, including ornamental wallpapers, embroidery, jewelry, fans, feathers, carved and painted wood furniture and faceted glass. A glance at the auction catalogue for Dante Gabriel Rossetti's belongings shows highly ornamented objects that have participated in his complex relations with other people, his translations of other cultures, and his paintings and poems themselves. The "Aesthetic" dress of American women in the eighties, often designed to mesh with the interior decorations of their houses, shows a mixture of styles, a literal layering of forms and patterns from far-flung places and times.[19] Pre-Raphaelite painters, instead of painting all parts of the canvas at once in order to keep the different parts related harmoniously, used a patchwork method like that of fresco, mosaic, quilt, or jigsaw puzzle. Such a technique allows "simultaneous, incompatible points of view and planes of orientation" and constantly shifting perspectives – in short, what we think of as Modernist painting.[20]

Ornament presents an interplay of different kinds of representation: a leaf that looks like a real leaf, a fanciful leaf that never was in nature, a leaf purified and abstracted.[21] Through this mixing of representational modes, the act of ornamentation encourages artists to think about freeing art from rigid categories. Realist, impressionist, and idealist notions of art intertwine in the "busy" surfaces of Victorian rooms. In addition a useful, if limited, critical narrative of modern painting has been the gradual rejection of illusionism in favor of a shallow or flat picture space, and this study explores such flatness in Victorian Modernist ornamentation.[22]

When we look back, for example, from Picasso's patterned furniture in his flattened portraits to the highly decorated surfaces of St. Elmo's rooms, the particularized and flattened surfaces of Rossetti's paintings, and the flourishing ornamentation on the exterior surfaces of Gothic cathedrals as they appear in Ruskin's word paintings and sketches, all, Picasso included, participate in a complex modernity. Because decorative form tends to be repetitive and conservative, one decorative convention can persist for a great length of time; witness the doorpull decorated with a lion's head, an ornament repeated over the centuries, down to their appearance in Calvin Klein earrings.[23] To the extent that early twentieth-century artists introduce "ornamental" patterns into paintings and literary works, such as the decorative borders and actual textile patterns of Matisse, or the incantatory repetitions or iconic images of modernist verse, these works of arts represent not a rupture from the immediate Victorian past, but its elaboration.

Samuel Beckett's speaker in *Watt*, telling something like a story about Watt's possible experience as a servant in a mysterious house, indulges in extravagant verbal fussiness that manages to convey metaphysical silliness, solemnity, and a rather hysterical aesthetic curiosity at the same time. Watt speaks of a picture (black circle, blue dot, "the rest was white") that decorates his bedroom, in prose that is itself a series of decorations into which a core of meaning seems to have dissolved:

And he wondered what the artist had intended to represent (Watt knew nothing about painting), a circle and its centre in search of each other, or a circle and its centre in search of a centre and a circle respectively, or a circle and its centre in search of its centre and a circle respectively, or a circle and its center in search of a centre and its circle respectively, or a circle and a centre not its centre in search of a centre and its circle respectively. . . . Watt's eyes filled with tears that he could not stem, and they flowed down his fluted cheeks unchecked, refreshing him greatly.[24]

Few heroines of sentimental and domestic novels have had a more fulfilling cry.

The ornamental is perhaps most powerful as an anti-essentialist force in Victorian Modernist literature. Because it is added on to the master plan or the basic structure, critics have often judged it to be inferior, feminine, contingent, excessive. Yet ornamentation gradually becomes in Victorian Modernism a celebration of surface as well as depth, of the local and the individual as well as the universal, and of the possibilities of addition, arrangement and rearrangement that challenge the fixities of essential or ideal form.[25] Decoration tends to raise questions of foreground and background, ordinary and extraordinary, passing fashion and eternal form. When we consider a teacup, do we register primarily the charm and attraction of its decoration, or the utility of its basic design? The answer, William James would argue, depends on what we intend to do with it. Often enough, Victorian Modernist writers don't make a clear choice between ornament and ground, but instead adopt a roving way between pure beauty and utter utility – pragmatism's and aestheticism's way.

It is not a matter of chance that, when William James describes the pragmatist process of truth as the creation of concatenated pattern, he adopts domestic metaphors. Nor is it a mere coincidence that when he considers "truth" itself – the process of testing and making true that leads one, however temporarily, to a resting place – he thinks of home. James personifies Pragmatism as "she" a genial hostess or a rural lass who leads us to a feeling of satisfaction. "Pragmatism gets her general notion of truth as something essentially bound up with the way in which one moment in our experience may lead us towards other moments,"[26] James explains, and the image for the present goal of this leading is none other than a house: "Following our mental image of a house along the cowpath, we actually come to see the house; we get the image's full verification" (*P*, p. 99).

Before we assume conscious or unconscious misogynist motivations on James's part, we might experiment with different preconceptions for a moment. Why *did* James choose feminized and domestic imagery throughout *Pragmatism*, indeed, throughout his oeuvre? Certainly, be- cause he wanted philosophy, like women, to serve men in everyday, practical ways. Yet he also tried to think beyond available cultural forms. To familiar accounts of his masculinist tendencies and yearnings for the strenuous life, we should add a careful analysis of his place in a feminine, home-centered culture in which he came to consciousness and actually wrote.

We'll find ourselves in familiar territory here, for James rehearsed issues of modernism, aestheticism, sentimentality, and sublimity, and drew them together into the association that became for him pragmatist methodology. James asks us to learn, as good pragmatists, to test ideas in our actual lives, not within the structures of analytical thought and philosophic system. For most of us, where, if not in the domestic, does the ordinary lie? How do we know when an idea has truth value? We pull a chair up to the table and taste it: "Just as certain foods are not only agreeable to our taste, but good for our teeth, our stomach and our tissues; so certain ideas are not only agreeable to think about ... but they are also helpful in life's practical struggles" (*P*, p. 42). Even when James travels to South America on expedition or quotes and rewrites W. H. Hudson's accounts of exotic forays into Patagonia, he simply claims the exotic as domestic, in much the same way that the Ruskin family travels to the Continent in order to transform it, by their family rituals, into part of home itself.

Pragmatism, with its texture of domestic metaphors, stages an ex- plicit conflict between feminine and masculine spheres. James tests how far he himself is able to go down the road of feminine and domestic culture, sentimentally intense and sublimely wide, as a means of philosophizing wisely. Nineteenth-century American domestic manuals often counseled women to become the peace-maker and harmonizer of the home. Pragmatism, James explained to his mixed audiences of amateurs and philosophers, is a "mediator and reconciler" of different philosophical positions (*P*, p. 43). Like a good Victorian woman, she brings differing parties (including those arguing within a single person) into conversation: empiricist with rationalist, sensationalist with intellectualist, materialist with idealist, and so on. Relations between ideas and things are as true as ideas and things themselves. Truth in an idea means successfully "marrying . . . previous parts of experience with newer parts" (*P*, p. 37), and this marriage is the continual refounding act of Victorian Modernist domesticity, the creation of "impalpable habitations" that have been, and continue to be, as real as home itself.[27] "I wish to speak . . . in sympathy with your desires," James tells his audience (*P*, p. 10). Relation is, for him, and for Victorian Modernism, a form of wisdom. And wisdom is itself a coming home.

CHAPTER 4

Recondite analogies: the Victorian Modernism of Augusta Evans

> While all melts under our feet, we may well catch at any exquisite passion, or any contribution to knowledge that seems by a lifted horizon to set the spirit free for a moment, or any stirring of the senses, strange dyes, strange colours, and curious odours, or work of the artist's hands, or the face of one's friend.
>
> Walter Pater, *The Renaissance*[1]

Beginning a study of Augusta Evans's novel *St. Elmo* (1866) within a larger study of Victorian Modernism lowers at least two common barriers: one standing between American and British literatures of the nineteenth century, and one dividing elite and popular literature. Once the processes of establishing relations among countries, authors, literatures, and genres become as important as the goal of demonstrating their integrities, we shall be well on our way to more expansive, nuanced, and useful literary truths. For example, although Ruskin disliked America and mentioned it infrequently, his own work was widely read, quoted, and appropriated there, in the same land from which Henry James separated himself in order to put down roots in England.[2] Furthermore, both Ruskin and James read popular literature, and it is impossible to distinguish clearly between elitist and popular influences and goals in their works. Similarly, women in nineteenth-century America who wrote best-sellers often had absorbed significant amounts of British, Continental, and Classical "high" culture – and it is as futile to try to separate native from foreign elements in their novels as it is to place that fiction neatly in the category of the popular, wholly apart from and below serious art. We may fruitfully consider Augusta Evans, as well as Walter Pater, to be disciples of Ruskin and we shall observe in the course of this study that she invented, in parallel with Pater, her own literary decadence.

St. Elmo is a good place to begin, again, to address these kinds of literary confusions, because it could be argued that Augusta Evans never heard of an "other" with which she did not wish to establish connection, even if it was domination she desired. The novel is a hodgepodge, as critics of the day testify:

> It is, we humbly confess, beyond our comprehension. It may be very beautiful, or only very obscure – at any rate it is too deep for us. We entreat Miss Evans to publish a key to her volume. Let us know what the fine talk which people use in this book is all about. Everyone cannot be expected to converse in Chaldee and Hebrew. Even the English has a wild and disordered aspect to our common eyes.[3]

Reading the book today, we are still often at a loss. We want to know why Evans writes so wildly, and whether the text's confusions may be usefully linked to the extended patternings of Victorian Modernism. To explore the why and whether of it, we will need to understand the sources of Evans's personal confusion, its expression in the texture of her novel, and its usefulness to her as she finds her way toward often conflicting goals.

St. Elmo has by now achieved canonical status within the critical ghetto of commentaries on popular novels by nineteenth-century American women.[4] Within the gates, *St. Elmo* is a respected book; outside, it is little known. That *St. Elmo* is so frequently discussed within its sub-field, indeed, to the exclusion of many related books that have received not one line of twentieth-century critical recognition, can be explained in three principal ways. First, it was immensely popular, even in a field crowded with bestsellers: it sold over a million copies and remained in print through the turn of the century.[5] Second, its subject – the trials of a writing, scholarly woman – would have a special appeal to writing, scholarly women. Third, it seems to expand the limits of the domestic novel.[6] *St. Elmo* states overtly what is only hinted at by similar novels: the rightful claim women can make to a life of intellectual accomplishment and a position of power not only apart from, but also over, men. In a literature which purveys the doctrine of separate spheres or the cult of domesticity with varying degrees of ambivalence and intelligence, *St. Elmo* flaunts the sharp contradictions of its dual polemics: one socially conservative, the other iconoclastic. Throughout her fiction, Evans imagines well-educated, economically and emotionally independent, artistic, and scholarly women. Yet she also insists upon their dutifully subordinate place in a society which she stalwartly maintains must be Christian, anti-woman's suffrage, and marriage-centered.

Most of the critics of *St. Elmo* share a certainty that Evans's contradictions play themselves out primarily in plot and characterization. The critical literature is strangely silent on the subject of prose style, tone, and setting. Such reticence may be attributed to misplaced critical anxiety. *St. Elmo* is an odd and often awkward book, and to analyze elements of style and narrative technique in it is perhaps to risk undermining critical claims for the novel's worth. Since the question of assessing the value of domestic fiction is still a vexed one, a formalist focus can (wrongly, I believe) appear threatening to the critical enterprise of returning this book to the scholarly eye.[7] This tendency to emphasize plot and character results in a criticism that continues primarily to seek "images of women." Such critics naively read fictional character as simply mimetic of human personality and situation; thus the female characters in these books can stand for nineteenth-century women, while plot can directly represent the vicissitudes of that always elusive phenomenon, the "daily life" of an earlier era. The "work of the artist's hands," her finer, texturing dissolution of the narrative line, goes unnoticed. It is in such patterning that we shall wish to dwell.

St. Elmo does have a striking stylistic problem: Evans seems deliberately to strew her narrative with erudite references and to empurple her diction. Even seasoned readers of pedantic prose can find themselves at a loss. Some of the citations and allusions are immediately identifiable, some elude us but seem just within our grasp, but many would require a trip to the reference room, and others are so abstruse as to defeat even dogged research. This is a *novel*, not a textbook, we begin to protest. Learning to read it, we discover, requires setting our calibrations firmly: we will go only so far to decipher its learned references, and past that point we will read over or through them, regarding them as piquant flavoring rather than learned discourse.

To add to the irritations or difficulties of absorbing such pedantry, Evans conceives most of the elements of her novel through a lens of learning. Much of the novel's action occurs within libraries or at desks. The two principal characters are scholars; St. Elmo speaks encyclopedically, and Edna Earl, a self-trained ethnologist, pores over ancient texts late into the night. The narrator continually situates the action of the novel within a vast series of references to Western and Eastern civilizations throughout time. Furthermore, Evans presents her learning with abandon: unidentified quotations from contemporary popular poetry nudge aside references to the Talmud; literary or historical allusions articulate awkwardly with one another and with snippets of scientific and philosophical discourse. Her confusions of details test the limits of pragmatist explorations – they are as much briar patch as they are pathways toward home truths.

A second apparent weakness of the novel involves the plot itself. The formulaic story tends to disappoint modern readers, even those with an eye to its telling dislocations, its intriguing rifts and bogs. Here is a novel that describes an arc with which we are all too familiar: Edna Earl, the innocent child of nature, soon orphaned, finds her way into the wide, wide world. Through luck and the attractions of her physical beauty and Christian character, she is informally adopted and then exquisitely educated. Extremely intelligent and even more diligent, she becomes a successful writer with a national reputation. She saves the Byronic and fallen St. Elmo Murray by wisely setting a good example and then leaving this wealthy, world-weary, and socially superior man to fight his own way back to Christian rectitude. Nearly writing herself into the grave, Edna rebuffs one dazzling suitor after another, until, as the novel ends, she gives up her career in order to marry St. Elmo, now a minister.

Such a plot summary reveals *St. Elmo* as a version of *Pilgrim's Progress* crossed with *Jane Eyre* (surely the *Ur*-texts of most domestic novels). But another *St. Elmo* shadows this orphan's tale, and this novel interests itself not in the journey of salvation but in stasis, not in Christian health but in exotic religions and disease, and not in plot but in narrative texture. Evans herself seems conscious of the contrast between the arc of her plot and the embroidery upon it. Encouraging her closest friend, Rachel Heustis, an Orthodox Jew and a Southerner, to write a novel of her own, she counsels, "Elaborate your plot, trace clearly to the end your grand leading aim, before you write *a line* and then you will find no trouble I think, in weaving the details, arranging your chiaro-scuro, in fine-polishing the whole."[8] This second novel, finally inseparable from the first, is a figuration of literary aestheticism of the decadent strain. What we think of as British and French decadence and modernism may well have made a parallel and even earlier appearance, and in an unexpected place: in this popular novel by a mid-century American woman. The domestic novel offered a rich site for the development of Victorian Modernism in both its mid- and turn-of-the-century forms; indeed Evans corroborates Schiller's claims for the domestic origins of the aesthetic.

In order to make the case for *St. Elmo* as a work of Victorian Modernism, we must look at some of its settings within rooms of exotic bric-à-brac, reconsider its plot and characters, and – removing it from the stiffened critical enclosures of both American fiction and women's popular fiction – consider its relations to a wider literary tradition of such writers as Byron, Rossetti, Ruskin, Huysmans, Pater, Joyce, and

Stevens. We will need as well to consider the particular conditions under which Evans simultaneously wrote the novel and created a writer's self with which she could make her peace.[9] Further, we must consider the narrative as Evans's account of the Civil War and its aftermath, though she mentions the war directly not once, instead painting, in the manner of the Symbolist Mallarmé, "not the object itself, but the effect it produces."[10]

Viewed from these other perspectives, *St. Elmo* is not only a book about women, it is also a novel about novels, a meditation on art and the artist, and a narrative whose studied silence on the subject of contemporary politics is actually coded speech. Just as British aestheticist writers created an art that bore witness to the strains and contradictions in their lives – Ruskin's mixed feelings about intimacy, Rossetti's confusions of art and life – so does Augusta Evans imagine a literary art of sensation, pose, illness, and impersonality in direct reaction to the world around her. This is the world of Mobile, Alabama, in 1865, with the South a shambles, the Confederacy a painful memory, and her own life as an artist still very much in the making.

The issues this study will touch upon, from the self-creation of the domestic writer and her calculated entry into the literary marketplace, to her narratives of contemporary history, religious experience, and practical aesthetics, together suggest that for Evans, literary aestheticism in its dark and decadent forms overlaps with literary domesticity. Further, an array of formal qualities binds *St. Elmo* to aestheticist and decadent literary productions that appear in England, France, and America from Evans's day to the turn of the century. Evans explores the significance of silence; the fascinations of the grotesque, the deadly, the diseased, and the over-wrought; the mirroring of characters; the counterpointing of plots; and the intricacies of self-reflexive narratives. These are only some of the luxury items of decadent formalist practice with which Evans has furnished her aesthetic novel of the 1860s.

Both literary decadence and literary domesticity thrive on moralities grounded in paradox. Evans struggles with a problem common to domestic writers: she must display in her novel the understanding that the good Christian housewife, busy creating a haven of morality for husband and children, should not spend time reading anything but the Bible and religious tracts. The domestic writer more often than not says, within her novel, that women should not read fiction; the paradoxical nature of the novelistic imperative "Read no novels!" appears, unglossed, as a topos of the domestic bestseller. Only if the novel is not really a novel, only if it becomes a spiritual handbook, conduct book, housekeeping guide, or Christian allegory (and, in the case of *St. Elmo*, also a pseudo-scholarly text) can it merit attention.

Along with domestic fiction's decadent embrace of generic discomfort (compare, for example, Wilde's unwillingness and eagerness to write a novel that would sell widely) goes a concern with audience reception that translates into style itself.[11] Critical of a society lacking in everything from good taste to spiritual strength (and sometimes suggesting that the two are identical), decadent artists regard themselves as an elite that can, through the very power of form, icily remove itself from the site of any modern degradation: utilitarianism, religious hypocrisy, market greed, the vulgarity of crowds. Evans imagines herself as improving a mass audience which she also hopes will never fully understand what she has to say. She creates a strangely learned narrative designed to insulate her from the same crowd that will, she hopes, blindly make her novel a bestseller.

In Evans's case, Southern pride as well as intellectual posing provide her with the certainty that she is superior to most readers by virtue of social class. Surely, she believes, the planter class would have supplied the world with both patrons and artists of high culture, had the North not destroyed the plantation system. And to the racial prejudice so often implicated in the decadent's notion of artistic aristocracy, we must add Evans's poisonous racism.

If it is a propensity to capture refined processes of feeling and consciousness rather than states of fixed belief that marks one of the decadent writer's important paths through literary history, then surely we can understand *St. Elmo* as a decadent work. Intellectual activity is one of its principal subjects; the very quality of its allusive texture insists upon our reading it as a novel about knowing. Yet for Evans knowing requires sentiment, as William James will argue in "The Sentiment of Rationality." Edna would master world knowledge, but we can never be sure of her method because sentiment and intellection are strangely synonymous in her being – those late nights in the library have a certain voluptuous meaning for her.

Edna lives her life at cross purposes: woman and writer. Her story's pattern is woven of contradictions, as if warp struggled with weft. A moralizing story told through illicit excesses of style, a domestic tale that seeks the deeply foreign, a chronicle of timelessness, a formulaic piece that would sell well but never be possessed, *St. Elmo* is in its contradictions a series of pragmatist experiments. Writing it, Evans invents her own form of literary ˙decadence in order to answer questions and solve problems she faces as a writer moored all too tenuously in her time and in her place.

IMAGINING WRITING

Evans charts within *St. Elmo* a field of artistic space, attempting there to define herself as a writer: to decide why, how, and for whom she was to write. Above all, this staunch secessionist wanted approval in a national literary market. In two recent newspaper articles, Evans had argued against sectionalism in literature. Urging the Southern writer to "rise above special pleading and write for the people who speak the English language," she warned that Southern literary chauvinism must eventually lower literary standards in the South.[12]

Evans also wanted a large audience. Her two most recent novels, *Beulah* (1859) and *Macaria; Or Altars of Sacrifice* (1864), had been popular successes. Both had been "problem" novels. The former, with liberal allusions to Ruskin's works, chronicles a young woman's intellectual and spiritual wandering in the wilderness. Beulah's story teaches that faith must be its own answer, that rational inquiry into religious belief is a terrible trap. The latter is a propagandistic account of the Confederacy, a rousing call for sectional pride. Both novels explore the lives of exceptionally intelligent, independent, forceful women who make their way painfully but surely through a world that seldom accords them either traditional womanly rewards or success in masculine terms.

With the writing of *St. Elmo*, Evans faced new problems. Her spiritual life firmly placed in Christian orthodoxy and the South humiliated and economically wounded, Evans had lost a clear sense of why she was writing at all. Readers who needed a vision of Christian womanhood could refer to *Beulah*; Southern readers no longer wanted propaganda of the sort she offered in *Macaria*; and a Northern audience had somehow to be wooed if Evans was to maintain and build upon her popularity. Only by examining the literary choices Evans made in the face of these difficulties can we begin to understand the curious quality of the novel she wrote.

Her needs struggled, one with another, at every juncture. All of the evidence suggests a woman who, in a state of turmoil, self-consciously created herself as a writer. Evans's need for funds and desire for fame contrasted with her Christian ethos of evangelical prose. Her desire to define herself as a superior being damaged her fantasy of a lovingly direct, domestic relation with a mass audience she wished to think of as "family."

Her Southern pride conflicted with her need for a Northern publisher; in parallel, her desire to discuss the Civil War competed with her certainty that she must, in order to survive as a national author, remain silent on the subject. The erosion of her faith in Southern compatriots during the war was deepened by a sense of loneliness and terrible loss at war's end. She had written to her confidante Rachel Heustis: "Oh! that we had a *government* capable of dealing with the [Union] wretches as they deserve" (Hoole, 22 January 1862); her criticism of Richmond, President Davis, and the Confederate Army makes troubling reading, embedded as it often is in letters of private worries or frolicsome accounts of parties with military men.

All these needs translated themselves into an inability to define her audience, and, concomitantly, a confusion in her definition of literary success. Evans leaves a record of an artist troubled by the questions of who is to read her, buy her, and follow her. Her needs translated as well into stylistic choices, most notably her invention of a decadent prose within *St. Elmo*. The writing of this novel is a curious chapter in literary history that requires gradual unfolding; first we must discover the questions which Evans herself pragmatically explored, often seeking answers by stirring sentimental domesticity and elitist aesthetic ambition into an unstable mixture.

The decadently reflexive strategy of writing a novel about writing a novel enables Evans to resolve some of the conflicts she feels. While domestic novelists typically portray themselves as humble and essentially private women, writing almost by accident or in dire financial need, Evans creates an image of a woman artist of vast will, deliberation, and solitude.[13] Like Ruskin, Evans wishes to discern the artist's optimal distance from other people. Edna Earl's coldness toward everyone in the novel (except a dying, crippled child) reflects Evans's own defensive turning away from potential antagonists: critics and mass audience alike. Evans's persona, Edna, writing in solitude at the Southern estate of "Le Bocage" and creating a fictional world of Oriental lore, distances herself physically from her audience and impersonally from her text as surely as did Flaubert writing *Salammbô* (1862) at Croisset, or Nabokov writing in the borrowed houses and motel rooms of his exile from Russia.

To say that Evans imagines herself a writer through the process of creating *St. Elmo* is also to speak of her self-annulment. As the novel ends her heroine apparently accepts St. Elmo's commandment that she never write again: "There shall be no more books written! No more study, no more toil, no more anxiety, no more heartaches!"[14] Edna's surrender of freedom mirrors another, less absolute surrender made by Evans, her creator: the entire arc of the novel's plot, formulaic in the extreme, expresses Evans's own apparent willingness to give up artistic autonomy and self-respect, in order to write what will sell. She offers a tried-and-true tale to a public wishing only as much novelty as will create in it the desire to consume yet another version of a familiar product. Although the trajectory of the novel's plot comes home to Edna's silencing by St. Elmo, its texture of conflict nonetheless traces a path across the space of freedom. Within the novel, Evans's Edna establishes, by setting *her* first novel in a middle East patterned on Ruskinian myth, her right to create freely, to write with imaginative abandon and scholarly intensity. Her "vindication of the unity of mythologies" she decides to cast in novelistic form:

A fair young priestess of the temple of Neith, in the sacred city of Sais – where people of all climes collected to witness the festival of lamps – becoming skeptical of the miraculous attributes of the statues she had been trained to serve and worship, and impelled by an earnest love of truth to seek a faith that would satisfy her reason and purify her heart, is induced to question minutely the religious tenets of travellers who visited the temple, and thus familiarized herself with all existing creeds and hierarchies. The lore so carefully garnered is finally analyzed, classified, and inscribed on papyrus. The delineation of scenes and sanctuaries in different latitudes, from Lhasa to Copan, gave full exercise to Edna's descriptive power, but imposed much labor in the departments of physical geography and architecture. (p. 108)

It is possible that Evans encountered Neith (the "Egyptian Athena") in Ruskin's *Ethics of the Dust* (1865). It is certain, though, that Evans read Ruskin and admired his mix of mythology and history.[15]

At the same time, the subject of Edna's scholarly novel, however arcane, places her squarely in the tradition of evangelical piety that informed contemporary ethnology: "the idea flashed across her mind that a rigid analysis and comparison of all the mythologies of the world would throw some light on the problem of ethnology, and in conjunction with philology settle the vexed question" (p. 85). The "vexed question" here is that of ethnology's very undertaking: whether it is possible to prove, using primarily printed records and philological evidence, that all of mankind, in all its diversity, is a single human species created by God. Evans, a Christian woman, clearly wanted to believe in what James would call a "through-and-through" Christian cosmos, although in the end she cannot. Ethnologists such as James Cowles Prichard, who published his *Researches into the Physical History of Mankind* in five volumes between 1836 and 1847, studied the "evolution of varieties" within the human species, using "similarities of physical type, religion, political institutions, and above all, language," which he insisted was the most reliable indicator of racial affinities.[16] Augusta Evans modeled her heroine's scholarly undertaking on a "science" that meant to prove Christian orthodoxy by a powerful, implicit metaphor: mankind considered as a tree, "with contemporary tribal twigs linked by major racial branches to the trunk of a single human species . . . [rooted] near the point where Noah's ark had come to rest in Southwest Asia."[17] Whether Evans read Prichard himself or others of his school, she is clearly a disciple. All of Edna's scholarly work, pre-Darwinian and creationist in its intellectual principles, is a type of Biblically based anthropology. Further, the very eclectic style of her learning is reminiscent of the ethnological discipline; as George Stocking points out, "ethnology may be viewed as a science of leftovers or residues. It was . . . a fusion of diverse styles of inquiry, derived from the natural historical, the moral philosophical, and the humanistic traditions" (p. 48).

Once launched as a successful novelist, however, Edna reneges on her artistic-ethnological freedom at the insistence of her mentor, Mr. Manning, who convinces her that she will never master world mythology. She proceeds to a traditionally domestic production, *Shining Thrones of the Hearth*. Writing this book, designed to soothe readers and sell well, constitutes a major step on the way to the full sacrifice of artistic power that closes the novel. Despite her willingness to propel her heroine into the free-fall of popularity-seeking, however, Evans never ceases to make grand claims for Edna, bestowing upon her qualities that unfailingly transport her directly out of the world of Christian domesticity. Although Edna Earl wishes to be a chastening, nurturing writer – "her high standard demanded that all books should be to a certain extent didactic, wandering like evangels among the people" (p. 107) – she also defines a space for herself that is autonomous rather than didactic. Because she wants to be seen as a *maker* of worlds, she creates an exotic world within her novel and also shuts herself off from polite society and her adoptive mother. This autonomy she claims in order to create fictions and scholarly articles which we, as readers, are never allowed to see. We hear about them, but the works themselves, like the arcane languages Edna masters, are hidden from our eyes. This (fictional) writer's work is both extremely public (when Edna begins to publish she is a popular success) and also private.

Given the astonishing amount of learning and research Edna Earl transmutes into her scholarship *qua* fiction, we probably wouldn't understand her writing anyway. Should we suffer from any delusions of our power to absorb what we would read had we a chance to see it, the *mise-en-abîme* of *St. Elmo* itself – Edna's own novels and articles mirror the scholarly novel by Evans in which they appear – disabuses us of our own pride as readers. Few among us can claim the fantastic breadth of knowledge that Evans attributes to Edna. To be a writer, then, is to give voice to nothing less than genius cultivated by superhuman powers of application. Edna, after mastering by the age of eighteen many branches of learning and several ancient and modern languages, works as a governess all day and writes all night for several years running.

This writer stands at the center of learned culture; Edna wishes to understand everything that mankind has ever been. Yet her fabulous learning also places her wholly apart and outside her culture, since no one – no other character and certainly no single reader – can meet her intellectual expectations. *Finnegan's Wake* comes to mind. This second writer's place is precisely apart from the arc of the domestic plot; it expands slowly, gorgeously, in the fascinating but unassimilable texture of allusion that constitutes the novel's narrative mode. Writing in Victorian America, Evans joins the Modernists in aspiring to an art of the elusive. Yet she is unable to deny the sentimental, relational, and didactic aspects of her art. Hence the complex truths of her novel, which will be echoed by the complex truth of high Modernism itself. It would be a mistake to read this novel as either sentimental/didactic or autonomous. Just as Modernism was not founded wholly on rupture, neither was domestic sentimentality solely a product of intimate connection. An important subject of *St. Elmo*, a novel about novel-writing, is the complex relation of such polarities.

Thus Evans straddles, as a writer, two worlds, each endlessly dissolving into the other. *St. Elmo* imagines itself and other worthy literary works as adjuncts to the Bible, like *Pilgrim's Progress*, that help make real and immediate some abstract Biblical lessons. The writer of such prose takes her place, personally, on the hearthstones of American homes. When one of her articles is accepted by a Northern magazine, Edna "thanked God that she was considered worthy of communicating with her race through the medium of a magazine so influential and celebrated" (p. 171). Evans's phrasing delicately balances Edna's authorial pride against her Christian humility.

In fact, Evans cannot avoid the kind of doubleness this statement delivers, because her every consideration of Edna as a domestic, Christian writer simultaneously resituates her in a realm that threatens safe,

domestic enclosures. When Edna spends a quiet evening at home reading, she serenely peruses not a gift album, domestic handbook, or novel,
but rather Aristotle's *Organon* (p. 145). When she modestly hopes for that
"certain" letter, it is an acceptance letter from a high-toned editor that
starts her heart's ardent beating. The authorial venue Evans chooses is
an impossible location, because it is neither here (domesticity) nor there
(the wide, wide world of high culture). Evans places Edna in a gracious
Southern mansion, but we learn soon enough that enclosing the orphan within that house is not unlike enclosing a field flower within the
adjacent hothouses: strange flowers with curious odors can be forced
to bloom. The literature Edna creates within the home will never
be simply domestic in nature; as she writes and studies in St. Elmo's
library/museum/mausoleum, that which she creates must deviate from
the wisdom of the hearth. Although Evans eventually imagines the space
of high literary culture as secular, cosmopolitan, and mercantile when
she sends her character to conquer literary New York, she begins by
imagining the space of elevated culture as the Southern home. Yet hers
is the home of wealth, extravagant seclusion, and, as we shall see when we
stroll through St. Elmo's rooms, a place which can itself deny the very
ideas of orthodoxy and stability. Let us examine just how Evans conducts a pragmatist experiment in decadence that leads outward from
the hearth to the far reaches of the earth and the imagination.

DECORATING ST. ELMO'S ROOMS

Writing soon after the horrors of the Civil War, Evans explores several
pathways away from the pain of recent history. One of her experiments
involves nothing less than the transformation of chronological history
itself, a vast, fictional experiment in synchronism. If time is to exist,
paradoxically, outside of time, what better way to effect this than to
pool time within her narrative? Evans slows and even stops the narrative
flow of her novel, as we have seen, by overstocking it with intellectual
bric-à-brac. Its accounts of local and contemporary events – the trivi-
alities of mid-century American domestic life – she arranges alongside
references to ancient and modern history across world cultures. When
Evans blithely – and to our ears, embarrassingly – compares the childish
Edna's face to that of Lorenzo de'Medicis [sic] (p. 6) or her dog's face
to that of the "Norse Managarmar" (p. 25), she implies that this girl
and her pet can be understood in terms of histories and myths wholly
outside a local scale of spatial and chronological reference. By making

such comparisons, Evans also presents her own credentials as a writer controlling vast stores of images. She is a writer of fancy, which "receives all its materials ready made from the law of association," and she is proud of it.[18] Like Rossetti and Ruskin, she tours mythologies, returning with complex images that she can first embroider or rearrange, and then place into the spaces, increasingly overstocked, of her works of art.

Writing in an ethnological tradition, Evans shows less interest in a chronological or developmental notion of human experience than in a spatial approach akin to Ruskin's filigree-work. And like Ruskin, she firmly centers all patterns in Christian doctrine, only to adopt, seemingly despite her orthodox belief, multiple centers. That is, Evans begins with a desire to demonstrate the diffusion of all civilization from a central point – that mooring place of Noah's ark – rather than the evolution of multiple, independent civilizations over time. Even domestic arrangements, including those of Victorian America, are for Evans so much evidence for the ethnological unity and original completion of the human race:

If the seers of geology are correct in assuming that the age of the human race is coincident with that of the alluvial stratum, from eighty to one hundred centuries, are not domestic traditions and household customs the great arteries in which beats the social life of humanity, and which, veining all epochs, link the race in homogeneity? (p. 116)

The "veining of all epochs" suggests as much a spatial as a chronological connection, Evans own "multiplex" whole of "differenced" parts, to borrow George Eliot's description of form. And this very similarity and linkage of (one) domestic tradition implies a *lack* of development or evolution that implies a deathly – or even potentially degenerate – stasis. All was set at the Flood; it remained only for conservative domesticity to pulse outward in time and space.

While Evans's goal is to study world mythology as an elaboration of one origin, she cannot be immune to what she discovers in the process, human cultural development in all its exotic complexity. The desire to jettison Christian didacticism in favor of a fascination with mythology for mythology's sake is everywhere evident in *St. Elmo*, in part because Christian ethology's spatializing principle potentially opposes the Christian will to think purposively or to act in time. Victorian Modernist textures reveal more of their complexity: while we must learn to see the relational energy of sentiment and didacticism in texts by men (Ruskin and Rossetti, for example), we must also learn to see the diffusion of sentimental energy toward languor and the departure from didacticism in texts by women such as Evans and others of her era. Having acknowledged what we have long known not to see, we must then accept the cross-gendered complexities of Victorian Modernist texts.

The ambivalence of Evans's narrative, reproducing as it does a tension within the very ethnology that informs her fiction (as well as her own lived tensions with Southern society), should not be underestimated. If the domestic writer judges actions by their consonance with the Ten Commandments and the Sermon on the Mount, surely *this* writer has something else, something potentially dangerous, in mind. The domestic, Christian, popular Evans seeks to join the cosmopolitan, exotic, and elitist Evans, to smooth the rift in the plot of her life, by experiments with a new battle strategy: not the silencing of history, but its utter reconfiguration in space. We can watch her at work as she decorates St. Elmo's rooms.

In the Murray household the reprobate St. Elmo has his own suite of rooms, and these we enter with trepidation. Since the domestic novel is understood to supply a warm, capacious, relaxing space into which the reader can sink, sure of having her expectations met, the creation of discomfiting, alien, threatening rooms within the household can signal the frailty of generic promises. Domestic novels occur around hearths, actual and symbolic, and their stories remove heroines from the hearth only in order to restore them there, hundreds of pages later. Not a circular journey, since the hearth gained at novel's end is that of adult womanhood, the progress between hearths ultimately traces a sure path, even if it involves some labyrinthine wandering. The point for reader and heroine alike is to move forward teleologically. By orphaning Edna, Evans signals early on that she has this story in mind; and indeed she propels Edna from Cumberland Gap to Le Bocage, New York City, and back to the Southern estate whose mistress she becomes.

Movement also occurs within the smaller context of the home itself. Passing from parlor to kitchen to bedroom and back again, maneuvering endlessly within the confined space of domesticity, the domestic heroine traces time's circularity. Domesticity reveals its dark underside of immobilization and incarceration, and their ties with Gothic sublimity. So it is that we enter St. Elmo's rooms with Edna, who wishes to replace his copy of Dante there, in a moment of uncertainty, for Evans utterly stops time at its threshold, and we cannot be sure to what effect. The frisson begins as standard period Gothic: St. Elmo's rooms are sinister, inhabited by the spirit of his ominous personality and threatening sexuality, certainly meant to thrill. But the room belies our comfortable expectations of discomfort when Evans simply suspends narration in an entire page of description. Not only do we linger in words that take us nowhere, but they describe arrested life, dead civilizations, denatured nature, thus doubly strangling narrative vitality. Even the eye's motion seems drugged:

The narrow, vaulted passage leading to Mr. Murray's [St. Elmo's] suite of rooms was dim and gloomy when Edna approached the partly opened door of the rotunda, whence issued a stream of light. Timidly she crossed the threshold and stood within on the checkered floor, whose polished tiles glistened under the glare of gas from bronze brackets representing Telamones, that stood at regular intervals around the apartment. The walls were painted in Saracenic style, and here and there hung specimens of Oriental armor – Turcoman cimeters, Damascus swords, Bedouin lances, and a crimson silk flag, with heavy gold fringe, surmounted by a crescent... near[by] was a circular [table] of black marble, inlaid with red onyx and lapis lazuli, which formed a miniature zodiac similar to that at Denderah, while in the middle of this table sat a small Murano hour-glass, filled with sand from the dreary valley of El Ghor.... (p. 46)

Evans interrupts the description in order to allow Edna to return the Dante to St. Elmo.

When the description resumes, St. Elmo paces through his strange cage, which seems to emanate directly from his tortured mind. The qualities of superfluity and exorbitant eclecticism are its principal messages:

When the echo of her retreating footsteps died away, St. Elmo threw his cigar out of the window, and walked up and down the quaint and elegant rooms, whose costly *bizarrerie* would more appropriately have adorned a villa of Parthenope or Lucanian Sybaris, than a country-house in *soi-disant* "republican" America. Oval ormolu tables, buhl chairs, and oaken and marquetrie cabinets, loaded with cameos, intaglios, Abraxoids, whose "*erudition*" would have filled Mnesarchus with envy, and challenged the admiration of the Samian lapidary who engraved the ring of Polycrates; these and numberless articles of *vertu* testified to the universality of what St. Elmo called his "world-scrapings," and to the reckless extravagance and archaistic taste of the collector. On a *verd-antique* table lay a satin cushion holding a vellum MS, bound in blue velvet, whose uncial letters were written in purple ink, powdered with gold-dust, while the margins were stiff with gilded illuminations... In the space between the tall windows that fronted the lawn hung a weird, life-size picture that took strange hold on the imagination of all who looked at it. A gray-haired Cimbrian Prophetess, in white vestments and brazen girdle... stood... watching, with divining eyes, the stream of blood which trickled from the throat of the slaughtered human victim down into the large brazen kettle beneath the scaffold.... On a sculptured slab, that once formed a portion of the architrave of the Cave Temple at Elephanta, was a splendid marble miniature, four feet high, of the miracle of Saracenic architecture, the Taj Mahal at Agra. The elaborate carving resembled lacework, and the beauty of the airy dome and slender, glittering minarets of this mimic tomb of Noor-Mahal could find no parallel, save in the superb and matchless original. (pp. 48–50)

This quotation presents less than a quarter of the entire description; even so, its excesses are apparent. St. Elmo's "museum" memorializes and even replicates for the observer his anomic, self-destructive and paradoxically static wanderings. St. Elmo has failed to place himself within a unified and still vital culture that would help him to live a meaningful life.[19] Yet it testifies as well to the Christian culture which he will embrace at novel's end, insofar as Evans believes that the pagan excess of the room is *potentially* subject to simplification by the Christian ethnologist who studies connections among just such diverse cultural artifacts of mankind's history. Such a potential discipline is not work for scholars only, however. Every Christian housewife, in ordering her domain (rugs from one source, furniture from another) establishes her own Christian cultural microcosm.

At the same time, St. Elmo's rooms, like those in Rossetti's house at 16 Cheyne Walk, testify to the impulse of exploring the layered, the intense, the grotesque, and the imaginative. Evans fills St. Elmo's rooms with that which can never be brought to a fixed order. Immediately the room announces itself as decadent, primarily because of its eerie similarities to the decadent rooms we know so much better. Looking backward from 1867 in literary history, we feel the presence of Poe – his beautiful, creepily intellectual, and dying women, his fascination with monomania and aristocratic doubles, his strange interiors furnished with tapestries, paintings, exotic objects from the east. But looking forward, we feel ourselves, here in St. Elmo's suite, uncannily at home in the rooms of Des Esseintes, of *À Rebours* (*Against Nature*) (1884). Indeed, Evans's entire tableau seems to echo a literary scene it actually precedes by eighteen years. We might say that the "Decadent Sixties" have come into view. Furthermore, the description of St. Elmo's rooms implies the values of Huysmans, Pater, and Wilde. Like Des Esseintes, who believes that true civilization ended in the west with the coming of the barbarians to Rome and Gaul, St. Elmo leads a monkish existence in his chambers because he hates the barbarian masses. St. Elmo is burning himself out in contempt for the world; his travels over the globe, his absences for years at a time from Le Bocage, testify to a goading from deep within his character. Like Des Esseintes, St. Elmo has radically reconceived good taste in order to try, by willed excess, to press back against the "pressure of [a distressing] reality."[20]

St. Elmo decadently surrounds himself with the iconography of death: his coffin-like suite of rooms encloses objects which, detached from their living context, constitute a graveyard of world culture. Further, every object itself speaks eloquently of death – if not specifically, as do the tombs and images of slaughtered victims, then by implication. The entire scene explores the transformation of real things into their deathly existence in art, embalming them in the ointments of exotic diction and hypnotic rhythm. We are reminded of the statement in *A Rebours* that, "as a matter of fact, artifice was considered by Des Esseintes to be the distinctive mark of human genius."[21]

This is a passage that strikes at the heart of sentimental domesticity in the attempt to kill it, too, into art. From time to time Evans allows a flicker of standard morality. She mentions the hypocrisy of "*soi-disant* 'republican' America," the "reckless extravagance" of the collector, and the "whim" of capturing lotus flowers on glass that "had cost a vast amount of time, trouble, and money," but in all cases the passage seems strangely to celebrate such deviance from common sense. Here, within the very stronghold of the home, Evans imagines a space antithetical to it.

Or is this space so foreign to domesticity? Certainly St. Elmo's rooms challenge the notion that the home is to be a pastoral retreat from the rigors of the public sphere; a contemporary reviewer in the *New York Times* complains, "What charm there can be in such uncomfortable furniture we are unable to divine. One cannot sit down on a scimitar, or dine off a sapphire. If a man chooses to surround himself with the trumpery of the stage, what has he done to entitle himself to our reverence?"[22] The central fact is that these theatrical rooms intensify domesticity in order to reveal to us the very energies that domesticity has always attempted to suppress. In St. Elmo's rooms literary domesticity and literary decadence meet, for if a limit of domesticity is decadence, it is also true that *a crucial source of decadence is domesticity*. The rooms of the home, carefully furnished, insulated from the sphere of bourgeois getting and spending, and providing an alternative system of morality to that of the marketplace, can be seen as the space in which domesticity sinks into decadence, or, alternatively, as the space in which decadence seeks its origins in a feminized world of marginality, first imposed, then imaginatively chosen.

St. Elmo's rooms, seen in this light, become the site of domesticity critically explored. They are both separate from and part of the domestic scene: Le Bocage, like 16 Cheyne Walk, features a menagerie of strange animals from around the world roaming its gracious lawns; the estate as a whole is a place of death into which the young Edna arrives, only to begin dying herself. These decadent rooms are always the site of surveillance, for in them St. Elmo hides when he returns from his travels, spies on Edna, and tests her with diabolical schemes. Surely the Christian home, likewise, is an enclosed space in which and for which woman must answer to the man who comes and goes. Indeed, in one of the moral tests St. Elmo continually stages for Edna, he leaves her with a golden key and instructions not to open a certain lock, a stunning image of woman's compromised freedom within her household.

These rooms constitute a museum filled with wonderfully useless objects. In this superfluity they resemble the idealized home in which labor gives way to gracious leisure and consumption for its own sake. As she figures forth St. Elmo's quarters, Evans points out the contradiction at the heart of domesticity, its dual goals of salvation by works and a sensitive, passive appreciation of comfort. Furthermore, as a museum these rooms testify to the spoils of the successful masculine life – St. Elmo has gone out into the world to win them – but also to the feminized nature of his "world-scrapings": these urns, manuscripts, and scimitars are not emblems of life in the marketplace or battlefield, but of an obsessive need to buy in order to make private the world itself.

Perhaps most significantly to Evans's self-creation as a writer, St. Elmo's rooms are a library. Many of their *objets* do double duty as things and as texts; they are literally written upon, usually in foreign languages. The books and manuscripts, conversely, are themselves things, made of ivory or dusted with gold. Here in this library-museum Edna discovers her vocation: "The hoary associations and typical significance of the numerous relics that crowded Mr. Murray's rooms seized upon Edna's fancy, linked her sympathies with the huge pantheistic systems of the Orient, and filled her mind with waifs from the dusky realm of a mythology that seemed to antedate all the authentic chronological computations of man"(p. 85). Here it is, under the "nepenthe influence" of books and sarcophagi, that "the idea flashed across her mind that a rigid analysis and comparison of all the mythologies of the world" would be her work (p. 85). Domesticity's enclosed spaces, like every kind of enforced limitation, become the spaces of transgression; all of (masculine) culture is possessed metonymically by Edna as she studies and writes in this room. Rigid analysis is precisely what Evans gestures toward but never practices. It comes as no surprise that Evans confuses these rooms and Edna's own richly decadent writings: "The manuscript was a mental tapestry, into which she had woven exquisite shades of thought, and curious and quaint devices and rich, glowing imagery that flecked the groundwork with purple and amber and gold" (p. 279).

Knowing full well that, with this passage, she has indulged herself and her characters in examining the forbidden underside of domesticity – home as the locus of imagination and deathly excess – Evans is quick to recant. Here, denial becomes the final luxury; having titillated and hypnotized us for several pages, Evans closes the passage with a paragraph of harsh, moralistic judgment: this is the site of death and unhappiness, a place where "light, childish feet" and "mirthful laughter" have never been heard, where all is "treacherously, repulsively lustrous; where "the dewy gleam of the merry morning of life" has never reached (p. 50).

It is this very site which, as the novel closes, Evans must take care to detoxify. Visiting Le Bocage during the time that St. Elmo is undergoing his moral transformation, Edna returns to the library, now a scene of domesticity:

Oxalis and heliotrope peeped at her over the top of the lotos vases; one of a pair of gauntlets had fallen on the carpet near the cameo cabinet; two or three newspapers and a meerschaum lay upon a chair; several theological works were scattered on the sofa. . . . Just in front of the Taj Mahal was a handsome copy of Edna's novel, and a beautiful morocco-bound volume containing a collection of all her magazine sketches. (p. 318)

The Cimbrian Prophetess, we learn, has been replaced by a copy of "Titian's Jesus." It is the presence of the newspapers and Edna's journalistic pieces that most strikes us, for with these ephemeral objects symbolizing the renewal of daily life, Evans reassures us that St. Elmo has reentered the present, the comfortable certainties of life measured in weeks and years rather than in millennia. The casual disorder of the room shows that he no longer values so highly the "mythology that seemed to antedate all the authentic chronological computations of man" (p. 85). He also telegraphs his willingness to dwell in bourgeois culture: the fine bindings gather only what everyone in America is reading and newspapers take the place of Aramaic paraphrases of the Old Testament. But in order to fully appreciate Evans's redecoration at novel's end, it might be helpful to understand in context her initial decoration of St. Elmo's rooms.

We might consider, for example, an actual house decorated "aesthetically": Olana, the summer home and studio of the American landscape

Figure 5 *Olana: Court Hall View*

painter Frederic E. Church (1826–1900).[23] Built during the 1870s and
expanded soon after, Olana reflected, in both its architecture and interior decoration, the Aesthetic movement in America. Looking to British
Aestheticism which had itself enjoyed the perquisites of empire by plun-
dering the Far East and the Islamic world, the American Aesthetic
movement incorporated architectural design and *objets* from Japan,
Turkey, Persia, and India. In order to justify (however unconsciously)
such imperialist aesthetics, "the designers of the Aesthetic movement in-
ternationalized the principles of the style. The vocabulary of art for art's
sake partially masked the degree to which this stylistic appropriation was
indeed a form of cultural appropriation."[24] Consider Olana's central
court Hall, a slightly younger cousin to St. Elmo's wing of Le Bocage.
With its arched windows, Turkish rugs, Egyptian ibis, Buddha, medieval
armor, "mosarabic floral stenciling on the spandul and across the interior
of the arches," Assyrian figures on stair risers (and all the rest), it engen-
ders in the viewer a pleasurable visual hysteria in which historical periods,
artistic styles, and cultural ideas never fully resolve into comfortable
harmony.[25]

The room might symbolize a vast syncretism, but for its insistence on sensation in the present moment over religious belief and its symbols. In fact, what both Olana and Le Bocage represent is a vision of sublime synchronicity in which things and styles are pulled out of context to form an exotic multiplexity, to use George Eliot's term. These rooms are endlessly extensive in their reach – anything imaginable can be brought in or taken out. Through interior decoration and *mise-en-scène*, Church and Evans create material and verbal manifestos of extensive sublimity: "*Peri Platous*." The immediate, aesthetic intensity of our experience of these objects and architectural details matters more than any scheme of classification that would depend on careful study of distant cultures or any accurate assessment of style and period.

While Le Bocage is a decadent room in comparison to the sprightlier, less death-obsessed Olana, it represents Evans's own flight from time and geography, a decade earlier than the generally accepted period for the advent of Aestheticism in America: the genteel era.[26] Evans attempts nothing less than the obliteration of chronology itself. As we have seen, the ethnological impulse guides her to the fascinations of the foreign and the old for their own sake, not just for the theological evidence they provide. To have so much of history present and unaccounted for is to reconceive historicity. Lest we believe that she limited this experiment to these few passages, it is important to remember that her entire narrative does just what Church attempts in his home: she deposits one cultural artifact after another in order to create a prose that is truly abstract, a pattern of glancing words, rebounding allusions, reverberating symbols, all of which in the end point to, but never fully claim, authorial power to fashion an utterly new world apart from actual time and place.

Through such a prose she has attempted, as we shall learn, to escape sectionalism and refurbish the realities of 1866, and she has also thrown into question the didactic Christianity she is at such pains to proffer. How to believe solely in Christianity when a vast eclecticism overtakes her novel like the sleep-protecting briars of fairytale castles? *St. Elmo* is a deep forgetting, a confusion made possible by the power of arrangement; it is equally a document in the history of literary decadence in its search for a way to express life's conflicting claims. Evans can effect the metamorphosis of home-centered Christian piety into a religion of art, itself unstable and subject to transformation, because domesticity has always carried within it the seeds of aesthetic rebellion.

A THOROUGHLY UNCOMFORTABLE PERSON

"The world of concrete personal experiences to which the street belongs is multitudinous beyond imagination, tangled, muddy, painful and perplexed," James tells his audience for the lecture that was to become the first chapter of *Pragmatism*, and he insists that a philosophy limited to the refinements of an intellectual system cannot be satisfying (*P*, p. 18). It would be a "monument of artificiality" (*P*, p. 18). Considering Evans as a pragmatist, we have begun with matters both artificial and abstract: the sub-genre of domestic fiction, the creation of a decadent domestic aestheticism by verbal means, nineteenth-century systematic ethnology, and literary ties to Ruskin and Rossetti.

Evans's novel, however, presents a warning to the scholarly Edna against such intellectualism with its dependence on rigid systems of abstractions. Edna's Northern editor advises her to "[b]urn the enclosed MS, the erudition and archaisms of which would fatally nauseate the intellectual dyspeptics who read my 'Maga,' and write sketches of home life – descriptions of places and things that you understand better than recondite analogies of ethical creeds and mythologic systems . . . " (p. 150). Both Evans and her fictional creation, Edna, follow this advice to avoid "recondite analogies" not by eliminating intellectualism altogether but by adding to it a good dose of painful and perplexed life on the street – or rather, in the house. We should not lose sight of the fact that the authorial space thus defined – domestic but foreign, comfortable but troubling, popular but unapproachable, evangelistic but self-absorbed – has everything to do with the actual geography in which Evans had to make her way as a Southern woman writer who needed to live by her pen. She needed, in Stevens's words, to believe that her "fragmentary tragedy" (*CP*, p. 324) was susceptible of expression (however disjointed) and remediation (however incomplete). What, then, was Evans's "world of concrete personal experiences," the perplexities attending her life of the street?

Simply stated, Evans, the oldest of eight children whose father gradually lost his health and his fortune, had to make money while retaining her self-respect as a Southern lady. Only by publication in the North, however, could her writing find the life she desired for it. Her publishing experiences prior to *St. Elmo* had been colored by sectional allegiances. *Beulah* had been first rejected by Appleton, a publishing house of high cultural pretensions, then accepted by Derby and Jackson only after an episode which Derby himself remembered as exotically vivid in a Southern manner. "In the summer of 1859," Derby recalls, "a young lady of pleasant address and marked intelligence" paid him a visit in New York, admitted that she had failed to place her manuscript elsewhere, and received his promise that "some members of the family" would read it. He continues:

When Miss Evans called for my decision, she was accompanied by her cousin, Colonel John W. Jones, of Georgia, who was the bearer of the manuscript at the first interview. Colonel Jones was a fiery young Southerner, and told me afterwards that although his back was turned while examining some books on the shelves, he had listened to the conversation and began to think by my tone and manner that I would reject the book, and in case I did, he intended to hurl one of my own publications at my head! Colonel Jones was a most estimable man, devotedly attached to his cousin. He fell at the head of his regiment at the sanguinary battle of Gettysburg, fighting for the cause which both of them believed to be sacred.[27]

The issue of Northern publication was painful in a variety of ways. *Macaria* had been published during the war by a Richmond house, on crude brown paper, and was seized and burned in the North.[28] Even friendly editors such as Derby, themselves victims of a romantic mythology, seemed condescendingly happy to meet Southern "characters" and to admire male military figures more than female authors. Evans had long watched Southern magazines fight unsuccessful battles for existence, while Southerners subscribed to Northern magazines. Part of this particular sectional battle involved the very phenomena of high culture, for Southern editors, proud of their classical educations, often favored highbrow material that could not compete with the contents of popular Northern magazines.[29]

The extravagantly displayed learning of *St. Elmo* would, then, have been in part a statement of regional identification: Southern gentlemen might have been quaintly fiery, but Southern gentlemen and ladies alike were certainly classically learned. Every allusion in the text is a mark of Southern pride, a political statement pervading the very substance of a novel that never directly raises the issue of sectionalism. As a writing woman and as a Southerner, Evans wanted to define herself as classically educated and more, yet she also desired to sell. With G. W. Carleton, the original publisher of *St. Elmo*, she reached as much of a compromise between these two positions as she could have hoped for. Although Carleton fell short of the high-cultured echelon of publishers such as Appleton or Stone and Kimball, it attracted its mass audience not just with fiction and humor, but also with dictionaries, handbooks, encyclopedias, and translations of French literature.[30] In a curious way, both of our authors, the fictional Edna and the real Evans, saw their work as a means of imparting information to readers, thus improving them. A powerful editor counsels Edna to remove the book-learning from her novel: "People read novels merely to be amused, not educated; and they will not tolerate technicalities and abstract speculation in lieu of exciting plots and melodramatic denouements" (p. 237). Edna, and her creator, Evans, are out to prove him wrong. Both succeed.

For it is true that *St. Elmo* is less melodramatic and exciting than many other novels of its type and era, and it is also true that Evans's novel was immediately successful. When Carleton realized how vulnerable the novel was to mockery by the critics, he did the best thing possible to increase its sales by commissioning a parody, Charles H. Webb's *St. Twel'mo; or, the Cuneiform Cyclopedist of Chattanooga* (1867), itself a success.[31] Hart reports that "a survey of booksellers in 1876 revealed that the most widely bought fiction included such tested works as *Jane Eyre*, *St. Elmo*, *The Scarlet Letter*, *Uncle Tom's Cabin*, *Barriers Burned Away*, *Griffith Gaunt*, *Under Two Flags* and *The Wide, Wide World* (pp. 168–169). Mott notes that "children were named 'St. Elmo'; towns, streets, hotels were christened with the magic name" (p. 127). And as late as 1923, *St. Elmo* was still polling among librarians as among the most popular novels in America.[32] Evans carefully plants within *St. Elmo* the idea of her own popular success; the New York City socialite Mrs. Andrews "declares she can't live without" the magazine in which Edna regularly publishes (p. 234); and Edna herself is urged by a "pertinacious young book vendor ... with his arms full of copies of her own books" (p. 339) to stop and buy.

The publishing history of *St. Elmo* suggests that Evans had arrived at a level neither so high as she liked to claim nor so low as she feared to fall. Carleton was not publishing the "best" authors, nor was it producing only morally suspect sensationalism. More agonized, perhaps, is Evans's assessment of the audience she courts. In her novel, she portrays the writer as one who turns to fiction (away from history, theology, and ethnography) specifically because she wishes to "popularize a subject bristling with recondite archaisms and philologic problems" (p. 108). Yet both Mr. Manning, the New York editor, and St. Elmo profess a disdain for the mass audience of novel-readers, the former observing, "the world of novel-readers constitute a huge hippodrome" (p. 238), and the latter quoting Dr. Johnson, "I am bound to furnish good definitions, but not brains to comprehend them" (p. 141). Although Edna repeatedly professes a respect for her audience, her humility as a nurturing mother-writer always exudes a whiff of condescension.

Thankful as Edna is for her audience – "While the critics snarled, the mass of readers warmly approved" (p. 287) – she never approves of either group. Similarly, Evans's authorial space is created not only by her profound sectional identity, but also by her intention to exclude readers, punish recalcitrant reviewers, and demonstrate her ability to reside in the community without being of it. Feeling her ideals betrayed by the South both during the war and also afterwards, when figures such as Congressman J. M. Curry capitulated too soon to Reconstruction; contemptuous and fearful of the North; and defensive as an intellectual woman intruding upon the male world of letters, Evans had no place to live, no place but home. "Home" became for her a series of reticulated enclosures within which she could nurse her rancor and develop an aesthetic that takes as its forming energy the bitter truth of dislocation. The abusive, jarring aesthetic that she developed must ever be cloaked in a velvety, soothing, evangelical domesticity.

Upon its publication, *St. Elmo* evoked two responses: a rapid acceptance by a mass audience, and an ambivalent reception by professional reviewers. The second response always focused on the book's inaccessible prose, and was often written in querulous tones, accusing Evans, for example, of "lugging in, on every occasion, a mass of odds and ends of knowledge . . . almost all of it, as she uses it, worse than useless."[33] Despite the book's popularity, this reviewer tells us that Edna Earl is detested by readers as a "thoroughly uncomfortable person." Another reviewer complains that "so overdrawn and unnatural are the characters introduced that they fail to live, move, and have their being, remaining to the end but the creations of an ill-regulated and heated fancy."[34] To a certain extent reviewers redraw the battle lines of the recent war. Although Southern reviewers do indict Evans for false learning, accusing her of cribbing knowledge from dictionaries and encyclopedias, they also urge readers to notice that Evans's moral message is admirable and to understand that the novel is not meant to be realistic: "With a fancy bold and fervid – with an imagination as warm and luxurious as the breath of the orange groves of her own sunny land – with a taste cultivated and refined by a thorough knowledge of classical and modern belles-lettres . . . we are ready to crown her Queen Regnant of Southern Literature."[35] Both Northern and Southern writers assume that the book's moralizing is its most important aspect; some Southerners, while wishing for simpler prose, at least allow that something other than a realist standard is being set within this novel, so susceptible to mockery yet so compelling at the same time.

But it is perhaps the anonymous reviewer in the *New York Times* of 5 January 1867, who inadvertently comes closest to the kind of insight into the novel we will find most interesting. He reckons Evans as one among "the most degraded school of modern novelists" and castigates her for creating St. Elmo as one of "the Corsair school of heroes." This reviewer wishes her to write with more originality, like Cooper or Hawthorne, and to save us from yet another clichéd Byronic hero, "the well-known gentleman who has exhausted every form of vice." We acknowledge that there *is* something degenerate about *St. Elmo*, but it is the paradoxically fresh odor of literary decadence that suffuses it, the artistic attempt to clear a way for the new by celebrating the intensity of what appears exotic, old, and *excessive*.

One point of origin for the decadence we have seen in *St. Elmo* is Evans's admiration for Byron as he teaches the world how to explore the importance of the individual's integrity.[36] That Evans pulls a stock character off the shelf for the delectation of the masses cannot be denied; the sunburnt, sexually thrilling, morally questionable St. Elmo is but a step removed from melodrama. But Evans also arrives, more profoundly, at a rewriting of Byron, an act of literary appropriation that gives her the foundation for an aestheticism continually ripening into decadence. Byron and Evans viewed the world with a similar moral intensity, and they also shared an understanding of how the self and its "life," its changing shades of consciousness, its shifting locales, its smallest actions, could be related to art. To the extent that Byron insists that the telling of his personal history as he inserts it into public history is a legitimate basis for art, the domestic novelists went to school in Byron, a poet notably popular among them. These novelists are Byron's heirs, for it is only a sort of illicit energy erupting through layers of silencing Christian propriety that would enable a nineteenth-century American woman to believe that the day-to-day chronicles of her orphaned heroine – cups of tea, dress fabrics, dinner menus, courtships, domestic misunderstandings, travels, tears – could ever be the stuff of art.

Further, Evans, like Byron, was unafraid of confronting defeat, crushed hope, or battered values as she traveled the Byronic hero's "curve of disappointment or disaster."[37] Evans invents Edna's life in *St. Elmo* by tracing an actual trajectory: from thrilled admiration and religious fervor for the Confederate cause ("Oh Rachel! I thank God that we are both *Southern Women*! My heart swells with exultation, in view of the future of our young Confederacy! Who shall presume to limit its extent and magnificence!" [Hoole, 20 August 1861]) to deep disappointment, even despair, as the war ended. Making use of Byron's new calculus of artist, art, and modern history, Evans patterned Edna's life on her own wartime experience, presented herself in prose. Edna's campaign to become a writer, at first thrillingly successful, ends in the chosen peace – which is the defeat of the writer – of marriage. It is this simultaneous self-creation and presentation that I hope to reveal, not in order to reduce the novel to allegory, but to trace Evans's patterns of analogy that link her many verbal abstractions to her actual experience.

For what Evans achieves in *St. Elmo* is nothing less than a story told within its silences: a novel of the Civil War and its immediate aftermath that does not once explicitly mention political conflict. Hence the "wild and disordered" feeling of the novel, its Victorian Modernist confusion. What it speaks is emotion repressed at several levels: Edna for St. Elmo, Evans for the Confederacy, the artist for her audience, romance for the "real" world. Throughout the novel Edna is divided, failing, agonized, but coldly triumphant; through her novel Evans tells and doesn't tell, insists upon order and courts disorder, conveys an unspeakable emotional state of foundering, willed passion. Purple prose, hyperbole, clotted erudition, material and emotional splendor that bespeak their own falsity: this is the fall from sincerity effected by the very voice of innocence. Relation is often distressing entanglement. To the extent that Evans intends this distress – and in her most intensely decadent passages she certainly does – she invents a style that, as we have seen in our tour of St. Elmo's rooms, takes us outside the domestic *locus amoenus*.

Pilgrim's Progress and the domestic novels it informs were written to make clear some difficult, abstract ideas. Yet the *St. Elmo* of such Christian didacticism is haunted by another *St. Elmo*, one which deliberately obfuscates. This shadow novel is in part about the Civil War and its ravages, present only in strange and deliberately unexplained images. In order to trace the lineaments of Evans's domestic aestheticism, it is this camouflaged battlefield we must walk.

With the defeat of the Confederacy, Evans lost her wartime roles: passionate propagandist; friend and advisor to generals (she was especially admiring of General Beauregard, who sent her his own pen in gratitude for her concern); gracious and flirtatious hostess to visiting military men; impetuous young woman (she cherished memories of her trip from Montgomery to Mobile during a period when such travel was quite dangerous and strictly forbidden: peremptory orders were "*to stop all ladies*"

["Hoole," 28 February 1864]). And, as wounded soldiers returned in ghastly waves, Evans became an outstanding nurse and medical administrator; the hospital near her home was named Camp Beulah in her honor.

The issue of what she was to do once the war ended soon became an issue of how she meant to be and feel in relation to the cataclysmic events of the recent past and the necessary reformulations of contemporary Southern society. "The sole enthusiasm of my life," she wrote, retrospectively constructing her wartime self,

> was born, lived, and perished in the four years of the Confederacy. Those solemn, anxious, torturing, yet holy, four years of tears, prayers, vigils beside hospital cots, of nights passed on my knees in prayer for dear ones in battle lines; those few vivid, terrible years constitute for me the most sacredly sacrificial portion of my life.[38]

Here, two chronicles might be told. The first recounts Evans's post-war life as a woman who stayed home and resumed a private life: nursing family members, running a household, writing when her domestic duties allowed, gardening, eventually marrying a wealthy widower and, with apparent grace, energy, and optimism, living out her days as a first lady of Mobile, Alabama. This is, indeed, the story of Augusta Evans (Wilson), happily married. The troubling narrative running parallel to such a domestic idyll we must seek in her novels. This Augusta Evans, writing *St. Elmo* as the war ends, deliberately buries recent events in a highly mannered prose but still manages to express the isolation and despair she feels. Needing both to admit and deny defeat, Evans in *St. Elmo* both reveals and hides the chronicle of recent events. Although critics have tended to assume that *Macaria* is her "war novel" and *St. Elmo* a study of woman's artistic vocation, I would argue instead that *St. Elmo* replaces the projected history of the Confederacy that Evans never produces.[39] Evans uses the genre with which she has had most success, the novel, to write her own history of the war, a chronicle deliberately intertwined with her character Edna's self-creation as a writer.

In the course of her lengthy novel, Evans specifically mentions four of Edna's literary works. The two novels – one describing the priestess Neith at Sais and the other, *Shining Thrones on the Hearth* – are mentioned above. Edna writes two belletristic articles as well, both of which appear in Northern magazines: "The Mutilation of the Hermae" and "Keeping the Vigil of St. Martin under the Pines of Grütli." We are given their titles only, not their texts. Both of these articles play an important role in

Edna's development as a writer; the former is her first publication, the latter assures Edna and us that she will continue to write, that she has a genuine vocation.

A visit to an encyclopedia reveals that "Keeping the Vigil" involves the William Tell story and a notable Confederacy of another time and place, thirteenth-century Switzerland. The "Everlasting League" of three Swiss forest cantons, Schweitz, Uri, and Unterwalden, met on St. Martin's eve in a mountain meadow at Rütli (not Grütli) and swore to claim the freedom of Helvetia from German oppression. Alluding to this tale of regional rebellion allows Evans to write into her novel a double message. Conscientious, learned (and all Swiss) readers will understand the implied political message of respect for noble Confederates; others may read this title in happy ignorance, assuming that it is merely part of the fantasy in which an orphan girl becomes a nationally celebrated writer. Readers of Ruskin will recognize Evans's allusion to his accounts of Swiss national mythology.[40] In retrospect, however, we can also read "Keeping the Vigil" as a sign that, in order to achieve a happy ending to her novel, Evans can refer only indirectly, in a detour through medieval Switzerland, to the actual unhappy ending she has just experienced. She cannot deny such recent history, for the recognition of Southern humiliation and death on a grand scale also, painfully enough, fuels her future development as a writer. The artist who has lost her familiar script thus attempts to make an honorable, if unstable, peace with the domestic novelist who always knows the end of every happy story: the projection of a timeless, mythical world of (marital) harmony.

With Edna's article "The Mutilation of the Hermae" Evans once again appeals to different audiences. Uneducated audiences will take it merely as evidence of Edna's scholarly attainments, but educated nineteenth-century readers will be reminded of the story of Alcibiades reported by Plutarch (even Edna's humble grandfather, the village smithy, owns a copy), George Grote, or any of a number of popular histories of the classical world. This latter group will perhaps remember the unsolved crime of the breaking of the Hermae in Athens the night before the disastrous expedition to Sicily. Here the light reflected from Athens to recent events at Fort Sumter vibrates vividly: the defeat of Athens in Sicily perhaps illuminates the ultimate defeat of the Confederacy. Further, Alcibiades is an inherently untrustworthy but talented general whose similarities to St. Elmo – his mockery of religious forms, his metamorphic qualities, his sexually charged aura, his general wiliness and questionable loyalties – suggest that Evans found in her reading of Grote and Plutarch sources for her devilishly attractive hero, American cousin to nineteenth-century French dandies.[41]

But beyond this kind of allusion-hunting there lies another, for with the mention of "The Mutilation of the Hermae" in her novel, Evans begins a Victorian Modernist experiment of deliberately trifling with her audience. One thinks of Nabokov, for example, as he buries bits of information and jokes within his novels primarily for his own delectation and only secondarily for those readers obsessed enough to ferret them out. For Evans actually published an article entitled "The Mutilation of the Hermae" in the *Gulf City Home Journal* of 9 September 1862. Here she writes, ". . . the Sicilian expedition was resolved upon, the doom of Athens sealed." Echoing Grote in his assessment that Alcibiades was framed in this particular incident because Athenians were offended by his mockery of the Eleusinian mysteries during an earlier episode, Evans closes with a strong rhetorical flourish in which she directly compares a contemporary American moment to that strange night in Athens: "a rude Iconoclasm shook the American nation to its centre and overthrew the noblest government which the wisdom of the world established." This is an iconoclasm of that "sacred instrument . . . dearer to every true American patriot, than Hermae to Athens, the hallowed Constitution of our forefathers . . . ." She adds, in a tone of outrage, that this "mutilation of the American Constitution by the depraved and unprincipled politicans of the North, was perpetrated openly at Washington," and that the only noble icon of Hermes still standing "is enshrined in the Southern Confederacy." Certainly Evans must have known that only the few readers of *St. Elmo* who happened to recall her newspaper article would grasp the full significance of the title of Edna's first publication.

It would be a mistake, however, to read the allusion simply as a hidden reference to a lost cause. It is, as well, a record of Evans's own self-creation as a writer. Why has she written the original *Gulf City Home Journal* article? According to an account she sends to Rachel, the article has been commissioned by a Dr. Powell who wishes to publish a book called *Voices from the South*, "composed of contributions from the literary women of the South." Evans tells Rachel that she has more pressing problems: "my thoughts run more on rifled cannon, Confederate cotton looms, and winter uniforms for our noble soldiery, than pen, and letters," but she has "by *sheer force of will* . . . contrived to throw together a few, dim, thought waifs." She then announces, with a note of coyness, that her article is "a *bona-fide* 'Mutilation' of a very classical and beautiful theme" (Hoole, 20 August 1861). And a year later when she sends a copy of the article to Congressman J. L. M. Curry, she complains that the printers "have *mutilated* my contribution almost as mercilessly as did the 'Hermakopids' my marble."[42]

The image of mutilation here reverberates in several ways. As political commentary: the North has mutilated the Constitution and is in the process of mutilating Southern soldiers. To describe her fictional technique: thoughts for the article she does not wish to write have been "drilled into line" (Hoole, 20 August 1861) like those soldiers who have been imperiled by Northern blasphemy. Evans herself has mutilated Greek history in "applying" it to the Confederacy, a kind of aggression she engages in throughout the embroidery of her text when she metaphorically uses ancient lore to describe contemporary subjects. To allude to the self-mutilation of the literary woman: Evans has used "mutilation" as a subject upon which to launch Edna's writing career, a vocation whose trajectory lies upward in public recognition, downward in ill health and in her eventual willingness to "kill" herself as a writer before she is killed by writing. Evans creates Edna as a writer in multifaceted images – victimized Southerner, artistic hoplite, angel in the house, public evangel, elusive priestess of high culture – that glimmer and flash among shifting perspectives of the type we associate with James Joyce, for example. Edna is herself a Victorian Modernist arrangement of possible selves.

"The Mutilation of the Hermae" is, then, a tale of identity – "*Who were the Hermokopid conspirators?*" she asks, – which she nests within the tale of Edna's search for an artistic self, this search itself reflective of Evans's own doubts and desires. *St. Elmo* is the history of the Confederacy and the history of artistic consciousness presented as domestic romance. Edna's first article is both a flaunting of her learning and a statement of skepticism so acute that its best image is an insoluble historical problem. Edna learns it all, but realizes that she can know nothing for sure.

These two examples, Swiss and Greek, establish a nucleus for veiled war talk in *St. Elmo*. One would not wish to catalogue here every instance, but merely to suggest enough examples that readers may begin to see for themselves the imperfectly hidden design. Consider, for example, the story of internecine warfare between St. Elmo and Murray Hammond; or Edna's rejection of Douglass Manning's marriage proposal, which autobiographically echoes Evans's rejection of James Reed Spaulding, primarily because she could not bring herself to marry a Yankee.[43]

Curiously emphasized, awkward, or wild aspects of Evans's writing often indicate the shadow war fought within the pages of *St. Elmo*, much as Samuel Beckett's *Watt* veils World War I.[44] Edna's proud intransigence on issues ranging from courtship to work schedules suggests a rehearsal of sectionalism. Writing to J. L. M. Curry in 1864, Evans complains that she is "pained and astonished" to discover how many of her countrymen were willing to "glide unresistingly" into a "dictatorship" of the North (Curry, nd); Edna Earl is a woman who speaks a resounding "no" to *any* usurpation of her freedom until the closing pages of the novel. Evans delays Edna's marriage for some four hundred pages not just the better to gratify consumers of the bestseller, but also to allow Evans to prove to herself that the South would bow to vicious Northern hegemony against its will and only when it had proof that the North, like St. Elmo, had adequately mended its ways. We can consider Evans's excessive reminders of Edna's self-destructive work habits as her means of both protesting the high price paid by the independent, literary woman and also warning women to stay within the domestic sphere. But we should also view Edna's exhaustion and heart disease as the result of "sectional" warfare between the divided parts of her being: dutiful, Christian helpmeet versus burgeoning, creative woman.

Like Ruskin, Rossetti, and William James, Augusta Evans not only brings things into relation, but also disturbs, complicates, and intermittently severs ties in order to reform or rearrange them. As James writes, the "common-sense world" is one in which we "find things partly joined and partly disjoined" (*P*, p. 79). Between conjunctions and disjunctions, Evans makes her pragmatist way toward the truths she can live by, her own supreme fictions.

Along the same lines, Evans presents Edna's development from uneducated country girl to exquisitely educated young woman to deeply committed writer as nothing less than a campaign she must wage against those who would deny her artistic and scholarly development, from the untutored folks at home in Tennessee, to St. Elmo and his mother, to New York editors. Even when Edna is not outflanked by adversaries, her responsibilities as daughter-substitute, governess, nurse, and mother-surrogate to a national audience can interfere with her writing. Describing her hopes for prompt Secession in a letter to Rachel, Evans reports that "the faces of the people are stamped with stern, desperate resolve" (Hoole, 13 November 1860). It is just this excessive and desperate resolve in Edna, who is always depicted as stony, aloof, preoccupied, which cannot be adequately explained by the plot and psychological motivation Evans offers us. Apparent awkwardness of novelistic technique represents a torsion of narrative line away from the certainties of domestic truths, toward an unstated plane upon which the unspeakable may be uttered.

In this way Evans furthers her decadently aestheticist venture, her intense attempt to wrest meaning from the comfortable realm of the accepted to a perspective from which hidden matters become strangely visible.

Any responsible discussion of the buried narrative of sectional passion must face the issue of slavery. Evans believed in the inferiority of "the low sensual African" and finds him apt to claim an importance "which the Creator has denied him by indications as strong as physical inferiority and mental incapacity could make them." She believed that slavery benefited mankind by freeing the planter class to pursue noble goals and make important contributions to society.[45] While one cannot imagine an Evans who understood that slavery was a vicious institution, the scenes in which St. Elmo beats his dog, the slave-like nature of Edna's years of serving others all day and writing all night, the violent separation of Edna from her family and her removal to another region, and Mr. Hammond's misguided view that Edna will be unable to survive on her own in the North as an independent woman do shade Evans's narrative with hints of humanitarian understanding. Evans, however, refuses to speak slavery's name, referring to slaves as "servants," even as she announces the status of Edna's maid by calling her "Hagar." Evans slips from time to time in her efforts to write her novel as if it took place in some vague era, neither ante- nor post-bellum. She has St. Elmo take a trip to "one of his plantations" (Le Bocage, because it is not a plantation, ostensibly could do without slaves). She slips agains when she has Hagar – alternately a sinister and warmly loving figure – warn Edna "Not to cross Mass' Elmo's path!" (p. 36).

The silence here is a means of self-protection, an effort to remove local coloration from a novel for which Evans sought a national market. This is the silence of repression, but it is also a void which Evans would fill with ideas that she cannot yet accept herself. Edna's rigid and seemingly excessive insistence on her own independence raises a challenge to all abridgments of human rights. Trapped in ideological conflicts, Evans avoided overt recognition of slavery in her novel not just in self-defense and sectional loyalty, but also as syncopated moments of silence, spaces in which she might have made the connection between Edna's and all people's need for freedom, but failed to do so. These repeated, brief stumblings into the arena of human equality, these silences so brief that she perhaps never noticed the interrupted rhythms, account in part for the "disorders" of her prose.

The links among Evans's triple concerns of war, writing, and womanhood, her tendency always to understand one in terms of the others, effect a subtle but thorough-going dissolution of the formulaic tale she tells, that of the orphan cast into the wide, wide world. The plot of this novel only begins to tell its story. To hide the events of recent history: this is the narrative challenge Evans faced in writing her first post-bellum novel. To mute the cacophony of war, Evans found, could mean simply to rewrite military campaigns as scholarly and romantic campaigns, to rewrite wounded soldiers requiring nursing as victims of a train wreck or dying children, and to transform slaves to servants. Recasting public history as private experience, transforming public events to a dark drama of the individual's consciousness, Evans leads the domestic novel to the strange terrain of domestic aestheticism as it twists into decadence.

RISKING AESTHETICISM

Evans imagines within St. Elmo's rooms, during an early chapter of a long novel, nothing less than "the dissociation of style from history."[46] Yet, as we have noted, Evans also reconnects with two particular histories – her own and that of the South. As Evans removes art from its historical context, she implies that it may comment on its own expanded moment outside of time. Buddha figures and Christ figures, Byzantine pictures and vellum manuscripts can be equally entrancing to the eye, equally involved in creating aesthetic harmony, and therefore, equally successful in conveying the only notion that matters: art for the sake of "pure" beauty. Never mind that her own art exists for other reasons as well, adumbrated above. Even within the given and cohesive aim of art for art's sake, Evans creates a texture of finer disjunctions. Having broached this possibility, Evans proceeds to split her narrative strategy in two. The arc of her plot attempts to describe the horrible error of St. Elmo's rooms, his need to understand that Christian text, not aesthetic texture, must rule his life. However, the imagery, diction, rhythm, and tone of her prose undermine this plot continuously.

A pagan excess disturbs even the most Christianized descriptions of the novel. Survey, for example, the house of kindly, effeminate Mr. Hammond, its structure almost buried by the sentimental language of flowers:

The old-fashioned house was of brick, with a wooden portico jutting out over the front door, and around the slender pillars twined honey-suckle and clematis tendrils, purple with clustering bells; while the brick walls were draped with lux-uriant ivy, that hung in festoons from the eaves, and clambered up the chimneys and in at the windows. The daily-swept walk leading to the gate was bordered with white and purple lilies – 'flags,' as the villagers dubbed them – and over the little gate sprang an arch of lattice-work loaded with Belgian and english [sic] honeysuckle, whose fragrant wreaths drooped till they touched the heads of all who entered. (p. 53)

What might have been a convincingly formulaic description of the good minister's cottage droops and tugs into luxuriant excess. Honeysuckle is not merely Southern, but Belgian and English: St. Elmo is not the only person involved in "world-scrapings," it seems, and the exterior of Mr. Hammond's house bears a family resemblance to the rooms of Le Bocage. What Evans has discovered is nothing less than the aestheticism (and hence amorality) implied within every domestic scene. Since the home must be *made* the locus of peaceful beauty, every homemaker is an artist, and therefore subject to the siren call of art for art's sake. Evans recognizes this implied seduction, and struggles both to resist it and to give way to it. She wills herself in opposing directions, thus beginning the decadent artist's argument with herself on the subject of art and morality. Is pursuit of the aesthetic a form of immoral self-gratification, or merely an intense means of appreciating God's creation?

Like so many Americans of her era who sought to define the place of art, especially European art, in their own culture, Evans read and reread Ruskin.[47] Wiley and Putnam had brought out the first American edition in 1847, and in 1859 Evans urges Rachel to get *Stones of Venice* and *Modern Painters* and let her know "whether you are [as] much fascinated as your far-off friend" (Hoole, 8 December 1859). Evans was charmed by Ruskin's exposition of European culture, for she had joined the growing group of Americans of the 1850s and '60s who wished to tour Europe: "From early childhood it has been a bright beautiful dream to me; that one day I should wander amid the ruins of the old world, and study art in the Galleries of Rome and Florence," she tells Rachel (Hoole, 4 January 1860). Although Evans stays home, she sends Edna Earl to Italy. But without a doubt it was Ruskin's Christianized aestheticism that reassured Evans in her yearning for wider culture; she writes of Beulah, during her religious crisis, that "it may safely be proclaimed that genuine aesthetics is a mighty channel, through which the love and adoration of Almighty God enters the human soul."[48]

Ruskin temporarily made America safe for Christian aesthetes, and he also enabled Evans to consider a wide variety of aesthetic questions. Ruskin's meaning was regularly "distorted or misinterpreted" according to the needs of his American readers, and Evans is in this regard a typical reader.[49] She uses Ruskin to buttress her Christianity in the face of the amoral or immoral impulses of artistic impressionism and autonomy she felt so strongly. She sees in him a popular writer whose works are deeply cultured; if Americans are unafraid to tackle Ruskin, certainly her own books will find a market. But she also adopts his values in an effort to understand the inherent strengths of the woman writer. His insistence, and that of his American followers, on rejecting crass materialism in order to search for beauty and feeling – still an important therapeutic strain in American culture – certainly would have registered with Evans as a feminized position. Pursuing beauty and harmony, developing an exquisite sensibility, was woman's work in nineteenth-century America.

For a woman who wished to retain her womanly prerogatives even as she carved out a place for herself in high culture, Ruskin would have been a powerful ally. Furthermore, in his social policy, especially his interest in the aesthetic education of the common worker, he provided a counter-argument to those who insisted that for a woman to concern herself too much with matters of the imagination was to shirk responsibility. The imagination could serve female humanity: thus in *Macaria* Irene Huntingdon sells her diamonds in order to endow a Ruskinesque "School of Design for Women" to enable them to learn dignified occupations other than mantua-making and school-teaching.[50]

Perhaps most important of all, under Ruskin's aegis Evans begins in *Beulah* to anatomize the aesthetic experience itself as a *substitute* for Christianity. The impoverished, lonely, and confused young woman has had a moment of grace during a walk in the woods: "Oh, what are Gothic cathedrals and gilded shrines in comparison with these grand forest temples, where the dome is the bending vault of God's blue, and the columns are these everlasting pines!" (p. 186).[51] That evening Beulah "pour[s] out the joy of her soul in song," and then analyzes the hours of delight she occasionally feels:

Sometimes she was conscious of their approach, while gazing up at the starry islets in the boundless lake of azure sky; or when a gorgeous sunset pageant was passing away; sometimes from hearing a solemn chant in church, or a witching strain from a favorite opera. Sometimes from viewing dim old pictures; sometimes from reading a sublime passage in some old English or German author. It was a serene elevation of feeling; an unbounded peace; a chastened joyousness, which she was rarely able to analyze, but which isolated her for a time from all surrounding circumstances. (pp. 186–187)

These hours of grace are notable for their genesis in the senses as they experience, first nature, then various forms of art. Christian texts do not enter the discussion. Here Evans considers the notion that aesthetic experience not only can be moral or ideal, but may also actually replace religious experience. If this is so, then it is but a short step to the understanding that religious experience may itself be aestheticized ("hearing a solemn chant in a church, or a witching strain from a favorite opera"), that one may treasure religion for its sensations rather than its moral and immortal truths. Evans has thus launched a stealth attack on the Christianity she has been at pains to defend, making common (if unconscious) cause with Swinburne and Pater.

Evans's thought converges with that of Stevens when he writes, "The final belief is to believe in a fiction, which you know to be a fiction, there being nothing else. The exquisite truth is to know that it is a fiction, and that you believe in it willingly."[52] And Willa Cather's Father Latour of *Death Comes for the Archbishop* is a French aesthete and epicurean whose tastes in food, drink, landscapes, art, and architecture are hallowed by God and by Ruskin alike. Cather writes of Ruskin, "To have lived so pure, so intense, so reverent a life as his is greater than to have written *Modern Painters*. For Ruskin is perhaps the last of the great worshippers of beauty."[53] Her ambivalence about popular women novelists arises in part defensively – Cather shares with them plots, character types, and a pagan worship of beauty learned at the feet of the moral aesthete, John Ruskin.

Evans joins to her world-shaking reevaluation of religious experience a fascination with the effects of living the aesthetic, as opposed to (but never wholly severed from) the Christian, life. Electra Gray, the painter of *Macaria*, claims, "I live, sustain myself by my art . . . . it feeds and clothes my body as well as my mind . . . Oh! aesthetics is a heavenly ladder" (p. 404). Yet Electra, like Edna, is wasting away. Art is a ladder extending outward, to beautiful yet painful things in the world, not upward to an all-fulfilling Neoplatonic beauty. However spiritually satisfying her art may be, Electra has also absorbed into her very face and being the strangeness of Mr. Clifton's *atelier* where she trains to be a painter, just as Edna studies in St. Elmo's library. She is plagued by melancholy, a disease that clearly fascinates Evans, since she gives it to Edna as well. Evans reminds us that "[t]here is no exquisite beauty without some strangeness in the proportions" (p. 133), quoting "Baron Verulam" but in actuality quoting Poe, who includes the line in "Ligeia." Evans packs Mr. Clifton's studio with a confusion of vases, paintings of pagan subjects, "a mimic aviary" of stuffed tropical birds, and other *objets* (p. 132). Not only is Clifton dying of consumption, but Electra, too, is dying in the venue of art, as would be expected of one who feeds her body with art. She is for Evans both the sentimental lovelorn maiden – "hope deferred maketh the heart sick" – and the dying woman who will become for turn-of-the-century culture the very shape of beauty, and the figure of the (decadent) artist herself.

Illness is a topos of the domestic novel, and the stock deathbed scene there usually functions to give women and children the moral and social power they so conspicuously lack while fully alive.[54] In a wholly decadent twist, Evans disperses the deathbed scene throughout the weave of *St. Elmo*. As she launches her writing career, Edna begins a slow decline, reversible only by substituting the work of marriage for that of literary creation. The child-aesthete Felix, given to quoting Ruskin, and a budding author himself, dies young. Both dying artists, adult and child, remind one of Baudelaire's "Painter of Modern Life," in which he compares the modern artist, the "genius for whom no edge of life is blunted" to the child and the convalescent, both of whom have especially acute sensory impressions.[55] Ailing modernist characters of the twentieth century – Henry James's Milly Theale, Virginia Woolf's Septimus Smith and Nabokov's Sebastian Knight – suffer Victorian maladies.

Illness is, like mutilation, another powerfully suggestive image for Evans. It makes of Edna a beautiful, strange, fragile woman, thus salvaging her ties to Christian other-worldliness. Yet illness also brings her into relation with dead civilizations (and the mortuary qualities of living civilizations), as if her learning had become so arcane, her sensations so intense, that they literally *are* her illness. Evans here creates the double edge of decadence: she associates it with the richness of decaying things – individual people and entire cultures – and with the new, with a challenge to the "givens" of cultural understanding. Edna is a Christian woman who undergoes trials and prospers within a sentimental and domestic novel, but she is also a dying woman, moving "downward to darkness" on the extended wings of world art-culture.

In particular, Evans uses Edna's illness to consider the taboo against woman's intellectualism. Edna suffers from heart disease, a suitably sentimental affliction for a woman who loves a man she refuses to marry. Yet we recognize that Edna suffers also from hysteria, a mark of the artist in nineteenth-century culture, and a defining device for the "deviant" artistic or sensual woman who cannot, by her very gender, easily forego or escape this condition. Edna works too hard, writes too much, turns down too many attractive suitors, sleeps and eats too little. Her "disease," then, is both her very artistic and scholarly activity and the physical effects it has upon her. She is literally dying from having chosen a forbidden line of work.[56] Dr. Howell prescribes with the voice of patriarchy: "There

must be no more teaching or writing" (p. 378). In depicting Edna's pun-
ishment for being a woman and for being, even worse, a writing woman,
Evans considers as well the strange rewards of sickness, hysteria as rebellion. For such a creature to lose a body is to gain a self. The more
Edna wastes away, the more she becomes herself. Surely we are meant
to feel at novel's end that St. Elmo becomes the doctor who will heal –
however much against her will – the woman whose very independence
is her illness. Significantly, although Edna embraces marriage, she never
responds directly to St. Elmo's commandment that she cease writing.
Silence – Edna's unspoken assent and unspoken *non serviam* – works to
dissolve formulaic certainty of plot.

The very hysterical texture of the novel, its over-written, abnormal
quality, may in part be explained by the extraordinary burden Evans
places upon her prose. In making Edna a sick woman Evans wants to
explore more possibilities than her prose can bear: aestheticist *askesis*,
decadent fascination with dying women and heightened forms of sensation, silenced memories of nursing dying soldiers ("many nights have
rolled away as I sat with my fingers on their feeble fluttering pulse" [letter
to Rachel Heustis, 22 January 1862]), misogynistic judgments of literary
women, indeed, of all women. Evans's deep ambivalence about every
one of these issues simply squares the complexity factor.

Perhaps, too, Evans wished to risk Edna's life in order to explore
endings: of wars, ways of life, life itself. To quote from a touchstone of
early Modernism published in England one year after *St. Elmo* appeared
in America: "Well! we are all *condamnés*, as Victor Hugo says: we are all
under sentence of death but with a sort of indefinite reprieve – *les hommes
sont tous condamnés à mort avec des sursis indéfinis* ... we have an interval, and
then our place knows us no more" (Pater [1986], p. 153). In Edna's case,
the reprieve comes in the form of marriage. Yet however high the plot
may soar toward the state of Christian matrimony, the novel's closing
pages imply a motion downward, a collection of the wages of female
creativity. Her place at a writing table knows her no more.

Between Edna's youthful ambition and her decline, Evans sets her to
exploring world religions. This task Edna undertakes with the intensity
of a Marius; furthermore, her first novel sounds uncannily like *Marius the
Epicurean*. Even the cadences of the description carry a Paterian intensity,
preciosity: "A fair young priestess of the temple of Neith, in the sacred
city of Sais – where people of all climes collected to witness the festival
of lamps – becoming skeptical of the miraculous attributes of the statues
she had been trained to serve and worship ... " (p. 108).

Such religious eclecticism becomes what William James would call a "live option" for Edna after she witnesses a fatal duel in the opening pages of the novel. Nothing in her experience helps her to make sense of the murders in the wood, nor can she ever fully reconstruct the lost (monistic, Christian) paradise of childhood unity. She cannot, like the young Ellen Montgomery in *Wide, Wide World*, find solace in Christianity when the person she loves best dies. If Beulah had to study philosophy in order to realize the futility of skepticism and the beauty and completeness of faith, Edna has to study world mythology in order to prove the primacy of Christianity. This strategy backfires, for having demonstrated the richness as well as the unity of world religions, Edna can no longer privilege the symbols and myths of Christianity without undermining her own writing. Like Marius, who dies a pagan with a deep appreciation of Christianity, Edna dies a Christian with a profound sympathy for all religions. Nervous intricacy and obsessive extension replace repose at one, fixed, center.

Perhaps Evans learned to entertain religious pluralism in a simple, even sentimental way: by loving her friend Rachel. "Your religion is so full of grand immemorial themes, exhaustless, ever attractive. I often wish that I might have been born a Jewess – you are a glorious old people; I would I belonged to you," she writes, rather startlingly for a devout Christian lady. Then she adds, " – though I would combine the Christian with the Mosaic dispensation" (Hoole, 28 August 1860). Attracted to Judaism's inspiring "themes," Evans clearly has been thinking about Judaism's artistic possibilites. Writing to Rachel a month earlier, she reports:

> I have often wondered why you *did not write*. Of course you know you *could* if you would; and my darling you have *such* a glorious field stretching out before you. Your nationality – ; your Grand Ancestral rights all of the sublime, that clusters around God's "chosen people." Rachel write a Jewish tale . . . . (Hoole, 30 July 1860)

The elitist religion practiced by Jews will provide for Rachel both artistic identity and artistic "material," not a code of public behavior or a promise of life after death. Rachel already inhabits an extensive sublime by virtue of her "chosenness;" she is a member of God's special family. Evans does not speak analogically, seeking to find the promise of Christianity in Judaism. In the end, not even her profound sense of synchronicity would enable Evans to find the origin of Judaism, or any older systems of belief, in Christianity. Once she has to accept the parity of Christianity with

Judaism, once she determines "to show the world that the true, good and beautiful of all theogonies and cosmogonies, of every system of religion that had waxed and waned since the gray dawn of time, could be traced to Moses and to Jesus" (p. 86), Christianity loses its absolute authority. It can be understood only in relation to Judaism; it is itself always slightly displaced from the center.

The Priestess of Neith in Edna's novel might well have failed – Evans is silent on the subject. What her project does make clear is that religions wax and wane, and that they are part of the human myth-making capacity. Religion, Evans implies, becomes a matter of desire, style, and the accidents of time and place. She even quotes Schiller, "man depicts himself in his gods." (p. 170). Or, as Wallace Stevens would say, "The mind that in heaven created the earth and the mind that on earth created heaven were, as it happened, one."[57]

Aesthetic sentimentalist and mythopoeic homemaker, Edna Earl confounds our comfortable distinctions between Victorian and Modern. James describes in *Pragmatism* a world made of many networks and little worlds, "little hangings together of the world's parts" (*P*, p. 67). "Whoever says the whole world tells one story" believes so at her own risk (*P*, p. 67). As Evans tells more than one story at a time in her novel, so may we in our criticism. Let us consider the hangings-together of the already complex and often elusive notions of the Victorian and the Modern. Perhaps we shall discover that, moving to a continuously rearranged house of criticism, we feel at home there.

Meditation: sentimentality

Sentimentality lives within a verbal family from which it can never be neatly excised. Its siblings are words such as emotionality, sentiment, sentimental, sensibility, sense, and sensible.[1] By now these related terms find shelter in a vast and rambling House of Criticism built by methodologies and political positions abounding. But why, then, choose sentimentality as the favored term? Because the words sentimental and sentimentality mean trouble – they are still largely words of aesthetic opprobrium – and where aesthetic trouble lies, an interesting story may often be found. And why pragmatist method? Because it is less a method than a flexible receptivity that enables it to move among other methodologies and positions. This study, however, links these two answers. Literary critics have largely understood pragmatist energy through metaphors of activity, as a matter of struggle or of constant dynamism. Evidence for this kind of interpretation abounds in William James and Ralph Waldo Emerson, for example, but other evidence – that pragmatism is also interested in drawing things together that they might dwell together – has been given less attention.[2] We may think of sentimentality as pragmatist dynamism in another style or mode – one that seeks connection, intimacy, and repose. It conducts a continual rather than a continuous dynamic.

We may relate the stories of sentiment and sentimentality that appear in our studies of Ruskin, Rossetti, Evans, and James to larger stories, including those told across the breadth of Western intellectual history. Historians of ideas often regard sentiment as a reaction against Plato's suspicion of poetry. Plato, so the argument goes, excoriates poetry as that which encourages irrationality in its audience, and in particular encourages hearers to "give way to sympathy" when their passions are aroused. In contrast, sentimentalists defend sympathy and passion. Their view holds that the arts of sentiment and sensibility argued, by showing and telling, a major change in traditional views of mind and reason: "new thoughts, whose...roots are in ancient sceptical philosophy, assume that no human action of any consequence is possible – including 'mental' action – that is not led and driven by feeling, affect, emotion."[3] Sentimentality is in this view an idea that arises across our cultural history widely construed as a challenge to the notion that a purified reason must triumph over feeling (and in parallel, form over material, male over female). One might say, for example, that late twentieth-century feminism has often posed itself as sentimental in order to launch its attacks on something called patriarchy, which views itself as operating within the superior domain of reason (however unreasonable patriarchal practices might be).

From this tracing of sentiment as a strand in the history of ideas, Victorian Modernists may tease out one small filament, that of the idea of sensibility in Great Britain in the eighteenth century: "the movement discerned in philosophy, politics and art, based on the belief in or hope of the natural goodness of humanity and manifested in a humanitarian concern for the unfortunate and helpless."[4] This narrower exploration looks backward to the cult of sensibility that flourished from the 1740s to the 1770s and was nourished by Scottish Common Sense Philosophy, including Lord Shaftesbury's "moral sense," an inborn faculty for knowing and choosing benevolence, and for seeing that the good and the virtuous are also the beautiful.[5]

In addition to historical approaches widely and narrowly construed, we may consider the aesthetic approach to sentiment and sensibility, which tends to explore artistic (including literary) conventions. In this second, largely formalist, methodology, sensibility tends to appear within a tableau in which one person who is highly susceptible to emotional impressions feels tenderly toward another, vicariously feeling the other's suffering. Sentimentality viewed formally as an aspect of artistic texts often begins as a singularly melancholy meditation on victimization and pity in which bodies express meaning through tears and palpitations. Within such conventions, tender emotings by subject (mother weeping at a little grave), artist (kneeling beside her and later recounting the experience), and audience (wondering what could possibly hurt more than losing a child) repeat and reinforce one another, often creating a *mise-en-abîme*. Real tears mingle with those of word and paint.

A third approach to sensibility and sentiment links two or more disciplines. To borrow George Eliot's term, "multiplex" problems respond well to complex approaches. Critical insights from within and across texts and disciplines form useful links as we view sentimental phenomena broadly, welcoming the work of any discipline that can help us understand the expression of emotion as part of culture. For example, Ellison links the literary conventions of sentiment to notions of "[a]n economy, a transaction, or a system" in which "connections among observation, mood and power are self-consciously traced."[6]

Thus, linking aesthetics with psychology, we might say that, in parallel with aestheticism's reflexivity, art which is about (among other things) art, sentimentality involves emotion which is about (among other things) emotion "itself." The phenomena of sentimentality appear not just in art but also in many kinds of cultural documents and often involve a "strategically choreographed" dance between emotional volatility and emotional discipline.[7] Because literary sentimentality is performative and thus blurs the distinctions between art and life, it tends to narrate its own growth within what we may call the scene of writing. Discussing the tableaux in which artists actually write and paint will be a way of discussing their art "itself" as entangled with – rather than mimetic or expressive of – the conditions of their ordinary lives. The biographical fallacy comes full circle to look more like biographical paradox. In order to understand Victorian Modernism we will need to grasp sentimentalities in all the fullness of their creators' circumstances: their stories will have to be told.

Not limited to an idea, a set of forms, or an emotional practice, sentiment emerges in Victorian Modernist works of art as a way of moving among categories, concepts, and forms in an effort to gather them into meaningful arrangement. It makes patterns. When William James teaches his students and wider popular audiences that the relations between things are as important as the things themselves, these things and relations eventually leading to a religious feeling of "More" at the fringes of things, he speaks in the language of a sublime sentimentality. If all encounters occur in a field of relations – and both Ruskin and James believe that they do – then the tradition of sentiment, with its practice of "mobile connection," may be seen as in part making pragmatism possible.[8] Furthermore, pragmatist processes of sentimentality merge with the experiences of sublimity as they mark the relations of human beings to extremes of height, depth, complexity, or breadth. James joins hands across this study with Ruskin, as the latter emblematically lies in a field of grass, flower, and weed, glorying in the complex texture of what he sees, "an infinite picture and possession to me" which he feels to be "the constant working of Omnipotent kindness in the fabric of the food-giving tissues of the earth."[9] Where sentiment and sublimity appear in

Victorian Modernism, the domestic is usually not far behind – often, as in Ruskin, uncomfortably to our ears.

The term "sentimentality" seems to have yearned for and received depreciating modifiers: mere, cheap, excessive, embarrassing. Since 1800 its use has been largely pejorative. To this day, the term "sentimental" often functions not as a considered formalist assessment, but rather as a marker for emotional discomfort in the viewer.[10] Victorian sentimentality, with its kittens boxing balls of yarn before a cozy hearth, has been notorious in evoking critical repugnance. Sentimentality is simply debased art in the view of high Modernists: "Sentimentality is a failure of feeling."[11] Sentimentalism is often associated with lax self-control, with a selfish giving-in to emotions that do no one any good: it is "the name of the mood in which we make a luxury of grief," states Sir Leslie Stephen.[12] His daughter, however, finds sentiment more difficult to dismiss. Virginia Woolf muses of a woman writer, "This terseness, this short-wordedness, might mean that she was afraid of something; afraid of being called 'sentimental' perhaps; or she remembers that women's writing has been called flowery and so provides a superfluity of thorns."[13] Woolf associates sentimentality with wordiness and prettiness, and although she does not stop to defend it, she does suggest that this woman writer has been somehow false to herself – defensively terse and thorny – in order to avoid it.

Because emotions are something that can happen to us, not something we always will or control, and because they have often been seen as a sign of reason's failure, emotionality and sentimentality have ironically been seen as *failures* of feeling.[14] They indicate a guilty, decadent, or improper emotion. Certainly William James apologizes for his vivid recounting of emotional states in *Varieties of Religious Experience*. "In re-reading my manuscript," he confesses, perhaps trying to beat his critics to the mark, "I am almost appalled at the amount of emotionality which I find in it. After so much of this, we can afford to be dryer and less sympathetic in the rest of the work that lies before us . . . . The sentimentality of many of my documents [recounting religious experience] is a consequence of the fact that I sought them among the extravagances of the subject."[15] James feels the need to defend the "palpitating documents I have quoted" (*VRE*, p. 396) by promising to move on to more arid matters, thus reassuring himself and his readers that he remains in control. Sentiment is crucial to a pragmatist approach, but it has its dangers

Much of James's pragmatist and radical empiricist philosophy and psychology, including "The Sentiment of Rationality," depend precisely

on sentimentality – not sense impression, but "mere" sentimentality itself, which he sometimes describes as feeling at home in our beliefs. For
any philosophy to succeed, James preaches, it must fulfill our "dearest
desires and most cherished powers,"[16] it must gratify our needs. As we
choose a philosophy by which to live, "[a]ll that the human heart wants is
its chance" (*WB*, 89) to sweep away philosophical skepticisms, pedantic
scruples, and vetoes, in order to live and act freely. An insistent diction
of desire, need, dearness, happiness, and feeling at home gradually in-
scribes a feminized texture of sentimental domesticity in James's writing.
Will American men inevitably be emasculated by thinking about things
dear and cherished; can the promptings of the heart, that troubling organ of sentimental popular culture in America, ever give rise to serious
philosophy? William James worries, but he also explores late nineteenth-
century and early twentieth-century women's sentimental culture and
discovers there some revolutionary ideas.

Dante Gabriel Rossetti, John Ruskin, and Augusta Evans join James
in anxiously exploring sentimentality as a source of rich possibility –
and so do Victorian Modernists in the twentieth century. For who can
separate sentimentality from fellow-feeling? W. H. Auden believes that
"the underlying reason for writing is to bridge the gulf between one
person and another," rather than leaving people "alone, cut off from each
other in an indifferent world where they do not live for very long."[17] As
people fail in their loneliness, so do nations. He beseeches the help of the
dead Yeats: "In the deserts of the heart / Let the healing fountain start, /
In the prison of his days / Teach the free man how to praise." Hearts,
healing, fountains of tears, poetry: Europe in 1939 may be mapped by
its failures of pity and love.[18]

In its linking of feeling and moral value, the culture of sensibility from
early on raised gender problems.[19] Many have believed it to be simply
the "natural order of things" that men think and act – in contrast to
women, who mostly feel. Seen in this light, judging a work of art to
be "merely" (or appallingly) sentimental may reveal a form of aesthetic
scapegoating: the work, like woman herself, communicates feeling in
excess of the facts.[20] Better to stay away. When Rousseau, for example,
argues the need for female qualities of tenderness and benevolence to
act on male society in order to form a good community, he casts male
superiority into doubt. Only discussion elsewhere of women's devious
and destructive qualities will right the balance.

It is important to note, however, that sensibility's links with gender
trace a complex filigree of relations between masculinity and femininity

throughout the centuries under discussion. The very word "passions," derives from, *pati*, to suffer, and relates through this stem to passive and patient.[21] An individual undergoing or suffering a change was thus an individual lacking power; and that individual, as three decades of feminist scholarship have established, was often considered to be woman herself. Yet the story is more complex. Eighteenth-century sensibility was also a mode of political legitimation in the civic life of men.[22] While sentimentality and sensibility might have been claimed by or assigned to a feminized sphere, it never lost its close associations with masculinity. Ruskin and William James may write from within a woman's world, but the very act of publication enables them to practice a "masculine" civic responsibility. We may see strange genderings of characters in nineteenth-century American sentimental and domestic fiction by women, such as the flaccid, asexual or incestuous male hero who nonetheless guides and supports a woman who must learn to give up her own, naturally strong, will. Although the man of feeling may take the woman's part, his nobility compensates for his effeminacy. Sympathy dispensed *de haut en bas*, to suffering women and poor men, restores masculinity wonderfully.[23] Yet by the mid-nineteenth century, sensibility in England and America had come to be associated strongly with the world of women, even if the "separate spheres" were never so separate as scholars once believed.[24]

The term "feminization," when it appears in this study, signals not a transformation from male to female, not the trumping of masculinity by femininity, but an illumination of shaded or occulted female elements. The so-called feminization of Victorian Modernism is an addition to the record, not a simple correction in favor of women rather than men in a gendered zero sum game. The retrieval of the feminine aspects of Modernism is far from complete. If we keep in mind that sentimentality may appear for many, and often opposing, political and aesthetic reasons (including the stifling and the celebration of women), we will be better prepared to tease out its complex patterns. Furthermore, we will be capable of seeing sentiment's intertwinements with sublimity. Far from marking aesthetic weakness, sentimentality can at times enable an artist to fly wide and high, taking willing readers with him.

The Victorian Modernism proposed in this study approaches sentimentality by admitting its shortcomings but exploring its strengths. This is not a mawkish exercise, but rather a careful look at what we too often have not known how to see. Understanding a twentieth-century form of sentimentality, kitsch, to be "Ersatz culture, destined for those who, insensible to the values of genuine culture, are hungry nevertheless for the diversion that only culture of some sort can provide," only begins our discussion.[25] While we may decry kitsch's manipulativeness, fakery, superficiality, or distortions, we must all the same recognize its artistic bona fides, especially among the very avant-garde and elitist artists who represent, for critics like Clement Greenberg, sentimentality's righteous scourge. Nabokov may have abhorred kitsch's Russian pal, "poshlust," but *Lolita* would not have been as fascinating – or worthy of our pity – without it. Flaubert may have railed against Madame Bovary's sentimental convent education, but he surrounded her lovely hair with a halo of light, especially pronounced at the fireside, that would have been remarkably familiar to readers of popular fiction.

Sentimentality's supposed shortcuts, its blueplate specials of vicarious experience,[26] were in fact served up by other "respectable" artists: e.g., Henry James (the effeminate Ralph Touchett of *Portrait of a Lady* dies as heart-rendingly as any heroine of sentimental fiction); and Wallace Stevens ("The mother's face, / The purpose of the poem, fills the room. / They are together, here, and it is warm, / With none of the prescience of oncoming dreams" [*CP*, p. 413]).[27] Those who attacked sentimentality also recreated its tableaux of benevolence and embodied knowledge. They explored the beauty of heart meeting heart. Oscar Wilde may tell his audience (1913) that it is "against the claims of mere sentiment and feeling that the artist must react,"[28] but the "mere" drops long before he attacks Lord Douglas's failure of feeling toward the suffering recounted in *De Profundis*. He mockingly *and* sincerely creates sentimental tableaux throughout his fiction and drama. Thus the mixed message of Mrs. Erlynne in *Lady Windermere's Fan*: "I have no ambition to play the part of a mother. Only once in my life have I known a mother's feelings. That was last night. They were terrible – they made me suffer – they made me suffer too much.... I thought I had no heart. I find I have, and a heart doesn't suit me, Windermere."[29] And those who specialized in sentimentality, such as popular domestic novelists, invented the new in their fictional parlors as surely as did their high cultural counterparts in the aggressive field exercises of the avant garde.

Once we venture down this path, we will begin to see the importance of sentiment to some of the central concerns of Modernism. For example, the notion of Modernist impersonality will require another look. Sentimentality, that mobile survey of the relations of emotion and power, supplies Victorian Modernist artists with tools for exploring perspectivism and human identity. Where does one person's emotion originate and with whom should it be shared? How much should one's inner emotional life count – and can the man who suffers really separate himself from the mind that creates?

Sentimental art in fact always carried within it the seeds of what we think of as Modernist impersonality, for the conventional images of sentimental poetry invite the reader to "read into" their generalized forms his own particular joys and sadnesses.[30] The Victorian Modernist invention of impersonality and masking is, as we shall come to understand, painstakingly – and painfully – pioneered by John Ruskin as he preaches the need for heartfelt art yet fears to reveal himself in his work. He counsels, "The whole function of the artist in the world is to be a seeing and feeling creature; to be an instrument of such tenderness and sensitiveness, that no shadow, no hue, no line, no instantaneous and evanescent expression of the visible things around him . . . shall either be left unrecorded, or fade from the book of record" (11.49).[31] Yet this seeing and feeling creature must, in order to create art, be able to leave his own personality behind and "enter . . . into the hearts and thoughts of each person; and in all this he is still passive" (11.49). Passivity, *pati*, passion: the paradox of sentimental impersonality finds its voice. Although Ruskin wishes at times to escape his own personality, he imagines doing so through heartfelt complications rather than by a pure "logic of the emotions."[32] Emotions can be brutish, irrational forces in human functioning, but they are also an integral part of reasoning.[33] In parallel, sentimentality can result in a debased art, but it can also be integral to the making and experiencing of beauty. As Rossetti says, implicitly questioning dispassionate judgment: "All poetry, that is really poetry, affects me deeply and often to tears."[34]

Artists themselves often both celebrate and attack sentimentality in a single work.[35] Sensibility and sentimentality have always been literary practices divided against themselves, hovering in contradictory extremes: Is nature the source of melancholy or its cure? Should we rhapsodize on a loving deity or wail in the face of human pain? Is sentiment primarily materialist (felt in the body) or idealist (felt by finer spirits)? Am I most or least myself when I lose myself in feeling with or for another? Do heartfelt condolences unduly torture the griever anew, or assuage his pain? The set of literary or artistic practices we choose to call sentimental inhabit a field rich in ambivalence and confusion, and therefore rich in the intermingling paths of truth-testing and truth-making that lead to and from it. The best of all possible worlds becomes, by the mid-nineteenth century – and well into the twentieth – a matter of possible worlds.

CHAPTER 5

Positions of repose: the Victorian Modernism of William James

Men always have attempted and always will attempt to make their minds dwell in a more reasonable world, just as they always have sought and always will seek to make their cities and their homes more beautiful.

William James, "Philosophers Paint Pictures"[1]

If his hand comes in contact with an orange on the table, the golden yellow of the fruit, its savor and perfume will forthwith shoot through his mind. . . . The voice of the violin faintly echoes through the mind as the hand is laid upon it in the dark.

Principles of Psychology[2]

A PHILOSOPHER'S VICTORIAN MODERNISM

William James began to publish in 1878 and continued until the year of his death, 1910. Important works appeared posthumously until 1943, with a flurry in the teens and twenties. Thus he stands chronologically in the Modernist period of literary studies. Yet as a psychologist and philosopher he captures the spirit of Victorian Modernism: its propensity toward interesting confusions, its pursuit of tender relations, and its certainty that our actual, lived, felt experience cannot and should not be separated from the work of art as it is made or as we later comment upon it. While Ruskin links the authors of this study historically, James links them theoretically, for it has been our practice to hypothesize the pragmatism of John Ruskin, Dante Gabriel Rossetti, and Augusta Evans in order to see what we may learn. A Jamesian pragmatism has arranged and rearranged the tentative patterns of this study. Since we have considered the other figures of this study as poets, painters, and novelists who philosophize, it is now time to consider a philosopher and psychologist who appreciates and creates art. As James himself declares, "Philosophers Paint Pictures."

A goal of this study is artfully to intermingle and confuse the categories of art and philosophy. Out of a "swarming continuum" of possible critical narratives about James's writings, the one presented here has been created for its extensive qualities. That is, it both adds to and grows out of the multiple and contingent centerings about artists (Ruskin, Rossetti, Alexander, Evans) and about concepts (sublimity, sentiment, aestheticism, domesticity). "Multiplexity," to borrow George Eliot's term again, describes the texture of the (ever incomplete) whole. The critical story told here begins with the James family's interest in sentimental domesticity and moves through James's solutions-in-progress to a cluster of problems having to do with the relation of peoples' "everyday" feelings to traditional philosophical questions about mind, metaphysics, epistemology, religion, and so on. Pragmatism is, James reminds his audience, "A New Name for Some Old Ways of Thinking." As a classical American philosopher, James developed Pragmatism with a capital P. The narrative presented here implies that, like Ruskin, Rossetti, and Evans, he also worked, thought, and wrote as a "lower-case" pragmatist. He worked with materials close to hand to respond to abstract philosophical questions through artistic undertakings.

The mind, including the philosophic mind, as James personifies it across the enormous stretch of *Principles of Psychology*, is not a scientist who assembles and interprets discrete components of reality manipulated as internalized, compact ideas. Rather, in its internal workings the mind is an impressionist painter who delicately makes meaning by fusing rather than separating, and it is also, somewhat confusingly, a classical sculptor in its relation to the "outside" world. Faced with a chaos of sensory experience, the mind chooses, chips away at the "swarming continuum" of experience until it has fashioned its world, "much as a sculptor works on his block of stone" (*PP*, 1:288). As mind meets world, fusion, not separation, is the final word. What remains after the mind sculpts the sensory flux has in a sense been there from the first – it has not been built of separate pieces but rather revealed through processes of attention, choice, and Parnassian purification. To simplify is to retain the originally "fused" quality of experience, in which "[c]olors, sounds, smells, are just as much *entangled* with other matter as the more formal elements of experience such as extension, intensity, effect, pleasure, difference, etc. . . . All are *embedded* in one world" (*PP*, 1:508). Thus James arrives at psychological law: "all things fuse that *can* fuse, and nothing separates except what must" (*PP*, 1:488, emphasis added).

The mind's created world bears a family resemblance to the high Modernist work of art when it is described as purely sculpted, durably masculine, paradoxically spiritual or cerebral for all its hardness, and set high on the shelf of self-sufficient and elitist autonomy. Yet we have seen the Victorian Modernist rejection of through-and-through monism, and James here speaks of fusion. It is crucial, therefore, to note that James uses the word *entangled*, and to understand that by fusion he means complex relation. Sensations and concepts are "embedded in," not overcome by. Fusion does not make the complex elements of experience and thought disappear into homogeneity. Nor has the "one world" in which they are embedded been created by a process that, like Coleridge's Primary and Secondary Imagination, effaces difference by dissolving, diffusing, dissipating, in order to recreate an ideal unity. Rather, as James will argue in *Pragmatism*, the mind's activity is inseparable from feeling and aims to add to an incomplete world rather than discovering an already fixed order. Across the years he meditates on just what it is that the mind and the feelings together can do.

These meditations often arise from James's experience of the quotidian, what he calls "the world of concrete experiences to which the street belongs," (*P*, p. 17), and they lead to aesthetic confusions of the sort that Alexander Baumgarten, an inventor of modern aesthetics, described when he said that "the more that is gathered together in a confused representation, the more extensive clarity the representation has, and the more poetic it is."[3] James's personal confusions grew out of his complex culture of letters, including the domestic and sentimental scenes in which he wrote, and as he mingled the personal and the professional he created a pragmatism that he hoped would bring "extensive clarity" to difficult issues. In its simplest form, that is the story here presented.

William James staked his professional career as a philosopher on artistic acts of attention concerned, from first to last, with the domestic and the sentimental. But then he came from a family that taught him to do so. In 1910, shortly before his death, James writes to his daughter Peg, "it is good sometimes to face the naked ribs of reality as it reveals itself in homes."[4] His statement rehearses a familial concern of exceptional intensity. Perhaps because Henry James, Sr., and Mary Walsh James reared their children in hotels and pensions in Europe as well as installing them in multiple residences in New York City, Newport, and Cambridge; and perhaps because these same children took up residence far apart from one another while attempting to retain a notion of the "central" home that had no secure geographical location, Alice, Henry, and William in their letters to one another frequently comment at length on domestic matters and dwell on the significance of home.

In this respect they were very much their mother's children; Mary Walsh James's letters are filled with domestic concerns. But they were also, in this case, repeating a less predictable pattern. When as a young man Henry James, Sr. (William's father) ran away from Union College, he announced his rebellion in a letter to his close friend Isaac Jackson, a college tutor, not by descriptions of filial conflict or theological frustration, but rather by the triumph of his own domestic arrangements:

Here I am in the good town of *Bosting* very comfortably situated on the first floor ... of a four story house in Hancock Street.... The room contains a very valuable and curious library (4 large cases). My bed stands in a neat recess, on either side of which opens a handsome closet. I am sitting on a snug sofa.... On my left is a cheerful Lehigh fire; under my feet a warm carpet and over my head a painting of Lorenzo de Medici, by Mrs. Jenks. This room is sacred to me.[5]

"Neat ... handsome ... snug ... cheerful ... warm," the landlady's painting on the wall – here is a sentimental and feminized scene. Like many a description in domestic fiction, this one features stock adjectives that lack specificity (they might be reshuffled among nouns with little effect on meaning) because the writer describes a sweetly contented frame of mind more than a particular room. Culminating in the "sacred," the scene anticipates Henry Senior's life's work. As William will later describe that work, it is a theology that tears down the structures of a coldly intellectual and professional theism, replaces it with a faith resistant to discursive formulation, and describes a Creator who lovingly shelters and redeems as "He" slowly becomes "we," an aggregate Humanity, one vast family.[6] So Henry Sr. begins to dream, aware, like Rossetti and Evans, of the strange – "a very valuable and curious library (4 large cases)" – within the site of the cozy. He is deliciously alone in his sacred room rather than in the home of that superior father, William of Albany. William sends this very letter to Henry many years later, remarking that "the document is intensely precious, sacred and to be treasured. I return it for the deepest drawer of the archives": domestic safekeeping across the generations (*CWJ*, III:51).

Alice, too, considers domestic security; unlike her father, she finds no domestic haven when she leaves home. Ill in England in 1886, Alice writes to William and his wife, who are setting up house in Cambridge, Massachusetts, requesting that they take from storage in Boston whatever furniture of hers they desire, since she will not be back soon to use it herself. When she learns that the couple has not only removed some of her belongings, as she has requested, but also moved the remaining items to Cambridge and paid to have them stored there, Alice reacts with rage:

I expressly requested that you shd. take *nothing whatever to store* . . . . . . I cannot therefore conceive how you felt free to transport the remainder to wherever it was most convenient for you, without a word of consultation with me . . . . My having chosen so expensive a lodgment for the things showed on the face of it that the objects were precious to me & that I had provided for their safety in a fire- & thief-proof building . . . . I made therefore another sad mistake in supposing that what was so plain to my order of mind could not be entirely unperceived by yrs. *I have no words to express my extreme annoyance at yr. having paid the storage.* You doubtless meant to be kind . . . [7]

Alice, suffering emotional and physical torments, cannot believe that her loving brother would fail to understand how desperately she needed to maintain her home, even when she is thousands of miles away. William has deprived her of her last scrap of domestic respectability, and this act is inseparable from his failure to read her letter, and herself, with proper sympathetic understanding. The distance from "home" measures the distance of one human soul from another.

A final instance of domestically embedded meaning: one of the most intense of the James family's soundings of the term "home" may be found in Henry James's correspondence as he arranges to buy Lamb House, the dwelling in Rye he had been renting. In August of 1899 he writes to William, who has cautioned him against paying more for the property than it is worth:

My whole being cries aloud for something that I can call my own – & when I look round me at the splendour of so many of the "literary" fry my confrères . . . & I feel that I may strike the world as still, at 56, with my long labour & my genius, reckless, presumptuous & unwarranted in curling up (for more assured peaceful production,) in a poor little $10,000 shelter – once for all & for all time – *then* do I feel the bitterness of humiliation, the iron enters into my soul, & (I blush to confess it), I *weep*! (*CWJ*, III: 79)

Henry James yearns for a home as mark of literary achievement; as literary workshop; as haven whose "thick old walls never give the faintest shudder & keep out the cold as well as the violence" (*CWJ*, III:48); and as family retreat: "Lamb House," he writes William, "is *Yours* utterly – interminately – absolutely – for *all* the time you are in Europe" (p. 94). Henry would be both masterly genius and angel in the house for visiting family members; when Alice Gibbens James visits him, he reports to William: "beautiful sunsets, neat frugal dinners, evenings as peaceful as the afternoons" (p. 132). The domestic "là-bas," the ordinary transformed by sheltering love to the beautiful and blissful, has been achieved.

Such letters from William James's family members indicate a rich source of imagery for James, a philosopher whose work depended, as we shall see, on the ordinary and the domestic aesthetically conceived. The Cambridge intellectual community, the wider European intellectual community, and genteel American culture of the second half of the nineteenth century are all presences in James's scene of writing, but he begins and ends in the domestic context of his family culture. Tracing the institutions, people, places, and actual situations that surrounded James as he worked is especially helpful in comprehending his thought because James's philosophical and psychological writings often blur the line between the circumstances of their creation and their substance. Like the fiction and poetry of other Victorian Modernists, James's philosophical writing confuses the frames of daily life and the frames of written creation. Matters of actual social import in genteel America entwine in his writing with the very psychological and philosophical notions he presents. Not just casually chosen "real world" examples or illustrations of abstruse philosophical claims, James's everyday observations and experiences provide the formative energy for the kinds of questions he asks, and tend to mingle with the answers he finds. Likewise, philosophical explorations of epistemology, metaphysics, aesthetics, and ethics metamorphose subtly into social commentary.

This quality of James's writing can best be characterized as a kind of "hyper" relevance: James does not merely connect his philosophical and psychological discourse to the ordinary experience of lay people or his own personal experience. Instead, he thinks and writes from a position that continually collapses and reconstructs the distance between substance and example, between "high" professional philosophy and "low" concerns of popular audiences. Throughout his Pragmatist philosophy James insists that such a mingling is necessary to the finding and making of true ideas.

Our representative texts will be three: "The Sentiment of Rationality" (1897), "On a Certain Blindness in Human Beings" (1899), and *The Varieties of Religious Experience* (1902). Published toward the end of James's career, they explicitly address issues of sentiment and genteel homemaking in ways that reverberate throughout the Jamesian oeuvre. *Varieties* catalogues and arranges people's actual accounts of their religious experience, including their sublime contact with what he calls the "More" that inhabits the extended fringes of consciousness. Like his sister Alice and John Ruskin before him, William will find that participation in the domestic culture of his day presents him with profoundly disturbing problems of self-definition. Alice's culturally inspired sense of humiliation at her failure to establish a home and family is the equivalent of William's own cultural lapse and attendant distress, born of his desire to ground his thought in what he regarded as the private, enervating, and, "unmanly" sphere of domestic sentiment. Indeed, he believes that to be a philosopher is in the first place to separate oneself painfully from the more manly spheres of action, whether they be construed as fresh-air adventure or as law, medicine, business, or public affairs. This conflict he makes explicit in "The Sentiment of Rationality." Alice was too little "at home"; William, too much.

Yet, like his father, William will forever feel attached to the venues of domestic sentiment and place them at the center of his religious philosophy. "On a Certain Blindness" explores a specifically aesthetic solution to both the hiddenness of the human heart and the emasculations of domesticity. *Varieties of Religious Experience* will mark the full-scale expedition into the heart of decadence, which is for James, as it was for Evans and Rossetti, the heart of home. And like Henry, Jr., who insists that his continued ability to create will be compromised if he fails to buy Lamb House and who describes the very enterprise of writing as the House of Fiction, William continually risks forays into the feminized preserve of late nineteenth-century American domesticity. He reveals this path to be at once the most familiar and the most strange a man can take. For William James, then, domestic and sentimental issues inform and invigorate philosophical and psychological thought. It is no coincidence that he furnishes the lectures of *Pragmatism* with household analogies, including the personification of Pragmatism as a peace-making, philosophizing, well-bred woman, comparable to a mother nature who is similarly a creature of artifice. Pragmatism is "a mediator and reconciler" *(P*, p. 43), and "She is completely genial. She will entertain any hypothesis, she will consider any evidence.... Her manners are as various and flexible, her resources as rich and endless, and her conclusions as friendly as those of mother nature" *(P,* 44). Who better to preside over the House of Philosophy?

But a second movement in our discussion is here required. James not only gathers the domestic and sentimental into the substance and momentum of his thought, but he does so aesthetically. I use the adverb because I wish to stress the fluid development of a complex mode of thinking, writing, and speaking, rather than James's subscription to any preordained set of "aesthetic" qualities. He develops aestheticism as a growing set of experiments, attitudes, and understandings within a space of vagueness or negative capability embracing his domestic situation, the public arenas he inhabited, and the imaginary worlds he brought into being as he wrote. The mind as he understands it is a creative force, an artist within each one of us, and it is also a critic/philosopher, testing notions of aesthetic truth as it creates.

THE SENTIMENTAL MAN

James takes intellectual strength from his domestic surroundings and the sentimental energies that pulse there. He describes the composition of some of the Gifford Lectures (delivered in Edinburgh in 1901 and 1902 and published in 1902 as *The Varieties of Religious Experience*) in his house in Cambridge:

When I get into my bare attic room, fifty-two feet long and nothing in it but a table, a standing desk, and an arm chair, paper, inkstand, and the books I bring up; flooded with warm white winter sunshine, I get a feeling of seclusion and power... (*CWJ*, III: 49–50)

The simplicity, order, and ease of the room belie the conflicts of its inhabitant. Power is indeed the issue: his status within both the growing profession of philosophy and society at large.[8]

From early on, James associates the best philosophy with beauty and art (he notes in his diary, upon reading Friedrich Schiller's *Loveliness and Dignity*, that his old "antinomian" trouble is "a dissatisfaction with anything less than grace").[9] Furthermore, James recognizes defensively that for the man of business, he who works in the marketplace rather than in a sunny attic, philosophy is "a superfluity, an ornament, like poetry or music, which one can turn his back on with impunity" (*MEN*, p. 3). James feels a diminishment of power when he is attacked from two sides: professional philosophers distrust his "antinomian" standard of aesthetic, quasi-religious feeling captured in the word "grace," while laymen see his philosophy as "merely" ornamental, useless in the "real" world. Like a woman's domestic graces – needlework or a turn at the keyboard – his learning counts for little.

James's straw men, those practical people who denigrate philosophy, are not entirely unfair in associating philosophy with beauty of the feminized and domestic sort. James himself associates beauty and taste not only with the most private of realms – each person's sensations – but also with the private realm socially construed. In his time this was primarily the world of women. Reviewing Santayana's *The Sense of Beauty*, James praises the philosopher's willingness to find diverse sources of aesthetic value rather than assuming that aesthetics is all about "the absolute supremacy of an abstraction called Beauty, with a big B." James tellingly gives as his example of a truer aesthetics the experience of "simple" people, who "appreciate the neatness of muslin curtains, shining varnish, and burnished pots. A rustic garden is a shallow patchwork of the loveliest flowers."[10] He applies Santayana's insight to metaphysics itself: radical empiricism and pragmatism both deny the absolute supremacy of any abstraction. Such humble simplicity, a proof of sincerity, is the beginning of good taste. Just so, James appreciates his own sun-filled, orderly study, while he writes within it *The Varieties of Religious Experience*. In that work, as we shall see, he conflates the domestic and the aesthetic through a sentimental performance that, reaching outward to seek sublimity as it is experienced by real people at the margins of their consciousness, enacts the very philosophical position it purports to present scientifically.

The problems James faces in negotiating his way through a world aesthetically and domestically construed he often signals by the words "sentiment" and the "sentimental." Toward the close of *Varieties*, James admits that he has perhaps crossed an unspoken line, that his documentary cases of religious experience have "literally bathed in sentiment" his audience. "I am almost appalled at the amount of emotionality which I find [in my own work]," he confesses (*VRE*, p. 383). Here, "sentiment" means excess emotion, but sometimes James appears to use it to mean more neutrally just "feeling," as in his title, "The Sentiment of Rationality." Sentiment is also linked to sensation to the extent that James opposes both of them to conceptual thought. Women and effeminate men are sentimental; all of us have sensations and sentiments. Yet these various distinctions never really hold; in fact, we can regard both "sentiment" and "sentimental" as place markers in James, indications that here he feels and wishes to convey a conflict about the place of men and women in his culture. James argues variously that any philosophy worth its salt is based upon sentiment; that all philosophies are necessarily based upon sentiment; and that the sentimental is a second-rate, craven, moralizing, effeminate, or just plain female, mode. James is both appalled by it and utterly sure that he will convince others of its importance to aesthetics, religion, philosophy, and psychology as they are pursued by "real" men.

He also fears sentiment. In 1868 he tells Henry, for example, that at one time, after reading Schiller and Goethe (in fact two of his direct sources for the literary and philosophical tradition of sensibility and sentiment) he had wished that Goethe had been more "sentimental, musical, visceral, whatever you please to call them." Now, however, in his maturity, "I smile . . . to think of my unhealthiness & weakness" (*CWJ*, 1:51).[11] Yet by the closing decade of his career, James writes an extravagant paean to emotionality and visceral thought – panics and raptures, enthusiasms and visions – entitles it *The Varieties of Religious Experience*, and therein celebrates the feeling, not the conceptualizing, mind. This is the mind of "sentiment," a word that by the mid-nineteenth century papers over immense social conflicts brewing in the realm of gender politics. It covers a multitude of meanings, some conservative of, some immensely threatening to, social arrangements through the turn of the century.

Domesticity, aestheticism, and sentiment: James lives and works perilously in spaces between the secure categories of public and private, male and female. Although scholarly treatments of James frequently mention his family life and his kind-hearted treatment of others, his life and thought are generally assumed to be masculine in character. Perhaps because commentators sense the dissonances of James's chosen positions, they wish all the more fervently to resolve them into a masculine harmony. He is thus frequently portrayed as a neurasthenic saved by manly activity, an advocate of the outdoor life and moral strenuousness, a son who transforms his father's intellectual legacy, and a dilettante who eventually finds moral, emotional, and financial security in professionalism, however critical he may be of institutions, titles, and degrees. Meliorism, voluntarism, pragmatism all have to do with action implicitly gendered masculine by his culture: willing (rather than submitting), building (rather than being or dwelling), having one's say (rather than remaining silent) in nothing less than the universe itself.

George Santayana presents a characteristically acute expression of this view. Writing of pragmatism, he explains, "Ideas are not mirrors, they are weapons; their function is to prepare us to meet events." Yet James, he tells us, chooses to dwell in the ideas of "sentimentalists, mystics, spiritualists, wizards, cranks, quacks, and impostors." Santayana's explanation: James becomes the "friend and helper . . . spokesman and representative" of these poor crazy individuals. "Yet the *normal practical masculine American*, too, had a friend in William James."[12] Those who are "groping, nervous, half-educated" are not straightforwardly masculine anymore than are sentimentalists. Nor, by association, is James, who demonstrates on their behalf the virtues of modesty, sympathy, and comfort-giving, questionable just to the extent that they are part of woman's work. Santayana redoubles his efforts to masculinize, i.e., invigorate and normalize, pragmatism: intelligence is an instrument of survival, "one kind of practical adjustment, an experimental act, a form of vital tension."[13] The pragmatism that Santayana then proceeds to question has at least been rescued from the charge of effeminacy. Yet far from embodying Santayana's notion of a masculine, pragmatic vigor, James was a man always attracted to languor, private intensities, and life indoors within a domestic, feminized scene. This James did not wish to separate himself from mysticism, sentimentality, or quackery, nor did he wish to surrender his masculinity.

It is by now a truism that nineteenth-century Americans imagined experience as divided between woman's private sphere of home and hearth, and men's public sphere of marketplace and professionalism. In fact, the two spheres overlapped, or, to present a more accurate metaphor, the two balls of yarn entangled frustratingly for men and women alike. But William James, more than most men of his day, believed that he lived, worked, and loved in both, rather than maintaining a rigid distinction between "life" in the private sphere and "work" in the public. Within his home, he blurred the lines between motherly and fatherly roles as he worked long hours in his study, often with his children present. At Harvard and, indeed, nationally and internationally, he was recognized by students and colleagues as exceptionally nurturing, tender-hearted, and modest even as he stood his intellectual ground.

William James's domesticity, his participation in "woman's" culture, should matter to this study only if it be reflected in his writing. The presence of the feminized and domestic within his thought must, for a mid-century American man of letters, be felt as a problem, and James indeed sets it out expressly as such in a pseudonymous passage within *The Varieties of Religious Experience.* James at times conducted his search for solutions in darkness and experienced them as decadent morbidity. Yet he never forgot that the lights might be rekindled to reveal the securities of home. Let us study, then, a "feminized" James who experienced the sentimental education of the aesthete.

A SYMPATHY WITH THE MORBID

In considering the significance of the domestic scene to James's thought, we must understand that for him it combined the repose of the familiar with the mingled threat and lure of the strange. The metamorphic quality of his daily life, its tendency to appear now as a maternal, domestic haven, now as a darkened theater of imagination, plays itself out not just in James's primary work of the sensationalistic margins, *The Varieties of Religious Experience*, but also throughout his oeuvre. Like Ruskin, Rossetti, and Evans, James explored the grotesque, a version of the sublime. Home is an important context in which to consider James's musings, both sunny and dark, on the many and the one, rationalism and materialism, the meaning of truth, and the meaning of faith.

In the famously disguised account of his own spiritual and emotional crisis in *The Varieties of Religious Experience*, James captures most intensely his feeling that the familiar tends to yield the disturbingly strange. Like popular women writers of the day who paradoxically announced in print the principle that woman's voice should be heard only in the private sphere, (we think of Augusta Evans's "There shall be no more books written"), James veils his words.[14] He bases *Varieties* on the value of personal testimony but denies his own, presenting autobiography as the "translated" words of a French (read decadent) journalist (read panderer to the public, not a serious thinker). The passage is worth quoting at length:

Whilst in this state of philosophic pessimism and general depression of spirits about my prospects, I went one evening into a dressing room in the twilight to procure some article that was there; when suddenly there fell upon me without any warning, just as if it came out of the darkness, a horrible fear of my own existence. Simultaneously there arose in my mind the image of an epileptic patient whom I had seen in the asylum, a black-haired youth with greenish skin, entirely idiotic, who used to sit all day on one of the benches, or rather shelves against the wall, with his knees drawn up against his chin, and the coarse gray undershirt, which was his only garment, drawn over them inclosing his entire figure. He sat there like a sort of sculptured Egyptian cat or Peruvian mummy, moving nothing but his black eyes and looking absolutely non-human. This image and my fear entered into a species of combination with each other. *That shape am I*, I felt, potentially. . . . I became a mass of quivering fear. After this the universe was changed for me altogether. I awoke morning after morning with a horrible dread at the pit of my stomach, and with a sense of the insecurity of life that I never knew before, and that I have never felt since. It was like a revelation; and although the immediate feelings passed away, the experience has made me sympathetic with the morbid feelings of others ever since. It gradually faded, but for months I was unable to go out into the dark alone.

In general I dreaded to be left alone. I remember wondering how other people could live, how I myself had ever lived, so unconscious of that pit of insecurity beneath the surface of life. My mother in particular, a very cheerful person, seemed to me a perfect paradox in her unconsciousness of danger, which you may well believe I was very careful not to disturb by revelations of my own state of mind. I have always thought that this experience of melancholia of mine had a religious bearing.... the fear was so invasive and powerful that if I had not clung to scripture-texts like "The eternal God is my refuge," etc., ... I think I should have grown really insane.[15]

The force of the passage develops precisely in its deviation from the domestic everyday: what should be an ordinary experience in that most ordinary of places, a dressing room, becomes a twilight experience of hallucinatory seizure, infectious madness.

The epileptic youth has become a thing on a shelf rather than a person in a chair; the very sign of madness is simultaneous proximity to and utter distance from the securities of home. The asylum where James has seen the creature – a sinister home where people are perhaps cared for but seldom loved – travesties a domestic haven just as, for the space of this vision, James's closet is home and not home. Sympathy, that most powerful of domestic virtues, here intensifies into horror; sensibility's fellow-feeling evoked in James by the memory of this patient makes of a man a small child: "for months I was unable to go out into the dark alone." He needs the security of home now more than ever, and, as if by imagistic power, his mother makes an appearance: "My mother in particular, a very cheerful person, seemed to me a perfect paradox in her unconsciousness of danger, which you may well believe I was very careful not to disturb...." As a man James must shelter her from the horror he knows; but he also may, like every male in genteel America, claim refuge in woman's sphere. His mother's cheerfulness and light are, with the Bible, ("if I had not clung to scripture-texts.... I think I should have grown really insane") the signs of his salvation.

To this plot of entitlement – the beset male may expect the domestic presence of the cheerful female – James adds a sensational twist: it is an interior cataclysm, not the vagaries of the market place, that causes the speaker to cling to his home. But home, usually the locus of sincerity in contrast to the slippery morality of the public sphere, here becomes a museum. James has seen the huddled figure as "a sort of sculptured Egyptian cat or Peruvian Mummy": within the mind within the closet within the house lurk the intense strangeness, beauty, and danger of the aesthetic, of life captured and slain into art.

James's commentators have from the first recognized his interest in "human life in the everyday world" (*P*, p. xxvii), his insistence that the amateur and the professional philosopher alike assent to philosophical beliefs on the basis of temperament, and his warnings against ignoring "everyday" experience. But the everyday world is of course always *an* everyday world; the "ordinary" is perhaps the most time- and place-bound of all concepts. One approach to parsing James's notion of the ordinary world of human feeling has been to examine the intellectual history of sentiment, to demonstrate that James's anti-intellectualist philosophy has a genealogy. Morton White, who never defines "sentiment" but uses the term as portmanteau for a varied set of "anti-scientific" positions, has admirably traced such a philosophical narrative from Lockian intuition, to Jonathan Edwards's "Sense of the Heart," to the Scottish Common Sense philosophers as they were transformed by the Transcendentalists, through Emerson's "sentimental" Reason.[16] William James then takes his place in a line of American philosophers who have granted sentiment a decisive role in theories of knowledge, metaphysical belief, and ethics. The representative passage of this intellectual heritage would be, for our purposes in establishing the importance of domestic culture in James's work, these words from Emerson's "American Scholar":

What would we really know the meaning of? The meal in the firkin; the milk in the pan; the ballad in the street; the news of the boat; the glance of the eye; the form and gait of the body; – show me the ultimate reason of these matters; show me the sublime presence of the highest spiritual cause lurking, as always it does lurk, in these suburbs and extremities of nature.[17]

About these homely yet sublime matters we know by feeling. Let us turn to one of William James's own essays about knowledge and feeling, "The Sentiment of Rationality," to explore with him the philosophical venue of the human heart.

DEAREST DESIRES AND "THE SENTIMENT OF RATIONALITY"

To the woman he hopes to marry, Alice Howe Gibbens, William James writes that he feels most intensely alive, most himself, when he experiences an "active tension" within and trusts outward things "to perform their part without any guarantee that they will." The absence of guarantee he feels as a "sort of deep enthusiastic bliss, of bitter willingness to do and suffer anything, which translates itself physically by a kind of stinging pain inside of my breast-bone." This mood or emotion is "to me as the deepest principle of all active or theoretic determination."[18] At letter's end he apologizes, as well he might, for his aridity and awkwardness; nevertheless he stands by his plan to make intellectual epistolary love, to describe his inner feelings as relevant both to his philosophy and to his acceptance by Alice.

After courting as a philosopher, James soon philosophizes as a family man in "The Sentiment of Rationality",[19] where he explores such topics as the nature and types of rationality, the contrasting temperaments of idealists and materialists, and the power of personal belief, in certain circumstances, to create truth. Yet at the same time he confronts a troubling contradiction at the heart of domestic life in genteel America: home is the haven that men wish for, but it is also the site of emasculation, of a peacefulness that might anaesthetize or even permanently cripple its male inhabitants.[20] The domestic and sentimental entwine as a leitmotif of the essay; through its philosophical music and its rhetorical patterns James returns us repeatedly to the site of the middle-class home.

Philosophical thought, James tells his audience, is inseparable from the ordinary experience of actual people. How do we recognize rationality? Through feelings of "ease, peace, and rest" (*WB*, 57). Such peacefulness and simplicity are aesthetically pleasing – "the relief of the musician at resolving a confused mass of sound" and domestically prudent – "the passion for parsimony, for economy of means in thought, is the philosophic passion par excellence" (p. 58). Yet this rational desire for simplification meets a conflicting desire for "distinguishing" which "loves to recognize particulars in their full completeness." Purely "theoretic rationalism" fails because it over-simplifies; we must consider rationality in its "practical" aspects as well (pp. 65–66). The notion of feeling widens to include not just mental ease, fluency, or lack of obstruction, but also the actual, complicated feelings of "the entire man" as he experiences daily life.

Simple conceptions here just won't do. We must leave the "insipid spaciousness" of theoretic rationality, a shelter that is no shelter, and pass into the "teeming and dramatic richness of the concrete world" (*WB*, p. 61). Here we find ourselves squarely in the world of custom, "the daily contemplation of phenomena juxtaposed in a certain order" (p. 66) which allows us to understand objects by what they have been and will probably become. This experience of daily life is now the very source of "whatever rationality the thing may gain in our thought" (p. 67); it is none other than rationality in its practical aspect. Every philosophical conception must "banish uncertainty from the future," must make us *feel* at home. "When we take up our quarters in a new room, we do not know what draughts may blow in upon our back, what doors may open, what forms may enter, what interesting objects may be found in cupboards and corners," he tells his audience. But after a few days "the feeling of strangeness disappears" (p. 67). Just as we inhabit rooms and grow to feel the balm of familiarity, so rational conceptions practically considered must also save us from the strange and unpredictable. James uses domestic analogies here as the very backbone of his argument, not as secondary elucidation or mere ornamentation, for the "sentiment" of rationality is in the end inseparable from the "sentimental," the private sphere of feeling experienced within rooms we actually inhabit.

As if with a dawning horror, James, safely tucked into the bed of home truths and predictable outcomes, suddenly sits upright. Too much reassurance, he counsels, is bad. The familiar and the customary now must play a different role: they must invite us to act upon them. Should we do so under the aegis of materialism or idealism? Neither – or both. Materialism, by denying that there is an eternal aspect under which we may consider our purposes, makes us feel *unheimlich*, unhoused, in the universe. Materialism allows us to act, but not to feel that our acts matter in the great scheme of things. Yet idealism, James argues, seems to obviate the need for action, as we dwell in our egos and minds, sure that our minds and absolute Mind are of one substance. Idealist "atonement" encourages utter passivity. In choosing between tough-minded materialism and tender-minded idealism, James explains, we find ourselves either distanced from a sympathetic home or paralyzed deep within one.

Neither alternative suffices; James wants both to rest at home and to live intensely, physically, strenuously. He embraces domestic security, but he must seek risk and challenge. Lest we underestimate his masculine striving, he closes with one last dichotomy. Do we wish to be moral skeptics (alarmingly foppish, epicurean, and superficial) or moral absolutists (energetic, if tragically rigid)? As between the skeptic's apathy and the absolutist's energy, James would have us choose the latter, but also choose to run risks, *make* truth in an as yet unfinished universe that defies the absolutist's tragic view. A tinge of skepticism will give us reason to make that choice. Yet even James's repudiation of the effeminate and foppish he couches in effeminate terms. For any philosophy to succeed, he explains, it must not disappoint our "dearest desires and most cherished powers" (*WB*, 70). The case for masculine spontaneity and power is made in the very bastion of the heart, the private sphere of home and hearth. "All that the human heart wants is its chance," he insists: a plaintive enough call to action (p. 89).

James observes, "Thousands of innocent magazine readers lie paralyzed and terrified, in the network of shallow negations which the leaders of opinion have thrown over their souls." If they pay attention to their feelings and intuitions, they will become "free and hearty again" as they sweep away "fastidious vetoes against belief" (*WB*, p. 89). In this lecture James mingles a host of oppositions: masculinity and femininity, logic and sentiment, will and paralysis. The question remains, whether the promptings of the heart, that throbbing organ of sentimental American popular culture, can ever send men up mountains to tax their endurance and prove themselves against the universe. Will a philosophy that takes seriously the feeling person forever be a trap?

Having explored the domains of sentiment and custom for their philosophical "cash value," James has opened a philosophical space which threatens him as a cultural prison. James still isn't sure about how rationality should be understood in relation to everyday feelings and hopes. His argument with himself about the place of softness in a discipline of rigor may be better understood by viewing his problem as a wider issue of mid- and late-nineteenth-century American culture, its argument with itself about the gender of feeling.

William James came to writing in a cultural milieu striking in its richness. First there is his widely documented personal situation: the influence of Henry James, Sr.; the rejection of careers in art, medicine, and, eventually, experimental psychology; the history of neurasthenic affliction; the fascinations of growing up in a family distinguished by its roving ways, waxing creativity, and waning material resources. Widening the scene of writing to include the set of institutions and people to whom James looked as he began to write, we may search the influences at work in Cambridge from 1860, beginning with various philosophical clubs of intellectual young men and developing toward the heyday of "Harvard Pragmatism" from 1898 to 1907.[21] Or, widening our explorations further still, we may examine James's position in the larger culture, focusing on James this time as a public philosopher who attempted to meet his anxious and listless society on the ground of its most pressing needs by creating "a discourse of heroism."[22] In the latter view, James set out his philosophy as therapy for so many American Hamlets: the will to believe, the strenuous life, and pragmatism would address the problem of the individual will. The attack on determinism, the emphasis on voluntarism and the anatomy of the sick soul can be understood in part as James's expression of and intervention in the ailing culture around him.

In these varied approaches to the culture of letters in which James gradually found his way, his experience in the private sphere, still considered "woman's" sphere in his day, tends to fade away, as if into one of the vague auras he describes in *Principles of Psychology*. As one of James's biographers has stated – and he might speak for almost every other commentator – "This is primarily a story about men, not because women are unimportant, but because the sources tell it that way."[23] "The" sources have long included William's sister and his wife (the two Alices), as well as a rich correspondence with Henry about such unmanly topics as living quarters, clothing, and illnesses. Anxiety at valuing this kind of information as part of any serious discussion of James's philosophy and psychology has often prevailed. Given our willingness to expand the record to womanly matters, the "so what" question rightly intrudes.[24] How are we to make useful connections between James's ordinary life at home and his life of the mind? James certainly advocates that we mingle the two.

We might well begin, as George Cotkin has, with the general social malaise of the period.[25] He sees James's solution (however problematical for James himself) in his exploration of strenuous experience that reads culturally as the rigors of outdoor life, martial energies redirected to peaceable ends, and a certain posture of lively feistiness toward the universe or, more modestly, toward's one own ennui. But we should also examine James's search for a renewal of failing energies within the domestic scene itself, and specifically within that scene's potential for intense, aesthetic experience. The American genteel home traps men and women alike, but James considers more than the traditional masculinist routes of escape. Pragmatism is a method predicated upon action and testing, and James wants to use it to free people even within the home.

Rather than dismissing mid-nineteenth-century domesticity – the private, pious, and pure realm of woman's culture, often considered "sentimental" – as part of the debasement of American culture against which James had to speak out in a discourse of masculine heroism, we might instead examine two aspects of such domestic culture. First, we might pause to remember that such culture, described and recreated in popular fiction of the day such as that of Augusta Evans, is never merely platitudinous or formulaic. It may embrace an idealized status quo, but it can also criticize, explore, and even undermine it. And second, we might consider James's chosen participation in domestic culture.

To understand William James's view of domestic matters, we ask, then, how he saw himself in relation to the "low" culture of domestic discourse. Like authors of domestic handbooks and like many a domestic novelist, he spoke directly, in familiar, even avuncular, tones to audiences whom he wished to convince of the importance of their humble experience, the legitimacy of their direct reactions to life. We recognize that James's essays often began as public lectures for a general audience, that he deliberately popularized his ideas on religion and ethics; and that he spoke therapeutically as well as scientifically of discipline, habit formation, and even metaphysics. Indeed, his commitment to such popularization of his ideas – like the domestic novelists, he spoke and wrote to support his family – actually stood in the way of his ever working out a technical philosophy for an audience of experts (*MEN*, p. xxvi).

James saw his philosophy's strength in its directness and accessibility, its deviation from the unstated codes of professional philosophy. Of *Pragmatism*, he writes to Henry, "It is a very 'sincere' and, from the point of view of ordinary philosophy-professorial manner, a very unconventional utterance, not particularly original at any point." Yet the volume has a "squeak or shrillness in the voice that enables the book to *tell*, when others don't" (*CWJ*, II:279). In the same letter in which he thus attributes *Pragmatism*'s strength to its effeminate voice, he announces how glad he is to have "thrown off the nightmare of my 'professorship'"; back in the privacy of his home, he feels "at liberty to be a *reality*, and the comfort is unspeakable" (*CWJ*, III:350).

James's frequent appearances on the lecture circuit carried more moral authority than present-day audiences would expect. The "profession" of lecturing, especially in its slant toward helping members of the audience, was often compared to the ministry.[26] His public lecturing meant that James would have been associated with the clergy, a feminized "helping" profession by mid-century, and thus with the private devotional sphere, woman's realm.[27] Indeed he writes to Henry of his speaking engagements, "Women's clubs are the great inviters" (*CWJ*, III:258).

Furthermore, James's personality, if not his metaphysics, was tender: people felt drawn to him because they believed he cared about them and understood their problems. Witnesses agree upon his gift of intimacy; even if we make adjustments for hagiographical tendencies, reports of former students depict James as wise, modest, and sympathetic. One of them writes, "His voice was so splendid, his use of words and the way he spoke them were so unique, and the problems which he discussed were at once so close to the common experience of man and so filled with his own peculiar wisdom, that his lectures were hailed as an intellectual treat."[28] Another writes of his teaching, "Always happy turns of intriguing phrases, a glow of warmth and meaning. . . . We were always thinking *together*. That sort of 'teaching' made us like the subject and love the instructor." He adds that James often inveigled students into "participating in the gracious hospitality of a perfect home. He was the consummate artist at living."[29] So popular was he that in 1904 he declined one hundred invitations to speak (*P*, p. xvi). Grateful readers and audience members wrote to him directly, just as the reading public in *St. Elmo* communicates directly with its adored Edna Earl.

Part of James's appeal would have been the comfort of hearing new ideas patiently explained in familiar terms and framed by traditional values. In book reviews and occasional essays he describes the home as man's haven, "one tranquil spot where he shall be valid absolutely & once for all" and the proper wife as subordinate to her husband (*ECR*, pp. 253–254). His own correspondence reveals that he believed he lived the ideal, that the premier domestic prize of the comely, intelligent, strong, and pure helpmate was actually his. When William, beset by nerves, fatigue, and ambition, leaves Alice in Cambridge with small children and a tight budget while he travels abroad, she writes:

you must not come home before spring. For your own sake it is a world better that you should stay. Wait till things are settled and you have done the work you desire to unhindered by the interruptions you would groan under here . . . I am happy to think of you in comfortable lodgings seeing these men you like. (Houghton, 22 December 1882)

William accepted uncritically the view of woman as man's intellectual inferior; in the "scale of culture" woman is below man (*PP*, II:368). Yet William respected and revered Alice, and he did so for just those qualities of feeling and intuition he would make so central to his philosophy. He answers her letters from Cambridge with a wish that she were there to judge the philosophers he meets, for with her "intuitive grasping of metaphysical and personal – *especially personal* – truth, I fairly long for your diagnosis" (Houghton, 28 June 1880).

Alice attends the deathbed of Henry, Sr., and then writes a letter to William (still in Europe when his father died) expressing grief, hope, and love worthy of the idealized heroine of popular fiction:

Be thankful dear, that in that real world in which he lived, he drew you to himself and your nature answered to his own. If you only could have seen his face with that mighty look of triumph upon it – It would have been a revelation to himself. To me it said life, *life, life everlasting!* (Houghton, nd)

Sentimental: yes, but not "merely" so: Alice ably reports and evokes the tender emotions. William James could speak directly to a general audience of domestic concerns popularly conceived because he knew them intimately and linked them to his work as a philosopher.

Yet James realized that popularity had its price. From a pleasure resort near Chautauqua, he writes to his wife, "I breakfasted with a Methodist parson with 32 false teeth . . . The wife said she had my portrait in her bedroom with the words written under it, 'I want to bring a balm to human lives'!!!!! Supposed to be a quotation from me!!!" (*CWJ*, II:43). He denigrated his "squashy popular-lecture style," resented speaking before crowds of Chautauqua visitors, and registered the cost of his public persona: "I have also just been offered 1500 dollars worth of lecturing in California . . . All this means hard labor & is inseparable from a social jigging which is rank poison to my nature" (*CWJ*, III:2). Lecturing, he muses, is "a sort of prostitution of one's person" (p. 233). He believes that respectable academic minds have come to loathe him (*CWJ*, II:300–301).

William James managed to situate himself within genteel domestic and popular culture – he married well, sold well, and, at least compared to his earlier periods of mental strife, he even slept and ate well. Yet he also sounded the limitations of such culture, yearned for more, sought to contribute to the "high" stream of philosophical achievement. A threat haunts the "Sentiment of Rationality": that sentiment, however central to the philosophical enterprise, might entrap the philosopher within an enervating domesticity. Indeed, the final image of "The Sentiment of Rationality" refers to escape, the seeking of "another realm into which the stifled soul may escape from pedantic scruples and indulge its own faith at its own risks" (p. 89). This realm he would describe in an essay about pleasurable repose which he himself labeled popular: "On a Certain Blindness in Human Beings."

THE SUBURBS AND EXTREMITIES OF NATURE: "ON A CERTAIN BLINDNESS"

The dilemma of James's "Sentiment of Rationality," that the attraction to the securities of home might extinguish American achievement with a vast yawn, had long been faced by American women who wrote domestic novels, including Augusta Evans. Like Evans, whose Edna Earl labors at home as a writer and caretaker for a dying boy while conquering the New York literary scene, William James absorbed energy from within the very enclosures he feared. The domestic scene may yield a shocking, but salutary, intensity of experience. There the mind may feel. "In passing the hand over the sideboard or in jogging the coal-scuttle with the foot, the large glossy dark shape of the one and the irregular blackness of the other awaken like a flash" (*PP*, I:556), William writes, revealing the wilderness of sensation to be explored at home. Simply touching an orange on the table may evoke synaesthetic theater, cause a "savor and perfume" to "shoot through [the] mind" (p. 556). The anaesthesia or anomie of the "epileptic patient" may be cured by the aesthetic flash of appreciation experienced at home, an invigorating novelty in the heart of familiarity.

Domesticity was as intrinsic to James's productivity as a thinker as it was threatening to his fondest philosophical ambitions. Most importantly, the conflict sent him in search of an aesthetic basis for his philosophy. He gives us reason to believe that his "tough-minded" and "tender-minded" types are revisions of Schiller's "naive" and "sentimental,"[30] and he explains in *Principles of Psychology* that "many of the so-called metaphysical principles are at bottom only expressions of aesthetic feeling" (*PP*, 1:672). While the "only" in that sentence strikes a diminishing note, James more often praises the aesthetic so long as it means the actual experiences people have of something they call beauty. He periodically attacks traditional philosophical aesthetics as a grim science that misses the point of beauty; in a review of Henry R. Marshall's *Pain, Pleasure and Aesthetics* (1894) he notes approvingly that the author expands the concept of beauty to include the actual experiences of people feeling pleasure, hinting, it seems, at a nascent *Varieties of Aesthetic Experience* (*ECR*, p. 490). James wishes to include the mundane in the continuum of aesthetic experience which might begin with a pleasant walk and culminate in appreciation of Michaelangelo or Beethoven (pp. 337–338).

William James explores the relation of domesticity and aesthetic experience in his essay "On a Certain Blindness in Human Beings." He states that in the essay lies "the perception on which my whole individualistic philosophy" is based.[31] Like Rossetti busily painting "potboilers" replete with domestic articles, James claims within this "rather popular" work an aesthetic way not beyond, but *into* the domestic. He simultaneously asserts domesticity's conservative and popular roots and exposes its transformative potential for the individual and for society.[32] To Dr. G. C. Ferrari he writes that the volume in which the essay appears "is better loved by me than any of my other productions, especially [valued is] the Essay on a certain blindness" (*TT*, p. 256). Here is the William James who believes that the tender can subsume the strenuous without paralyzing the man of feeling. That he "loved" both his essay and the essay by Robert Louis Stevenson he quotes at length within it; that it sold extremely well; that he believed his individualistic philosophy to be based upon it; that in form it pays lip-service to logical development but in performance early on gives way blissfully to a stream of metamorphosing tableaux and echoing images; that these tableaux, however exotic (James takes us all the way to Patagonia), are presented within a context of homemaking: all of these matters testify to James's realization over the years that domesticity, aesthetically experienced, provides an opportunity, not a trap. The heroic and the energetic may be located within the tender heart of domestic security.

In "On a Certain Blindness" James preaches the messages of tolerance and respect for others. The world we know and appreciate is the world each one of us makes; we cannot expect ever to experience the world as someone else, whether stranger or intimate, "knows" it to be. As Alice's letter about her stored belongings testifies, we have difficulty knowing another's feelings. Henry's impassioned defense of his right to home-ownership takes William, his intimate, by surprise. Rather than developing traditional philosophical arguments about the nature of human identity or knowledge, James instead chooses in "On a Certain Blindness" to paint with words a familiar and individual form of knowing the world: homemaking. As he figures forth the five major tableaux of the essay – homemaking scenes set in North Carolina, Brooklyn, Scotland, Russia and Patagonia – James meditates upon aesthetic practice as the surest route to one's truest self. Homemaking involves nothing less than one's imagination in intimate and changing relation with the universe.

James displays in "On a Certain Blindness" then, not just the site of homesteading, but also of claiming and arranging the world, of arriving at that "custom" he has introduced in "The Sentiment of Rationality." Yet each time that he rehearses the domestic imperative – to claim the here and now by making it fit for human habitation – he expands its realm and abstracts its goals. Eventually he portrays in "On a Certain Blindness" something like the pleasurable habitation he describes in an 1873 letter to Henry:

How people can pass years without a week of that *Normal* life I can't imagine. Life in which your cares and responsibilities and thoughts for the morrow become a far off dream, and you *are* simply, floating on from day to day, and "boarded" you don't know how, by what Providence, washed clean without and within, by the light and the tender air. (*CWJ*, 1:215)

Such a lodging embraces the world of dream and irresponsibility in the open and tender air, the very ether claimed as home.

It is a place of repose remarkably similar to another dwelling, one that appears at the close of "On a Certain Blindness." James depicts the naturalist W. H. Hudson, who has gone (manfully) exploring in the desert wilderness of Patagonia. No domestic acedia for Hudson. The land he explores provides an antithesis to the genteel parlor: it is an unformed "grey waste, stretching away into infinitude, a waste untrodden by man" (*TT*, p. 147). Hudson "explores" without object or motive; indeed he rides about for hours at a slow pace in "aimless wanderings," open to every sensation. The summit of a hill reveals undulating grey sameness to the very horizon. But the narrative takes a turn: Hudson finds a grove on a hill that looks different from neighboring hills; he makes a "point of finding it and using it as a resting place every day at noon" (p. 148). As the habit forms, he begins to conceive of his special site as tidy, "that particular clump of trees, with polished stems and clean bed of sand beneath" (p. 148). It is a place of repose from which he would watch and listen in a state of suspense both strange and elating. Hudson believes that he has "*gone back*" to a savage condition (p. 149); like James, he desires a life in which "you *are* simply, floating on from day to day, and 'boarded' you don't know how."

Home is now a bed of sand at the end of the earth; the explorer who energetically strikes out from his "insipid existence" at home now lies in utter languor which is simultaneously savage. But what a Schillerian savagery: he is "in perfect harmony with nature" (*TT*, p. 149). His daily drama played out for irrational reasons has taken him home to a sheltered grove and to all of nature, home to the concentered self and to the egoless being of a "wild animal." Like Baudelaire's dandy-savage of *The Painter of Modern Life*, Hudson practices "the centralization and vaporization of the self."[33] Of this savagery more later.

James has prepared us to grasp intuitively the limit at which domesticity sublimely opens upon the imaginative habitation of the cosmos in the long passage he quotes in "On a Certain Blindness" from Stevenson's "Lantern Bearers." Stevenson describes in his essay a favorite childhood pastime: he would hide a lantern under his topcoat, walk by himself through the darkness, meet in hidden places with friends similarly equipped, and just talk in the lantern-light. "Man's true life," Stevenson writes, "for which he consents to live, lie[s] altogether in the field of fancy ... the true realism, always and everywhere, is that of the poets: to find out where joy resides" (*TT*, p. 137). The tin bull's-eye lanterns hidden inside the coats of Scottish boys surely offer James a powerful metaphor for the hiddenness of the human heart, but as "some golden chamber" at the heart of life, the image of the lantern (Romantic emblem of the Imagination itself) echoes Stevensons's emblem of the "warm, phantasmagoric chamber of [man's] brain, with the painted windows and the

storied walls" (p. 137). Both insist upon the imaginative quality of every
site of deep security. The boys who hide the lanterns gather in "some
hollow of the links" or in the "belly of a ten-man lugger" (p. 135) in
order to escape the blasting winds. Their secret lantern-bearing fellowship within sheltered spaces is practical (they seek shelter from the cold),
utterly and importantly whimsical (Schillerian play is serious), and ever
dramatically and aesthetically conceived: lanterns for lanterns' sake.

James repeats this pattern of aestheticized domesticity throughout
"On a Certain Blindness." Only when Peter of *War and Peace*, another
of James's featured homemakers, inhabits the most constricting home
imaginable, a jail cell, can he experience "powerful and ineffaceable
sensations" at daybreak that infuse his life, for the first time, with joy (*TT*,
p. 135). Whitman leaves his room "about 12 and loafe[s] somewhere,"
taking it easy until he can imagine the entire city intimately, "face to
face" (pp. 142–143). Such joy and repose will become defining elements
of mystical religious experience itself as James presents it in *The Varieties
of Religious Experience*.

A theme with variations, "On a Certain Blindness" is also a collage of
essay, poetry, fiction, and travelogue. By quoting voluminously, James,
like Ruskin in *Roadside Songs of Tuscany*, appropriates the voices of his
chosen writers. As he points the "morals" of these borrowed passages,
he also lets them speak for themselves and contradict the logical scheme
of his essay, which aims to document the solitude of the human heart
as a first step in urging us to overcome barriers between ourselves and
others. One of James's domestic settlers, Walt Whitman, for example,
celebrates his oneness with, rather than distance from, members of the
crowd: "Just as you feel when you look on the river and sky, so I felt"
(*TT*, p. 142); but James himself, by quoting at length, causes us to lose
track of where his voice ends and Whitman's or Tolstoy's or Stevenson's
begins. He *is* these others; their vision is his vision, Patagonia, Brooklyn,
Russia are his worlds. Even an ugly cabin built by a homesteader in
North Carolina is his; who more than the tender William could understand the man who wishes only to gather his family safely about him?
James's Victorian Modernist subject, complex yet familiar and simple,
fragmented yet cohesive, elusive but appropriated, takes shape – as ten-
tatively yet as deliberately as did Ruskin's Francesca. Like Ruskin, James
conducts experiments in domestic sentiment in order to understand others. He has, however, additional aims in mind.

In order to explore the fullness of James's Victorian Modernism in
"On a Certain Blindness," we must return to W. H. Hudson's volume

Idle Days in Patagonia, a combined memoir, travelogue, and nature essay that James quotes at length. It is worth remembering that like Hudson, an ornithologist from Buenos Aires who chronicles the year he spent in Patagonia, James, too, had gone exploring as a naturalist when he joined Louis Agassiz's expedition to the Amazon. From Obidos, Brazil he writes to his mother of his own experience of monotony:

You have no idea, my dearest mother, how strange that home life seems to me from the depths of this world buried as it is in mere vegetation and physical needs & enjoyments . . . Here all is so monotonous, in life and in nature that you are rocked into a kind of sleep – but strange to say, it is the old existence that has already begun to seem to me like a dream. (Houghton, n.d.)

Although the old, fevered social life at home in Massachusetts ("people swarming about me . . . killing themselves with thinking about things . . . studying themselves into fevers") seemed so unattractive, James rejected his new life in favor of it. Feeling himself unsuited to the expeditionary work, disoriented and adrift, made testy by long days of enforced idleness due to eye trouble, James returned home early. Perhaps his memories of enforced invalidism in an exotic South American setting made him especially interested in Hudson, who, shortly after arriving in Patagonia, accidentally shoots himself in the knee and thus experiences an enforced idleness, moving from his bed in a hut to various spots outside, where he lies, staring at the sky and listening to birds. Even when he is ambulatory, even when he recommences hunting, gathering specimens, and exploring, he continues in the mode of idle, Schillerian play. It is the convalescent Hudson we meet in James's 'On a Certain Blindness," a man, like James himself once was, far from the fret of civilization.

James has left out a great deal of Hudson's narrative. First, the frame of the larger work: the passage occurs in the thirteenth of Hudson's fourteen chapters. Second, significant passages from within the episodes of *Idle Days in Patagonia* that he does present. One missing passage – and James chooses not to indicate its absence by ellipses – explains what Hudson means by the term "pure savage," and it speaks directly to the question of manliness at home (quoted in *TT*, p. 149). It is a far more brutal and bestial state than that implied by the material James actually quotes. Although Hudson merely lies and dreams, he experiences a revelation of his atavistic self, a revival of a "purely animal" instinct of courage. One need not travel to Patagonia, he tells us; the soldier "who goes into battle inflamed with instinctive, joyous excitement" achieves the state of instinctive courage. "Man and the inferior animals alike, confronted with almost certain death, act courageously." Such instinctive courage, "inherited by a very large majority of the male children born into the world,"[34] is rarely called into activity in civilized life. But not only warfare and impending disaster elicit such behavior: sportsmen, too, when confronted by a wild animal when they have no firearms suitable for killing in "the usual civilized way" will neverthelesss attack brutally with whatever is at hand, "driven by a sudden uncontrollable impulse" (Hudson, *Patagonia*, p. 219). Having done so, the killer will remember "the keen feeling of savage joy" (p. 220). The escape of the "continual repression of civilized life" brings with it elation, even "mad joy, like animals newly escaped from captivity"(p. 220).

James chooses to emphasize the idleness and sensory lushness of Hudson's domestic tableaux. What the omitted section of the Hudson chapter reveals is a fiercer version of the primitive. Yet such atavism, "going back," is for Hudson a homecoming, and therein lies his principal attraction for James, however wary he may be of letting his genteel audience know the full extent of Hudson's primitivism. By idling and dreaming his way into a desolate landscape, Hudson proves that one can achieve cognitive savagery minus the bloodshed, and that such savagery may be understood in gentle terms. Hudson, for all his talk of blood lust, sees a new world about him, the oldest world any of us can know:

to see it all is like returning to a home, which is more truly our home than any habitation we know. The cry of the wild bird pierces us to the heart; we have never heard that cry before, and it is more familiar to us than our mother's voice. (p. 223)

When we experience this "going back," we feel a "shock of pleasure" and then a "profound and mysterious melancholy" that indicates the personal and psychical nature of this first home (p. 223).

Here Hudson indicates a turn to the decadent; the savage's "keen feeling of joy" becomes Hudson's fin-de-siècle moodiness. The profundity of mood becomes the profundity of human history, for we carry within us, like Pater's Mona Lisa, the entire story of the race:

And we ourselves are the living sepulchres of a dead past – that past which was ours for so many thousands of years before this life of the present began; its old bones are slumbering in us . . . and the bones rejoice and dance in their sepulchre. (p. 223)

Like Edna Earl of the decadent novel *St. Elmo*, Hudson wishes to recapture all of the past, and he finds that enforced convalescence helps. Where Ruskin sees stone walls as breathing with the lives they have witnessed across time, Hudson sees the human being as a stony sepulchre. Going home, for Hudson, involves a morbid visit to the depths of time which are one with the depths of the human psyche: "What has truly entered our soul and become psychical is our environment – that wild nature in which and to which we were born at an inconceivably remote period" (p. 225). Furthermore, it is an ascension to utter aesthetic sensitivity; in the primitive state, all rational obstructions removed, we watch and listen with no dulling filters in place. The brain becomes a mirror in which the world is reflected with "miraculous clearness" (p. 230).

The full sequence thus emerges: Hudson leaves home in the city for a desolate place which he fashions into a temporary home, only to grasp, through long idle days, that the escape from civilization and its repressions is a returning to a "truer" home buried deep within us. The tale of this journey, including a fin-de-siècle meditation on the threatening and entrancing dance of the bones, marks a journey home that James both desires and fears. So desirable is the sense of belonging at home, yet so suspicious is James of being trapped at home or lost within the dark depths of psyche, that he imagines home in psychical terms as the site of imaginative release and vast exploration. That such a release might free brutal instincts James tries to ignore by deleting a lengthy section of Hudson's account. That such a release is related to extremes of emotion – melancholy, savage joy, aberrant behavior by "civilized" standards – he will continue to acknowledge, placing such matters at the heart of his Gifford Lectures, published as *The Varieties of Religious Experience*.

Varieties, with hardly a passage that speaks directly of domestic matters, is James's long meditation on what he calls the "More," the beyond which lies at the margins of our conscious thoughts, for him a desired home. One need not travel to South America, to the depths of time, or to a metaphysical realm to experience this "More," nor does James regard it as a foundational space, the origin of everything that is. Rather, it is a path we might choose to take if we are able. Madness, religious transport, hypnosis, imaginative power: a variety of experiences may force a chink in the thick wall of consciousness within us, freeing us to explore and inhabit that widest of domestic sites, a wild "Patagonian" space. The extreme of savagery is the extreme of domesticity. Another early twentieth-century text, Freud's meditation on the uncanny, is surely germane here: "the usage of speech has extended *das Heimlich* into its opposite *das Unheimlich*; for this uncanny is in reality nothing new or foreign, but something familiar and old-established in the mind that has been estranged only by the process of repression."[35] Just as for Freud the "canny" refers to that which is friendly, intimate, and homelike as well as that which may suddenly reveal the uncannily vast, frightening, and unsheltered, so for James the "More" as he theorizes it in *Varieties* represents both a place of gentle ease and a space of potentially cosmic dimensions in which all that we know and are might be lost. His own experience of the uncanny ("I went one evening into a dressing room in the twilight to procure some article that was there; when suddenly there fell upon me without any warning . . . a horrible fear of my own existence" [*VRE*, p. 134]) must somehow be amended, and this process he has begun in writing "On a Certain Blindness" some time between 1896 and 1898.[36]

In quoting Hudson for the purposes of this essay, James had to leave something out. Knowing how he minimized the chronicle of brutal savagery and psychical atavism can help us understand the terms of the argument he carried on with himself, an argument that required the writing of *The Varieties of Religious Experience* to work through. Thirty years before composing the Gifford Lectures, James recorded in a notebook, later sent to his fiancée, Alice, his reactions at Barnum's menagerie:

Sight of elephants 6 tigers, whose existence, so individual and peculiar, yet stands there, so intensely and vividly real, as much so as one's own. So that one feels again poignantly the unfathomableness of ontology. . . . They *are*, *eadem jure* with myself, & yet I with my pretensions or at least aspirations to adequately represent the world, can *never hope to sympathize in a genuine sense of the word with their being*. And the want of sympathy is not as in the case of some deformed or loathsome human life, for their being is admirable, so admirable that one yearns to be in some way its sharer, partner, or accomplice. (Houghton, n.d.)

Like the naturalist Hudson, James wishes to study and to sympathize with alien species, yet he finds his powers of sensibility wanting. As late as the writing of *Varieties*, James the fervent Pragmatist is still attempting to fathom the "unfathomableness of ontology." *Varieties* is a book of aestheticized, even decadent natural history, a companion piece, as it were, to Hudson's speculations, empirical and metaphysical, on the exotic bird species of desert places. James's alien and exquisite beings belong to various human subspecies, as it were, some of them first sighted by himself and his pupil Edwin Starbuck, others historical and mythical beings of repute, but all roaming the uncharted territory of religious experience itself. His *Gifford Lectures*, by all accounts, succeeded in conveying the aesthetic pleasure of the pursuit which led by way of sentiment, sickness, intensity, and repose, to the margins of consciousness – and past them, through a doorway into the wilderness of home.

THE VARIETIES OF RELIGIOUS EXPERIENCE:
WITH MAP AND COMPASS

Asked in a 1904 questionnaire what he means by "religious experience," James replies, "Any moment of life that brings the reality of spiritual things more 'home' to me" (*CWJ*, 11:215). Home in this instance carries a variety of meanings. The paragraphs written for the opening of the Gifford Lectures (but not included in the published version) reveal the insurmountable difficulty James believes he faces as he himself tries to bring the reality of spiritual things home to an audience.

Language cannot adequately capture the feeling of home-dwelling central to religious experience. He depicts the philosopher as a hunter with inadequate weapons who stalks what can only be glimpsed and felt, not told: "everytime he fires his volley of new vocables out of his philosophical shot-gun . . . he secretly kens at the same time the finer hollowness and irrelevance of his phrases." He cannot translate religion, "the very inner citadel of human life" because "spread-out conceptual terms" cannot convey "a kind of experience in which intellect, feeling and will, all our consciousness and all our subconsciousness together melt in a kind of chemical fusion" (*VRE*, p. 480). Religious experience occurs inwardly, in melting moments of homecoming akin to the richly static world of *Roadside Songs*, a place where Ruskin explores experiences of melting and fusion: saints with God and his creatures, lovers with each other, and artists with the world they depict and the audience they touch. Ruskin's desire to learn how one person may touch another is but a version of James's desire to learn how different people experience the "inner citadel of human life." Both look to the tales and songs of saints, lunatics, and lovers.

Before he has finished, James will have expanded the notion of domestic indwelling to include a homecoming to the universe, a finding of a niche, like those of Stevenson's lantern-bearers and Hudson's swooning ornithologist, that will be protected and private, but also wild, full of March's expectancy and dissolution. He will create, as well, his own mode of philosophical discourse that attempts a sympathetic dwelling in, rather than a target practice aimed at, the experience of the exotic religious figures he studies. James argues throughout *Varieties* that people come home to religion through imagination, sensation, and sentiment, not theology, system, and rationality; likewise James himself will not reason his way to a philosophical grasp of religion, but instead asks us to sympathize with his appreciations, to "melt," as he does, into the testimony he proffers. "Sacrifices and surrenders...are our only permanent positions of repose" (*VRE*, p. 49), he writes of the religious propensity to give way. As a philosopher James practices what he describes, sacrificing all but the most general lines of argument, surrendering himself to the fascination of arraying before our eyes the rich and suggestive reports of religion made by individuals speaking from the inner field of religious experience.

Throughout his life James wrestled with the demands of propriety and achievement as they conflicted with disorganization, wildness, and risk. *Varieties* is perhaps his strongest vote for the latter, for the life of what he elsewhere calls "the passionate tumultuous blunderers."[37] *Varieties* is meant to be read as a kind of freak show. James returns to Barnum's menagerie, sure that he can this time stand with the "other," even make the madness and incoherency of his subjects, their simple *oddness*, accessible to the proper philosopher and psychologist within himself, to his audience at Edinburgh, and ultimately to the popular audience at home. Self-recognition will take his various audiences part of the way: "the sanest and best of us are of one clay with lunatics and prison inmates, and death finally runs the robustest of us down" (*VRE*, p. 46). But what gives him the courage of his undertaking in the wild and the mad is his inner certitude of repose, the notion that religion as "the habitation of our safety" (p. 46) is a phenomenon potentially within his grasp as a feeling man.

The horror in the dressing-room vision has been almost overcome; that is why he can write of it. Perhaps even his immediate situation serves as inspiration: he writes the opening lectures in Henry's London flat, which he reports "means safety, space, everything to us just now" (*CWJ*, III:89) after uncomfortable lodgings on the Continent. In *Varieties* William ventures "out" professionally (subject matter, style, argument – are all risky) because he believes that he will undoubtedly recognize "in" when he eventually achieves it, just as the human oddities in his sideshow most often do. *Varieties* is a work about, but also of, faith.

In James's case, the leap is to decadence, a turn-of-the-century aestheticism in which *Varieties* should be considered a primary text. Whereas earlier in his career James, as we have noted above, discusses the sentiment of rationality as a homecoming in which "the feeling of strangeness disappears" (*WB*, p. 68), James now explores a homecoming that exaggerates the *Unheimlich*:

Our civilization is founded on the shambles, and every individual existence goes out in a lonely spasm of helpless agony ... Forms of horror ... fill the world about us today. Here on our very hearths and in our gardens the infernal cat plays with the panting mouse, or holds the hot bird fluttering in her jaws. Crocodiles and rattlesnakes and pythons are at this moment vessels of life as real as we are; their loathsome existence fills every minute of every day that drags its length along. (*VRE*, p. 137)

The crocodiles and pythons of Cambridge, Massachusetts, are creatures of the mind, but "real" nonetheless. Here James, remarking on the dressing room episode, speaks in the persona of a desperate melancholic, as one of the gallery of lunatics in whom he has professed to recognize "a common clay."

James seeks a habitation of safety by facing the monster, by pursuing extreme and troubling cases, many of them pathological. In his opening lecture he defends this turn to the strange with the still controversial argument that the abnormal can yield the fullest truth about religious experience. Normal religious people, he insists, experience only second-hand religious life; we must instead look for:

the original experiences which were the pattern setters to all this mass of suggested feeling and imitated conduct. These experiences we can only find in individuals for whom religion exists not as a dull habit, but as an acute fever rather. . . . Such religious geniuses have often shown symptoms of nervous instability [and are] subject to abnormal psychical visitations. Invariably they have been creatures of exalted emotional sensibility. (*VRE*, p. 15)

James's first specimen is George Fox, "a psychopath and *détraqué* of the deepest dye" (p. 16). Fox's world, as James conveys it by quoting from his *Journal*, is one of apocalyptic horror: "afterwards I came to understand that in the emperor Dioclesian's time a thousand Christians were martyred in Lichfield. So I was to go, without my shoes, through the channel of their blood" (p. 16). As if wrenching his audience out of its genteel religiosity, James paints a lurid picture. Even when he describes the cheerful, optimistic religious experience, "sanguine and muscular", of healthy-minded people, he reverts to decadent form, mentioning the "luxury of woe," the sentimentally voluptuous melancholy of Marie Bashkirtseff, and Robert Louis Stevenson's vision of the "broad, bawdy, and orgiastic," the "Mænadic-foundations" rising up to threaten genteel religious life, "a spectacle to which no habit reconciles me" (p. 81n).

Why this emphasis upon the extreme, troubled, or pathological? In part James is still solving the problem he set for himself in "The Sentiment of Rationality." Dwelling in truth sounds disturbingly akin to a slow, indoors death. He still seeks the elements of vigor and heroism that define manhood and answer to a need for danger and excitement. Part of the power residing in the images of "On a Certain Blindness" issues from the pain of coming home – the frigid and relentless winds of coastal Scotland, the debauched clearing of North Carolina, the prison cell of Russia, the sinister and harsh landscape of Patagonia. Pain elicits hardihood, even valor: it makes men. In *Varieties* James simply explores at length the potentially heroic qualities of arranging "habitations of safety," the homes his subjects have made. An anecdote from *Idle Days in Patagonia* sheds light on James's intentions. Hudson, suffering from a gunshot wound to his knee, spends a night of agony and anguish alone in a hut while his companion leaves to seek aid. During the night, in which he imagines himself asleep in a coffin ten feet under the vast Patagonian wilderness, evil in its very desolation, he hears a peculiar sound, like that of a rope being dragged over the floor. An hour after sunrise his friend returns, and out from Hudson's poncho glides the venomous "Craspedocephalus alternatus," called "*serpent with a cross.*" Hudson regards the snake as evil – "something had touched me, and . . . virtue had gone out from me" – but he nevertheless "rejoices to think that the secret deadly creature, after lying all night with me, warming its chilly blood with my warmth, went back unbruised to its den."[38]

Repose in dangerous situations, repose that is intimate with evil: such is the decadent Baudelairean ideal which, held up to religious experience, sends James in search of the bizarre, deformed, and mad. Hudson's image must have pleased James the philosopher who argued for a pluralistic universe in which supernaturalism and evil are both parts of a concatenated whole rather than infusions through and through of an homogeneous universe. It must have pleased the James who wrote always of "ordinary" life, for him a decidedly domestic and bourgeois existence, because it captures the courage of a sick man in bed, as well as his ability, unlike the youthful James at Barnum's menagerie, to sympathize with a fellow creature, however loathsome.

Repose in danger, acceptance of a universe that harbors evil without itself being essentially evil, recognition of the human yearning for negativity (religious ascetics, James argues, demonstrate the need for "austerity and wintry negativity, some roughness, danger, stringency, and effort" (*VRE*, p. 240) – James anatomizes religious experience as would a naturalist. He proceeds, at great professional risk, to pace through an uncharted wilderness where the fauna, religious people of various spiritual coloration, will reward him with the explorer's prize: the certainty that he can heroically make a home amid the untamed and the dangerous, that he can find a habitation of safety both as a philosopher and as a man who actually writes at home of the home.

This domestication James effects by linking himself to his human subjects, as Ruskin has identified with the *contadini* of *Roadside Songs of Tuscany*. Those who give themselves up to trances and visions, fevers and masochisms, are akin to James, the Harvard psychologist and professor who turns from normal professional activity to "abnormal" practices, among them, listening to the voices of pathological types not as nosology, but as the basis for a science of religion, and including those voices as a major part of his text. The daring of redefining a field from an eccentric perspective shared by researcher and subject can be measured by the difficulty of conveying the new picture as "truth" to the world of normality and professionalism. His various specimens may be likened to the exotic menagerie that Rossetti painstakingly assembled in the garden at 16 Cheyne Walk.

This very choice of perspective invites, indeed requires, a change in presentation of data and argument: a change in style. Like Hudson, who writes of the impossibility of capturing birdsong in communicable form, James's rare birds speak in a language that can never tell their experience. Pater's "thick wall of personality" grows denser in proportion to the abnormality of the subject. The solution, for James, as for Ruskin, Pater, and Proust, lies in art: if one person can paint a picture, perhaps another, in experiencing the canvas, can meet the artist there in a moment of shared feeling. James is a psychologist and philosopher of religion, but he is also an artist who has assembled a vast collage of portraits: "philosophers paint pictures." Like Rossetti's portraits of odd-looking women never quite at home in their painted enclosures, like Ruskin's nature in which we "always see something, but . . . never see all" (3.329), James's portraits both welcome and repel.

The text of *Varieties* presents at least as much quotation as it does commentary, and although the quoted material is only a crude verbal equivalent of the experience it chronicles, it does present a degree of immediacy. Or degrees: some testimony is first-person, elicited in a kind of man-on-the-street series of written interviews conducted by Edwin Starbuck. Some is journal entry, some autobiography – experience recaptured and certainly crafted in tranquillity. Some is biography. Even excerpts from fiction and philosophy have a place. These varying degrees of immediacy in the end take on a certain equivalence; each block of quotation stands as an expanded moment to which we respond as we might to a visual image. That is, James's psychological and philosophical commentary never quite controls this material as we read it through time. Psychology recedes as quoted testimony takes the stage; although we know that every example supports or illustrates a part of James's argument, we often are not sure of or do not care to make the logical connection. The effect is to thrust us into a presentness. As Hudson lies at the base of a tree, listening to the song of a bird whose Latin name he has just given us, the presence of Linnaean authority gradually fades. Similarly, a kind of feverish repose sets in as we hear James's natural history of religious people. A relentlessly unfolding testimony, much of it strange and unsettling ("the heart of a horse slain by a witch, taken out of the yet reaking carcase" [*VRE*, 392n]) gradually convinces us that the most we can really keep in mind is the notion that actual religious experience vividly matters.

Even the division of the book into five or six major topics does not enable us to fit each example into a rational framework. We would be hard pressed to identify any given quotation with just one of these topics in particular. The mixture of types of subjects – acknowledged saints, theologians, historical figures, country preachers, mystics both Eastern and Western, scientists, "ordinary" people; these types taken from "time immemorial" (p. 317) to the present day and presented in the context of many disciplines – history, anthropology, medicine, literature, metaphysics, psychology, sociology; so much variety ensures that we never really know where we are. The hodgepodge extends, perhaps, to a sublime breadth. Like Rossetti, James freely arranges exotica from various traditions, countries, and genres within a small space. A seductive stasis and vagueness sets in, a sense of settling into religious experience for its own sake. We are once again safely caught in intricacy; confusion has done its useful work. The work, in sum, is performative. James takes us home rather than merely demonstrating that home is a theologically useful concept.

Yet James surely keeps up professional standards; like many a turn-of-the-century explorer, including Hudson's "Mr. Abel" of *Green Mansions*, he constantly fears "going native." He continually reminds us of his intellectual imperialism. Not a deeply religious man himself, he must establish an outpost in an alien land. Thus, like Ruskin, he resorts to lists, classifications, divisions, and generalizations. At times, and according to our particular reasons for reading, these distinctions order and register. But the indigenous population must never be fully quelled. That is, after all, James's central message, and a sincere one. Religious experience regarded systematically is religious experience denied. *Varieties*, like many a work of decadent art, exists in the mode of paradox: James systematically demonstrates the ills of system, and his work is an arrangement more than a proof. Hence the difficulties he faces when he tries to bring *Varieties* to a close by telling us how we may generalize from all that we have witnessed. The work ends by petering out.

James does seek closure, but of a paradoxically potential sort. One achieves it only in a most unhygienic relaxation. James's religious subjects surrender themselves and experience an influx of religious relaxation; indeed, the "abandonment of self-responsibility seems to be the fundamental act in specifically religious, as distinguished from moral practice" (*VRE*, p. 233).

It is important to remember that the idleness and vagueness attendant upon religious repose, the "equanimity, receptivity, and peace" (p. 233), are domestically conceived as home-dwelling. Self-surrender allows one to feel a "habitation of safety" (p. 46), or, in more familiar language, to dwell in the house of the Lord. But idleness and vagueness are aesthetic states of receptivity and negative capability as well. Here we can understand more fully why James's professional leap of faith – his radical reassignment of authority from philosophers and theologians to ordinary people and to fringe figures – is a leap to decadence. In part, he depicts severely troubled, even "insane," people because their "twice-born" experience, their movement from yearning and confusion to religious equanimity, is far clearer than in "healthy-minded" people. In part James takes the decadent as subject and mode because of its pleasurably self-contradictory character: sophisticated, artificial, and heightened artifacts sometimes miraculously convey simplicity and innocence. Thus James adopts a common goal of decadent artists, to reclaim in an art of extremity what the world has cheapened, sullied, or misunderstood. Thus he reports to Henry:

It is a touching thing in Titian and Paul Veronese, who paint scenes which are a perfect *charivari* of splendor and luxury, and manifold sensations as far removed from what we call simplicity as anything well can be, that they preserve a tone of sober innocence, of instinctive single-heartedness, as natural as the breathing of a child.[39]

Neither Rossetti nor Pater could have said it better. The decadent *frisson* of the overwrought that circles through to "finiteness and serenity and pleasure" indicates to James a religious experience as well. His religious visionaries display a painful richness of spiritual need that, by their own testimony, metamorphoses to the simple answer of the faith state, of innocence regained. And one suspects that for James personally the aesthetic experience must stand in for the religious. The measure of his religious fervor is his growing ability to reject hygiene in favor of decadent aestheticism. During the period when he composes the Gifford Lectures, he writes to Frances R. Morse that he adores Rome: "the things the eyes most gloat on, the inconceivably corrupted, besmeared and ulcerated surfaces, and black and cavernous glimpses of interiors, have no suggestions save of moral horror, and their 'tactile values,' as Berenson would say, are pure gooseflesh. Nevertheless the sight of them delights" (*CWJ*, ii:138).

Eight years earlier, he had written to James F. Putnam: "How good Switzerland is, is something that can't be described in words. The healthiness of it passes all utterance – the air, the roads, the mountains, the customs, the institutions, the people. Not a breath of art, poetry, esthetics, morbidness, or 'suggestions'! It is all there, solid meat and drink for the sick body and soul, ready to be turned to, and do you infallible good when the nervous and gas-lit side of life has had too much play" (*CWJ*, i:327–328). Yet when he reaches Florence, he reneges on his hygienic passion. Although the city seems to suffer from stale air and a general debility, "the charming sunny manners, the old-world picturesqueness wherever you cast you eye, and above all, the magnificent remains of art, redeem it all, & insidiously spin a charm round me" (p. 330).

By the time he finishes *Varieties*, Italian decadence (inseparable from Italian "sober innocence") has triumphed, as it were, over Swiss hygiene, and James's "healthy-minded" subjects are judged inferior to the tormented "twice-born" who earn their repose. But James makes a far more radical claim than the blending of decadence and religious experience. When we consider *Varieties* in the context of James's psychology, the religiously intense person, the actor in his aestheticist scenario, becomes the exemplar of human cognition itself. Not only are we of one clay with lunatics, but they are perhaps our cognitively better selves.

One last step in our reading of *Principles* in the context of James's pragmatism remains. The notions of chemical fusion James does not apply to notions of the self. Most people, he tell us "mentally inhabit more than one world, each with its own special and separate style of existence, such as the world of sense, of science, of the supernatural, of abstract truths," but "the various worlds themselves ... appear to most men's minds in no very definitely conceived relation to each other" (*PP*, ii:292). We simply attend now to one, now to another, according to what matters to us, what best meets our emotional needs or enables us to function in the world. Most of us, out of habit, choose one world as supreme, but we regularly file away some bit of data in another mental "world" which exists in only a casual connection to the primary world. Worlds within us do not fuse, they coexist.

Seen in the light of James's "normal" psychology in which each one of us fashions a world or series of loosely connected worlds by eliminating extraneous matter and then roving fluidly among the penumbrae of images, James's subjects in *Varieties* may be seen as abnormal, but also as "super" normal, that is, as more passionate in their sculptural activities, more complicatedly fused in their consciousness, and more intensely involved in their construction of the one true world, that of religious insight. They need more reality of a certain sort, and they therefore create more. They break the templates, eschew imitation, dwell in entanglements until the world burgeons in sublimity.

The vagueness that James places at the center of *Principles* swells in *Varieties* until it comes to represent the possible existence of a "MORE" beyond the fringes of consciousness, an unseen realm that is "really" there. If everyone's reality depends upon relation, the religious genius's reality develops from a case of "hyper" relation: the melting mood within him, the self-surrender that puts him in touch with something he labels divine. If consciousness itself indicates that each one of us is an artist, making a world by acts of choice and attention, religious consciousness defines artistic obsession and, where its fruits are deemed valuable, artistic genius. James is willing to go even a step farther. The *mind* works in flowing, "melted" non-distinctions; the *person* chooses a reality that is from the first "entangled," and even loosely connects to that world another entangled world or worlds; the *religious genius* creates one world, a supernatural reality, in which the vagueness engendered by fusion becomes the final reality. But for the *saint*, whom James examines as the most intense figure of religious experience, the object is wholly gone and relation is all; artist, medium, and object form an abstract texture. The saint transforms self into religious art:

The greatest saints . . . are successes from the outset. They show themselves, and there is no question: everyone perceives their strength and stature. Their sense of mystery in things, their passion, their goodness, irradiate about them and enlarge their outlines while they soften them. They are like pictures with an atmosphere and background. (*VRE*, p. 299)

As Francesca Alexander and John Ruskin together demonstrate in *Roadside Songs of Tuscany*, saints are personified epiphanies. Like minds, they carry a penumbra or halo in which meaning inheres; as people, they fashion their own lives; and like works of art, they admit the observer into a gorgeous mystery, they are a showing. If a sign of decadence be the insistence upon art as intense, cultic activity, often mythically or magically framed, that places its devotees in what they consider to be a superior world, James's saint embodies decadence.

For both James and his religious geniuses, vagueness is both a method and a goal. The very negative capability James brings into play as an investigator ("we are dealing with a field of experience where there is not a single conception that can be sharply drawn . . . . the boundaries are always misty" [*VRE*, 392n]) – will lead him to understand that last and greatest of unexplored desert spaces, the unseen "MORE" lying at the borders of consciousness. To study such a "place" requires an atavism of method, if not all the way back to a primitive state, at least proceeding in that direction. For all James's championing of the scientific work of Frederic Myers and the Society for Psychical Research,[40] *Varieties* testifies to another kind of exploration: a return to irrational, mythical thought, a "going back" of the sort James describes by quoting Stevenson and Hudson in "On a Certain Blindness." "The pretension . . . to be rigorously 'scientific' or 'exact' in our terms would only stamp us as lacking in understanding of our task," James cautions (*VRE*, p. 39).

As soon as scientific rigor is abandoned as a standard, as soon as James drops the mask of professional certitude, his text, from the reader's point of view, enters free fall. The very texture of the prose, its multiple points of view, its rhetorical lingering within an aesthetic, rather than a logical, framework, encourages judgment of the work for its pleasures and intensities as they pulse, and only secondarily as a developing doctrinal argument.

But exactly how does James want his work judged? As a performance to be appreciated rather than analyzed? Not quite: for all his disclaimers, he never wholly abandons scientific method. As a professional contribution to the philosophy of religion? Not quite: for all his erudition, reflected in sophisticated references across the professional literatures, James writes as an artist of artists, and invites readers to feel before they reason. While the phrasing of these questions implies an answer – James wants his book read as both artistic performance and intellectual document, as both sentimental gift and professional statement – the issue of judgment returns us to the buried tale of domesticity within *Varieties*. We return to a final understanding of James's domestic aestheticism as revisionary energy.

James always frames within the context of utter familiarity his forays into the exotica of religious experience. However *détraqué* the religious genius, his experience, James repeatedly notes, has its sources in common and well-documented psychological phenomena such as attention, impulse and inhibition, instinctive action, memory, and conception – all of them treated at length and with utter professional propriety in *The Principles of Psychology*. Religious cognition may be an extreme example of human cognition, but it is also to be understood as simply one variant of the "natural" or "normal." "Like love or fear, the faith state is a natural psychic complex," states James the psychologist (*VRE*, p. 225).

Like other turn-of-the-century explorers, Hudson among them, James domesticates the wilderness even as he urges us to appreciate its exoticism. Far from, say, practicing Loyola's spiritual exercises in the hope of achieving enlightenment, James stays at home and constructs, with the help of sophisticated philosophical and psychological concepts, the notion of a margin through which many have sought transcendence and discovered it to be home. He studies, as a pluralist, religious monists, and this is an important and fruitful confusion in his work. Throughout the magic lantern show that is *Varieties*, James, the returned explorer, depends heavily on our common sense and everyday notions of behavior. Recognizing both the religious and the abnormal or exalted as variations on a widely shared emotional state, we are effective explorers in a strange land because we carry with us the image of home and can form connections between the two. James handles the potentially conflicting modes of his study – call them the "scientific" and the "mythic" – by placing his faith in the realm of the ordinary and in the sentiment of the familiar. Domesticity generously expands its patterns to enable a position of repose, the "big easy" that effects a truce between science and religion, mind and body, self and other, profession and play. Wallace Stevens understands the sublimity of such repose when he writes, "The house was quiet and the world was calm. / The reader became the book."[41] Perhaps Stevens echoes James: "We pass into mystical states... as from a less into a more, as from a smallness into a vastness, and at the same time as from an unrest to a rest" (*VRE*, p. 330).

The faith state is "the habitation of our safety," entered at "the verge of the mind" (*VRE*, p. 334), where mystery circles round to seize the tail of utter familiarity. James celebrates both verges and habitations at once, by imagining the graceful dance of aestheticism, domesticity, and ultimately, religion, as a going out, a sublime ecstasy, that is nothing but a homecoming experienced by actual people in familiar terms.

Within the "painted windows and the storied walls" of the mind, William comes home to faith, beauty, and even truth. We might even begin to rethink the importance of domesticity to pragmatism itself as a method of imaginatively determining the truth. He writes, "If I am lost in the woods and starved, and find what looks like a cow-path, it is of the utmost importance that I should think of a human habitation at the end of it, for if I do so and follow it, I save myself" (*P*, p. 98). A fascination with human habitation infused with sentiment provides for James the occasion, the subject, and the mode of his art: the House of Philosophy.

Meditation: sublimity

During the mid- and late-nineteenth century, artists began to challenge the Longinian notion of sublimity as *"hypsos,"* or elevation, with a set of ideas that associated sublimity with beauty, terror before the vast with interest in the local, and heights and depths of extraordinary and lonely human experience with lowlands of ordinary, social interaction. *Platos*, or extension, is the term I use to point toward these developing complications of the sublime.

Depending heavily on fragments of Longinus's *Peri Hypsous, On the Elevated,* theories of sublimity had, by the eighteenth century, permeated what we would now call the disciplines of psychology and philosophy, including ethics, aesthetics, epistemology, and metaphysics.[1] Issues of sublimity migrated into many sorts of discussions, including those of economics, theatrical and oratorical performance, perspective in drawing, and the proper education of women.[2] Within this web of inquiry and prescription several ideas dominated, among them Longinus's belief that sublimity had to do with things so elevated that they beckoned (or threw) the viewer under the temporary sway of powerful forces. People experienced the sublime when they surpassed themselves.[3] Sublimity required things high, grand, thrilling or frightening, and, except for the moment outside time of the subject's transport, inaccessible. While theorists acknowledged sublimities of mathematical infinity (including the infinitesimal), they usually agreed that sublimity was not to be associated with the low, small, or merely additive. Lord Kames writes, for example, that the "capital rule for reaching the sublime ... [is to] present those parts or circumstances only, which make the greatest figure, keeping out of view every thing low or trivial ... for the mind, from an elevation inspired by important objects, cannot, without reluctance, be forced down to bestow any share of its attention upon trifles."[4] Sublimity, it appears, took shape in opposition to ordinary life.

By the mid-nineteenth century, however, an important theorist of the sublime, John Ruskin, posits the "noble grotesque" and asserts that it "giv[es] the highest sublimity even to the most trivial object so presented and so contemplated."[5] Sublimity in Ruskin's thought gradually migrates from its primary eighteenth-century location in high, vast, or overwhelming things as they transport the human subject out of this world to its nineteenth-century home: the consciousness of the observer as he experiences things both high and low, grand and even trivial. Such a mid-century understanding had been itself prepared for by some Romantic poets, whose sublime hopes generated by the French Revolution were dashed by the end of the eighteenth century.[6] They created oxymorons of the humble grand and the trivial sublime as they struggled with what to make of their disappointment.

This poetic project of recovery slowly metamorphoses into a sublimity of breadth that begins as much in hope as in disillusionment.[7] Ruskin provides an example of such sublimity by quoting Jeremiah 1.13, 14: "I see a seething pot; and the face thereof is toward the north. Out of the north an evil shall break forth upon all the inhabitants of the land" (5.133). He chooses to quote the Bible which, as the word of God, is available to all who claim it as guidance within their daily lives. Sublimity, here in the form of a fearful divine revenge, is figured by a lowly cooking pot that leads outward to northern latitudes, not upward to topographical or celestial elevation. Overwhelming power and crippling fear have metamorphosed to anxious threat: seething, not volcanic eruption, actual armies, not divine thunderbolts. Ruskin writes in his diary, "I wish Vesuvius could love me, like a living thing; I would rather make a friend of him than any morsel of humanity."[8] The sublime still holds out for Ruskin the possibility of surpassing mere human relation, but – ironically, even paradoxically – only at the cost of being itself humanized, becoming friendly. A sublime aesthetic of lonely extremity meets a sentimental aesthetic of relation, transforming both.

Twentieth-century critics have often argued that Longinian and Burkean sublimity begin to dissipate during the nineteenth century. By the twentieth century, "true" sublimity is in eclipse, and any sublimity making its appearance after the turn of the century must be a "moribund aesthetic."[9] From a Victorian Modernist perspective, however, sublimity does not fail, it changes. Ruskin prepares us to see sublimity in the twentieth century, and so do the other figures of this study as they lead readers to consider what would have been an impossibility in the eighteenth century: the sublime of everyday life. What I shall call *Peri platous*, a sublime discourse of breadth, not elevation, comes to life during Victoria's reign, and it grows steadily through the twentieth century. The distinctions among beauty, sublimity, and the picturesque which are strongly, if at times confusedly, established by eighteenth-century commentators, begin to blur. In Burkean terms neither (masculine) sublimity nor (feminine) beauty, neither utterly important nor sadly trivial, hardly captured by the term "picturesque," a relational sublime is born.

In fact, Longinus had discussed an "extensional" sublime in his treatise, but he held that it was not true sublimity, and critics have ever since taken him at his word. Yet his own rhetoric confuses the sharp distinction he makes between sublimity and "aggregation," or breadth. Sublimity for him depends on elevation, to be distinguished from amplification, "an aggregation of all the details and topics which constitute a situation, strengthening the argument by dwelling on it."[10] Yet as he gives an example of each, Demosthenes representing sublimity or elevation and Cicero representing aggregation or extension, Longinus implies that Cicero may be just as powerful, just as truly sublime in his rhetoric, as Demosthenes. "Demosthenes," he writes, "has an abrupt sublimity; Cicero spreads himself. Demosthenes burns and ravages . . . Cicero, on the other hand, is like a spreading conflagration. He ranges everywhere and rolls majestically on." *Hypsos* (elevation) becomes *platos* (breadth), and the latter rolls majestically on, with no apparent diminishment in its power to thrill.[11] Longinus seems ambivalent as well about the relation of the sublime to the ordinary. On one hand, he states that "the useful and necessary are readily available to man, [but] it is the unusual that always excites our wonder"; on the other hand he asserts that in literature of genius, such as Homeric epic, "grandeur is not divorced from service and utility."[12]

The celebration of sublime breadth, suggested by Longinus and characteristic of much Victorian Modernist sublimity, can be linked to domesticity and ordinary life, since *platos* does not require the subject's ecstasy, his transitory loss of self, before the extraordinary. One can simply stay at home, marvel, and find that the self has changed. Admiration for a sublimity that broadens majestically rather than mounting the heights has, however, been difficult for us to see. The willingness of writers to explore the trivial or the low as potential sources and goals of sublimity is not simply a process of relabeling older concepts. Ruskin's "noble

picturesque," "grotesque," and "parasitical sublime" are not merely sub-
categories of the traditional sublime, but instead represent new ways of
thinking about sublimity.[13]

Or, rather, old ways of thinking about sublimity. They are in part
a renewal of a source of sublimity that gradually lost ground in the
eighteenth century: its importance to the art of rhetoric. Sublimity grew
out of a rhetorical tradition of a grand style meant to sway audiences. It
had to do with a text as embodied in and through the orator, and with the
effects of texts on the emotions of hearers. As such it was practical and
of this world, meant to sway real people in their actual circumstances as
listeners – even if the goal was to make them feel transported directly
to higher truth. A fortuitous confusion characterizes the discourses of
sublimity throughout the eighteenth century: is it a quality of things
in the world (mountains, seas), texts (orations, poems), or artists and
audiences (as they experience mountains or poems)? Given the difficult
questions raised by such sets of interlocking sublimities, commentators
on the sublime react over time by complicating, rather than simplifying,
the concept of sublimity.[14] It comes to involve more emotions and more
objects; the notion of the picturesque itself might be seen as a *deus ex
machina* meant to deliver us from some of sublimity's knottier problems.
It is no wonder that a limit had to be established somewhere, and so it
was – the exclusion of whatever one thinks of as the useful, the convenient,
or the ordinary. Sublimity, despite its source in the practical problem of
how to sway audiences, must suppress the practical, the messily human,
the worldly.

In parallel to the Modernist claims of autonomous art that were to
come, commentators on the sublime have tended to insist that it exists in a realm apart. Iris Murdoch, however, disagreed. Neither art nor
sublimity should aim for freedom from the disorders of human experience. Challenging Kantian notions of autonomy in art, she corrects
them by identifying a social sublime. "The work of art is conceived by
Kant, and mostly by the Romantics, on the analogy of a fairly small
perceptual object," she notes, and the "Kantian enjoyment of art is an
analogon of the free rational act, in that it is something clean, free, empty,
self-contained, not contaminated by the messiness of emotion, desire, or
personal eccentricity."[15] Rejecting the notion that true art must be small,
shapely, and careful of its reader's emotions, she transforms Kant's theory
of the unboundedness of the sublime into a theory of art. Her example
is the novel, and she argues that fiction should attempt to capture the
"contingent, messy, boundless, infinitely particular, and endlessly still to

be explained" quality of human existence (p. 274). Allowing herself these "impurities," a writer can explore a social sublime: "'The sublime' is an enjoyment and renewal of spiritual powers arising from an apprehension of the vast formless strength of the natural world. How close all of this is indeed to being a theory of tragedy, if we think of the spectator as gazing not at the Alps, but at the spectacle of human life" (p. 282).

Murdoch's is a pragmatist sublimity, in that "[t]o understand other people is a task which does not come to an end" (p. 283). Nor is such sublimity necessarily tragic: "the man that I have in mind, faced by the manifold of humanity may feel, as well as terror, delight, but not, if he really sees what is before him, superiority" (p. 283). The state of awed paralysis before a vast nature metamorphoses into the state of ongoing interest in a "manifold" of people that includes their relations with one another.

Murdoch insists that "[e]xperience of the art of the novel is spiritual experience" which comes from the spectacle of the human manifold that exhilarates and "reminds us, to use Kant's words, of our supersensible destiny" (p. 282). So it is that Murdoch places tantalizingly off center in many of her novels a powerful religious figure of no certain sect of belief, a lay saint or visionary who seems at times to hold the key to life, at times to be a charlatan. He appears in an early and especially evil form as Mischa, in *The Flight from the Enchanter*. Whether or not this figure is unmasked as a fraud, his powers lie in his ability to bring people together in a supreme confusion: a manifold. When he is not the director of a community where people actually assemble as in a murder mystery's country house, he is often a moving void in the novel into which all manner of richly flawed people are sucked. Like Rossetti, Murdoch overfills her canvas with the details, hints, and mysteries of everyday unboundedness.

The denial of the ordinary as a contender in sublime realms is gradually reversed in the nineteenth century. What was a discourse of the rupture of habitual relations becomes an affirmation of the building out of habitual relations. Rupture, the transport from every-day experience and even from one's own sense of identity effected by thrillingly powerful sights, continues to exist as a quality of sublimity. But sublimity expands to include more centrally the experience of making fascinating and compelling connections within everyday experience, and within a shared and, therefore, social life. Adopting on faith the Burkean distinction between the beautiful and the sublime, critics have all too readily overestimated the clarity of the distinction itself and the resulting significance of its two psychological manifestations.

"The beautiful initiates reconciliation . . . the sublime splits consciousness into alienated halves," Weiskel asserts.[16] If it's sublime, something must break.

A lesson to be learned here is the difficulty of trying systematically to divide the world of artistic experience into categories. Sublimity has never been fully distinguished from beauty, from Longinus's day to ours.[17] While the distinction between the sublime and beautiful might hold up reasonably well in describing certain relations of human beings to the wild power of nature, it becomes less satisfactory as theorists consider rhetorical and textual sublimity, perhaps because nature offers actual heights and grandeurs that texts offer only tendentiously or metaphorically. An exemplary text in illustration of such difficulty would be Rousseau's "Seventh Walk" in *Reveries of a Solitary Walker*, in which, during one of his botanizing expeditions, the walker's experience of a traditionally sublime mountain landscape is interrupted by his discovery of a textile factory half hidden within the scene. He must acknowledge in his state of distress that the apparently wild mountains of Switzerland have actually all been settled, but his response is not to turn away, frustrated by the dashing of his hopes for sublimity. Instead he feels joy "like a flash of lightning," then paranoid distress, then a liberating sense of gentle self-mockery.[18] The experience of sublimity disappointed then generates a field of linked episodes, each "about" botanizing, each with its own emotional flavor. Way leads to way – through reverie, memory, and story. The world on high (sublime Swiss mountains) because the world traversed in extended textual forays. Rousseau does not simply relabel the scene picturesque and retreat from it; instead, he chooses to understand the sublime in a new way. "It is the chain of accessory ideas that makes me love botany" (p. 120), he concludes. It is the making of just such chains that characterizes the extended sublime of Ruskin, who tells us that he learned his sentimental love of nature from Rousseau.

Questions of authentication arise as the power of God the Creator recedes. The progression of powers authenticating the sublime may be roughly sketched: from God to Nature/Spirit to the Egotistical Sublime to text itself, whether it be the text of nature or the texts of man. These texts over time continue to refer to something that cannot be wholly contained within them, yet that something neither issues from a transcendent realm nor floats entirely free of it. Wordsworth writes of "a sense sublime/Of something far more deeply interfused" as he reads the text of a landscape casually located "a few miles above Tintern Abbey." This "dwelling in an unconfined space"[19] will become, over the decades, a search for the Jamesian sense of "More" within actual dwellings, including the Victorian parlor, and hence sublimity will be domesticated. Rossetti will trace Blakean sublimity to that visionary's humble dwelling place.

When Victorian Modernist artists create texts of sublimity, they often do so, like Edmund Burke before them, in a secular attempt to serve the human spirit, to find a worldly language for the expression of other-worldly experience. Sublimities of breadth tend to deny religious dogma while searching for spiritual experience. Even Augusta Evans, the sole dogmatic Christian of this study, imagines her heroine's sublime experience as inhering in her wide reading – including her explorations of other gods besides the Christian God – and in her daring act of writing for mass publication and distribution. Where her heroine Edna sees only *hypsos* – "The glittering pinnacle of consecrated and successful authorship seemed to her longing gaze as sublime, and well-nigh inaccessible, as the everlasting and untrodden Himalayan solitudes appear to some curious child of Thibet"[20] – Augusta Evans herself imagines *platos*. Yet many of Edna's readers write to her, asking for advice, and she responds. Himalayan solitude yields to aesthetic social work.

Although Evans exercises throughout her novel *St. Elmo* the rhetoric of eighteenth-century sublimity and of nineteenth-century, heaven-seeking Christian rectitude, she concentrates on her heroine's relations in the mundane: with her benefactress, teacher, employer, publisher, audience, and eventually husband. The diction of elevation is everywhere leveled, not by turning away from the sublimely elevated, but by that elevation's metamorphosis into the extensive, continuing and complicated. Such is Evans's *platos*: a reticulated plotting of personal relationships in domestic settings and the invention of a decadent aesthetic expressed as a manifold of languages, rituals, and objects.

D. H. Lawrence, like Murdoch and Evans, believes that reading novels can be a spiritual experience, particularly if one can feel the sublime spirituality of eroticism. As a Modernist, Lawrence writes of crisis: "man struggles with his unborn needs and fulfilment . . . we are now in a period of crisis. . . . The people that can bring forth the new passion, the new idea, this people will endure."[21] The new passion is nothing if not "Eros of the sacred mysteries" (p. vii). Yet within *Sons and Lovers* he muffles the terrible drumbeat of sublime sexual mastery with hyperbole, or shatters and wildly multiplies it by heaping pulsating image on image: wet boughs on naked backs, beasts within, swoonings into darknesses, and stonings of the moon. When Gerald announces, after the erotic "gladitorial" match with Birkin, "I always eat a little before I go to bed ... I sleep better" (p. 265), this is not so much a deflation of what might have been sublime as an Antaeus-like touching of the domestic ground that means he will always be able sublimely to "rise" before other people again.

When William James writes of the many forms of religious experience, he depends on the entire British tradition of sublimity and more particularly on what we have called Victorian Modernist sublimity as it had been developing since mid-century. Looking to the accounts of actual people swept up in intense states of awe rather than to a religious code or body of dogma, James seeks out the extreme: religious fanatics, prophets, and madmen. Eventually he generalizes by saying that the life of religion they describe "consists of the belief that there is an unseen order, and that our supreme good lies in harmoniously adjusting ourselves thereto. This belief and this adjustment are the religious attitude in the soul."[22] Deity may be experienced as the sublime voice in the whirlwind or as extreme, sudden, or weird states of possession, but such experiences of sublimity are impossible unless they issue from actual experience "located" in daily life.

Lived religious belief, far from denying the possibility of continued relation with the sublime, demands it. Kantian sublimity lies ultimately in the analytic purity of a free human reason, but James writes in the chewier tradition of a Burkean sublimity that tries to ascertain "*how objects affect us.*"[23] After consulting numerous first-person accounts of religious episodes, James concludes that such experience often involves "a mood of welcome" to ideas and experiences of "the More," and that the experience of a conversion, even of an abrupt and soul-wrenching transport to faith, is often also described as a homecoming, a feeling of "affective peace" (*VRE*, p. 202), a dwelling in certitude. The converted person feels that the "mysteries of life become lucid" and that "an appearance of newness beautifies every object" (202). The sublime moment is extended, teased out into the actualities of domestic life. While the Victorian Modernist world is perhaps constricted by the loss of religious faith and by a rupture with certainty, it is also expanded by the will to believe, a deliberate rescue operation carried out in complexities, across the gaps and through the connections of the quotidian.

It is dangerous to assume that the concept of sublimity remains constant over time. The concept and experience of sublimity vary across the decades, and are understood differently by each writer, depending on the specific culture of writing in which she participates. If "[a] humanistic sublime is an oxymoron," then Victorian Modernism presents us with just this difficulty. Delimiting mid-nineteenth-century sublimity as

"secondary or problematical sublime" implies the superiority of sublimity's earlier forms rather than exploring how a complicated tradition
continues to develop.[24] What must at one time have been a useless
contradiction in terms (i.e., a human-sized, even sentimental or domestic sublime) began to feel like a path worth taking during the
Victorian period, and continued to feel that way through much of high
Modernism and beyond.

As sublimity gradually became a matter of extension, its filaments
entered into the patern of other Victorian Modernist discourses. While
distinctions between sublimity and sensibility are for the most part respected by poets and novelists of the eighteenth century, the differences
weaken as time passes. Because intensity of feeling and complications
of subject–object relations are common to sublimity and sentimentality,
and because both sentimentality and sublimity originate in notions of
passivity (the sentimental figure passively overtaken by his emotions, the
sublime experience obliterating the spectator's will), significant bonds
between the two begin to develop. When popular domestic novelists
of nineteenth-century America speak of feelings of the heart as the
most important thing in the world, and as a vast, complicated and
often painful source of inspiration, they are developing a Victorian
Modernist sublimity that will attract writers such as Henry James and
James Joyce. Isabel Archer is a brilliant metamorphosis of the heroine of conventional domestic melodrama, an orphan at large in the
wide, wide world. The children, lonely women, and disappointed men
of *Dubliners* pull at our heartstrings while they stumble about, primitive
eschatologists all.

Such an association of sentimental, social relation with traditionally
sublime, autonomous power exists from early on, however widely the
notions of sublimity and sensibility were to diverge before they recon-
verged. Adam Smith discusses in *The Theory of Moral Sentiments* two sets
of virtues, one corresponding to the beautiful (soft, gentle, amiable) and
one that begins by corresponding to the sublime (great, awful) but that
shades imperceptibly into the social and thence to the altruistic and sentimental. Sublime virtue involves "the great, the awful and respectable,"
and the exercise of "self-denial, of self-government . . . [the subjection] of
all the movements of our nature to what our own dignity and honour, the
propriety of our own conduct requires."[25] Self-denial enables social harmony; both honor and altruism require tenderness and fellow-feeling.
Richard Payne Knight writes that "[a]ll sympathies, excited by just and
appropriate expression of energetic passion; whether they be of the
tender or violent kind, are alike sublime."[26]

Such blendings of sublimity and sentimentality occur throughout the
works of this study. Rossetti intersperses images of storms at sea with
images of tearfully loving parents and children in *The House of Life*, liken-
ing each set of images to the other. Ruskin went to school in Turner,
who placed small cottages and tiny human figures in the midst of his
sublime mountain vistas. Ruskin's ekphrasis of Tintoretto's *Massacre of
the Innocents*, a traditionally sublime subject, lingers in one detail of the
canvas: a mother gazing at a dead child. Is this then a scene of traditional
sublimity or conventional sentimentality? Both: it is a scene of Victorian
Modernist intensity, in which the connecting of hitherto disconnected
notions is part of the meaning. A sublimity of breadth requires entwinement with that which feels, at first, distant: other people, different kinds
of experience, and, not least, with sentimentality itself. The solitary self,
storms, battles, mountains, deities appear in concatenated unity with
close human relations and intimate settings. Beauty, sublimity, and sentimentality intermingle. Yet it is not the case that they always do so happily.
Common life and exalted life warily circle about each other in the works
of these writers.[27] Connections are not always made. Forms fail. The
finding of what will suffice, what will work, can be despairing work, yet
its motivations are as much those of healing and relation as they are of
pride and independence.

Nor do hierarchies, autonomies, systems and orders, monisms, polarities – a panoply of fixities – disappear as we study Victorian Modernists.
They all appear, motivated by arrogance or fear (John Ruskin); by social anxiety or frustrated economic desire (Evans); or sometimes simply
by a love of what Yeats would call "the ancient ways" and "eternal
beauty wandering on her way." (Rossetti).[28] It is important to realize,
however, that the very needs satisfied by traditional or reactionary ideas
and practices of many sorts also fueled pragmatic explorations of the
new-within-the-old, and that is why we must study the actual conditions
in which each writer developed his *Weltenschauung*. The sublime tends to
develop as an answer to a set of pressing questions about beauty, God,
human identity, and moral action as Victorian Modernist artists seek,
and thereby create, pragmatist truths in the patched together unions of
their works and days.

CHAPTER 6

Afterword

It is never too late to begin again – a statement, coming at the close of this book, meant to convey a variety of related meanings: sentimental, philosophical, formal. Wittgenstein, one of many twentieth-century ghostly figures in *Victorian Modernism*, tells us that his style of investigation "compels us to travel over a wide field of thought criss-cross in every direction. The philosophical remarks in this book are, as it were, a number of sketches of landscapes which were made in the course of these long and involved journeyings."[1] Like Ruskin and his beloved Turner, Wittgenstein finds that his travel "precipate[s]" in sketches (ixe). William James tells us that philosophers paint pictures. My own sketches have converged with some frequency in two areas: crisis and its etymological brother, criticism.

Crisis – with its clear turning points or its gaping stress lines often associated with disease, difficulty or insecurity – has often given way here to ongoingness, a patient connecting or rearrangement across gaps. Pragmatism has not been a crisis-oriented philosophy; in place of sharp distinctions and dramatic upheavals it has tended to see the finer adjustments of constancy or incursions of novelty.[2] Criss-crossing the borders of the Victorian and Modern periods does not mean denying the changes that come with time, rather it means following time's lines in multiple directions as they measure what lives on or circles back as well as what fades away. I have traveled across several complex concepts, including but not limited to that of time. In spatial terms, I have tended to see concepts themselves as participating in a kind of delta culture. Neither distinct river nor universal sea, concepts move and pool. Both liquid and solid, delta water and delta earth, concepts burgeon, metamorphose, and fall away, and not necessarily in that order.

Criticism appears most frequently as appreciation in my travels. "It is not only difficult to describe what appreciation consists in, but impossible," Wittgenstein tells us, and "To describe what it consists in we would have to describe the whole environment."[3] In the eyes of many within the academy, appreciation means at best mere belles-lettristic musings which ignore sophisticated thought about literature, at worst a code word for concerted reactionary responses to literary scholarship of the past quarter century. What I mean by "appreciation" cannot be sharply defined, but it involves sympathy with works of art and with what artists do. Appreciation involves a thinking and feeling with rather than a separation from – although, once again, "with" and "from" may themselves intersect. "The whole environment" is surely at issue here.

The current environment of critical activity does honor connection: between works of art and acts of social justice, among members of hitherto marginalized groups, among disciplines, among "national" literatures. But the current environment also encourages severe ruptures of several kinds. First, critics and artists are often assumed to inhabit separate worlds, joined only temporarily when critics work "on" the creations of artists. We have largely suppressed the possibility that critics write as artists themselves. Second, in order to survive and prosper professionally, we have too often and too thoroughly separated our professional and extra-professional selves in a multitude of ways, despite all our politically engaged writing and teaching. Third, we have experienced – even chosen – a distancing from the beauty and pleasure-giving qualities of artistic works, as well as from audiences outside our sub-fields and outside the academy.

It is such gaps that appreciation may begin to bridge. Far from ignoring the fruits of various critical approaches and far from rejecting knowledge about literature both deep and wide, those who write appreciations may, in my view, develop and express expertise of many kinds, yet also recognize themselves as the kin of artists. We might *take care and take pleasure* in and with our own written texts, ourselves, whatever it is that each of us experiences as beauty, and those we address.

Looking back and beginning again, I see another area of multiplexity in this work: that of aesthetic interest and disinterest. The varieties of aesthetic experience I have touched upon have been interested – not just in a political sense, but also in their participation in multiple realms that include everyday things and practical concerns. Yet to the extent that aesthetic experience differs from quotidian experience, it generates an energy of disinterest. Connection, after all, implies distance to be bridged.

Let us take instruction for a moment from an aesthete and critic, the Nova Scotian seal in Elizabeth Bishop's "At the Fishhouses," as he acts in an almost allegorical drama of appreciation. At the ocean's edge, the poem's speaker sings hymns to a seal she has seen "evening after evening" because he "was interested in music; / like me a believer in total immersion."[4] The seal is interested in her: "He stood up in the water and regarded me / steadily, moving his head a little. / Then he would disappear, then suddenly emerge / almost in the same spot, with a sort of shrug / as if it were against his better judgment." The seal's interest is exactly what interests the speaker; it is a kind of attention granted which the speaker half creates from a distance (anthropomorphized seal) and which the seal half creates (*he* regards her, and the connection between them is mutually fashioned). He lives in a realm apart, deep water, but he surfaces and makes contact "with a sort of shrug." And his humanly alien element, cold and dark water is, by poem's end, the source of all human knowledge. If the appreciative yet diffident seal were not so very much himself, we would be tempted to say that he is a work of art, an audience, and an artist – and an emblem of all three.

To know him in his setting, his aesthetic "environment" as Wittgenstein would call it, is to know Bishop – at a complex distance certainly, yet, miraculously and paradoxically, with an immediacy we cannot deny. Bishop redeemed the imperfections of her experience by coming to know them again, through her poetry. Losing things – parents, lovers, homes, and even continents – she called her "One Art." All of these diminishments were marked by her extended and losing fight against alcoholism and depression. After worrying that her first book of poetry, *North & South*, lacked substance (she wrote to Marianne Moore that it "says so very little, actually"), she evidently set out in 1946 to write a weightier poem, on the subject of what knowledge is, thereby surely beckoning artistic disaster.[5]

Instead, it was triumph. Between 1946 and 1952 she wrote two of her greatest works, the poem "At the Fishhouses" (first published in 1947) and the long prose poem or short story, "In the Village" (1953), both set in Nova Scotia where she lived for a time as a child. Both join "wrongnesses" with what is beautiful and right, harmonizing them into imperfect wholes akin to the many imperfect unifications this study has traced. Both poem and story mysteriously take on a rolling sublimity that cannot be accounted for, only recognized. And what each work achieves independently of the other, together they bring to greater intensity.

Bishop sets "In the Village" in the summer of 1916, when, as a child of five living in Nova Scotia with relatives, she saw her mother for the last time. The events of her mother's nervous breakdown and placement in a sanitorium are juxtaposed, by the child aesthete-narrator, with the events and scenes of an idyllic, Victorian village life (where kindly cows and dogs have such highly developed interior lives that they do everything but speak English). The small Great Village of 1916, with its unpaved streets, one-room schoolhouse, blacksmith shop, and agricultural economy was, as Bishop later wrote, "a pocket of Time," and that time was nineteenth-century in its sense of British propriety and its rural simplicity. But "Time made a sudden gesture; / His nails scratched the roof / Roughly his hand reached in / and tumbled me out."[6] Here is Modernism's familiar record of crisis and rupture. She found herself in the twentieth century, both hungering for and horrified by that past. "At the Fishhouses" describes the adult's walk along Lockeport Beach during her first visit to Nova Scotia after her mother's death. The "in" of her Victorian childhood meets the "at" of modern adulthood, with its houses where nobody really lives. That prepositional force-field enables Bishop to ameliorate life: to know it as a matter of addition and complication as well as a matter of stark loss.

Always braced for another scream from her mother, the child of "In the Village" deliberately loses herself in the domestic patterns of her world: "My grandmother's hair is silver and in it she keeps a great many celluloid combs, at the back and sides, streaked gray and silver to match. The one at the back has longer teeth than the others, and a row of sunken silver dots across the top, beneath a row of little balls."[7] She helps her grandmother brush her hair as a means of solace for them both after the old woman has cried and the child has, kissing her, tasted her tears.

But the nineteenth-century scene inside the house is also the twentieth-century domestic scene "At the Fishhouses":

> All is silver: the heavy surface of the sea,
> swelling slowly as if considering spilling over,
> is opaque, but the silver of the benches,
> the lobster pots, and masts, scattered among the wild jagged rocks,
> is of an apparent translucence.

The repainted rocking chair in the kitchen is "as smooth as cream – blue, white, and gray all showing through"; equipment at the fishhouses is coated with "creamy iridescent coats of mail," silvery herring scales. The grandmother's patterned combs, "a row of sunken silver dots across the top, beneath a row of little balls," have metamorphosed from "the long ramp / descending into the water, thin silver / tree trunks . . . laid horizontally / across the gray stones, down and down / at intervals of four or five feet."

The village child hopes that the saving and beautiful "Clang" of the blacksmith's shop will drown out the "Scream" of her mother's nervous breakdown; that clang "sounds like a bell buoy out at sea. It is the elements speaking: earth, air, fire, water." These elements sound again in her adult stroll at the water's edge, and they taste of salt, like the grandmother's tears:

> I have seen it over and over, the same sea, the same,
> slightly, indifferently swinging above the stones,
> icily free above the stones,
> above the stones and then the world.
> If you should dip your hand in,
> your wrist would ache immediately,
> your bones would begin to ache and your hand would burn
> as if the water were a transmutation of fire
> that feeds on stones and burns with a dark gray flame.
> If you tasted it, it would first taste bitter,
> then briny, then surely burn your tongue.
> It is like what we imagine knowledge to be:
> dark, salt, clear, moving, utterly free . . .

The water burns as the blacksmith's fire burns – and as the child's shame and fear burn and ache as she carries a package to be mailed to her lost mother:

> Every Monday afternoon I go past the blacksmith's shop with the package under my arm, hiding the address of the sanitorium with my arm and my other hand. . . .
> Clang.
> *Clang.*
> Nate is shaping a horseshoe.
> Oh, beautiful pure sound!
> It turns everything else to silence. . . . Now there is no scream.
> . . . .
> It sounds like a bell buoy out at sea.
> It is the elements speaking: earth, air, fire, water.

But perhaps the child does not wish for the sound of the scream to be silenced. The "it" that sounds like a bell buoy out at sea is many things: the scream, the "beautiful pure sound," and the grace of memory: "Oh, beautiful sound, strike again!"

It is "the elements speaking," but it is also "All those other things – clothes, crumbling postcards, broken china; things damaged and lost, sickened or destroyed; even the frail almost-lost scream – are they too frail for us to hear their voices long, too mortal?" The answer seems to be no: the imperfections of these bric-à-brac, painfully catalogued at the close of "In the Village," are gathered by memory and art into the dark, salt, clearness of icy water that Bishop chants as she brings "At the Fishhouses" to a close in feeling that is knowledge. Bishop's "beautiful sound" strikes repeatedly: 1916, 1947, 1953, 2002, but also back through the nineteenth century, "The old man accepts a Lucky Strike. / He was a friend of my grandfather" the latter a line that Bishop said came to her "in a letter dream."[8] The "dignified tall firs," "associating with their shadows," are kin to the trees of a poem by her close friend, Marianne Moore. In "An Octopus" Moore writes "The fir trees. . . . 'each like the shadow of the one beside it.'"[9] But Moore's trees live in her poem as a precise quotation from Ruskin's *Modern Painters*: "The pines rise in serene resistance, self-contained . . . in quiet multitudes, each like the shadow of the one beside it" (7.105–106). Ruskin says that "you cannot reach them, cannot cry to them," but Bishop could walk up and touch them. Appreciation for Bishop involves closely attending to the writing of others as part of the scenes of her environment, and speaking that appreciation in poem, story, and watercolor. Appreciation involves appropriation.

While Victorian Modernism has led me on travels across many borders, those very travels have provided a means of pausing at the wayside of literary criticism. Finding repose there, I have only begun to experiment with a kind of watching, learning, and touching guided by the very works that are ostensibly the object of my scrutiny. Rossetti's paintings and sonnets, William James's philosophical tableaux, Augusta Evans's didactic tales, Ruskin's highly wrought prose: these works are not wary of dispensing literal, sensual, ghostly advice. Some of their dicta are useful and some not, but many seem of the sort we have been encouraged to talk around, rather than into. My style of reading these works has been pragmatist, because pragmatism holds for me an encouraging possibility: perhaps we can be amateurs again.

Notes

1 INTRODUCTION

1 William James, *Pragmatism*, eds. Frederick H. Burkhardt, Fredson Bowers, and Ignas K. Skrupskelis (Cambridge, MA: Harvard University Press, 1975), p. 44. This work is hereafter cited parenthetically in the text as *P*.

2 Alexander Baumgarten, *Reflections on Poetry*, trans. Karl Aschenbrenner and William B. Holther (Berkeley and Los Angeles, CA: University of California Press, 1954), p. 43.

3 Marcel Proust, *On Reading Ruskin: Prefaces to La Bible d'Amiens and Sésame et les Lys*, trans. and eds. Jean Autret, William Burford, and Phillip J. Wolfe (New Haven, CT: Yale University Press, 1987), pp. 58–59. Proust changed his mind about Ruskin; for an account of his various positions, see Carlo Lauro, "Proust and Ruskin: a Controversial Admiration" in Toni Cerutti, ed., *Ruskin and the Twentieth Century: the Modernity of Ruskinism* (Vercelli: Edizioni Mercurio, 2000), pp. 25–36.

4 Proust, *On Reading Ruskin*, p. 28.

5 For a representative anthology of "canonical" American philosophers, see John J. Stuhr, *Classical American Philosophy: Essential Readings and Interpretive Essays* (New York and Oxford: Oxford University Press, 1987). For a study based on the premise that we may expand the canon of Pragmatists, see Charlene Haddock Siegfried, *Pragmatism and Feminism: Reweaving the Social Fabric* (Chicago, IL: University of Chicago Press, 1996).

6 This capsule account of Pragmatism I have taken directly from Richard Rorty, "Pragmatism," *Routledge Encyclopedia of Philosophy*, URL: http://etext. lib.virginia.edu/encyphil/. For another useful overview of Pragmatism, see Stuhr, *Classical American Philosophy*, pp. 4–11. For the evolutionary optimism of Victorian poetry and its relations to modernity, see Daniel Karlin, ed., *The Penguin Book of Victorian Verse* (London and New York: Allen Lane, Penguin Press, 1997), pp. l–liv. The optimism he describes itself evolves, in my view, into the meliorism of Victorian Modernism.

7 For an excellent discussion of the nineteenth-century aesthetic turn, see Allan Megill, *Prophets of Extremity: Nietzsche, Heidegger, Foucault, Derrida* (Berkeley, CA: University of California Press, 1985), pp. 1–64.

8 Wallace Stevens, "How to Live. What to Do," *The Collected Poems of Wallace Stevens* (New York: Alfred Knopf, 1969), pp. 125–26.
9 M. H. Abrams, *The Mirror and the Lamp: Romantic Theory and the Critical Tradition* (New York: W. W. Norton and Co., 1953), p. 4.
10 For a collection of essays addressing the topic of whether and how to address the question of beauty after a long silence on the subject, see Bill Beckley, ed., *Uncontrollable Beauty: Toward a New Aesthetics* (New York: Allworth Press, 1998). For an early and still interesting work that brings the Victorian and the Modern into relation, see Carol T. Christ, *Victorian and Modern Poetics* (University of Chicago Press, 1984).
11 For narratives that base chronological continuity between Victorian and Modern on the shared experience of discontinuity, especially psychological fragmentation, disorientation, or rupture, see, for example, Marshall Berman, *All That Is Solid Melts Into Air: The Experience of Modernity* (New York: Simon and Schuster, 1982). To be modern in Berman's view is to find one's world and oneself in a "maelstrom of perpetual disintegration and renewal, of struggle and contradiction, of ambiguity and anguish" (p. 15). See, too, Isobel Armstrong, *Victorian Poetry: Poetry, Poetics and Politics* (London: Routledge, 1993). She explores the affinities of Victorian and Modern cultures in their shared experiences of crisis, anxiety, alienation, and loss of certainty and finds a particular way of reading useful: "A text is endless struggle and contention, struggle with a changing project, struggle with the play of ambiguity and contradiction" (p. 10). For an example of a recuperative reading of the Victorian presence in Modernism see, for example, Giovanni Cianci and Peter Nicholls, eds., *Ruskin and Modernism* (Basingstoke and New York: Palgrave, 2001), who explain "for while Modernism defines itself in terms of a definitive break with the nineteenth-century past, it habitually reworks and reinvents the legacy from which it recoils" (p. xvi).
12 For studies of Modernism which have taken sentiment seriously, see Gregg Camfield, *Sentimental Twain: Samuel Clemens in the Maze of Moral Philosophy* (Philadelphia, PA: University of Pennsylvania Press, 1994); Morton White, *Science and Sentiment in America: Philosophical Thought from Jonathan Edwards to John Dewey* (New York: Oxford University Press, 1972); Fred Kaplan, *Sacred Tears: Sentimentality in Victorian Literature* (Princeton, NJ: Princeton University Press, 1987); Shirley Samuels, ed., *The Culture of Sentiment: Race, Gender, and Sentimentality in Nineteenth-Century America* (New York and Oxford: Oxford University Press, 1992); and Julie K. Ellison, *Cato's Tears and the Making of Anglo-American Emotion* (Chicago, IL: University of Chicago Press, 1999).
13 For different approaches to the problem of "handling Modernism" see, for example, Matei Calinescu, *Five Faces of Modernity: Modernism, Avant Garde, Decadence, Kitsch, Postmodernism* (Durham, NC: Duke University Press, 1987); Michael Levenson, ed., *The Cambridge Companion to Modernism* (Cambridge and New York: Cambridge University Press, 1999); Malcolm Bradley and James McFarlane, *Modernism: a Guide to European Literature 1890–1930* (London and

New York: Penguin Books, 1991); Marjorie Perloff, "Modernist Studies," in Stephen Greenblatt and Giles Gunn, eds., *Redrawing the Boundaries: The Transformation of English and American Studies* (New York: Modern Language Association of America, 1992) 154–78.

14 George Levine, *Aesthetics & Ideology* (New Brunswick, NJ: Rutgers University Press, 1994), p. 12.

15 Pragmatist literary critics have found chronological and psychological continuities across the nineteenth and twentieth centuries, but they have tended to see Pragmatism as primarily dynamic. Richard Poirier, *Poetry and Pragmatism* (New Haven, CT: Harvard University Press, 1992) describes a Pragmatist modernism that is recuperative and meliorist, yet he sees it as a phenomenon of endless, energetic repositionings, with little room for being, dwelling, absorbing. Jonathan Levin, *The Poetics of Transition: Emerson, Pragmatism, and American Literary Modernism* (Durham, NC: Duke University Press, 1999) describes transition as a phenomenon of both fixity and vitality, but his emphasis is still on the dynamic, that which is in the process of continuous change. David Kadlec, *Mosaic Modernism: Anarchism, Pragmatism, Culture* (Baltimore, MD: Johns Hopkins University Press, 2000), p. 2, discusses Pragmatist writers as they resist "the stasis of representation," thereby joining those who see Modernism as struggle. For a political reading of Pragmatism, see Brian May, *The Modernist as Pragmatist: E. M. Forster and the Fate of Liberalism* (University of Missouri Press, 1997).

16 Megill, *Prophets of Extremity*, p. 2

17 Marcus Bullock, "Benjamin, Baudelaire, Rossetti and the Discovery of Error," *Modern Language Quarterly* 53 (1922): 220.

18 See Francis G. Townsend, "The American Estimate of Ruskin, 1847–1860," *Philological Quarterly* 32:4 (1953): 77, for a brief history of *The Crayon* and Ruskin's place in it.

19 Andrew Leng, "Pater's Aesthetic Poet: the Appropriation of Rossetti from Ruskin," *Journal of Pre-Raphaelite Studies* 2 (1989): 42–48.

20 Roger B. Stein, *John Ruskin and Aesthetic Thought in America, 1840–1900* (Cambridge, MA: Harvard University Press, 1967) and Eileen Boris, *Art and Labor: Ruskin, Morris, and the Craftsman Ideal in America* (Philadelphia, PA: Temple University Press, 1986) give rich accounts of Ruskin's embrace by Americans seeking aesthetic guidance.

21 Augusta J. Evans, *Beulah*, 1864, reprint, ed. Elizabeth Fox-Genovese (Baton Rouge, LA: Louisiana State University Press, 1992), p. 179.

22 For a useful discussion of Ruskin's myth and mythography in its relation to modernity, see Dinah Birch, "Ruskin, Myth and Modernism" in Cianci and Nicholls, *Ruskin and Modernism*, pp. 32–45. See also Dinah Birch, ed., *Ruskin and the Dawn of the Modern*, and Birch, *Ruskin's Myths* (Oxford: Clarendon Press, 1988).

23 John Ruskin, *The Works of John Ruskin*, eds. E. T. Cook and Alexander Wedderburn, 39 vols. (London: George Allen, 1903), 3:509. Subsequent references will appear in the text by volume number and page only.

24 William James, *Essays in Radical Empiricism*, eds. Frederick H. Burkhardt, Fredson Bowers, and Ignas K. Skrupskelis (Cambridge, MA: Harvard University Press, 1976), p. 52. This work is hereafter cited parenthetically in the text as *ERE*.

25 Ruskin, too, speaks of arrangement and a "noble whole" which is imperfect: "The question is, therefore, how the art which represents things simply as they are, can be called ideal at all. How does it meet that requirement stated ... as imperative on all great art, that it shall be inventive, and a product of the imagination? It meets it pre-eminently ... [when it accepts] the weaknesses, faults, and wrongnesses in all things that it sees, [and] so places and harmonizes them that they form a noble whole, in which the imperfection of each several part is not only harmless, but absolutely essential, and yet in which whatever is good in each several part shall be completely displayed" (5.111).

26 Samuel Taylor Coleridge, *The Portable Coleridge*, ed. by I. A. Richards (New York: Penguin Books, 1978), p. 516.

27 See David Summers, "Form and Gender," *New Literary History* 24 (1993): 243–71 for a succinct history of the gendering of notions of form and matter.

28 See Naomi Schor, *Reading in Detail: Aesthetics and the Feminine* (New York: Methuen, 1987) for a history of ornamentation and detail in art, and their relation to gender issues.

29 Vladimir Nabokov, *Pale Fire* (New York: Library of America, 1996), p. 460.

30 Dante Gabriel Rossetti, *The Collected Works of Dante Gabriel Rossetti*, ed. William M. Rossetti, 2 vols. (London: Ellis and Elvey, 1897), 1:444.

31 Marcel Proust, *Remembrance of Things Past*, trans. C. K. Scott Moncrieff and Terence Kilmartin (New York: Vintage Books) vol. I, p. 379.

32 Works discussing sentiment that have been useful to me include: Patricia Spacks, *Desire and Truth: Functions of Plot in Eighteenth-Century English Novels* (Chicago, IL: University of Chicago Press, 1990); Jerome McGann, *The Poetics of Sensibility: A Revolution in Literary Style*, (Oxford: Clarendon Press, 1996); Janet Todd, *Sensibility: an Introduction* (London: Methuen and Company, 1986); David J. Denby, *Sentimental Narrative and the Social Order in France, 1760–1820* (Cambridge University Press, 1994); John Mullan, *Sentiment and Sociability: the Language of Feeling in the Eighteenth Century* (Oxford University Press, 1988).

33 George Eliot, "Notes on Form in Art," in *Selected Essays, Poems, and Other Writings*, eds. A. S. Byatt and Nicholas Warren, p. 232. Emphasis added.

2 A SWEET CONTINUANCE: JOHN RUSKIN'S VICTORIAN MODERNISM

1 John Ruskin, *The Works of John Ruskin*, 39 vols. (London: George Allen, 1903), 7:427. Subsequent references will appear in the text by volume number and page only.

2 For a discussion of the importance of detail in revealing the gendered nature of aesthetic issues, see Naomi Schor, *Reading in Detail: Aesthetics and the Feminine* (New York: Methuen, 1987), pp. 3–22.

3 For a helpful essay on the subject of centers and margins, see Lawrence Lipking, "The Marginal Gloss," *Critical Inquiry* 3, no. 4 (1977): 609–656.

4 For a discussion of pragmatism outside of classical American philosophy, see Charlene Haddock Siegfried, *Pragmatism and Feminism: Reweaving the Social Fabric* (University of Chicago Press, 1996). I am throughout indebted to George P. Landow, *The Aesthetic and Critical Theories of John Ruskin* (Princeton University Press, 1971). For an excellent discussion of the Calvinist tenets of heartfelt faith, see C. Stephen Finley, *Nature's Covenant: Figures of Landscape in Ruskin* (University Park, PA: Pennsylvania State University Press, 1992), p. 41. Ruskin's evangelical faith meshed well with his sentimentalism. Jeffrey L. Spear, in *Dreams of an English Eden: Ruskin and his Tradition in Social Criticism* (New York: Columbia University Press, 1984), explains Ruskin's interest in domesticity, "the concept of household is, as we shall see, as essential a part of Ruskin's ideal polity as it was of Carlyle's organic social order" (p. 134).

5 See Nicholas Shrimpton, "Ruskin and the Aesthetics," in Dinah Birch, ed., *Ruskin and the Dawn of the Modern* (Oxford: Oxford University Press, 1999), pp. 131–151, for a discussion of the relation of Ruskin the aesthete to Ruskin the moralist. He explains, "a simple binary division between a Swinburnian or Whistlerian Aestheticism, on the one hand, and the Theoretic or moral view of art, on the other, will not suffice" (p. 147).

6 Ruskin warns that while sentiment is necessary to good painting, it is hardly sufficient. See, for example, his discussion of William Holman Hunt's *The Scapegoat* (14.65).

7 For the concept of the scene of writing, see Richard H. Brodhead, *Cultures of Letters: Scenes of Reading and Writing in Nineteenth-Century America* (University of Chicago Press, 1993), pp. 4–12.

8 For an opposing view, see K. O. Garrigan, *Ruskin on Architecture: his Thought and Influence* (Maddison, WI: University of Wisconsin Press, 1973), p. 22. Ruskin did occasionally contradict his own position that Gothic Architecture originated in the domestic: see, for example, 10.272. Such contradictions do not trump his celebration of the domestic heart of the Gothic, they instead reveal his desire not to force every case into a pre-determined pattern.

9 William Rossetti, ed., *Dante Gabriel Rossetti: his Family-Letters with a Memoir by William Michael Rossetti* (New York: AMS Press, 1970), 1:416. Ruskin, never plagued by the "hobgoblin of little minds," also denigrates the decorative (3.89). He consistently, however, dismisses household furnishings, which he considers largely as signs of the "illth" of modern society (4.7–8).

10 For an important discussion of Ruskin's interest in the details rather than the larger structures of architecture, see Garrigan, *Ruskin on Architecture*. I have also consulted Susan P. Casteras, Susan Phelps Gordon and Authony Lacy Gully, *John Ruskin and the Victorian Eye* (New York: Harry N. Abrams; Phoenix: Phoenix Art Museum, 1993).

11 For a discussion of why I use the words sentiment, sentimentality, and sensibility as very nearly interchangeable, see "Meditation: Sentiment" in this study. For Ruskin's derisory comments on the sentimental in art and literature, see: 5.191, 5.231, 14.56, 14.152–153.

234 *Notes to pages 24–33*

12 For examples of Ruskin's relation of art to sentimental domesticity, see 6.63, 7.306, 7.406, 10.xxxviii.
13 For examples of Ruskin's blending of sensibility and sentiment, see 3.142–143 and 14.152–153.
14 John Ruskin, *The Diaries of John Ruskin*, eds. Joan Evans and John Howard Whitehouse, vol. I (Oxford: Clarendon Press, 1956), I:220.
15 Although most studies of Ruskin assume or point out his lifelong immersion in the Bible, I am particularly indebted to Francis Townsend's *Ruskin and the Landscape Feeling; a Critical Analysis of his Thought during the Crucial Years of his life, 1843–1856*, vol. xxxv, no. 3 of Illinois Studies in Language and Literature (University of Illinois Press, 1951). William Wordsworth provided another source of sentimental tradition for Ruskin, as did Sir Walter Scott; for the latter see Patricia Spacks, *Desire and Truth: Functions of Plot in Eighteenth-Century English Novels* (University of Chicago Press, 1990), pp. 203–234.
16 For Ruskin's knowledge of (and occasional publication in) popular annuals see *The Ruskin Family Letters*, ed. Van Akin Burd (Cornell University Press, 1973), II:563–564; and Fredrick W. Faxon, *Literary Annuals and Gift Books: a Bibliography* (Middlesex: Pinner, Private Libraries Association, 1973).
17 To be sure, Ruskin was capable of faulting Landseer for his sentimental focus on a dog; see 7.337. Ruskin's own interest and pleasure in describing at admiring length Landseer's painting cannot, however, be denied.
18 David Denby, *Sentimental Narrative and the Social Order in France, 1760–1820* (Cambridge University Press, 1994), p. 78.
19 Spacks, *Desire and Truth*, p. 144.
20 Quoted in Denby, *Sentimental Narrative*, p. 197.
21 For "iridule," see my introductory chapter.
22 Spacks, *Desire and Truth*, p. 11.
23 For a more rigid account of allegorical (earlier, faith-based) versus analogical (later, faith-deprived) thinking in Ruskin's works, see Landow, *Aesthetic and Critical Theories*, pp. 321–369.
24 For an important study of Ruskin's spectatorship that deeply informs my own, see Elizabeth Helsinger's *Ruskin and the Art of the Beholder* (Harvard University Press, 1982).
25 William James, *Essays in Radical Empiricism*, eds. Fredson Bowers and Ignas K. Skrupskelis (Harvard University Press, 1976) p. 52. William James, *Pragmatism*, eds. Frederick Burkhardt, Fredson Bowers, and Ignas K. Skrupskelis (Cambridge, MA: Harvard University Press: 1975), p. 79. (Future references will appear in the text as *P*.) I will explain at length why I can only differ with critics who believe that Ruskin is purely an essentialist. See, for example, Spear, *Dreams*: "Ruskin was, of course, an essentialist in his art criticism as well as in his science" (p. 114).
26 John James Ruskin perhaps best expressed his son's interest in discontinuous continuities, in a letter to W. H. Harrison, 25 May 1846: "He is cultivating art at present . . . It will neither take the shape of picture nor poetry. It is gathered in scraps hardly wrought, . . . fragments of everything from a Cupola

to a Cart-wheel, but in such bits that it is to the common eye a mass of hieroglyphics – all true – truth itself, but Truth in mosaic" (8.xxiii).

27 Elizabeth Bishop, *The Complete Poems*, (New York: Farrar Straus and Giroux, 1969 [1933]), pp. 72–74.

28 Jerome McGann, *The Poetics of Sensibility: a Revolution in Literary Style* (Oxford: Clarendon Press, 1996), pp. 189–190. See Janet Todd, *Sensibility: an Introduction* (New York and London: Methuen, 1986), p. 52, where she points out that even in eighteenth-century sentimental verse, there is a yearning for isolation from direct human contact, "Praise is given to society and domestic affections, but the poet himself is alone, withdrawn, sleepless, and unconversing."

29 Denby, *Sentimental Narrative*, p. 83

30 Helsinger, *Art of the Beholder*, p. 68. Helsinger characterizes the excursive sublime as "a multiplication of limited perspectives, an expansion, through compassion, of a deliberately partial but stubbornly human point of view" (p. 134). My intent is not merely to rename Helsinger's "excursive sublime" as "sentimental sublime," but rather to build upon her important insight by exploring the specifically domestic, sentimental, and stay-at-home quality of Ruskin's "excursions," however far afield they took him.

31 Helsinger, *Art of the Beholder*, pp. 112–131.

32 "The beholder's limitations of sight and understanding govern two kinds of aesthetic response ... the 'grotesque' and the 'noble picturesque.' ... [They] are nonetheless versions of sublime experience ... [and] are equal in emotional force to the experience of the Burkean sublime" See Helsinger, *Art of the Beholder*, pp. 112–131, for a discussion of positive sublimity. See also, Peter Nicholls, "Ruskin's Grotesque and the Modernism of Ezra Pound and Wyndham Lewis," in Giovanni Cianci and Peter Nicholls, eds., *Ruskin and Modernism*, (Basingstoke and New York: Palgrave, 2001), pp. 165–180.

33 Helsinger, *Art of the Beholder*, p. 134.

34 Wallace Stevens, *The Collected Poems of Wallace Stevens* (New York: Alfred Knopf, 1969), p. 216.

35 See also 5.38–84, 1.178, 11.157–58.

36 John Rosenberg, "Style and Sensibility in Ruskin's Prose," in George Levine and William Madden eds., *The Art of Victorian Prose* (Oxford University Press, 1968), p. 187. See also Rosenberg, *The Darkening Glass: a Portrait of Ruskin's Genius* (New York: Columbia University Press, 1961). I move beyond interpretations of Ruskin that consider his psyche through metaphors of polarization. Rosenberg, for example, speaks of Ruskin's "polarization of reality"; of "his own divided consciousness, split into a heightened awareness of felicity and pain" (p. 190). The pain of sentiment and domestic life are not so neatly culled from their pleasures; I would describe the two as confused, not polarized, in Ruskin's understanding. Further, I do not divide Ruskin's life into clearly defined phases as does, for example, Dwight Culler: "By 1848, when the combined efforts of revolutionaries and restorers seemed to threaten all the heritage of the great cathedrals, Ruskin's evolution was complete. He had

shifted his attention from nature to man in society" ("The Darwinian Revolution and Literary Form," in George Levine and William Madden eds.,
The Art of Victorian Prose, [Oxford University Press, 1968], p. 161).

37 Carol T. Christ, "'The Hero as Man of Letters': Masculinity and Victorian
Nonfiction Prose," in Thaïs Morgan, ed., *Victorian Sages and Cultural Discourse:
Renegotiating Gender and Power* (New Brunswick, NJ: Rutgers University
Press, 1990), pp. 29, 30. See, too, Sharon Weltman, "John Ruskin and the
Mythology of Gender" (PhD dissertation, Rutgers University, 1992) for the
feminization of the Victorian sage: "the role Ruskin assigns women as men's
conscience resembles his own as social and art critic, prophet, and sage"
(p. 118).

38 E. T. Cook and Alexander Wedderburn, editors of *The Works of Ruskin*,
have placed *Wayside Songs* in a volume which they have entitled *Studies of
Peasant Life*, containing three other works edited by Ruskin, two of them by
Francesca Alexander, and one by Jeremias Gotthelf (Alfred Bitzius).

39 I shall refer to Francesca Alexander throughout as "Francesca" – in part
because I dislike "Miss Alexander," in part because referring to her as
"Alexander" not only makes her seem masculine, but also prevents me from
communicating the intimate appeal she seemed to have for everyone who
met her, including Ruskin.

40 The publishing history of Francesca's work may be read in detail in Cook
and Wedderburn's "Introduction" (32.xvii–xxxv) and Bibliographical Note
(32.44–48). Francesca or her work are mentioned in eight volumes of Cook
and Wedderburn's edition.

41 See Helsinger, *Art of the Beholder*, for a discussion of Ruskin's identification
of the audience as crucial focus, the reader as part of the book: "Once
the reader becomes a character in the book, the book can dramatize the
conditions under which perceptions and judgments are made" (p. 150).

42 Alexander Baumgarten, *Reflections on Poetry*, trans. Karl Aschenbrenner and
William B. Holthen (Berkeley, CA: University of California Press, 1954),
p. 43.

43 For a discussion of the feminization of sentimental heroes, see Claudia
Johnson, *Equivocal Beings: Politics, Gender, and Sentimentality in the 1790s: Wollstonecraft, Radcliffe, Burney, Austen* (University of Chicago Press, 1995).

44 For an excellent discussion of a parallel inhabitation of another – Ruskin's
appropriation of Sir Walter Scott in *Fors Clavigera* – see C. Stephen
Finley, "Scott, Ruskin, and the Landscape of Autobiography," in *Studies
in Romanticism* 26, no. 4 (1987), pp. 549–572, who argues that for Ruskin,
to learn to know Scott is to learn to know innerness itself, including his
own. It is what Finley calls a "biographical/autobiographical synapse"
(p. 560).

45 Lucia Gray Swett, *John Ruskin's Letters to Francesca and Memoirs of the Alexanders*
(Boston, MA: Lothrop, Lee and Shepard, 1931), p. 28.

46 Critics who accuse Ruskin of misogyny often call attention to his sinister
belief in an essentialized femininity. See, for example, Paul Sawyer, "Ruskin

and the Matriarchal Logos," in Thaïs Morgan, ed., *Victorian Sages and Cultural Discourse: Renegotiating Gender and Power*, (New Brunswick, NJ: Rutgers University Press, 1990), pp. 140–141. Without denying Ruskin's sexism, I must insist that it is only part of the story, and I argue for a more complex picture which includes the positive feminization of Victorian Modernism that Ruskin and the other figures of this study effected. See Sharon A. Weltman, *Ruskin's Mythic Queen: Gender Subversion in Victorian Culture* (Athens, OH: Ohio University Press, 1998) and Dinah Birch, "Ruskin's 'Womanly Mind,'" *Essays in Criticism* 38, no. 4 (1988), for nuanced discussions of Ruskin's attitudes toward women.

47 For a discussion of Ruskin's myth-making and its similarities to that of T. S. Eliot, H. D, and Virginia Woolf, see Dinah Birch, "Ruskin, Myth and Modernism" in Giovanni Cianci and Peter Nicholls, eds., *Ruskin and Modernism* (Basingstoke and New York: Palgrave, 2001), pp. 32–47.

48 Rimbaud, "Car Je est un autre" [sic] in *Rimbaud: Complete Works, Selected Letters*, Translation, Introduction and Notes by Wallace Fowlie (University of Chicago Press, 1966), pp. 304–305; Baudelaire, "De la Vaporisation et de la centralisation du *Moi*. Tout est là," *Oeuvres Complètes*, ed. Claude Pichois (Paris: Editions Gallimard, 1975), vol. i, p. 676.

49 See *Fors Clavigera 31* (27.564) for a similar overlapping of identities among Sir Walter Scott, his biographer Lockhart, and Ruskin himself. Once again, I am indebted to Finley, "Scott, Ruskin, and the Landscape of Autobiography," pp. 549–572.

50 Swett, *Letters to Francesca*, pp. 76–77.

MEDITATION: AESTHETICISM

1 For a discussion of the "metaphysics of relation" in modern art that sets forth a pragmatist aesthetics, see John McDermott, "To be Human is to Humanize: a Radically Empirical Aesthetic," in Michael Novak, ed., *American Philosophy and the Future: Essays for a new Generation*, (New York: Scribner, 1968), pp. 21–59. See also Richard Shusterman, *Pragmatist Aesthetics: Living Beauty, Rethinking Art*, 2nd edn. (Lanham, MD: Rowman and Littlefield Publishers, 2000).

2 William James, *Pragmatism*, eds., Frederick H. Burkhardt, Fredson Bowers, and Ignas K. Skrupkelis (Cambridge, MA: Harvard University Press, 1975), p. 32. This work hereafter is cited in the text as *P.*

3 I am well aware that important antechambers number more than three: psychological, structuralist, and feminist criticism come quickly to mind, and there are others. My purpose here is not to survey methods and schools, but rather to suggest one hall of doorways in Hotel Literary Theory.

4 For examples of criticism skeptical of the purity of art, see, Jonathan Freedman, "An Aestheticism of Our Own: American Writers and the Aesthetic Movement," in Doreen Bolger Burke, ed., *In Pursuit of Beauty:*

Americans and the Aesthetic Movement, (New York: Metropolitan Museum of Art and Rizzoli, 1986) and *Professions of Taste: Henry James, British Aestheticism, and Commodity Culture* (Stanford University Press, 1990); Regina Gagnier, *Idylls of the Marketplace: Oscar Wilde and the Victorian Public* (Stanford, CA: Stanford University Press, 1986); Talia Schaffer and Kathy Psomiades, eds., *Women and British Aestheticism* (University Press of Virginia, 1999).

5 Peter Bürger, *Theory of the Avant-Garde*, trans. Michael Shaw (Minneapolis: University of Minnesota Press, 1984), p. 27.

6 Terry Eagleton, *The Ideology of the Aesthetic* (Oxford and Cambridge, MA: Blackwell, 1990), p. 20.

7 Allan Megill, *Prophets of Extremity: Nietzsche, Heidegger, Foucault, Derrida* (Berkeley, CA: University of California Press, 1985), p. 101. "As it is usually employed, the word aestheticism denotes an enclosure within a self-contained realm of aesthetic objects and sensations, and hence also denotes a separation from the 'real world' of nonaesthetic objects." In contrast, Megill writes, "I am using it to refer not to the condition of being enclosed within the limited territory of the aesthetic, but rather to an attempt to expand the aesthetic to embrace the whole of reality. . . . . I am using it to refer to a tendency to see 'art' or 'language' or 'discourse' or 'text' as constituting the primary realm of human experience" (p. 2).

8 Talia Schaffer, in *The Forgotten Female Aesthetes: Literary Culture in Late Victorian England* (Charlottesville, VA: University Press of Virginia, 200), opens our eyes to the various ways in which the works of female aesthetes were ignored, plagiarized, and devalued. For a broader view, see Rita Felski, *The Gender of Modernity* (Cambridge, MA: Harvard University Press, 1995).

9 See Lawrence Rainey, *Institutions of Modernism: Literary Elites and Public Culture* (New Haven, CT: Yale University Press, 1998); Freedman, *Professions of Taste*; and Gagnier, *Idylls of the Marketplace*.

10 Peter De Bolla, *The Discourses of the Sublime: Readings in History, Aesthetics and the Subject* (Oxford and New York: Basil Blackwell, 1989), pp. 27–58. Linda Dowling, *The Vulgarization of Art: the Victorians and Aesthetic Democracy* (University Press of Virginia, 1996).

11 See, for example Luc Ferry, *Homo Aestheticus: the Invention of Taste in the Democratic Age*, trans. Robert de Loaiza (Chicago and London: University of Chicago Press, 1993).

12 John Ruskin, *The Works of John Ruskin*, eds., E. T. Cook and Alexander Wedderburn, 39 vols. (London: George Allen and New York: Longmans, Green, and Co., 1903), 35.50. This work is hereafter cited in the text according to the numbering standard used by Ruskin scholars.

13 Nicholas Shrimpton, "Ruskin and the Aesthetics," in Dinah Birch, ed., *Ruskin and the Dawn of the Modern*, (Oxford University Press, 1999), p. 147, explains, "a simple binary division between a Swinburnian or Whistlerian Aestheticism, on the one hand, and the Theoretic or moral view of art, on the other, will not suffice."

14 Friedrich Schiller, *Essays*, eds., Walter Hinderer and Daniel O. Dahlstrom, vol. XVII of The German Library (New York: Continuum, 1993).

15 See "Introduction" by Elizabeth M. Wilkinson and L. A. Willoughby in Friedrich Schiller, *On the Aesthetic Education of Man, in a Series of Letters* (Oxford: Clarendon Press, 1967), pp. xi.–cxcvi.

16 Wallace Stevens, *The Collected Poems of Wallace Stevens*, (New York: Alfred Knopf, 1969), p. 317.

17 Schiller, *Essays*, pp. 165–166.

18 Oscar Wilde, *Essays and Lectures*, 4th edn. (London: Methuen, 1913), p. 152.

19 Mary Warner Blanchard, *Oscar Wilde's America: Counterculture in the Gilded Age* (New Haven, CT and London: Yale University Press, 1998), p. 166. These novelists wrote aesthetically before the 80s and 90s, which is when Blanchard believes that aestheticism really arrived in America. Blanchard, too, sees a division between Victorian and genteel or aesthetic culture, yet when she argues that Victorian domesticity was challenged by aesthetic style, I find that I must disagree. Aesthetic style did not begin one day in order to challenge Victorian style – it was always intrinsic to Victorian style. Looking at what women wrote in the 60s and 70s, as well as what they wore and how they decorated their homes at the turn of the century, will reveal an aestheticism of greater breadth.

20 Gertrude Stein, *Writings 1903–1932* (New York: The Library of America, 1998), pp. 313–325, 333.

21 Mario Praz, *The Romantic Agony*, trans. Angus Davidson (New York: Meridian Books, 1956).

22 Alfred Garvin Engstrom and Clive Scott, "Decadence," *The New Princeton Encyclopedia of Poetry and Poetics* (Princeton University Press, 1993), pp. 275–276.

23 For a discussion of decadence across the ages, see Robert Martin Adams, *Decadent Societies* (San Francisco, CA: North Point Press, 1983).

24 For views of women and decadence that emphasize the victimization of women see Bram Djikstra, *Idols of Perversity: Fantasies of Feminine Evil in Fin-de-Siècle Culture* (New York and Oxford: Oxford University Press, 1986), Praz, *Romantic Agony*. Elaine Showalter, ed., *Daughters of Decadence: Women Writers of the Fin-de-siècle* (Rutgers University Press, 1993), pp. vii–xix, points out that women writers countered the misogynist views of male decadents.

3 ARRANGEMENTS: DANTE GABRIEL ROSSETTI'S VICTORIAN MODERNISM

1 Walter Pater, *Selected Writing of Walter Pater*, ed. Harold Bloom (New York: New American Library, 1974), p. 204.

2 Dante Gabriel Rossetti, *Letters of Dante Gabriel Rossetti*, eds. Oswald Doughty and John Robert Wahl, 4 vols. (Oxford: Clarendon Press, 1965–1967), p. 252. This work is hereafter cited in the text as *LDGR*.

3 See Claudia Johnson, *Equivocal Beings: Politics, Gender, and Sentimentality in the 1790s: Wollstonecraft, Radcliffe, Burney, Austen* (University of Chicago Press, 1995) for a history of sentiment in the eighteenth century that takes gender into account. See also J. Ellison, *Cato's Tears and the Making of Anglo-American Emotion* (University of Chicago Press, 1999).

Notes to pages 69–74

4 R. L. Stein, *The Ritual of Interpretation: the Fine Arts as Literature in Ruskin, Rossetti, and Pater* (Boston, MA: Harvard University Press, 1975), p. 124.

5 Virginia Surtees, *The Paintings and Drawings of Dante Gabriel Rossetti 1828–1882: a Catalogue Raisonné* (Oxford: Clarendon Press, 1971), vol. II, plate 198. Plates from this work is hereafter cited in text as Surtees II, plate #.

6 Iris Murdoch, "The Sublime and the Beautiful Revisited," in Peter Conradi, ed., *Existentialists and Mystics: Writings on Philosophy and Literature* (New York: Penguin Books 1999), p. 263.

7 Gertrude Stein, *Writings 1932–1946* (New York: The Library of America, 1998), p. 197.

8 For interpretations that stress the bleakness and entrapment of Rossetti in his own subjectivity or in a constantly replicating world of signs see, for example: Stephen J. Spector, "Love, Unity, and Desire in the Poetry of Dante Gabriel Rossetti," *English Literary History* 38 (1971): 432–458 and J. Hillis Miller, "The Mirror's Secret: Dante Gabriel Rossetti's Double Work of Art," *Victorian Poetry* 29 (1991): 333–349. For accounts of Rossetti's self-loathing as a result of "selling out" in his art, see, for example, Jerome McGann, "Dante Gabriel Rossetti and the Betrayal of Truth," *Victorian Poetry* 26 (1988): 339–361; and William Fredeman, "What is Wrong with Rossetti? A Centenary Reassessment," *Victorian Poetry* 20 (1982): xxiii.

9 David Riede, *Dante Gabriel Rossetti Revisited* (New York: Twayne Publishers, 1992), p. 117.

10 See Baker's reading of *The House of Life* ("The Poet's Progress: Rossetti's *The House of Life*," *Victorian Poetry* 8 [1970]: 1–14) underscoring the sequence's didactic message of the salutary power of self-discipline and work, for a critical narrative that takes into account Rossetti's simultaneous participation in and rebellion against the surrounding Victorian culture.

11 Miller, "Mirror's Secret," p. 335.

12 Debora L. Silverman, *Art Nouveau in Fin-de-Siècle France: Politics, Psychology, and Style* (University of California Press, 1989); and Cecil Lang, *The Pre-Raphaelites and their Circle*, 2nd edn. (University of Chicago Press, 1975), pp. xxiv–xxvi.

13 For example, "the paintings seem to represent a genuine switch of allegiance from an art that worships and instructs to an art that exists for the sake of its own nobility and beauty," David Riede, *Dante Gabriel Rossetti and the Limits of Victorian Vision* (Cornell University Press, 1983), p. 71.

14 Stein, in *The Ritual of Interpretation*, portrays a Rossetti who engages in a subtle moralizing that enables him to escape despair and nihilism. He discusses Rossetti's understanding of wholeness and his "rituals of interpretation" that create "a momentary but total aesthetic environment in which . . . the reader can achieve wholeness of being" (p. 18). I would add that this educative and therapeutic role places Rossetti in the position of Victorian woman who ameliorates, encourages, and heals in passing moments of ritualized domestic life.

15 Dante Gabriel Rossetti, *The Collected Works of Dante Gabriel Rossetti*. ed. William M. Rossetti, 2 vols. (London: Ellis and Elvey, 1897), vol. I, p. 76. This work is hereafter cited in text as *CW*.

16 Herbert Jennings Rose, "Lustration," in N. G. L. Hammond and H. H. Scullard, eds., *The Oxford Classical Dictionary*, 2nd edn., (Oxford: Clarendon Press, 1970), p. 626.
17 Fredeman, "What is Wrong?" pp. xv–xxviii.
18 Riede, *Limits*, p. 159.
19 Charles Baudelaire, *Paris Spleen*, trans. Louise Varèse (New York: New Directions, 1970), pp. 5–7. It is important to understand that Walter Benjamin's interpretation of Baudelaire, however significant, is but one of many important interpretations and not the final word on this poet, as so many theorists of Modernism assume, especially those who have not read Baudelaire's oeuvre, but only Benjamin's accounts of it.
20 Pater, *Selected Writing*, pp. 199–200.
21 Wallace Stevens, *The Collected Poems of Wallace Stevens* (New York: Knopf, 1969), p. 10.
22 Robert Essick, "Dante Gabriel Rossetti, Frederick Shields, and the Spirit of William Blake," *Victorian Poetry* 24 (1986): 170. See Essick, also, for valuable information about the history of the sonnet's composition, including a list of pictures on which Rossetti might have based the sonnet and an account of its earlier versions. I disagree, however, with Essick's view that Rossetti felt himself in competition with Blake.
23 Johnson, *Equivocal Beings*.
24 For the home as narcissist expression, see Mario Praz, *An Illustrated History of Furnishing, from the Renaissance to the Twentieth Century* (New York: G. Brazillier, 1964). For discussions of commodity culture and aestheticism in England, Jonathan Freedman, "An Aestheticism of our Own: American Writers and the Aesthetic Movement," in D. B. Burke, ed., *In Pursuit of Beauty: Americans and the Aesthetic Movement* (New York: Rizzoli, 1986); see Regina Gagnier, *Idylls of the Marketplace: Oscar Wilde and the Victorian Public* (Stanford University Press, 1986); Terry Eagleton, *The Ideology of the Aesthetic* (Oxford: Blackwell, 1990); Thomas Richards, *The Commodity Culture of Victorian England: Advertising and Spectacle, 1851–1914* (Stanford University Press, 1990); and Jerome McGann, "Betrayal of Truth."
25 See Sarah H. P. Smith, "Dante Gabriel Rossetti's Flower Imagery and the Meaning of his Painting, (PhD diss., University of Pittsburgh, 1978) for an exhaustive account of the meaning of flower imagery in Rossetti's paintings.
26 John Bryson, ed., *Dante Gabriel Rossetti and Jane Morris: their Correspondence* (Oxford: Clarendon Press, 1976), p. 146.
27 See Jerome McGann, *The Poetics of Sensibility: a Revolution in Literary Style* (Oxford: Clarendon Press, 1996), pp. 136–142, for a discussion of the sentimentalists' tendency to create such verbal vessels.
28 William E. Fredeman, ed., *The P. R. B. Journal: William Michael Rossetti's Diary of the Pre-Raphaelite Brotherhood, 1849–1853* (Oxford: Clarendon Press, 1975), p. 106.
29 Charles Wells, *Joseph and his Brethren. A Dramatic Poem*, 1824, reprint (New York: Oxford University Press, 1908), pp. xix–xx. For a brief biography of Wells

and a history of Rossetti's association with him and his works, see Janet
Butler, "A Pre-Raphaelite Shibboleth: Joseph," *The Journal of Pre-Raphaelite
Studies* 3, no. 1 (1982): 78–90.
30 Wells, *Joseph and his Brethren*, p. 32.
31 Ibid., p. 115.
32 Ibid., p. 214.
33 Ibid., p. 176.
34 Theodore Watts, "The Truth About Rossetti," *The Nineteenth Century: A
Monthly Review* 13 (1883): 405.
35 William Michael Rossetti, *Dante Gabriel Rossetti as Designer and Writer* (London:
Cassell, 1889), p. 30.
36 T. Hall Caine, *Recollections of Dante Gabriel Rossetti* (Boston, MA: Roberts
Brothers, 1898). For a balanced view of Rossetti's character and personality,
there can be no substitute for reading widely in biography, memoir, and correspondence. See William Fredeman, "Biographies and Studies Principally
Biographical" and also his "The Rossetti Family," both in *Pre-Raphaelitism:
a Bibliocritical Study* (New Haven, CT: Harvard University Press, 1965),
pp. 98–106.
37 Barbara Gelpi, "The Feminization of Dante Gabriel Rossetti," in *The
Victorian Experience: The Poets*, ed. Richard A. Levine (Ohio University Press,
1982), pp. 94–114.
38 Dante Gabriel Rossetti, *Dante Gabriel Rossetti and Jane Morris: Their
Correspondence*, p. 109.
39 Ibid., p. 63.
40 Quoted in Caine, *Recollections of Dante Gabriel Rossetti*, pp. 202–203.
41 For a useful discussion of this issue, see Mary Kelley, *Private Woman, Public
Stage: Literary Domesticity in Nineteenth-Century America* (New York: Oxford
University Press, 1984).
42 See Anne Mellor's reading, in *Romanticism and Gender* (New York: Routledge,
1993), of the masculine plots of Romanticism.
43 Henry Treffry Dunn, *Recollections of Dante Gabriel Rossetti and His Circle*, ed.,
Gale Pedrick (New York: James Pott, 1904), p. 64.
44 William M. Rossetti, *Rossetti Papers 1862 to 1870* (New York: Charles
Scribner's Sons, 1903), p. 201.
45 Rossetti, *Rossetti Papers*, pp. 62, 70.
46 B. C. Williamson, *Murray Marks and his Friends: a Tribute of Regard* (New York:
John Lane, 1919), p. 54.
47 Walter H. Godfrey, *The Parish of Chelsea*, 1909, reprint (New York: AMS
Press, 1971).
48 H. C. Marillier, *Dante Gabriel Rossetti: an Illustrated Memorial of his Art and Life*
(London: George Bell and Sons, 1899), pp. 121, 224–227.
49 Caine, *Recollections of Dante Gabriel Rossetti*, pp. 210–211.
50 Dunn, *Recollections of Dante Gabriel Rossetti and his Circle*, pp. 17–18.
51 Quoted in Oswald Doughty, *Dante Gabriel Rossetti: a Victorian Romantic*
(Yale University Press, 1949), p. 310.

52 Praz, *Illustrated History*, p. 368.
53 *16, Cheyne Walk, Chelsea. The Valuable Contents of the Residence of Dante G. Rossetti*
 [Catalogue of the Sale]. (London: T. G. Wharton, Martin and Co., 5–7 July
 1882). Hereafter cited as *Contents*, item #).
54 Rossetti, *Rossetti as Designer and Writer*, p. 8.
55 Fredeman, "What is Wrong?," pp. xv–xxviii.
56 Silverman, *Art Nouveau*, p. 24.
57 Baudelaire, *Selected Writings*, pp. 423–434.
58 Doughty, *Victorian Romantic*, pp. 84–85.
59 Maryan Ainsworth, *Dante Gabriel Rossetti and the Double Work of Art* (New
 Haven, CT: Yale University Press, 1976), p. 99.
60 Marillier, *Illustrated Memorial*, p. 197.
61 Graham Ovenden, *Pre-Raphaelite Photography* (London: Academy Editions,
 1972), p. 44.
62 Marillier, *Illustrated Memorial*, p. 197.
63 Rossetti, *Rossetti and Jane Morris*, pp. 145–146.
64 Ibid., p. 154.
65 Algernon Charles Swinburne, *Essays and Studies* (London: Chatto and
 Windus, 1876), pp. 63–64.
66 For a suggestive discussion of writing artfully about art, see Paul Barolsky,
 Walter Pater's Renaissance (University Park, PA: Pennsylvania State University
 Press, 1987), pp. 93–199.

MEDITATION: DOMESTICITY

1 George Eliot, *Selected Essays, Poems and Other Writings*, eds. A. S. Byatt and
 Nicholas Warren (London: Penguin Books, 1990), p. 232.
2 Emmanuel Le Roy Ladurie, *Montaillou: the Promised Land of Error*, new edn.
 (New York: Vintage Books, 1979), p. 24.
3 For this argument about words of interiority and visual images of interiority,
 see John Lukacs, "The Bourgeois Interior," *The American Scholar* 39, no. 4
 (1970): 623.
4 Arthur Danto, *The Transfiguration of the Commonplace: a Philosophy of Art*
 (Cambridge, MA and London: Harvard University Press, 1981), p. 113.
5 John Ruskin, *The Works of John Ruskin*, eds. E. T. Cook and Alexander
 Wedderburn, 39 vols. (London: George Allen and New York: Longmans,
 Green and Co., 1903), 12.387. This work is hereafter cited in the text
 according to the numbering standard used by Ruskin scholars.
6 Henry James, *The Portrait of a Lady*, 1908 (Boston: Houghton Mifflin, 1963),
 p. 17.
7 I am indebted throughout the following discussion of domesticity and
 feminism to Iris Marion Young, *Intersecting Voices: Dilemmas of Gender, Political
 Philosphy, and Policy* (Princeton University Press, 1997).
8 Ibid., p. 164.
9 Ibid., p. 161.

10 See, for example, Tamar Katz, "'In the House and Garden of His Dream': Pater's Domestic Subject," *Modern Language Quarterly* 56 (June 1995): 167–188.

11 For this view, and for her analysis of the function of disembodiment in nineteenth-century views of women's labor, see Gillian Brown, *Domestic Individualism: Imagining Self in Nineteenth-Century America* (Berkeley and Los Angeles, CA: University of California Press, 1990).

12 Augusta Jane Evans, *St. Elmo*, 1896, reprint (University of Alabama Press, 1992), p. 49.

13 For a series of discussions of the place of the domestic in modern art and architecture that is useful to students of literature, see Christopher Reed, ed., *Not at Home: the Suppression of Domesticity in Modern Art and Architecture* (New York: Thames and Hudson, Inc., 1996).

14 George P. Landow, *William Holman Hunt and Typological Symbolism* (New Haven, CT: Yale University Press, 1979), p. 9.

15 Mary Warner Blanchard, *Oscar Wilde's America: Counterculture in the Gilded Age* (New Haven, CT and London: Yale University Press, 1998).

16 Talia Schaffer tells it well in *The Forgotten Female Aesthetes, Literary Culture in Late-Victorian England* (Charlottesville, VA: University Press of Virginia), pp. 73–122.

17 For a history of ornament, see E. H. Gombrich, *The Sense of Order: a Study in the Psychology of Decorative Art* (Ithaca, NY: Cornell University Press, 1979). See also Adolf Loos, "Ornament and Crime," in Ludwig Münz and Gustave Künstler eds., *Adolf Loos: Pioneer of Modern Architecture*, (New York and Washington, DC: Frederick A. Praeger, 1966), pp. 226–231.

18 Richard Ellmann and Charles Feidelson, Jr., *The Modern Tradition: Backgrounds of Modern Literature* (New York: Oxford University Press, 1965), p. 122.

19 Blanchard, *Oscard Wilde's America*, p. 143.

20 See W. F. Axton, "Victorian Landscape Painting: a Change in Outlook," *Nature and the Victorian Imagination*, eds. U. C. Knoepflmacher and G. B. Tennyson (Berkeley, Los Angeles, CA, and London: University of California Press, 1977), pp. 301–305, for this analysis.

21 Gombrich, *Sense of Order*, p. 162.

22 See Kirk Varnadoe, *A Fine Disregard: What Makes Modern Art Modern* (New York: Abrams, 1989), pp. 12–15 for a dismissal of this "goal-oriented" view of the march of Modern Art. I present it here not as credo, nor as "ordained progress," but rather as one possible, if incomplete, way to think about modern painting, and one that is especially germane to the issues of domesticity and ornamentation that I intend to take up.

23 Gombrich, *Sense of Order*, pp. 271–272.

24 Samuel Beckett, *Watt* (New York: Grove Press, 1953), pp. 128–129.

25 See Naomi Schor, *Reading in Detail: Aesthetics and the Feminine* (New York: Methuen, 1987) for a superb exposition of the place of ornamentation in aesthetic doctrine. Her discussion of the gendered nature of ornamentation's subordination is especially helpful.

26 William James, *Pragmatism*, eds. Frederick H. Burkhardt, Fredson Bowers, and Ignas K. Skrupskelis (Cambridge, MA: Harvard University Press, 1975), p. 98. This work is hereafter cited in the text as *P.*

27 Wallace Stevens, *The Collected Poems of Wallace Stevens* (New York: Alfred Knopf, 1969), p. 466.

4 RECONDITE ANALOGIES: AUGUSTA EVANS'S VICTORIAN MODERNISM

1 Walter Pater, *The Renaissance: Studies in Art and Poetry*, ed., Adam Phillips (Oxford and New York: Oxford University Press, 1986), p. 152.

2 For discussion of the impact of Ruskin's works in the United States, see two studies in particular: Roger B. Stein, "Artifact as Ideology: the Aesthetic Movement in its American Cultural Context," in Doreen Bolger Burke, ed., *Pursuit of Beauty: Americans and the Aesthetic Movement*, (New York Metropolitan Museum of Art and Rizzoli, 1986), pp. 22–51; and Eileen Boris, *Art and Labor: Ruskin, Morris, and the Craftsman Ideal in America* (Temple University Press, 1986).

3 *New York Times*, 5 January 1867.

4 This is a world proximately formed by the critical impact of Nina Baym's *Woman's Fiction: a Guide to Novels by and about Women in America, 1820–1870* (Cornell University Press, 1978) and Ann Douglas's *The Feminization of American Culture* (New York: Knopf, Avon Books, 1977), a terrain still primarily feminist. Susan Avery Phinney Conrad, *Perish the Thought: Intellectual Women in Romantic America, 1830–1860* (New York: Oxford Universitiy Press, 1976); Alfred Habegger, *Gender, Fantasy and Realism in American Literature* (New York: Columbia University Press, 1982); Nina Baym, *Novels, Readers, and Reviewers: Responses to Fiction in Antebellum America* (Cornell University Press, 1984); See also Mary Kelley, *Private Women, Public Stage: Literary Domesticity in Nineteenth-Century America* (Oxford University Press, 1984); Jane Tompkins, *Sensational Designs: the Cultural Work of American Fiction, 1790–1860* (Oxford University Press, 1985); Gillian Brown, *Domestic Individualism: Imagining Self in Nineteenth-Century America* (Berkeley, CA: University of California Press, 1990); Susan Harris, *Nineteenth-Century American Women's Novels: Interpretive Strategies* (Cambridge University Press, 1990); Elizabeth Moss, *Domestic Novelists in the Old South: Defenders of Southern Culture* (Baton Rouge, LA: Louisiana State University Press, 1992); Richard Brodhead, *Cultures of Letters: Scenes of Reading and Writing in Nineteenth-Century America* (University of Chicago Press, 1993); and Joyce Warren, ed., *The (Other) American Tradition: Nineteenth-Century Women Writers* (New Brunswick, NJ: Rutgers University Press, 1993).

5 I take this sales figure from Frank Luther Mott's *Golden Multitudes: the Story of Best Sellers in the United States* (New York: Macmillan, 1947), p. 127. See also Susan Geary, "The Domestic Novel as a Commercial Commodity: Making a Best Seller in the 1850s," *The Papers of the Bibliographical Society of America* 70 (1976): 365–393.

6 I will call *St. Elmo* and related works of fiction "domestic" novels, not to set these novels apart, but instead to study their mingling with works of "high" art – British and continental as well as American – that we might also see as domestic. For studies of *St. Elmo* as marking the limit of the domestic novel, see Beverly Voloshin, "The Limits of Domesticity: the Female *Bildungsroman* in America, 1820–1870," *Women's Studies* 10 (1984): 283–302; and Moss, *Domestic Novelists*.

7 For a contrasting view, see Tompkins, *Sensational Designs*. While I would agree with Tompkins that sentimental novels are not "just like" other novels, I object to her wish to remove them utterly from the same system of judgments we make about literary works of "high culture." In fact, I want to judge works of literary modernism through the lens of sentimentality and domesticity, not remove a novel such as *St. Elmo* to a domestic *cordon sanitaire*.

8 Augusta Evans, *Letters to Rachel Heustis* (Tuscaloosa, AL Hoole Special Collections Library, University of Alabama) (hereafter cited as Hoole), 13 November 1860. The Collection houses the lively correspondence between Evans and Rachel Heustis; the two were close friends throughout Evans's life.

9 Brodhead, *Cultures of Letters*. I am indebted throughout to his study; see especially his discussion of the necessity for placing women's writing in the context of writing by other groups, and for realizing as well that there is no monolithic woman's culture, but "plural and divergent women's cultures, each defined by a host of other social determinants" (p. 144).

10 Stéphane Mallarmé, *Selected Prose Poems, Essays, and Letters*, trans. Bradford Cook (Baltimore, MD: Johns Hopkins University Press, 1956) p. 83.

11 For a discussion of Wilde's relation to contemporary markets, see Regina Gagnier, *Idylls of the Marketplace: Oscar Wilde and the Victorian Public* (Stanford University Press, 1986).

12 Augusta Evans, "Northern Literature," *Mobile Daily Advertiser*, 11 and 16 October 1859; "Southern Literature," *Mobile Daily Advertiser*, 30 October and 6 November 1859.

13 See Ann Douglas Wood, "The 'Scribbling Women' and Fanny Fern: Why Women Wrote," *American Quarterly* 23, no. 1 (1971): pp. 3–24; and Kelley, *Private Women*, for discussions of the ways in which nineteenth-century American women attempted to legitimize the very fact of their literary activity.

14 Augusta Evans, *Saint Elmo*, 1867 reprint (Tuscaloosa, AL: University of Alabama Press, 1992), p. 365.

15 Evans might also have read of Neith in any of a number of popular accounts of Egyptian history, including two that we know Ruskin consulted, Bunsen's *Egypt's Place in Universal History* and Sidney Gray (Annie Keary), *Early Egyptian History for the Young*. See Ruskin, 18.36, 18.231–232.

16 George Stocking, *Victorian Anthropology* (New York: Free Press, 1987), p. 51.

17 Ibid., p. 52.

18 Samuel Taylor Coleridge, *The Portable Coleridge*, ed., I. A. Richards (New York: Penguin Books, 1978), p. 516.

19 See Christopher Herbert, *Culture and Anomie: Ethnographic Imagination in the Nineteenth Century* (University of Chicago Press, 1991) for a history of notions of culture in the nineteenth century and the tendency to contrast "culture" with varieties of "anomie" whose symptoms are variously restlessness, aimlessness, uncontrolled desire, absence of desire.

20 Wallace Stevens, *The Necessary Angel: Essays on Reality and the Imagination* (New York: Vintage Books), p. 20.

21 Joris-Karl Huysmans, *Against Nature*, trans. Robert Baldick (Harmondsworth: Penguin, 1959), p. 36.

22 *New York Times*, 5 January 1867.

23 See Stein, "Artifact as Ideology," for the intensive and imaginative study of Olana upon which I base my analysis of Olana and its relation to St. Elmo's study.

24 Ibid., for a discussion of such appropriation.

25 I in part paraphrase Stein, ibid., p. 24.

26 For an excellent account of Aestheticism in America, see Mary Warner Blanchard, *Oscar Wilde's America: Counterculture in the Gilded Age* (New Haven, CT: Yale University Press, 1998). I do take issue, however, with her claim that Aestheticism did not develop in the United States until the 1880s.

27 J. C. Derby, *Fifty Years among Authors, Books, and Publishers* (Hartford, CT: M. A. Winter and Hatch, 1886), pp. 389–390.

28 Fidler, *Augusta Evans Wilson*, pp. 106–107.

29 Rhoda Coleman Ellison, "Propaganda in Early Alabama Fiction," *The Alabama Historical Quarterly* 7 (1945): 93–94.

30 Madeleine Stern, *Publishers for Mass Entertainment in Nineteenth-Century America* (Boston, MA: G. K. Hall, 1980), pp. 84–87.

31 Ibid., p. 84.

32 James D. Hart, *The Popular Book: a History of America's Literary Taste* (Oxford University Press, 1950), pp. 168–169; Mott, *Golden Multitudes*, p. 127; Esther Jane Carrier, *Fiction in Public Libraries* (Littleton, CO: Libraries Unlimited, 1985), p. 200.

33 *The Nation*, 21 March 1867, pp. 232–233.

34 Quoted in Jay Hubbell, *The South in American Literature 1607–1900* (Duke University Press, NC, 1954), p. 615.

35 Ibid.

36 See Jerome McGann, "The Book of Byron and the Book of a World," in Robert F. Gleckner, ed., *Critical Essays on Lord Byron* (New York: G. K. Hall, 1991), pp. 266–282. He argues that Byron is interested in "the idea of the renewal of human culture in the west at a moment of its deepest darkness. This means for Byron the renewal of the value of the individual person, and the renewal of Greece as an independent political entity becomes Byron's 'objective correlative' for this idea" (p. 268). The parallels between *Childe Harold* (1812) and Evans's *St. Elmo* are many, and beyond the scope of this study. Surely, however, Evans also writes at a moment of deep darkness, even though she conveys that message by silencing modern history rather than

adopting it as a vehicle for literary expression. For her, war must be hidden, the figure in the carpet.

37 McGann, "The Book of Byron," p. 276.

38 Quoted in Ellison, "Propaganda," pp. 179–180.

39 Here I would disagree with Elizabeth Moss, *Domestic Novelists*, who argues, "Evans's decision to write a history of the Confederacy even after acknowledging that *Macaria* was her best book so far was revealing. The most outspoken of the five Southern domestic novelists [Caroline Gilman, Caroline Hentz, Maria McIntosh, Mary Virginia Terhune, and Augusta Evans] was the first to realize that the Southern domestic novel provided an inadequate explanation of the recent past and to seek out an alternative means of expression" (p. 218). I believe that *St. Elmo is* an historical endeavor, but one which has been forced to extreme indirection once a rousing Southern chauvinism was no longer an option for Evans.

40 See John Ruskin, *The Works of John Ruskin*, eds., E. T. Cook and Alexander Wedderburn, 39 vols. (London: George Allen and New York: Longmans, Green, and Co., 1903), 22.258–59, 7.111–114, 5.415, 16.190. This work is hereafter cited in the text according to the numbering standard used by Ruskin scholars. See also Elizabeth Helsinger, "Lessons of History: Ruskin's Switzerland," in Michael Cotsell, ed., *Creditable Warriors: 1830–1876* (London: Ashfield, 1990), pp. 187–208.

41 She writes to Rachel, "I am very much engaged my darling, for my two sisters Carrie & Sarah have left school and are under my charge. They are reading to me a course of History and Philosophy, which requires at least *half the day*. We are now deep in Grotes [sic] Greece, (12 volumes!) and in connection with it, I am reading the Iliad to them" (Hoole, 29 May 1860).

42 Augusta Evans, (*Letters to the Honorable J. L. M. Curry*, Curry Collection, Washington, D. C.: Library of Congress 10 November 1862). Hereafter cited in text as Curry.

43 Moss, *Domestic Novelists*, p. 196.

44 Marjorie Perloff, *Wittgenstein's Ladder*, pp. 115–143.

45 "Northern Literature" (no page given); "Southern Literature" (no page given).

46 Stein, "Artifact as Ideology," p. 24.

47 Stein notes in *John Ruskin and Aesthetic Thought in America, 1840–1900* (Cambridge, MA: Harvard University Press, 1967) that "by 1855 Ruskin felt that he had a more significant audience in America than in England" (p. 263). Certainly many of Evans's readers, coming across the numerous references to Ruskin's works in *Beulah*, *Macaria*, and *St. Elmo*, would be able to appreciate her heroine's discourses on *Modern Painters* and *The Stones of Venice*, as well as identify more general allusions to Ruskin. "Probably the only English authors whose works were more popular with American readers and publishers were novelists like Scott and Dickens" (p. ix).

48 Augusta Evans, *Beulah*, ed., Elizabeth Fox-Genovese, 1859 reprint, (Louisiana State University Press, 1992), p. 267.

49 Stein, *Ruskin and Aesthetic Thought*, p. vii.
50 Augusta Evans, *Macaria; or, Altars of Sacrifice* (New York: J. Bradburn, 1864), p. 463.
51 One is reminded of Baudelaire's "Correspondances":

> La Nature est un temple où de vivants piliers
> Laissent parfois sortir de confuses paroles;
> L'homme y passe à travers des forêts de symboles
> Qui l'observent avec des regards familiers.
> [(*Oeuvres Complètes*, ed. Claude Pichois
> (Paris: Editions Gallimard, 1975], p. 11)

52 Wallace Stevens, *Opus Posthumous*, ed., Milton J. Bates, rev. edn. (New York: Knopf, 1989), p. 163.
53 Willa Cather, *The Kingdom of Art: Willa Cather's First Principles and Critical Statements 1893–1896*, ed., Bernice Slote (Lincoln: University of Nebraska Press, 1966), p. 400.
54 Here, the classic text is Douglas, *Feminization*; see too, Brown, *Domestic Individualism*. Critics of domestic fiction must account for the regularity with which sick women make appearances in its pages.
55 Charles Baudelaire, *Baudelaire: Selected Writings on Art and Artists*, trans. P. E. Charvet (Cambridge University Press, 1981), p. 399.
56 See Martha Evans, *Fits and Starts: a Genealogy of Hysteria in Modern France* (Cornell University Press, 1991), and Janet Beizer, *Ventriloquized Bodies: Narratives of Hysteria in Nineteenth-Century France* (Cornell University Press, 1994), for discussions of the cultural construction of hysteria and especially its relation to intellectual activity. Beizer establishes the very "textual" quality of hysteria, which, as she demonstrates, is constructed in nineteenth-century France as a series of cultural phenomena floating among medical texts, novels, women's bodies, and men's needs. Evans's character Edna displays the symptoms of hysteria, but so does Evans's prose itself.
57 Wallace Stevens, *Opus Posthumous*, ed., Samuel French Morse (New York: Knopf, 1971), p. 176.

MEDITATION: SENTIMENTALITY

1 See Jean H. Hagstrum, *Sex and Sensibility: Ideal and Erotic Love from Milton to Mozart* (University of Chicago Press, 1980), pp. 6–10. As Janet Todd in *Sensibility: an Introduction* (London and New York: Methuen, 1986) points out, "The adjective 'sentimental' is the cause of much of the confusion of terms. It does duty for 'sentiment,' 'sentimentalism,' 'sensibility,' and 'sentimentality' – and cannot discriminate amongst them" (p. 9).
2 See, for example, Jonathan Levin, *The Poetics of Transition: Emerson, Pragmatism, and American Literary Modernism* (Durham, NC: Duke University Press, 1999) and Richard Poirier, *Poetry and Pragmatism* (Cambridge, MA: Harvard University Press, 1992).

3 Jerome McGann, *The Poetics of Sensibility: a Revolution in Literary Style* (Oxford: Clarendon Press, 1996), p. 5.

4 Charles Taylor, *Sources of the Self: the Making of the Modern Identity* (Cambridge, MA: Harvard University Press, 1989), pp. 248–84.

5 For histories of sensibility, see Todd, *Sensibility*; Patricia Spacks, *Desire and Truth: Functions of Plot in Eighteenth-Century English Novels* (University of Chicago Press, 1990); David Denby, *Sentimental Narrative and the Social Order in France, 1760–1820* (Cambridge University Press, 1994); and G. J. Barker-Benfield, *The Culture of Sensibility: Sex and Society in Eighteenth-Century Britain* (University of Chicago Press, 1992).

6 Julie K. Ellison, *Cato's Tears and the Making of Anglo-American Emotion* (University of Chicago Press, 1999) pp. 8, 20.

7 Ibid., p. 20. For timely and convincing arguments for widening the subject of sentiment and sensibility and viewing it in interdisciplinary ways, see also June Howard, "What is Sentimentality?" *American Literary History* 11 (1999): 63–81. See Hagstrum, *Sex and Sensibility*, p. 6, for a discussion of the meanings through time of sentiment, sentimental, sense, sensible, and sensibility.

8 Ellison, *Cato's Tears*, p. 123.

9 John Ruskin, *The Works of John Ruskin*, ed. E. T. Cook and Alexander Wedderburn, 39 vols. (London: George Allen and New York: Longmans, Green and Co., 1903), 35.429. This work is hereafter cited in the text according to the numbering standard used by Ruskin scholars.

10 See Todd, *Sensibility*, p. 8. See Eve Kosofsky Sedgwick, *Epistemology of the Closet* (Berkeley and Los Angeles, CA: University of California Press, 1990), pp. 142–155, for a discussion of the gendered nature of sentimentality and the structural principles of its practices, especially those of scapegoating.

11 Wallace Stevens, *Opus Posthumous*, ed. Milton J. Bates, rev. edn. (New York: Knopf, 1989), p. 162.

12 Quoted in Todd, *Sensibility*, p. 7.

13 Virginia Woolf, *A Room of One's Own, Three Guineas*, ed., Michèle Barrett (New York: Penguin Books, 1993), p. 73.

14 See Ronald de Sousa, "The Rationality of Emotions," in Amelie Oksenberg Rorty, ed., *Explaining Emotions* (Berkeley, Los Angeles, CA and London: University of California Press, 1980), pp. 37–38, for a discussion of the etymologies and cultural histories of words having to do with emotion.

15 William James, *The Varieties of Religious Experience*, eds., Frederick H. Burkhardt, Fredson Bowers, and Ignas K. Skrupskelis (Cambridge: Harvard University Press, 1985), p. 383. This work is hereafter cited in the text as *VRE*.

16 William James, *The Will to Believe and Other Essays in Popular Philosophy*, eds., Frederick H. Burkhardt, Fredson Bowers, and Ignas K. Skrupskelis (Cambridge: Harvard University Press, 1979), p. 70. This work is hereafter cited in the text as *WB*.

17 Quoted in Jahan Ramazani, *The Poetry of Mourning: the Modern Elegy from Hardy to Heaney* (University of Chicago Press, 1994), p. 178.

18 W. H. Auden, "In Memory of W. B. Yeats," in Edward Mendelson, ed., *Collected Poems* (New York:Vintage International, 1991), pp. 247–249.

19 Barker-Benfield, *Culture of Sensibility*, p. xix identifies within the culture of sensibility a "tendency toward the aggrandizement of feeling and its investment with moral value."

20 Sedgwick, *Epistemology of the Closet*, pp. 142–155.

21 James R. Averill, "Emotion and Anxiety: Sociocultural, Biological and Psychological Determinants," in Rorty, *Explaining Emotions*, pp.37–38.

22 Ellison,*Cato's Tears.*

23 See Claudia Johnson, *Equivocal Beings: Politics, Gender, and Sentimentality in the 1790s: Wollstonecraft, Radcliffe, Burney, Austen* (University of Chicago Press, 1995).

24 Linda K. Kerber, "Separate Spheres, Female Worlds, Woman's Place: the Rhetoric of Women's History," *The Journal of American History* 75 (1988): 9–39.

25 Clement Greenberg, "Avant Garde and Kitsch" and "Towards a Newer Laocoon," in vol. I, *Receptions and Judgments, 1939–1944* of *The Collected Essays and Criticism*, ed., John O'Brien, (Chicago and London: University of Chicago Press, 1986), p. 13.

26 Greenberg, *Receptions and Judgments*, p. 17

27 For some interesting defenses of kitsch and sentimentality, see Robert C. Solomon, "On Kitsch and Sentimentality," *The Journal of Aesthetics and Art Criticism* 49 (Winter 1991): 1–14. I take my list of principal objections to sentimentality and kitsch from his essay, p. 5.

28 Oscar Wilde, *Essays and Lectures*, 4th edn. (London: Methuen, 1913), p. 126.

29 Oscar Wilde, *Complete Works of Oscar Wilde* (New York: Harper and Row, rpt. 1989), p. 425.

30 McGann, *Poetics of Sensibility.*

31 Early in his career, when Ruskin sees his mission as convincing his audience that painting has a serious moral quality, he writes "I say that the greatest picture is that which conveys to the mind of the spectator the greatest number of the greatest ideas . . ." (3.91). He spends much of the rest of his writing life insisting that tender and sincere feelings lead artists to those great ideas while abstract conceptual systems, generalizations, and abstractions do not.

32 T. S. Eliot, *The Sacred Wood: Essays in Poetry and Criticism* (London: Methuen and Co., Ltd., 1972), p. 116.

33 Martha Nussbaum, "Emotions and Women's Capabilities," in Martha C. Nussbaum and Jonathan Glover, eds., *Women, Culture, and Development: a Study of Human Capabilities* (Oxford: Clarendon Press, 1995), pp. 360–395.

34 William Rossetti, ed., *Dante Gabriel Rossetti: his Family Letters with a Memoir by William Michael Rossetti* (New York: Ams Press, 1970) p. 416.

35 See, for example, Gregg Camfield, *Sentimental Twain: Samuel Clemens in the Maze of Moral Philosophy* (Philadelphia, PA: University of Pennsylvania, 1994).

5 POSITIONS OF REPOSE: WILLIAM JAMES'S VICTORIAN MODERNISM

1 William James, *Manuscript Essays and Notes*, eds., Frederick H. Burkhardt, Fredson Bowers, and Ignas K. Skrupskelis (Cambridge, MA: Harvard University Press, 1988), p. 3. This work is hereafter cited parenthetically in the text as *MEN*.

2 William James, *The Principles of Psychology*, 2 vols. (New York: Dover Publications, 1918), 1:556. This work is hereafter cited parenthetically in the text as *PP*.

3 Alexander Baumgarten, *Reflections on Poetry*, trans. Karl Aschenbrenner and William B. Holthen (Berkeley and Los Angeles, CA: University of California Press, 1954), p. 43.

4 William James, *The Correspondence of William James* [1897–1910], eds., Ignas K. Skrupskelis and Elizabeth Berkeley, 4 vols. to date (Charlottesville, VA: University Press of Virginia, 1992), II:339. This series is hereafter cited parenthetically in the text as *CWJ*.

5 Austin Warren, *The Elder Henry James (1811–1882)* (New York: Macmillan, 1934), p. 19.

6 William James, *Essays in Religion and Morality* (Cambridge, MA: Harvard University Press, 1982), pp. 3–63.

7 Ruth Bernard Yeazell, *The Death and Letters of Alice James* (Berkeley and Los Angeles, CA: University of California Press, 1981), pp. 147–148.

8 Bruce Kuklick, *The Rise of American Philosophy, Cambridge, Massachusetts, 1860–1930* (New Haven, CT: Yale University Press, 1977). Kuklick provides a fine account of the professionalization of philosophy centered in Harvard University during James's day.

9 Ralph Barton Perry, *The Thought and Character of William James, as Revealed in Unpublished Correspondence and Notes*, 2 vols. (Boston, MA: Little Brown and Company, 1935), II:259.

10 James here quotes Santayana. William James, *Essays, Comments, and Reviews*, eds. Frederick H. Burkhardt, Fredson Bowers, and Ignas K. Skrupskelis (Cambridge, MA: Harvard University Press, 1978), pp. 536–537. This work is hereafter cited parenthetically in the text as *ECR*.

11 For a literary history of concepts of sensibility and sentiment, and for distinctions between the two, see Jerome McGann, *The Poetics of Sensibility: a Revolution in Literary Style* (Oxford: Clarendon Press, 1996).

12 George Santayana, *The Genteel Tradition: Nine Essays*, ed., Douglas L. Wilson (Cambridge, CA: Harvard University Press, 1967), p. 205. Emphasis added.

13 Ibid., p. 206

14 Augusta Evans, *St. Elmo*, reprint (Tuscaloosa, AL and London: University of Alabama Press, 1992). For discussions of the problems inherent in the very process of publishing for nineteenth-century American women, see Ann Douglas Wood, "The 'Scribbling Women' and Fanny Fern: Why Women Wrote," *American Quarterly* 23, no. 1 (1971): 3–24 and Mary Kelley, *Private*

Woman, Public Stage: Literary Domesticity in Nineteenth-Century America (New York: Oxford University Press, 1984).

15 William James, *The Varieties of Religious Experience*, eds. Frederick H. Burkhardt, Fredson Bowers, and Ignas K. Skrupskelis (Cambridge, MA: Harvard University Press, 1976), pp. 134–135. This work is hereafter cited parenthetically in the text as *VRE*.

16 Morton White, *Science and Sentiment in America: Philosophical Thought from Jonathan Edwards to John Dewey* (New York: Oxford University Press, 1972).

17 Ralph Waldo Emerson, *Essays and Lectures* (New York: Library of America, [1837] 1983), p. 69.

18 William James to Alice Howe Gibbens, 7 June 1877, James Family Collection, Houghton Library. This work is hereafter cited in the text as Houghton.

19 *The Will to Believe and Other Essays in Popular Philosophy*, eds. Frederick H. Burkhardt, Fredson Bowers, and Ignas K. Skrupskelis (Cambridge, MA: Harvard University Press, 1979), pp. 57–89. This work is hereafter cited parenthetically in the text as *WB*.

20 For accounts of American malaise and fear of emasculation, see T. J. Jackson Lears, *No Place of Grace: Antimodernism and the Transformation of American Culture 1880–1920* (New York: Pantheon Books, 1981); George Cotkin, *William James, Public Philosopher* (Baltimore, MD: Johns Hopkins University Press, 1990); and Tom Lutz, *American Nervousness, 1903: an Anecdotal History* (Ithaca, NY: Cornell University Press, 1991).

21 For a thorough account of such a context, see Kuklick, *Rise of American Philosophy*. See also Louis Menand, *The Metaphysical Club* (New York: Farrar, Straus, and Giroux, 2001).

22 George Cotkin, *William James, Public Philosopher* (Baltimore, MD: Johns Hopkins University Press, 1990), p. 11.

23 Howard Feinstein, *Becoming William James* (Ithaca, NY: Cornell University Press, 1984), p. 16.

24 For Alice's place in William's story, see Jean Strouse, *Alice James, a Biography* (Boston, MA: Houghton Mifflin, 1980); Yeazell, *Alice James*; and R. W. B. Lewis, *The Jameses: a Family Narrative* (New York: Farrar Straus; Anchor Doubleday, 1991).

25 Cotkin, *Public Philosopher*, pp. 7–17, 19–39.

26 For a discussion of the place of professional lecturing in American culture, see Donald M. Scott, "The Popular Lecture and the Creation of a Public in Mid-Nineteenth-Century America," *The Journal of American History* 66, no. 4 (1980): 255–282.

27 See Ann Douglas, *The Feminization of American Culture* (New York: Knopf, Avon Books, 1977), pp. 1–196.

28 Elizabeth Glendower Evans, "William James and his Wife," *The Atlantic Monthly*, September 1929: 377.

29 Edwin D. Starbuck, "A Student's Impressions of James in the Middle '90's," *Psychological Review* 50 (1943): 128–129.

30 Friedrich Schiller, *On the Naive and Sentimental in Literature*, trans. Helen Watanabe-O'Kelly (Manchester: Carcanet New Press, 1981). For the evidence linking James's terms to Schiller's thought, see Paul Weigand, "Psychological Types in Friedrich Schiller and William James," *Journal of the History of Ideas* 13 (1952): 376–383.

31 William James, *Talks to Teachers on Psychology and to Students on Some of Life's Ideals*, eds., Frederick H. Burkhardt, Fredson Bowers, and Ignas K. Skrupskelis (Cambridge, MA: Harvard University Press, 1983), p. 224. This work is hereafter referred to in the text as *TT*.

32 For recent discussions of Jamesian Pragmatism's and aestheticism's political meanings and leanings, see David Kadlec, *Mosaic Modernism: Anarchism, Pragmatism, Culture* (Baltimore, MD: Johns Hopkins University Press, 2000); and Isobel Armstrong, *The Radical Aesthetic* (Oxford: Blackwell, 2000). They provide excellent bibliographical information, and they also take part in debates about the political resonances of Pragmatism which lie beyond the scope of this study.

33 Charles Baudelaire, *Oeuvres complètes*, ed. Claude Pichois (Paris: Editions Gallimard, 1975), 1:676.

34 W. H. Hudson, *Idle Days in Patagonia* (London: Chapman and Hall, 1893), p. 219.

35 Sigmund Freud, "The Uncanny," in *An Infantile Neurosis and Other Works*, vol. XVII of *The Complete Psychological Works of Sigmund Freud*, standard edition, ed., James Strachey, (London: Hogarth Press, [1919] 1953), p. 394.

36 For the dating of "On a Certain Blindness," see *TT*, pp. 242–244.

37 Perry, *Thought and Character of William James*, II:258.

38 Hudson, *Idle Days in Patagonia*, p. 27.

39 Perry, *Thought and Character of William James*, I:268.

40 William James, *Memories and Studies* (New York: Longmans, Green, 1911), pp. 145–208.

41 Wallace Stevens, *The Collected Poems of Wallace Stevens* (New York: Alfred Knopf, 1969), p. 358.

MEDITATION: SUBLIMITY

1 The name Longinus must stand for whomever actually wrote the fragments we have assembled as "On the Sublime."

2 Peter De Bolla, in *The Discourse of the Sublime: Readings in History, Aesthetics and the Subject* (Oxford and New York: Basil Blackwell, 1989), argues convincingly that "[i]f one were to locate the continuation of the eighteenth-century debate it would be in the social and economic theory of the 1840s where one would find the same obsessions with the interrelations between ethics, aesthetics and rhetoric." He asks us to consider the "trajectory of eighteenth century aesthetics, or the discourse on the sublime, from ethics via rhetoric and empirical psychology to political economy" (p. 34).

3 For a discussion of the tendency of the discourse of the sublime to migrate into many areas of culture, see ibid., pp. 9–11.

4 Quoted in Andrew Ashfield and Peter De Bolla, eds., *The Sublime: a Reader in British Eighteenth-Century Aesthetic Theory* (Cambridge University Press, 1996), p. 230.

5 John Ruskin, *The Works of John Ruskin*, edited by E. T. Cook and Alexander Wedderburn, 39 vols. (London: George Allen and New York: Longmans, Green and Co., 1903), 5.133. This work is hereafter cited in the text according to the numbering standard used by Ruskin scholars.

6 For specific poets and poems, see M. H. Abrams, "English Romanticism: the Spirit of the Age," in *The Correspondent Breeze: Essays on English Romanticism* (New York and London: W. W. Norton and Co., 1984), pp. 44–75, the source of my argument about Romantic experiments with a "low" sublimity.

7 For my initial understanding of an extensional sublime, I am indebted to Elizabeth K. Helsinger, *Ruskin and the Art of the Beholder* (Cambridge, MA: Harvard University Press, 1982), who demonstrates Ruskin's interest in "a response to landscape and art somewhere between picturesque taste and sublime comprehension or poetic invention" (p. 128). I would add to her list of examples of alternative ways of seeing – "Dreams, visions, fantasy, wit, humor, satire, Gothic grotesqueness" (p. 128) – the artist's intense apprehension of the ordinary and the trivial until patterns emerge.

8 John Ruskin, *The Diaries of John Ruskin*, eds., Joan Evans and John Howard Whitehouse (Oxford: Clarendon Press, 1956), 1:166.

9 Thomas Weiskel, *The Romantic Sublime: Studies in the Structure and Psychology of Transcendence* (Baltimore, MD: Johns Hopkins University Press, 1976), p. 6.

10 Longinus, "On Sublimity," in *Ancient Literary Criticism: the Principal Texts in New Translations*, eds., D. A. Russell and M. Winterbottom (Oxford: Clarendon Press, 1972), p. 474.

11 Patricia Yaeger, "Toward a Feminine Sublime," in Linda Kauffman, ed., *Gender and Theory: Dialogues on Feminist Criticism*, (Oxford and New York: Basil Blackwell, 1989), pp. 191–212, writes of the feminist background to the notion of a horizontal sublime: "The burden of French feminist writing is that women must create a new architectonics of empowerment – not through the old-fashioned sublime of domination, the vertical sublime which insists on aggrandizing the masculine self over others, but instead through a horizontal sublime that moves toward sovereignty or expenditure, that refuses an oedipal, phallic fight to the death with the father, but expands toward others, spreads itself out into multiplicity" (p. 191). I would not limit such a sublimity to the writing or experience of women, nor would I agree that the sublime is an unequivocally male genre until women begin to appropriate it in the modern period. Sublimity, like sentimentality, has always had a more complex history of gendered concerns than the simple dichotomy of male and female can capture.

12 Longinus, "On Sublimity," p. 494.
13 See Helsinger, *Ruskin and the Art of the Beholder*, for an account of Ruskin's "beholder's sublime," one that describes and prescribes a way of seeing that occurs associatively and across time (pp. 111–139). Ruskin tends to label such experiences as instances of the "grotesque" or "noble picturesque," but Helsinger argues that "the grotesque and the noble picturesque are nonetheless versions of sublime experience" (p. 111).
14 Samuel H. Monk, *The Sublime: a Study of Critical Theories in Eighteenth-Century England* (Ann Arbor, MI: University of Michigan Press, 1960), p. 61.
15 Iris Murdoch, "The Sublime and the Beautiful Revisited," in Peter Conradi, ed., *Existentialists and Mystics: Writings on Philosophy and Literature* (New York: Penguin Books, 1997), p. 263. For a feminist reading of Kant, see Timothy Gould, "Intensity and its Audiences: Toward a Feminist Perspective on the Kantian Sublime" in Peggy Zeglin Brand and Carolyn Korsmeyer, eds., *Feminism and Tradition in Aesthetics* (University Park, PA: Pennsylvania State University Press, 1995), pp. 66–87.
16 Weiskel, *Romantic Sublime*, p. 48.
17 "Though Burke lucidly asserts their difference in a series of neat oppositions – the sublime involving pain, admiration, and greatness, the beautiful [involving] positive pleasure, love, and often smallness – a certain similarity becomes impossible to ignore" (Adam Phillips, "Introduction," in Edmund Burke, *A Philosophical Enquiry into the Origin of our Idea of the Sublime and Beautiful*, ed. Adam Phillips [(Oxford and New York: Oxford University Press, 1990], p. xxiii).
18 Jean-Jacques Rousseau, *Reveries of the Solitary Walker*, trans. Peter France (New York: Penguin Books, 1979), p. 118.
19 Albert O. Wlecke, *Wordsworth and the Sublime* (Berkeley, Los Angeles, CA, and London: University of California Press, 1973), p. 30.
20 Augusta Jane Evans, *Saint Elmo*, 1867, rept. (Tuscaloosa, AL, and London: University of Alabama Press, 1992), p. 107.
21 D. H. Lawrence, *Women in Love* (New York: Viking Press, 1950), p. viii.
22 William James, *The Varieties of Religious Experience*, eds., Frederick H. Burkhardt, Fredson Bowers, and Ignas K. Skrupskelis (Cambridge, MA: Harvard University Press, 1985), p. 51. This work is hereafter cited in the text as *VRE*.
23 Monk, *The Sublime*, p. 92.
24 Weiskel, *Romantic Sublime*, p. 3.
25 Quoted in Ashfield and De Bolla, *The Sublime*, p. 244.
26 Quoted in George P. Landow, *The Aesthetic and Critical Theories of John Ruskin* (Princeton University Press, 1971), p. 209.
27 See Frances Ferguson, *Solitude and the Sublime: Romanticism and the Aesthetics of Individualism* (New York and London: Routledge, 1992), for a discussion of Burke's association of functional and dysfunctional social forms. Burke's "*Enquiry* finally resolves aesthetic experience into more and less explicitly social formations – beauty being the conspicuously functional social form,

the sublime being the apparently dysfunctional social form"(p. 63). During the mid- and late-nineteenth century, artists signal their unwillingness to support the binaries so long associated with the *ur*-binary of sublime/beautiful by replacing the notion of hypsos with a set of ideas that deliberately, even eagerly, confuse the seer with the seen, the individual with society, the sublime with the beautiful. *Platos* is the term I use to point toward this confusion.

28 See for example, 3.128 and 3.130, where Ruskin discusses the sublime and the beautiful as overlapping, and, in contrast, and 4.369 where he explains that they are mutually exclusive.

6 AFTERWORD

1 Ludwig Wittgenstein, *Philosophical Investigations*, trans., G. E. M. Anscombe (New York: Macmillan, 1958) m p. ix**e**, quoted in Marjorie Perloff, *Wittgenstein's Ladder: Poetic Language and the Strangeness of the Ordinary* (University of Chicago Press, 1996), p. 65.

2 Richard Poirier, *Poetry and Pragmatism* (Cambridge, MA: Harvard University Press, 1992), p. 132.

3 Ludwig Wittgenstein, *Lectures and Conversations on Aesthetics, Psychology and Religious Belief,* ed. Cyril Barrett and as reported by Yorick Smythies, Rush Rhees and James Taylor (Oxford: Basil Blackwell, 1966), p. 7.

4 Elizabeth Bishop, "At the Fishhouses," *The Complete Poems 1927–1979* (New York: Farrar Straus Giroux, 1979), pp. 64–66.

5 Biographical information in this "Afterword" comes from Brett C. Millier, *Elizabeth Bishop: Life and the Memory of It* (University of California Press, 1993), pp. 1–40, 181–194; and from *Elizabeth Bishop: One Art, Letters*, ed., Robert Giroux (New York: Farrar, Straus, and Giroux, 1994), pp. 133–146.

6 Unpublished fragment quoted in Millier, *Bishop*, pp. 16–17, 19.

7 Elizabeth Bishop, "In the Village," *The Collected Prose* (New York: Farrar, Straus, and Giroux, 1984), pp. 251–274.

8 Millier, *Bishop*, p. 193.

9 Marianne Moore, "An Octopus," in *The Complete Poems of Marianne Moore* (New York: Macmillan), p.71.

Index

Abstractionism 3
aestheticism 3, 5, 6–7, 14–16, 21, 48, 54,
        56–65, 69, 73, 84, 93, 130, 141–142,
        156–163, 179, 181, 202
    and domesticity 3, 31, 64n.19, 69, 72, 84,
        111, 202
    and pragmatism 7–8
    and religious belief 158–159
    and sentimentality 54–55, 60
    and sublimity 60
    versus aesthetics 7–8
    see also art; decadence
Alexander, Francesca 41–55, 102, 209
architecture
    see Ruskin, John: architecture.
arrangements 10–11, 11n.25, 19–20, 22–24, 33,
        34, 47, 50, 54, 66–111, 114, 135, 143,
        153–154, 175–81, 194, 206–207
    see also pattern; ornamentation
art 16, 68–69, 171
    and philosophy 172–212
    and Rossetti 67–68, 99–107, 107–111
    and the everyday 3–4, 66–67, 69–70, 71–72,
        95, 125, 174, 177
    as criticism (and vice versa) 12, 17–18
    for art's sake (alias l'art pour l'art) 56, 57, 58,
        72–73, 99
    high/low distinction 67, 72–73, 123, 177
    high Modernist idea of 6, 174
Art Nouveau 101
artifice 79–85
Auden, W. H. 168

Baudelaire, Charles 51, 59, 75, 101, 195
Baumgarten, Alexander 1, 8, 174
Beardsley, Aubrey 63
beauty 57–58, 60, 62, 73, 78, 171, 180
Beauvoir, Simone de 115
Beckett, Samuel 44–45, 120, 153
Bible 9, 10, 26, 36, 47, 65, 82, 125, 127, 132,
        133, 184, 214

Bishop, Elizabeth 8, 34, 224–228
Blake, William 77–79, 105, 107
Brontë, Charlotte 9, 126, 146
Bunyan, John 9, 126, 133, 149
Burke, Edmund 40, 214–215, 219, 220
Byron, Lord 9, 25, 26, 126, 148–149

Cameron, Julia Margaret 105
Cather, Willa 6, 159
Church, Frederic E. 142
Coleridge, Samuel Taylor 11, 19, 68, 76, 174
Conrad, Joseph 33
Cooper, James Fenimore 148
Cornforth, Fanny 95
Cotkin, George 189
Crayon, The 9

Danto, Arthur 113
decadence 3, 63–65, 72, 123–163, 178,
        182–183, 198, 200, 202, 204, 207, 208,
        219
decoration 11, 23n.9, 68, 95–98, 100, 101,
        134–143
    see also arrangements; ornamentation;
        pattern
Dewey, John 2
didacticism 123–163
domestic novelists 6, 9, 31, 40, 64n.19, 64, 118,
        124n.6, 123–163, 169, 170
    see also Evans, Augusta; popular literature;
        Stowe, Harriet Beecher
domesticity 3, 14, 20, 21, 23, 30–34, 52, 72–73,
        84, 85, 90–91, 99–103, 112–122, 127, 130,
        132, 134–143, 174–182, 192–201, 205, 210
    and aestheticism 3, 61–62, 66, 69, 72, 84,
        111, 181
    and arrangement 71–72
    and decoration 134–143
    and sentimentality 15, 66, 77, 181
    and sublimity 15, 73–78, 91, 92–93, 110, 136
Duchamp, Marcel 113

Edwards, Jonathan 185
Eliot, George 16, 117, 135, 142, 165, 173
Eliot, T. S. 34, 51
Emerson, Ralph Waldo 164, 185
Evans, Augusta 9, 40, 62, 123–163, 115, 117, 192
  and aestheticism 130, 141–142, 156–163
  and arrangement 135, 143, 153–154
  and decadence 123–163
  and decoration 134–143
  and domesticity 130, 132, 134–143
  and imagination 129–134
  and pragmatism 125, 128, 134–143, 144, 154
  and Ruskin 9, 129, 131, 135
  and sentimentality 128, 130, 133, 164, 168
  and sublimity 219, 222
  and writing 129–134, 183
  works: *Beulah* 129, 144, 158; *Macaria; Or Altars of Sacrifice* 129, 145, 159; *Shining Thrones of the Hearth* 132, 150; *St. Elmo* 9, 123–163, 191, 198

fancy 2, 11, 19, 68
Faulkner, William 6
feminist criticism 4, 5, 115–16, 165
feminization (*alia feminine, the; femininity*) 21, 32, 64, 121–122, 168–169, 186
  feminine ideal 44
  of works 85
  of authors and artists 45, 48, 85; James, William 178–182, 186–189; Rossetti 73, 73n.14, 85–98; Ruskin 17, 44n.46
Fielding, Henry 25
Flaubert, Gustave 34, 130, 170
folk traditions 43–44, 48
friendship 94–95, 102
Freud, Sigmund 20, 199–200

Gautier, Théophile 56
gender 3–4, 11, 58–59, 63–65, 68, 73, 78, 79, 83, 85, 99–101, 123–163, 174–182, 186–192
  see also masculinity; feminization
Greenberg, Clement 170

Hake, Dr. Thomas Gordon 79–81
Hawthorne, Nathaniel 148
Helsinger, Elizabeth 32n.24, 39n.30, 40
Hopkins, Gerard Manley 108
Hudson, W. H. 194–200, 201, 204–206, 210, 211
Huysmans, Joris-Karl 63, 126, 138

illness 159–161
imagination 11, 68, 74, 129–134, 174
  see also fancy

impersonality 18, 34–41, 51, 52, 127, 171
  and sublimity 34–41
intimacy 12, 87, 94

James, Henry 52, 70, 113–114, 123, 160, 170, 207, 221
James, William 25, 33, 39, 47, 56, 61, 62, 115, 117, 162, 163, 172–212, 223
  and aestheticism 193, 200
  and arrangement 11, 75, 175, 177–178, 181, 194, 206–207
  and decadence 178, 182–183, 198, 200, 202, 204, 207, 208
  and domesticity 174–182, 189, 193, 205, 211
  and family 8, 174–175, 189, 191; *see also* James, Henry
  and morbidity 182–185
  and nature 192–200
  and patterns 12
  and Rossetti 175, 193, 206
  and Ruskin 10, 19, 49, 172, 178, 196, 209
  and sentimentality 164, 166, 167–168, 179–192
  and sublimity 219, 220
  Lamb House 176–178
  works: *Essays in Radical Empiricism* 11; "On A Certain Blindness in Human Beings" 177, 178, 192–200, 204, 210; *Pragmatism* 1, 2, 5, 8, 12, 32, 35, 120–122, 174, 178, 184, 212; *Principles of Psychology* 11–12, 173, 189, 191, 193, 208–211; "Sentiment of Rationality, The" 10, 128, 177, 178, 180, 185–192, 203; *Varieties of Religious Experience, The* 25, 177, 178–184, 199–212; "Will to Believe, The" 10, 186–188
Joyce, James 8, 18, 34, 70, 126, 133, 153, 221

Kames, Lord 213
Kant, Immanuel 57, 70, 216–217, 220
Keats, John 56, 76
Knight, Richard Payne 221

Landseer, Sir Edwin 26–27
Lawrence, D. H. 219
Leighton, Frederick 67
literary theory 3–7, 56–59
  see also feminist criticism; Marxist criticism; Poststructuralism
Locke, John 185
Longinus 15, 213–216, 218

Mallarmé, Stéphane 103, 127
marketplace 5, 57, 66, 71, 71n.8, 74, 78, 82, 92, 94, 127–134, 182

Marshall, Henry R. 193
Marxist criticism 56, 57, 58
masculinity 42, 169, 181–182, 186–189,
    194–195, 197–198
    see also feminization; gender
McGann, Jerome 34n.28
mirrors, mirroring 52, 66, 93, 96, 102, 105, 127
Modernism 1–16, 69–71, 126
    see also individual authors
Moore, Marianne 228
morbidity 182–185
Morris, Jane 81, 86, 103–107
Morris, William 86
multiplexity 16, 64, 98, 117, 135, 143, 165, 173
Murdoch, Iris 40, 216–217, 219
mythology 9, 51, 64, 65, 71, 73, 98, 100, 103,
    135

Nabokov, Vladimir 8, 12, 29, 130, 152, 170
nature 15–16, 20, 21, 23, 29, 74, 84, 98, 100,
    102–103, 105–107, 118, 126, 132, 203, 204
    aesthetic response to 32
    extremities of 192–200
neo-classicism 40

O'Connor, Flannery 25
"Olana" 142
ornamentation 10–11, 23, 65, 68, 75, 117
    see also arrangements; decoration;
        ornamentation

Papini, Giovanni 56
Pater, Walter 18, 38, 66, 71, 107, 111, 123, 126,
    138, 159, 161, 198, 205, 207
pattern 3, 4, 8, 10–13, 17–21, 23, 29, 34, 44–45,
    54, 55, 61, 65, 71, 98, 106, 109, 124, 166
    see also arrangements; ornamentation
Peirce, Charles Sanders 2
Picasso, Pablo 119–120
Plato 164
Poe, Edgar Allan 59, 111, 138
popular literature 25, 26, 82, 123, 129, 146,
    170
    see also domestic novelists; Evans, Augusta;
        Stowe, Harriet Beecher
Poststructuralism 56, 58
Poussin, Nicolas 32
pragmatism 5, 7n.15, 18, 19, 23, 30–34, 56–65,
    78, 125, 128, 134–143, 154, 172–212, 217
    definition of 2–3, 2n.6, 5
    and aestheticism 7–8
Praz, Mario 63, 96
Pre-Raphaelitism 3, 8, 38, 56, 69, 79, 82, 119
    see also Rossetti, Dante Gabriel; Rossetti,
        William Michael

Prichard, James Cowley 131
Proust, Marcel 1–2, 1 n.3, 8, 13–14, 16, 51, 70,
    105, 205
Prout, Samuel 24
purity 57

rationality 185–192
religious belief 9–10, 19n.4, 30, 43, 46, 51, 60,
    71, 114–115, 123–163, 178, 186, 199,
    201–212
    see also Bible
repose 18, 25, 31, 172–212
Reynolds, Sir Joshua 40
Richardson, Samuel 25
Rimbaud, Arthur 51
Romanticism 11, 73, 75, 195, 214
    see also individual authors
Rossetti, Dante Gabriel 38, 39, 62, 63, 66–111,
    117, 126, 127, 217
    and aestheticism 7, 66, 73, 75
    and arrangement 66–111
    and art 99–107, 107–111
    and artifice 79–85
    and charity 68, 72, 75–76, 86–87
    and decoration 68, 97, 100, 101
    and domesticity 71–78, 99–103, 113–119
    and the feminine 67–68, 73, 78, 85–98, 101
    and ornamentation 68
    and pattern 12–13, 98
    and pragmatism 78
    and Ruskin 10, 23, 67, 74, 78
    and sentimentality 79–85, 164, 168, 171
    and sublimity 73–78, 98, 222
    and William James 175, 193, 206
    home at 16 Cheyne Walk 33, 66, 68, 72, 78,
        85, 91, 95–99, 102, 105, 138, 205
    paintings: *Astarte Syriaca* 103; *Aurea Catena* 79;
        Bower Meadow 93; *Day Dream, The* 78,
        103–107; *Ecce Ancilla Domini!* 99; *Gate of
        Memory, The* 79; *"Hist!", Said Kate the Queen*
        99; *Joli Coeur* 79; *La Bella Mano* 102; *La
        Donna della Fiamma* 93; *Lady Lilith* 71, 102;
        Loving Cup, The 79, 102; *Marigolds* 79, 80,
        90, 102; *Monna Rosa* 69; *Monna Vanna* 93;
        Passover in the Holy Family, The 99; *Proserpine*
        87; *Rosa Triplex* 102; *Sibylla Palmifera* 71;
        Venus Verticordia 93; *Vision of Fiammetta* 79;
        *Wedding of St. George and the Princess Sabra,
        The* 102
    writing: *Day-dream, The* 106; *House of Life, The*
        33, 40, 74, 78, 85, 88, 106–111, 222; *Five
        English Poets* 39–40, 76
Rossetti, Mrs. Gabriele, 85, 88–90
Rossetti, William Michael 9, 68, 78, 86, 89, 91,
    92, 96, 100

Rousseau, Jean-Jacques 20, 168, 218
Ruskin, John 3, 9–16, 17–55, 56, 59–60, 62, 64,
   69, 113–119, 123, 126, 127, 157–158, 223
   and aestheticism 3, 7, 18, 31
   and architecture 22n.8; domestic (*alia*
      suburbs; cottages; villas) 115, 192–200;
      religious (*alia cathedrals; churches*) 10, 22, 31,
      34, 54, 115
   and arrangement 11 n.25, 17, 19–20, 22–24,
      33–34, 47, 50, 54
   and Augusta Evans 9, 129, 131, 135
   and domesticity 18–23, 30–34, 121
   and Francesca Alexander 41–55, 102
   and impersonality 18, 34–41
   and painting 26–27, 28; *see also*
      Turner, J. M. W.
   and pattern 13, 17–21, 23, 29, 34, 44–45, 54
   and pragmatism 18, 19, 30–34, 39, 50
   and Rossetti 9, 10, 23, 67, 74, 78
   and sentimentality 15–16, 20n.6, 23, 24–34,
      164, 166–167, 168, 169, 171
   and sublimity 18, 21, 23, 34–41, 98, 214–216,
      218, 222
   and William James 10, 19, 172, 178, 196, 207
   Brantwood, home of John Ruskin 45, 49
   works: *Art of England, The* 43, 44; *Bible of
      Amiens, The* 1; "Essay on Literature" 25;
      Ethics of the Dust 131; *Fors Clavigera* 41–42,
      43, 44, 49; "Law of Help, The" 19;
      Modern Painters 17, 22, 26, 29, 42, 45, 46,
      50, 54; "Mystery of Life and Its Arts,
      The" 49; "Of Queens' Gardens" 50; "Of
      Water, as Painted by Turner" 28; *Poetry
      of Architecture, The* 20–21, 33; *Praeterita* 15,
      21, 22, 23, 35, 39, 43, 52; *Roadside Songs
      of Tuscany* 18, 28, 41–55, 201, 205, 207;
      Seven Lamps of Architecture, The 37; *Stones
      of Venice*; *Studies of Peasant Life* 43
Ruskin, John James 33n.226

Santayana, George 180–182
Schiller, Friedrich 60–62, 126, 179, 193, 196,
   197
Scott, Sir Walter 25, 26, 54
sentimentality 3, 5, 13–16, 20, 21, 23, 24–30,
   34, 37, 76, 128, 130, 133, 164–171, 179–182
   and aestheticism 66, 165, 169
   and arrangement 67–68, 101
   and art 20n.6, 51, 109
   and artifice 79–85
   and domesticity 15, 30–34, 50, 66, 77,
      174–182
   and Modernism 5, 13

   and morbidity 182–185
   and pragmatism 30–34
   and rationality 185–192
   and sublimity 3, 15, 64
   negative associations of 79, 81, 167, 169–170
   silent sentimentality 27–28
Siddal, Elizabeth 9, 88, 113
Smetham, James 86–87, 111
Smith, Adam 29, 221
Spartali, Maria 95
Stein, Gertrude 8, 45, 62, 71
Stephen, Sir Leslie 167
Sterne, Laurence 25
Stevens, Wallace 4, 8, 58, 61, 126, 144, 170,
   211
Stevenson, Robert Louis 193, 195, 196, 201,
   203
Stocking, George 132
Stoker, Bram 65
Stowe, Harriet Beecher 9, 40, 146
sublimity (*alia reverie; grotesque*) 3, 14–15, 21, 23,
   34–41, 111, 182–185, 213–228
   and aestheticism 60
   and impersonality 34–41
   and decadence 65
   and domesticity 15, 73–78, 91–93, 98, 106,
      110, 136
   and gender 215n.11
   and sentimentality 3, 15, 64
Swinburne, Algernon Charles 59, 91, 107–108,
   159

Tennyson, Alfred, Lord 81, 83
Tintoretto 46, 222
Titian 207
Tolstoy, Leo 196
Turner, J. M. W. 27–30, 32, 38, 39, 45, 47, 48,
   54, 87, 222, 223

Veronese, Paul 22, 207

Wells, Charles J. 82–85
Warner, Elizabeth
   Wide, Wide World, The 162
Whistler, James 21
White, Morton 185
Whitman, Walt 196
Wilde, Oscar 3, 58, 62, 65, 128, 138, 170
Wittgenstein, Ludwig 223
Woolf, Virginia 44, 70, 118, 160, 167
Wordsworth, William 26, 89, 118, 218

Yeats, William Butler 16, 18, 70, 168, 222